by

Robert H. Marshall

Donald H. Jacobs

Allen B. Rosskopf

Charles J. LaRue

AGS Publishing
Circle Pines, Minnesota 55014-1796
800-328-2560

About the Authors

Robert H. Marshall, M.Ed., teaches high school physics and algebra for the Baltimore School for the Arts. He is coauthor of several AGS textbooks including *Earth Science, Physical Science,* and *Matter, Motion, and Machines.*

Donald H. Jacobs, M.Ed., taught mathematics for many years in the the Baltimore City Public Schools. He is currently with the Upton Home and Hospital School Program in the technology department. Other AGS textbooks that he has coauthored include *Basic Math Skills,* and *Life Skills Math.*

Allen B. Rosskopf, M.L.A., has taught English, journalism production, and desktop publishing for 30 years in the Baltimore City Public Schools. He is a coauthor of the AGS textbook *Earth Science.*

Charles J. LaRue, Ph.D. The late Charles J. LaRue held a Ph.D. in science education, zoology, and botany from the University of Maryland, and an M.A. in zoology and botany from the University of Texas. He taught biology.

Photo and illustration credits for this textbook can be found on page 647.

The publisher wishes to thank the following consultants and educators for their helpful comments during the reviews of AGS Publishing science textbooks. Their assistance has been invaluable.

Physical Science: Rebecca Abreu, Timber Creek High School, Orlando, FL; Bonnie Buratti, Jet Propulsion Laboratory, California Institute of Technology, Pasadena, CA; Barbara Cassius, Hoover High School, San Diego, CA; Norman Gelfand, Fermi National Accelerator Laboratory (Fermilab), Batavia, IL; Brian P. Johnson, Centennial High School, Circle Pines, MN; Gary A. Mansergh, Ed.D., Professional Development Center for Academic Excellence, St. Paul, MN; Thomas E. Rock, John Marshall High School, San Antonio, TX; Lorraine S. Taylor, Ph.D., State University of New York at New Paltz, New Paltz, NY; Katherine L. Turley, Timber Creek High School, Orlando, FL; Dr. Alex Vera, Templeton Secondary School, Vancouver, BC, Canada

Earth Science: Susan B. Board, Terry Parker High School, Jacksonville, FL; Bonnie Buratti, Jet Propulsion Laboratory, California Institute of Technology, Pasadena, CA; Sean Madden, Summit School, St. Laurent, Quebec; Suzanne McKinley, El Capitan High School, Lakeside, CA; Esterina Mignacca, Summit School, St. Laurent, Quebec; Harrison H. Schmitt; Lorraine S. Taylor, Ph.D., State University of New York at New Paltz, New Paltz, NY; Wayne Wendland, University of Illinois at Champaign-Urbana, Urbana, IL

Biology: Susan B. Board, Terry Parker High School, Jacksonville, FL; Brenda Bowman-Price, Milby High School, Houston, TX; Trish Duncan, Freedom High School, Tampa, FL; Brian P. Johnson, Centennial High School, Circle Pines, MN; Johnny McCarty, Flour Bluff I.S.D. High School, Corpus Christi, TX; Daniel A. McFarland, Durant High School, Plant City, FL; Helen M. Parke, Ph.D., Meriwether Educational Designs, Greenville, NC; Mary Schroder, St. Aloysius Gonzaga Secondary School, Mississauga, ON, Canada

Publisher's Project Staff

Vice President, Product Development: Kathleen T. Williams, Ph.D., NCSP; Associate Director, Product Development: Teri Mathews; Senior Editor: Julie Maas; Editor: Susan Weinlick; Assistant Editor: Jan Jessup; Development Assistant: Bev Johnson; Senior Designer: Daren Hastings; Senior Designer/Illustrator: Diane McCarty; Senior Designer/Illustrator: Tony Perleberg; Desktop Production Artist: Jack Ross; Production Coordinator/Designer: Katie Sonmor; Production Coordinator/Designer: Laura Henrichsen; Creative Services Manager: Nancy Condon; Purchasing Agent: Mary Kaye Kuzma; Senior Marketing Manager/Secondary Curriculum: Brian Holl

Printed in the United States of America
ISBN 0-7854-3646-4
Product Number 93960
A 0 9 8 7 6 5 4 3

Contents

How to Use This Book: A Study Guide

Welcome to *General Science*. Science touches our lives every day, no matter where we are—at home, at school, or at work. This book covers the areas of physical science, earth science, life science, and the human body. It also focuses on science skills that scientists use. These skills include asking questions, making predictions, designing experiments or procedures, collecting and organizing information, calculating data, making decisions, drawing conclusions, and exploring more options. You probably already use these skills every day. You ask questions to find answers. You gather information and organize it. You use that information to make all sorts of decisions. In this book, you will have opportunities to use and practice all of these skills.

As you read this book, notice how each lesson is organized. Information is presented in a straightforward manner. Examples, tables, illustrations, and photos help clarify concepts. Read the information carefully. If you have trouble with a lesson, try reading it again.

It is important that you understand how to use this book before you start to read it. It is also important to know how to be successful in this course. Information in this first section of the book can help you achieve these things.

How to Study

These tips can help you study more effectively.

◆ Plan a regular time to study.

◆ Choose a quiet desk or table where you will not be distracted. Find a spot that has good lighting.

◆ Gather all the books, pencils, paper, and other equipment you will need to complete your assignments.

◆ Decide on a goal. For example: "I will finish reading and taking notes on Chapter 1, Lesson 1, by 8:00."

◆ Take a five- to ten-minute break every hour to stay alert.

◆ If you start to feel sleepy, take a break and get some fresh air.

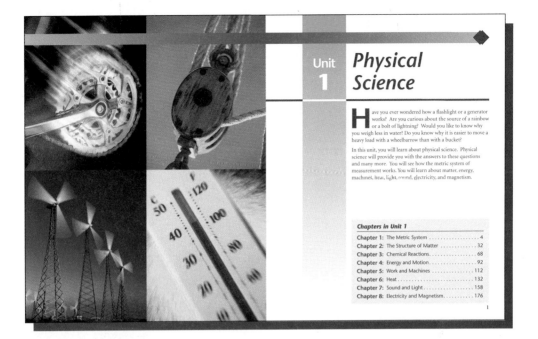

Before Beginning Each Unit

◆ Read the unit title and study the photograph or photographs.

◆ Read the opening paragraphs.

◆ Read the names of the chapters in the unit.

◆ Read the Unit Summary to help you identify the key ideas.

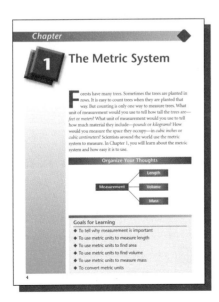

Before Beginning Each Chapter

◆ Read the chapter title and the introductory text.

◆ Study the Goals for Learning. The Chapter Review and tests will ask questions related to these goals.

◆ Read the Chapter Review. The questions cover the most important information in the chapter.

Note These Features

Note

Points of interest or additional information that relates to the lesson

Did You Know?

Facts that add details to lesson content or present an interesting or unusual application of lesson content

Science Myth

Common science misconceptions followed by the correct information

Technology Note

Technology information that relates to the lesson or chapter

Science in Your Life

Examples of science in real life

Achievements in Science

Historical scientific discoveries, events, and achievements

Science at Work

Careers in science

Investigation

Experiments that give practice with chapter concepts

Before Beginning Each Lesson

Read the lesson title and restate it in the form of a question.

For example, write:
Why use metric units to measure length?

Look over the entire lesson, noting the following:
◆ bold words
◆ text organization
◆ notes in the margins
◆ photos and illustrations
◆ lesson review questions

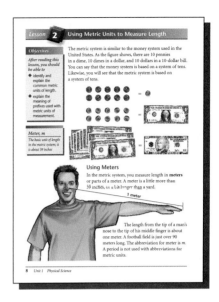

Using the Bold Words

Knowing the meaning of all the boxed vocabulary words in the left column will help you understand what you read.

These words are in **bold type** the first time they appear in the text. They are often defined in the paragraph.

Chemistry is the study of matter and how it changes.

All of the words in the left column are also defined in the **glossary.**

Chemistry (kemʹə strē) the study of matter and how it changes (p. 3)

Bold type
Words seen for the first time will appear in bold type

Glossary
Words listed in this column are also found in the glossary

Word Study Tips

◆ Start a vocabulary file with index cards to use for review.
◆ Write one term on the front of each card. Write the chapter number, lesson number, and definition on the back.
◆ You can use these cards as flash cards by yourself or with a study partner to test your knowledge.

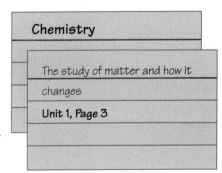

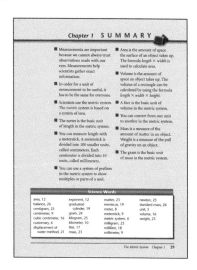

Using the Summaries

◆ Read the summaries from your text to be sure you understand the main ideas in the chapter or unit.

◆ Make up a sample test of items you think may be on the test. You may want to do this with a classmate and share your questions.

◆ Read the vocabulary words in the Science Words box with each Chapter Summary.

◆ Review your notes and test yourself on vocabulary words and key ideas.

◆ Practice writing about some of the main ideas.

Using the Reviews

◆ Answer the questions in the Lesson Reviews.

◆ In the Unit and Chapter Reviews, answer the questions about vocabulary under the Vocabulary Review. Study the words and definitions. Say them aloud to help you remember them.

◆ Answer the questions under the Concept Review and Critical Thinking sections of the Reviews.

◆ Review the Test-Taking Tips.

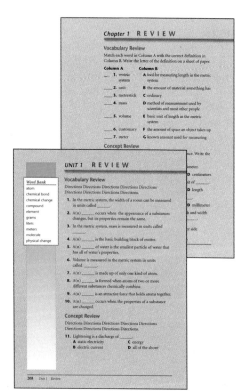

Preparing for Tests

For each unit:

◆ Complete the Investigations.

◆ Go over your answers to the Reviews and Investigations.

◆ Test yourself on vocabulary words and key ideas.

◆ Use graphic organizers as study tools.

Using Graphic Organizers

A graphic organizer is a visual representation of information. It can help you see how ideas are related to each other. A graphic organizer can help you study for a test or organize information before you write. Here are some examples.

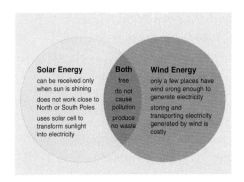

Venn Diagram

A Venn diagram can help you compare and contrast two things. For example, this diagram compares and contrasts solar energy and wind energy. The characteristics of solar energy are listed in the left circle. The characteristics of wind energy are listed in the right circle. The characteristics that both have are listed in the intersection of the circles.

Four Biomes			
Tundra	**Grassland**	**Tropical Rain Forest**	**Desert**
cold, dry frozen below the surface	temperate humid	warm wet	very dry
lichens, low shrubs	grasses	palms, tree ferns, vines	cacti
polar bears, caribou, wolves	antelopes, bison, coyotes	bats, birds, monkeys	lizards, snakes, kangaroo rats

Column Chart

Column charts can help you organize information into groups, or categories. Grouping things in this format helps make the information easier to understand and remember. For example, this four-column chart groups information about each of the four biomes. A column chart can be divided into any number of columns or rows. The chart can be as simple as a two-column list of words or as complex as a multiple-column, multiple-row table of data.

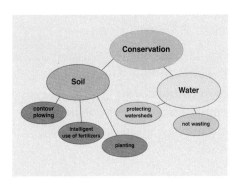

Network Tree

A network tree organizer shows how ideas are connected to one another. Network trees can help you identify main ideas or concepts linked to related ideas. For example, this network tree identifies concepts linked to the concept of conservation. You can also use network trees to rank ideas from most important to least important.

The Nature of Science

Science is an organized body of knowledge about the natural world. It encompasses everything from atoms to rocks to human health. Scientific knowledge is important because it solves problems, improves everyday life, and uncovers new opportunities. For example, scientists develop vaccines and antibiotics to prevent and cure diseases. Scientific knowledge helps farmers grow better and more crops. Science is behind the electricity we depend on every day. And science has launched space exploration, which continues to offer new opportunities.

Scientists use a logical process to explore the world and collect information. It is called the scientific method, and it includes specific steps. Scientists follow these steps or variations of these steps to test whether a possible answer to their question is correct.

1. Ask a question.
2. State a hypothesis, or make a prediction, about the answer.
3. Design an experiment, or procedure, to test the hypothesis.
4. Perform the experiment and gather information.
5. Analyze the data and organize the results.
6. State a conclusion based on the results, existing knowledge, and logic. Determine whether the results support the hypothesis.
7. Communicate the results and the conclusion.

As a scientist researches a question, he or she may do these steps in a different order or may even skip some steps. The scientific method requires many skills: predicting, observing, organizing, classifying, modeling, measuring, inferring, analyzing, and communicating.

Communication is an important part of the scientific method. Scientists all over the world share their findings with other scientists. They publish information about their experiments in journals and discuss them at meetings. A scientist may try another scientist's experiment or change it in some way. If many scientists get the same results from an experiment, then the results are repeatable and considered reliable.

Sometimes the results of an experiment do not support its hypothesis. Unexpected observations can lead to new, more interesting questions. For example, penicillin was discovered

accidentally in 1928. Alexander Fleming observed that mold had contaminated one of his bacteria cultures. He noticed that the mold had stopped the growth of the bacterium. Since the mold was from the penicillium family, he named it penicillin. A decade later, researchers found a way to isolate the active ingredient. Since then, penicillin has been used to fight bacteria and save people's lives.

Once in a while, scientists discover something that dramatically changes our world, like penicillin. But, more often, scientific knowledge grows and changes a little at a time.

What scientists learn is applied to problems and challenges that affect people's lives. This leads to the development of practical tools and techniques. Tools help scientists accurately observe and measure things in the natural world. A new tool often provides data that an older tool could not. For example, computers help scientists analyze data more quickly and accurately than ever before. Our science knowledge grows as more advanced tools and technology make new discoveries possible.

Scientists use theories to explain their observations and data. A theory is a possible explanation for a set of data. A theory is not a fact. It is an idea. Theories are tested by more experiments. Theories may be confirmed, changed, or sometimes tossed out. For example, in 1808, John Dalton published a book describing his theory of atoms. His theory stated that atoms are solid spheres without internal structures. By the early 1900s, however, new tools allowed Ernest Rutherford to show that atoms are mostly empty space. He said that an atom consists of a tightly packed nucleus with electrons whizzing around it. This theory of the atom is still accepted today.

Theories that have stood many years of testing often become scientific laws. The law of gravity is one example. Scientists assume many basic laws of nature.

In this book, you will learn about physical science, earth science, and biology. You will use scientific skills to solve problems and answer questions. You will follow some of the steps in the scientific method. And you will discover how important science is to your life.

Unit 1

Physical Science

Have you ever wondered how a flashlight or a generator works? Are you curious about the source of a rainbow or a bolt of lightning? Would you like to know why you weigh less in water? Do you know why it is easier to move a heavy load with a wheelbarrow than with a bucket?

In this unit, you will learn about physical science. Physical science will provide you with the answers to these questions and many more. You will see how the metric system of measurement works. You will learn about matter, energy, machines, heat, light, sound, electricity, and magnetism.

Chapters in Unit 1

Unit 1

What Is Physical Science?

Physical science is the study of the things around you. It deals with **matter** and energy. Matter is anything that has **mass** and takes up space.

The Study of Matter and Energy

Look around you. What do you have in common with all the objects you see—your desk, the floor, the air? At first, you might think you have very little in common with these objects. But, in fact, all of them—including you—are made of matter. Other examples of matter appear in the photograph.

All matter has mass. Mass is the amount of material that an object has. All of the objects in the photo have mass. The cat has more mass than the potted plant.

Energy is different from matter. You cannot hold energy or measure it with a ruler. Energy is needed to make things move. You use it to move your body. A car uses energy to move, too.

What do all these objects have in common?

Two Areas of Physical Science

Physical science can be divided into two areas. One area is **chemistry.** Chemistry is the study of matter and how it changes. Chemistry can explain how a cake rises or how acid rain forms. Chemistry is also the study of how matter can be made into new materials. By studying chemistry, scientists have made new medicines, food, clothing, fragrances, and soaps. They have even made artificial skin and bones for people.

A second area of physical science is **physics.** Physics is the study of energy and how it acts with matter. Physics can explain why helium balloons rise or how lasers work. Scientists studying physics have developed television, cellular phones, stereo systems, computers, space satellites, microwave ovens, and jet airplanes.

Computers and cell phones are among the many products physical scientists have developed.

The Metric System

Forests have many trees. Sometimes the trees are planted in rows. It is easy to count trees when they are planted that way. But counting is only one way to measure trees. What unit of measurement would you use to tell how tall the trees are—*feet* or *meters*? What unit of measurement would you use to tell how much material they include—*pounds* or *kilograms*? How would you measure the space they occupy—in *cubic inches* or *cubic centimeters*? Scientists around the world use the metric system to measure. In Chapter 1, you will learn about the metric system and how easy it is to use.

Organize Your Thoughts

Measurement
- Length
- Volume
- Mass

Goals for Learning

◆ To tell why measurement is important

◆ To use metric units to measure length

◆ To use metric units to find area

◆ To use metric units to find volume

◆ To use metric units to measure mass

◆ To convert metric units

Unit

A known amount used for measuring

Did You Know?

In ancient times, the Arabs used carob beans as a standard to measure small amounts. Carob beans are very consistent in size. They usually weigh the same no matter when or where they were grown.

Look at the poles in the photo. Which one is the tallest? Use a ruler to measure each one.

Are the poles the same height?

Though some look taller than others, in reality the poles are the same height. Measurements are important because we cannot always trust observations made with our eyes. Measurements help us gather exact information. Exact measurements are especially important to a scientist.

Units of Measurement

When you measured the poles in the photo above, you probably measured with a ruler marked in inches. You compared the length of the pole to a known measurement, the inch. A known amount in measurement, such as the inch, is called a **unit.** Other units you might be familiar with are the yard, mile, minute, and day.

Science Myth

The metric system is the most accurate way to measure.

Fact: The metric system is one of many ways to measure. Once you know it, it is an easier way to measure. Also, people use it around the world. But it is no more or less accurate than any other measurement system.

If you had lived thousands of years ago, you most likely would have used units of measurement that were based on the length of certain parts of your body.

For example, Egyptians used the cubit to measure length. A cubit was the distance from the elbow to the tip of the middle finger. The Romans used the width of their thumb to measure length. This unit of measurement was called an uncia.

Compare the widths of the thumbs of each person in your classroom. Do you think they are all the same? Probably not. So you can see why using units of measurement based on body parts does not work very well. The exact length of an uncia or a cubit could vary from person to person.

In order for a unit of measurement to be useful, it has to be the same for everybody. When one scientist tells another scientist that something is a certain length, that measurement should mean the same thing to both of them.

Systems of Measurement

You probably measure in units based on the **customary** system. Some customary units for measuring length are the inch, foot, yard, and mile. Customary units also can be used to measure time, weight, and other amounts.

In the customary system of measurement, it is difficult to convert one unit to another because the units are very different. The units of measure also are not clearly related to each other.

Scientists and most other people throughout the world use a different system of measurement. They use the **metric system.** Metric units are the most common units of measurement in the world. The metric system is simpler to use and easier to remember than the customary system. You will use the metric system in this book. You will find conversion information about some metric and customary measurements in Appendix B on pages 604–605.

Write your answers to these questions in complete sentences on a sheet of paper.

1. Why are measurements important?

2. Why is it important to use units of measurement that are the same for everyone?

3. What are some common units in the customary system of measurement?

4. What is the name of the system of measurement that scientists use?

5. Name the unit of measurement you would use to measure the length of your finger.

Answer these questions to find out how familiar you are with the customary system.

6. How many inches are in 1 foot?

7. How many feet are in 1 yard?

8. How many minutes are in 1 hour?

9. How many seconds are in 1 minute?

10. How many seconds are in 1 hour?

Technology Note

Digital measurers use sound waves to measure distance. A laser beam points at the spot from which you want to measure. At the same time, a sound wave bounces off that spot. The measurer calculates the distance the sound wave traveled. Then it displays the measurement digitally.

After reading this lesson, you should be able to

◆ identify and explain the common metric units of length.

◆ explain the meaning of prefixes used with metric units of measurement.

The metric system is similar to the money system used in the United States. As the figure shows, there are 10 pennies in a dime, 10 dimes in a dollar, and 10 dollars in a 10-dollar bill. You can say that the money system is based on a system of tens. Likewise, you will see that the metric system is based on a system of tens.

 =

 =

Meter, m

The basic unit of length in the metric system; it is about 39 inches

Using Meters

In the metric system, you measure length in **meters** or parts of a meter. A meter is a little more than 39 inches, or a bit longer than a yard.

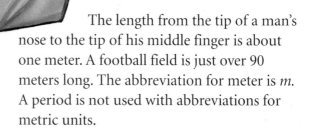

1 meter

The length from the tip of a man's nose to the tip of his middle finger is about one meter. A football field is just over 90 meters long. The abbreviation for meter is *m*. A period is not used with abbreviations for metric units.

Did You Know?

The way scientists define the meter keeps changing. It used to be one ten-millionth of the distance from the North Pole to the equator. Now it is how far light travels during a small fraction of a second.

The common tool for measuring length in the metric system is the **meterstick.** It is one meter long.

The figure below shows part of a meterstick. Notice that it is divided into equal units. Each of these units is a **centimeter.** A centimeter is $\frac{1}{100}$ of a meter. You can use centimeters when the meter is too long a unit. For example, it might be difficult to measure the width of your book in meters, but you could easily use centimeters. The abbreviation for centimeter is *cm*.

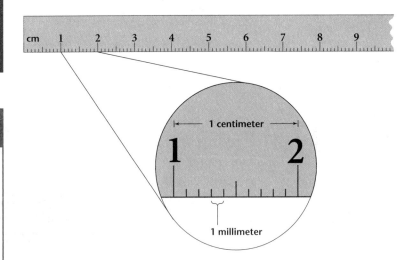

Sometimes, even the centimeter is too large a unit to measure an object. You need a smaller unit. Look at the meterstick again. Notice that each centimeter is divided into 10 smaller units. Each of these smaller units is a **millimeter.** A millimeter is $\frac{1}{1,000}$ of a meter. You would measure the width of a pencil in millimeters. Use *mm* as an abbreviation for millimeter.

Using meters to describe the distance from your school to your home would likely result in a large number of units. It would be more convenient to use a unit larger than a meter. The **kilometer,** which is equal to 1,000 meters, would be more useful. The abbreviation for kilometer is *km*.

Length Equivalents	
10 millimeters	1 centimeter
1,000 millimeters	1 meter
100 centimeters	1 meter
1,000 meters	1 kilometer

Did You Know?

Only three countries do not use the metric system as their official measurement system. They are the United States, Myanmar (Burma), and Liberia.

Using Metric Prefixes

Once you understand how the meterstick is divided, you know how to use other units of measurement in the metric system. The prefixes in front of the word *meter* have special meanings. They are used to show how many times the meter is multiplied or divided. Just as a cent is $\frac{1}{100}$ of a dollar, a centimeter is $\frac{1}{100}$ of a meter. The prefix *centi-* means $\frac{1}{100}$. You will learn how to use the prefixes shown in the table with other units of measurement later in this chapter.

Any measurement of a physical quantity must include two things. The measurement must include a number followed by a unit.

Some Metric Prefixes		
Prefix	Meaning	Unit and Its Abbreviation
kilo- (k)	$1,000 \times$	kilometer (km)
centi- (c)	$\frac{1}{100}$ (0.01)	centimeter (cm)
milli- (m)	$\frac{1}{1,000}$ (0.001)	millimeter (mm)

Write your answers to these questions in complete sentences on a sheet of paper.

1. Which letter in the figure below marks 1 millimeter?

2. Which letter shows 1 centimeter?

3. How many millimeters are there in 1 centimeter?

4. How many millimeters are there in 10 centimeters?

5. What is the measurement in millimeters of the match? What is it in centimeters?

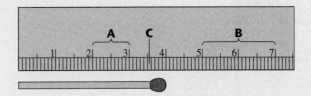

Achievements in Science

Measurement Standards

Every measurement compares an unknown quantity with a standard. A measurement standard defines the size of a unit. People based early standards on local customs. They sometimes used body parts to create standards. They also used objects like grains and stones.

In the 1400s, King Edward I of England created what may have been the first uniform standards. He ordered a measuring stick made of iron to be a master yardstick. The first metric standards were a standard meter bar and kilogram bar. The French government officially adopted them in 1799. The international kilogram bar and meter bar are made of a mixture of metals.

The Bureau of Weights and Measures in France keeps standards of length and mass. In the United States, the National Institute of Standards and Technology keeps these same standards. All metersticks and scales are checked against these standards.

Objectives

After reading this lesson, you should be able to

◆ explain and define area.

◆ calculate area in metric units.

You can use measurements of length to calculate other measurements. One example of a calculated measurement is **area.** Area is the amount of space the surface of an object takes up.

For example, each side of a square measures 1 cm. To find the area of the square, multiply the length by the width.

EXAMPLE

$$area = length \times width$$
$$= 1 \text{ cm} \times 1 \text{ cm}$$
$$= 1 \text{ cm}^2$$

Area

Amount of space the surface of an object takes up

Exponent

A number that tells how many times another number is a factor

When you calculate area, the units of length and width must be the same. Express the answer in square units. To do this, write a small 2 at the upper right of the unit. This is called an **exponent.** An exponent is a number that tells how many times another number is a factor. In the example above, the unit is read *square centimeter.* Square centimeter (cm^2) means centimeter $\times$ centimeter. The area of the square is 1 square centimeter (1 cm^2).

You can find the area of a rectangle by using the same formula you used to find the area of a square.

EXAMPLE

$$area = length \times width$$
$$= 3 \text{ cm} \times 2 \text{ cm}$$
$$= 6 \text{ cm}^2$$

The area of the rectangle is 6 square centimeters.

What is the area of a rectangle with a length of 8.5 mm and a width of 3.3 mm?

EXAMPLE

$$area = length \times width$$
$$= 8.5 \text{ mm} \times 3.3 \text{ mm}$$
$$= 28.05 \text{ mm}^2$$

The area is 28.05 square millimeters.

Find the area for each of the rectangles in the table. Write your answers on a sheet of paper. The first one is done for you.

	Length	Width	Area (length × width)
1.	8 cm	7.2 cm	8 cm × 7.2 cm = 57.6 cm^2
2.	8 m	8 m	
3.	3.4 mm	5.2 mm	
4.	2.6 m	4.7 m	
5.	13 m	5.1 km	

Science in Your Life

Do you have enough paint?

If you have ever gone to a store to buy paint, you know that first you have to figure out how much paint you need. It is easy to do if you use what you learned about calculating area.

Suppose you have a wall that measures 3.5 m long and 8 m high. You want to paint it. The instructions on the paint can say that the paint will cover 32 m^2 of surface area. Do you have enough paint to cover the wall?

3.5 meters

8 meters

INVESTIGATION

Materials
- safety glasses
- small sheet of paper
- ruler
- safety scissors

Counting Squares and Calculating Area

Purpose
How is area related to square units? This investigation will show the relationship between area and the number of square units.

Procedure

1. Copy the data table on a sheet of paper.

	Length	Width	Area (length × width)	Total Number of Squares
original paper				
rectangle 1				
rectangle 2				

2. Put on your safety glasses. Obtain a small sheet of paper from your teacher. The size of your paper will be larger or smaller than your classmates' papers. Use a ruler to measure the length and width of the paper. Record these two measurements in centimeters in your table.

3. Use the following formula to calculate the area of the paper.

$$\text{area} = \text{length} \times \text{width}$$

Record this area. Remember that the units should be square centimeters (cm^2).

4. Use the ruler to mark off all four sides of the paper in 1-cm units. Using the ruler as a straightedge, draw straight lines to connect the marks from side to side. Now connect them from top to bottom. You will create a grid of squares similar to the one on the next page.

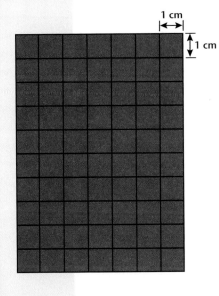

1 cm

1 cm

5. Count the squares on the paper. The area of each square is 1 square centimeter. That is because area = length × width = 1 cm × 1 cm = 1 cm². The area of the sheet of paper is the number of squares. Record that number in your table. The answer should be in square centimeters.

6. Cut the paper into squares along the lines you drew. Use all the individual squares to make two smaller rectangles of different lengths and widths. To do this, carefully place the squares next to each other in rows and columns. Make sure the squares have almost no space between them and that they do not overlap.

7. Measure the length and width of each new rectangle you create. Find the area of each one.

Questions and Conclusions

1. Does the area for the original paper in step 5 match the area calculated in step 3? Do you think it should? Explain your answer.

2. How does the sum of the areas of the two new rectangles compare to the total number of squares in the two rectangles? How does it compare to the calculated area of the original sheet of paper? Explain these results.

Explore Further

Repeat steps 1 through 5. Divide the grid in half. Use a ruler to draw a line from one corner to the opposite corner. Cut along the diagonal line. Measure the area of each triangle using the following formula.

$$area = base \times \frac{height}{2}$$

Calculate the sum of the two triangles. How does it compare to the area of the rectangle?

Objectives

After reading this lesson, you should be able to

◆ explain what volume is.

◆ calculate volume in metric units.

◆ convert metric units of volume.

◆ explain how to use a graduated cylinder to measure volume

Volume

The amount of space an object takes up

Cubic centimeter, cm³

A metric unit of measure that means centimeter × centimeter × centimeter

In 1975, the United States Congress passed the Metric Conversion Act. The act made the metric system the preferred system of measurement for U.S. commerce. It also directed government agencies to use the metric system.

Another calculation that you can make using metric measurements is **volume.** Volume describes the amount of space an object takes up.

Volume of a Solid

The small green box in the figure below measures 1 cm on each edge. You can find out how much space the box takes up—its volume—by using a simple formula.

EXAMPLE
$$\text{volume} = \text{length} \times \text{width} \times \text{height}$$
$$= 1 \text{ cm} \times 1 \text{ cm} \times 1 \text{cm}$$
$$= 1 \text{ cm}^3$$

The small 3 written to the upper right of the centimeter unit means cubic. It is read **cubic centimeter** or *centimeter cubed.* Cubic centimeter means centimeter × centimeter × centimeter. The volume of the small green box is 1 cubic centimeter.

1 cm
1 cm
1 cm
1 cubic centimeter

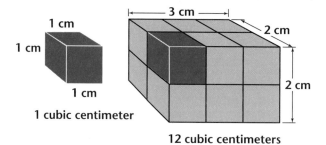

3 cm
2 cm
2 cm
12 cubic centimeters

Now look at the larger box above. Its length is 3 cm. Its width is 2 cm. Its height is 2 cm. You can see that 12 small boxes will fit into the larger box. If each small box is 1 cm³, then the large box would have a volume of 12 cm³.

You also can use the formula to find the volume of the larger box.

EXAMPLE   volume = length × width × height
= 3 cm × 2 cm × 2 cm
= 12 cm^3

Volume of a Liquid

You might be familiar with another unit of volume in the metric system—the **liter.** You can see liter containers at the supermarket, especially in the soft-drink section. A liter is slightly more than a quart. The abbreviation for liter is *L*. The liter is the basic unit of volume in the metric system. It is often used to measure the volume of liquids.

As you can see in the figure, one liter of water will exactly fill a box that measures 10 cm on each side. A liter occupies the same amount of space as 1,000 cubic centimeters.

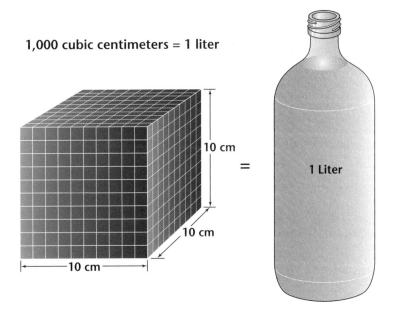

1,000 cubic centimeters = 1 liter

10 cm

10 cm

10 cm

=

1 Liter

4006400147571 2

Milliliter, mL

A metric unit of measure that is $\frac{1}{1,000}$ of a liter; it equals one cubic centimeter

You can use the same prefixes you used with the meter to form other units of measurement. The only prefix that is commonly used to measure volume is *milli-*. Remember that *milli-* means $\frac{1}{1,000}$. A **milliliter** is $\frac{1}{1,000}$ of a liter. The abbreviation for milliliter is *mL*. There are 1,000 milliliters in a liter. Since there are also 1,000 cubic centimeters in one liter, a milliliter is the same as one cubic centimeter.

Volume Equivalents	
1 liter (L)	1,000 cubic centimeters
1 cubic centimeter (cm³)	$\frac{1}{1,000}$ liter (0.001 L)
1 milliliter (mL)	$\frac{1}{1,000}$ liter (0.001 L)
1 milliliter (mL)	1 cubic centimeter (cm³)

Sometimes you will have to convert cubic centimeters to liters. Since one cubic centimeter is $\frac{1}{1,000}$ of a liter, you can convert by dividing by 1,000.

EXAMPLE   Express 1,256 cm³ as liters.
1,256 ÷ 1,000 = 1.256 L

You can also convert liters to cubic centimeters. Simply multiply by 1,000.

EXAMPLE   Express 4.3 L as cubic centimeters.
4.3 L × 1,000 = 4,300 cm³

Measuring with a Graduated Cylinder

To measure the volume of a liquid, you can use a **graduated cylinder.** Graduated cylinders come in many different sizes. The largest ones usually hold 1 L of a liquid. More common sizes hold 100mL, 50 mL, or 10 mL. Follow this procedure.

1. Pour the liquid into the graduated cylinder.

2. Position yourself so that your eye is level with the top of the liquid. You can see the correct position in the figure below.

3. Read the volume from the scale that is on the outside of the cylinder. The top of the liquid usually is curved. This curve is called a **meniscus.** You can see the meniscus in the figure to the left. Read the scale on the bottom of the curve as shown. The volume of this liquid is 16 mL.

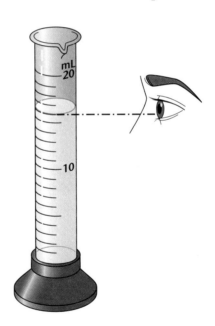

To measure the volume of a liquid in a graduated cylinder, you need to know what the spaces between the lines represent. In other words, you need to be able to read the scale. It is easy to do if you follow this procedure.

1. Subtract the numbers on any two long lines that are next to each other.

2. Count the spaces between the two long lines.

3. Divide the number you got in step 1 by the number you counted in step 2. In the figure below, each space equals 2 mL.

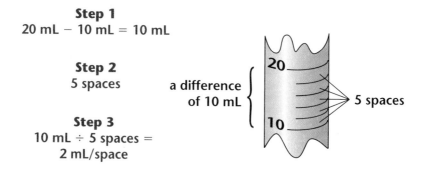

Step 1
20 mL − 10 mL = 10 mL

Step 2
5 spaces

a difference of 10 mL

20

10

5 spaces

Step 3
10 mL ÷ 5 spaces =
2 mL/space

Achievements in Science

The Metric System

The metric system is the first standardized system of measurement based on the decimal. Before the metric system, units of length, area, and weight varied from country to country. Ways of measuring were sometimes different even within a country. England had three different systems. In order to trade goods fairly, merchants and tradesmen needed a uniform system. Scientists needed a way to exchange information.

In France, the idea of the metric system first was suggested around 1670. No action was taken, however, for more than 100 years. In the 1790s, the French Academy of Sciences proposed a new system of measurement. The French revolutionary assembly adopted the metric system in 1795.

At first, the people of France had a hard time changing to a new system. For a time in the early 1800s, France went back to the old units of measure. But in 1837, the metric system became the rule in France. Soon other countries throughout the world began using the metric system.

Displacement of water method

Method of measuring volume of irregularly shaped objects

Volume of an Irregular Solid

You have learned the formula for finding the volume of a rectangular solid. You cannot use a formula to find the volume of a solid with an irregular shape. Instead, you can use the **displacement of water method** to find the volume of irregularly shaped objects.

Figure A

If a glass is partially filled with water and you place an object in the glass, the level of the water will rise. In fact, the water level will rise by an amount equal to the volume of the object that was placed in the glass.

To measure the volume of a small, solid object using the displacement of water method, follow the procedure below. Remember to cover the object completely with water.

1. Pour water into a graduated cylinder. Record the volume of the water. (Figure A)

$$volume = 10 \text{ cm}^3$$

Figure B

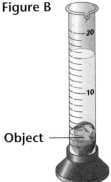

Object

2. Place the object in the cylinder. The water level will then rise. Record this new volume. (Figure B)

$$volume = 16 \text{ cm}^3$$

3. Subtract the volume of the water from the volume of the water and the object. The difference will be the volume of the object.

$$16 \text{ cm}^3 - 10 \text{ cm}^3 = 6 \text{ cm}^3$$

The volume of the object is 6 cm³.

Lesson 4 R E V I E W

Write your answers to these questions in complete sentences on a sheet of paper.

1. A box measures 8 cm by 9 cm by 12 cm. What is its volume?

2. What is the volume of a stainless-steel container with a length of 18 mm, width of 20 mm, and height of 10 mm?

3. Find the volume of a cabinet that measures 1.20 m by 5 m by 75 cm. (Hint: Convert meters to centimeters. Remember that 1 m = 100 cm.)

4. Explain how you could use a graduated cylinder to find the volume of a small rock.

Convert each of these measurements. Write the answers on your paper.

5. 3 L = _____ mL

6. 5.5 L = _____ mL

7. 3,000 cm^3 = _____ L

8. 3,700 cm^3 = _____ L

9. 0.72 L = _____ mL

10. 350 mL = _____ cm^3

▼◄▲▼◄▲▼◄▲▼◄▲▼◄▲▼◄▲▼◄▲▼◄▲▼◄▲▼◄▲▼◄▲▼◄▲▼◄▲▼

Science at Work

Instrument Calibration Technician

Instrument calibration technicians calibrate, or check the accuracy of, three types of instruments. The instruments make measurements, control equipment, or give information about what equipment is doing. All these instruments must be exact.

Instrument calibration technicians first test an instrument by comparing it with another instrument. They study the test results and keep a record. Instrument calibration technicians maintain and repair instruments so they stay calibrated.

Instrument calibration technicians must earn a two-year degree in electronics technology.

They must be able to handle details and must have strong fine-motor skills. They also must understand electronics.

Weight
_____
The measure of how hard gravity pulls on an object

Newton
_____
The metric unit of weight

Everything around you is made up of matter. Matter is anything that has mass and takes up space. The mass of an object refers to the amount of material it has. For example, the mass of the man in the figure is 65 kg. But what is the man's **weight?** Are mass and weight the same?

Mass and Weight

Mass and *weight* are often used to mean the same thing. However, scientists have different meanings for these two words. Mass measures how much matter is in an object. Weight is a measure of how hard gravity pulls on an object. The force of gravity depends on the mass of an object. Objects with a large mass will have a strong pull of gravity.

You may have seen a scale like the one shown here at the grocery store or supermarket. You can use a scale like this to measure the weight of produce such as grapes or tomatoes.

Scientists use the **newton** when describing weight. A mass of 1 kg has a metric weight of 9.8 newtons.

The mass of an object never changes under normal conditions. But the weight of an object can change when it is moved to some other place. For example, the pull of gravity on the moon is less than the pull of Earth's gravity. So when the astronaut in the photograph went to the moon, he weighed less on the moon than he did on Earth. But his mass did not change.

This astronaut weighs less on the moon than on Earth, but has the same mass.

In the metric system, the **gram** is the basic unit of mass. Look at the figure below. One gram equals the mass of one cubic centimeter of water. That is about the same mass as a large wooden match or a small paper clip. There are 454 grams in one pound. The abbreviation for gram is *g*.

1 cm³ water
1 g   =   1g   =   1g

Technology Note

Most electronic scales have a load cell. A load cell changes force or weight into an electrical signal. An indicator reads the signal. The indicator shows how much an object weighs. Scales in grocery stores have load cells. So do scales used to weigh large trucks on highways.

Did You Know?

Deimos, a moon of Mars, has very low mass. This makes its gravity much less than the earth's gravity. On Deimos, you would weigh very little. You could jump a great distance off the surface on a pogo stick.

Mass Equivalents

Recall that the meter sometimes is too large or too small to measure the length of certain objects. The same is true for the gram. For example, a person may have a mass of 85,000 grams. That's a large number!

You can use the same prefixes you use with meters to show parts of a gram or multiples of a gram. The table below shows these units of mass.

Mass Equivalents	
1 kilogram (kg)	1,000 g
1 centigram (cg)	$\frac{1}{100}$ g (0.01 g)
1 milligram (mg)	$\frac{1}{1,000}$ g (0.001 g)

To measure the mass of a person, you probably would use **kilograms.** One kilogram equals 1,000 grams. The abbreviation for kilogram is *kg.* However, the mass of a single hair from your head would be measured in smaller units called **milligrams.** A milligram is $\frac{1}{1,000}$ of a gram. The abbreviation for milligram is *mg.* A **centigram** is $\frac{1}{100}$ of a gram. The abbreviation for centigram is *cg.*

If 1 cubic centimeter of water has a mass of 1 gram, then 1,000 cubic centimeters will have a mass of 1,000 grams, or 1 kilogram. Remember that there are 1,000 cubic centimeters in 1 liter. Therefore, as the figure below shows, 1 liter of water will have a mass of 1 kilogram.

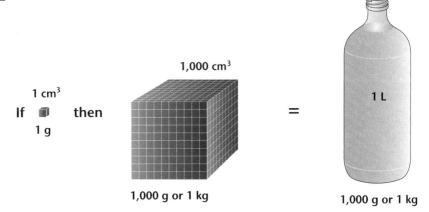

Using a Balance to Measure Mass

You can use an instrument called a **balance** to measure mass. There are many different kinds of balances. But the simplest kind often looks like the one in the figure below. When you use this kind of balance, you find the mass of an object by balancing it with objects of known masses.

A **standard mass** is a small object that is used with a balance to determine mass. The object is usually a brass cylinder with the mass stamped on it. Look at the standard masses in the figure. Most people use standard masses when they use a balance. You can place standard masses on the pan opposite the object to be measured until the two pans are balanced. The mass of the object is equal to the total of the standard masses.

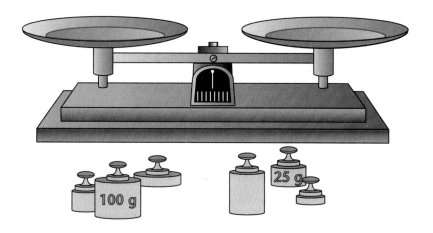

Measuring Liquid Mass

You can find the mass of a solid by using a balance. But how do you find the mass of a liquid? You can use a similar procedure.

1. Measure the mass of an empty container, such as a beaker.

2. Pour the liquid you want to measure into the beaker.

3. Measure the mass of the liquid plus the beaker.

4. Subtract the mass of the empty beaker from the mass of the beaker plus liquid. The answer will be the mass of the liquid.

mass of liquid = mass of liquid plus beaker − mass of beaker

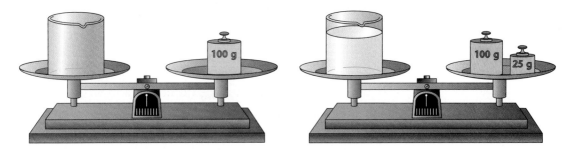

Mass of empty beaker = 100 g   Mass of beaker plus liquid = 125 g

The mass of the liquid is 125 g − 100 g = 25 g

Achievements in Science

Balances

The first scales were used more than 4,500 years ago in ancient Egypt. The oldest kind of scale is the balance.

The first balance was the equal-arm balance. Egyptians made the equal-arm balance around 2,500 B.C. An equal-arm balance has a bar with a pan hanging from each end. The bar is held up at the center by a piece of metal or other hard material. The object whose mass is being measured is put in one pan. Standard masses are placed in the other pan until the two pans balance. A pointer shows that the pans are balanced.

About 2,500 years later, the Romans invented the steelyard balance. A steelyard balance has a bar with arms that are not the same length. The shorter arm has a pan or hook to hold the object that is being measured. A small standard mass is moved along the longer arm until it balances. Markings on the arm show the object's weight.

Lesson 5   R E V I E W

Convert each of these measurements. Write the answers on a sheet of paper.

1. 6 g = _____ mg

2. 80,000 g = _____ kg

3. 90 g = _____ cg

Write the answers to these questions on your paper.

4. How does mass differ from weight?

5. Are you measuring mass or weight when you use a grocery scale?

6. What is the weight in newtons of a 5 kg mass?

7. A container has a mass of 150 g. What is the mass of a liquid if the container plus the liquid has a mass of 185 g?

8. A container has a mass of 125 g. When a liquid is added, the mass becomes 163 g. What is the mass of the liquid?

9. Suppose the mass of a certain liquid is 35 g. You place it in a beaker that has a mass of 75 g. What is the mass of the beaker plus the liquid?

10. A beaker has a mass of 100 g. Liquid is poured into the beaker. The mass of the liquid and the beaker is 135 g. What is the mass of the liquid?

■ Measurements are important because we cannot always trust observations made with our eyes. Measurements help scientists gather exact information.

■ In order for a unit of measurement to be useful, it has to be the same for everyone.

■ Scientists use the metric system. The metric system is based on a system of tens.

■ The meter is the basic unit of length in the metric system.

■ You can measure length with a meterstick. A meterstick is divided into 100 smaller units, called centimeters. Each centimeter is divided into 10 units, called millimeters.

■ You can use a system of prefixes in the metric system to show multiples or parts of a unit.

■ Area is the amount of space the surface of an object takes up. The formula *length × width* is used to calculate area.

■ Volume is the amount of space an object takes up. The volume of a rectangle can be calculated by using the formula *length × width × height.*

■ A liter is the basic unit of volume in the metric system.

■ You can convert from one unit to another in the metric system.

■ Mass is a measure of the amount of matter in an object. Weight is a measure of the pull of gravity on an object.

■ The gram is the basic unit of mass in the metric system.

Science Words

area, 12	exponent, 12	matter, 3	newton, 23
balance, 26	graduated	meniscus, 19	standard mass, 26
centigram, 25	cylinder, 19	meter, 8	unit, 5
centimeter, 9	gram, 24	meterstick, 9	volume, 16
cubic centimeter, 16	kilogram, 25	metric system, 6	weight, 23
customary, 6	kilometer, 10	milligram, 25	
displacement of	liter, 17	milliliter, 18	
water method, 21	mass, 23	millimeter, 9	

Chapter 1 R E V I E W

Vocabulary Review

Match each word in Column A with the correct definition in Column B. Write the letter of the definition on a sheet of paper.

Column A

Column B

_____ **1.** metric system

A tool for measuring length in the metric system

_____ **2.** unit

B the amount of material something has

_____ **3.** meterstick

C ordinary

_____ **4.** mass

D method of measurement used by scientists and most other people

_____ **5.** volume

E basic unit of length in the metric system

_____ **6.** customary

F the amount of space an object takes up

_____ **7.** meter

G known amount used for measuring

Concept Review

Choose the answer that best completes each sentence. Write the letter of the answer on your paper.

8. There are 10 _____ in a centimeter.

    A milligrams **B** millimeters **C** kilometers **D** centimeters

9. In the metric system, the gram is the basic unit of _____.

    A volume   **B** mass   **C** weight   **D** length

10. The longest of the following units is the _____.

    A meter   **B** centimeter **C** kilometer **D** millimeter

11. After using a meterstick to measure the length and width of a rectangle, you can find its area by _____.
    A adding the length and width
    B subtracting the shorter side from the longer side
    C multiplying the length by the width
    D dividing the longer side by the shorter side

12. The measurement _____ describes the area of a square or rectangle.

    A 25 mm   **B** 25 cm   **C** 25 cm^2 **D** 25 cm^3

13. One _____ is equal to 1,000 grams.

    A kilogram   **B** milligram   **C** kilometer   **D** milliliter

14. The basic unit of volume in the metric system is the _____.

    A quart   **C** liter

    B cubic centimeter   **D** A and C

15. If 1 cubic centimeter of water has a mass of 1 gram, then a liter of water has a mass of _____ gram(s).

    A 1   **B** 10   **C** 100   **D** 1,000

Critical Thinking

Write the answer to each of these questions on your paper.

16. Some ancient civilizations used units of measure based on the length of certain seeds. What kinds of problems might you expect with such a system?

17. How is the relationship between units in the money system in the United States similar to the metric system?

18. For each of the following objects, tell which unit of measurement you would use:

    A length of an ant   **C** volume of a large jug of milk

    B mass of a postage stamp   **D** mass of a truck

19. Calculate the volume of the rectangular object shown in the figure.

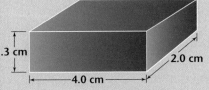

20. If one candle has a mass of 2.5 grams, and all of the candles in a box have a combined mass of 1 kilogram, how many candles are in the box?

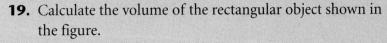

Test-Taking Tip Drawing pictures and diagrams is one way to help you understand and solve problems.

2 The Structure of Matter

Have you ever looked closely at a snowflake? It looks like one large ice crystal. In fact, a snowflake is made up of thousands of small particles of matter called molecules. Each molecule is made of even smaller parts called atoms. In Chapter 2, you will learn more about the particles that make up matter—molecules, atoms, elements, and compounds.

Organize Your Thoughts

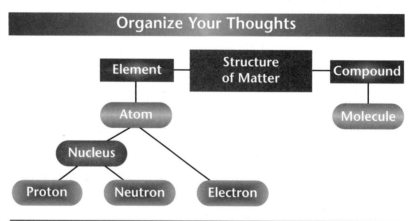

Goals for Learning

◆ To describe various objects by listing their properties

◆ To explain molecules, elements, and compounds

◆ To tell how scientists use models

◆ To describe the parts of an atom

◆ To identify the symbols used to represent different elements

◆ To explain the meaning of atomic number and mass number

◆ To explain what a compound is

Property

A characteristic that helps identify an object

Matter has many properties. One property of matter is the temperature at which something melts. Another property of matter is how it dissolves. How well something conducts electricity is also a property of matter.

If someone asked you to describe sugar, what would you say? You might say "It is a solid made of small, individual pieces." Each part of that description tells a **property** of sugar. A property is a characteristic that helps identify an object. The above description identifies two properties of sugar.

◆ It is a solid.
◆ It is made of small individual pieces.

This description of sugar is correct. But it isn't enough to accurately identify sugar. As you can see in the photo, sand has the same properties. The description could be made more useful by adding other properties. For example, you might add color and taste. Your description of sugar becomes, "It is a white solid made of small, individual pieces that have a sweet taste." Sand could be described as "a tan solid made of small, individual pieces that have no taste."

Sugar and sand have some of the same properties.

Scientists group the properties of matter into two categories. Properties that describe how one kind of matter reacts with another are called chemical properties. All other properties are called physical properties.

Some Common Properties

The photo on this page shows some of the more common properties that you might use to describe matter. Scientists prefer to use some properties more than others. For example, scientists often use mass. The reason is because mass can be measured easily. If someone asked you to describe a rock you saw, you might say it was big. But how big is big? And would someone else think the same rock was big? By using specific measurements of mass, everyone can agree on the measurement. For example, everyone can find the mass of the rock and agree on its mass. Another property that can be measured easily is volume (length, width, and height).

Color: yellowish-red
Shape: almost round
Volume: about 20 mL
Feel: fuzzy, soft

Size: similar to a baseball
Mass: about 0.023 kg
Taste: sweet
Smell: pleasant, sweet

Which of these properties are easy to measure?

Some properties, such as color, cannot be measured as easily. Because of this, descriptions based on color can be misunderstood. For example, how would you describe the color of the fruit in the photo above? One person might describe the color as "pink," while another would call it "yellowish-red." When describing properties, it is important to be as exact as you can. Use measurements whenever possible.

Write your answers to these questions on a sheet of paper.

1. For each of the following statements, tell whether it is a good description. Explain your answer.
   A It is a large, colorful box.
   B The rock has a mass of 25 kilograms.
   C The solid that formed was dark, shiny, and lumpy.

2. A baseball has several properties. Write one property that a baseball has.

3. Could the property you wrote for question 2 also be a property for another object? If yes, write a second property that a baseball has.

4. Choose an object. Write a detailed description of the object.

5. Read your description from question 4 to the class. Can classmates identify the object from your description?

Objectives

After reading this lesson, you should be able to

◆ describe the size of molecules.

◆ explain what a molecule is.

◆ explain how molecules move in each of the three states of matter.

◆ describe plasma.

Molecule

The smallest particle of a substance that has the same properties as the substance

How would you describe the sugar shown in the figure below? You might mention that sugar is a material made of matter. You might tell about its properties, such as its color, taste, or texture. Now think about how you might describe a single grain of sugar. You probably would say that it is very small. But how small is the smallest piece of sugar?

Size of Molecules

Each grain of sugar is made of even smaller particles that are too tiny for you to see. These tiny particles are called **molecules.** Molecules are the smallest particles of a substance that still have the properties of that substance. Each molecule of sugar has exactly the same properties. How small can molecules be? Molecules of some substances are so small that billions of them could be placed side by side on a line one centimeter long.

Describing Molecules

Look at the water spraying out of the fountain in the photo. Imagine dividing one drop of this water into smaller and smaller drops. The smallest drop you could make that still had the properties of water would be one molecule of water.

This fountain contains billions of molecules of water.

In general, all water molecules are alike. A water molecule from the fountain is the same as a water molecule in a raindrop, in a lake, or in the water you drink. The figure on the left shows a molecule of water. You can see that each water molecule has three parts—one large part and two smaller parts.

If you divided a water molecule into its three parts, it would no longer be a molecule of water. The parts would no longer have the properties of water. When a water molecule is divided into its separate parts, each individual part is called an **atom.** An atom is a building block of matter. A water molecule has three atoms. Each kind of atom has its own properties. All matter is made of atoms.

Molecule of water

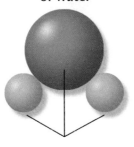

Atoms

States of Matter

You can describe matter by telling about its properties. For example, you might tell about its mass or **density.** The form that matter has is another one of its properties.

There are three forms of matter in the photo below. Can you find them? The boats and rocks are **solids.** A solid is a form of matter that has a definite shape and volume. The molecules in a solid attract, or pull toward, each other. In a solid, molecules vibrate, which means that they move back and forth quickly, but stay close together. For this reason, a solid keeps a certain shape and volume.

Density

A measure of how tightly the matter of a substance is packed into a given volume

Solid

A form of matter that has a definite shape and volume

Liquid

A form of matter that has a definite volume but no definite shape

Science Myth

Gases do not have mass.

Fact: A gas is one of the four states of matter. All matter has mass, even if we cannot see the matter.

How many solids, liquids, and gases do you see?

The water in the photo is a **liquid.** A liquid is a form of matter that has a definite volume but no definite shape. The pull between the molecules is weaker in liquids than it is in solids. The molecules can slide past each other. A liquid can change its shape because its molecules can move around easily.

Suppose you had a liter of water in a container. If you poured the liter of water into a container that had a different shape, the water would still take up one liter of space. But its shape would be different. The water would take the shape of the new container.

Notice the shape of the helium balloon in the photo on page 38. Helium is a **gas** that fills the balloon. Gas is a form of matter that has no definite shape or volume. The molecules of a gas are much farther apart than they are in a liquid or a solid. The attraction between the molecules in a gas is very weak. The gas molecules will always fill a container completely. A container of water can be half full, but a container of a gas will always be completely full. The volume of a gas can change.

Solid   Liquid   Gas

These forms of matter—solid, liquid, and gas—are called the **states of matter.** The figure illustrates how the molecules move in each of these three states of matter.

Plasma

Matter can exist in a fourth state called **plasma.** Plasma is a very hot gas made of particles that have an electric charge. The particles of plasma shake violently at very high temperatures. Plasma is very rare on Earth. But all stars, including the sun, are balls of plasma. Scientists estimate that 90 percent of all matter in the universe is plasma.

Lesson 2   R E V I E W

Write your answers to these questions in complete sentences on a sheet of paper.

1. Can you see a single molecule of sugar? Explain your answer.

2. What parts make up a molecule of water?

3. Describe how molecules move in each of the three states of matter.

4. What is plasma?

5. In which form of matter are the molecules close together?

6. Which form of matter has a definite shape and volume?

7. Which form of matter has no definite shape, but has a definite volume?

8. Which form of matter takes the shape of its container?

9. Where is most plasma located?

10. In which state of matter is the attraction between molecules weakest?

Technology Note

The scanning electron microscope, or SEM, uses electron beams to look at very small items. The SEM makes a sharply detailed, 3–D picture. An SEM picture can show an item up to 200,000 times bigger than it is. The item is magnified so much that you can see molecules.

Objectives

After reading this lesson, you should be able to

◆ describe what a model is and explain how scientists use it.

◆ explain how models of the atom have changed.

◆ describe the electron cloud model.

Model

A picture, an idea, or an object that is built to explain how something else looks or works

Since atoms are too small to be seen with the eyes alone, people have wondered for a long time what atoms look like. In fact, scientists have been studying atoms since the 1800s. But if scientists can't see an atom, how do they know what atoms look like?

Using Models

Sometimes scientists can tell what things look like by studying how they act. For example, have you ever seen wind? What does it look like? You might say that wind is leaves blowing or your hair getting messed up. If you say that, you are describing what wind does, not what it looks like. You use the effects of wind to describe it. You know that wind is there because of its effects even though you can't see it. You use evidence.

Scientists use the same kind of evidence to study things they can't see, such as atoms. Scientists study how atoms act and then decide what an atom must look like. Scientists make **models.**

You have probably seen models of cars or airplanes or buildings. In science, a model is an idea, a picture, or an object that is built to explain how something else looks or works. The model may not look exactly like the object it is built to describe, but it helps people understand the way the object acts.

Models of Atoms

Nucleus

The central part of an atom

Proton

A tiny particle in the nucleus of an atom

Electron

A tiny particle of an atom that moves around the nucleus

In 1827, Robert Brown found the first sign that atoms exist. While· studying pollen under a microscope, he noticed that particles were always moving. This *Brownian* motion comes from the movement of atoms and molecules.

Scientists use models of atoms to show how atoms look and act without having to actually see them. Many scientists have developed models of atoms. The first model was developed over 2,000 years ago. But as scientists gather new information about atoms, they change their models.

In the early 1900s, a scientist developed a model of an atom like those shown at the bottom of the page. Although scientists know more about atoms today, this kind of model is still useful for describing atoms.

Find the center of each atom. This central part of an atom is called the **nucleus.** The nucleus of an atom contains small particles called **protons.** Protons are labeled with the letter *p* in the figures below. Another symbol for a proton is a plus (+) sign. Protons have a positive charge. Look for the letter *e* in the figures below. This letter stands for **electrons.** Electrons are particles in an atom that move around the outside of the protons. The mass of an electron is much less than the mass of a proton. Another symbol for an electron is a minus (−) sign. Electrons have a negative charge. The protons and electrons of an atom stay together because they attract each other.

Notice that the numbers of protons and electrons in the models are different. Figure A shows a model of an atom of hydrogen. You can see that hydrogen has one proton and one electron. Figure B shows an atom of helium, a gas that is often used to fill balloons. How many protons and electrons does helium have?

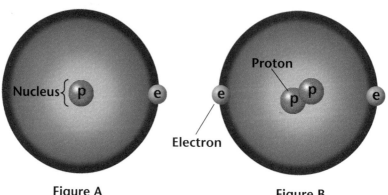

Figure A
An atom of hydrogen

Figure B
An atom of helium

In 1932, scientists had evidence that the nucleus of an atom had another kind of particle. This particle is called a **neutron**. It is similar to a proton in size. Because of the new evidence, scientists changed the model of the atom. In Figure C, an atom of boron shows how the model changed. Find the neutrons, labeled with the letter *n*.

You can see in Figure C that the electrons seem to be on certain paths around the nucleus of the atom. Scientists thought that electrons moved in different layers around protons, sometimes jumping from one layer to another.

Today scientists use another model of atoms. You can see this new model—the electron cloud model—in Figure D. The dark center area represents the nucleus. However, you can't see different layers of electrons like you see in the models in figures A, B, and C. The electron cloud model was developed because of evidence that electrons behave in more complicated ways than scientists previously thought. Because of this new evidence, scientists are not sure how electrons move around the nucleus. As scientists continue to learn more about atoms, perhaps the model will change again.

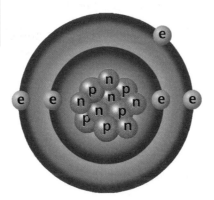

**Figure C
An atom of boron**

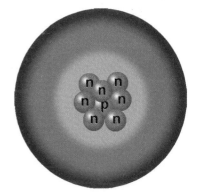

**Figure D
Electron cloud model
of an atom**

In an electrically neutral atom, the number of protons equals the number of electrons. When an atom gains electrons or loses electrons, the charge becomes unbalanced.

You have looked at models showing the number of protons and electrons in a few different atoms. The table below lists some other atoms and tells the numbers of protons and electrons in each. Find the number of protons in carbon. How many electrons does carbon have? Compare the numbers of protons and electrons in nitrogen. How many of each does it have? Now look at the numbers of protons and electrons in each of the atoms listed. What do you notice? The number of protons in an atom is equal to the number of electrons in the atom.

Number of Protons and Electrons for Some Atoms			
Atom	Number of Protons	Number of Electrons	Number of Neutrons
hydrogen	1	1	0
helium	2	2	2
lithium	3	3	4
beryllium	4	4	5
boron	5	5	6
carbon	6	6	6
nitrogen	7	7	7
oxygen	8	8	8
fluorine	9	9	10
neon	10	10	10

Write your answers to these questions in complete sentences on a sheet of paper.

1. If scientists cannot see atoms, how do they know what atoms look like?

2. How do scientists use models?

3. How many protons are in the atom shown in the figure?

4. How many electrons are in the atom?

5. What is the name of the atom? (Hint: Use the table on page 44.)

Achievements in Science

The History of the Atom Model

Democritus, a Greek philosopher, first used the term atom around 400 B.C. In 1803, English schoolteacher John Dalton showed that materials were made of atoms. Ideas about the atom have continued to change. Scientists, at different times in history, have thought about what an atom looks like. In recent years, scientists have done experiments to prove information about atoms.

Over the years, scientists discovered that atoms were made of smaller parts. They also created models for the atom. In the late 1800s, English physicist J. J. Thompson discovered the electron. He also suggested the "plum pudding" model of the atom. He imagined the electrons scattered inside an atom like bits of plum in plum pudding. Fourteen years later New Zealand physicist Ernest Rutherford disproved the plum pudding model. He showed that atoms have a nucleus in the center with electrons on the outside.

Later, Danish scientist Niels Bohr offered his planetary model of the atom. It was based on speculation that seemed to be supported by experiments. Later, however, mathematical calculations led to the electron cloud model.

Objectives

After reading this lesson, you should be able to

◆ explain what an element is.

◆ explain what a natural element is.

◆ give examples of natural elements.

◆ explain what the atomic number of an element is.

Element

Matter that has only one kind of atom

In Lesson 2, you learned that atoms are very tiny. In fact, they are one of the smallest particles that make up matter. Remember the balloon that was filled with helium? A balloon as small as a softball would hold many billions of atoms of helium.

One Kind of Atom

Most of the matter you see around you is made up of many different kinds of atoms. However, some matter has only one kind of atom. Matter that is made of only one kind of atom is called an **element.** All atoms of the same element are alike. For example, all atoms of oxygen are the same. The atoms of oxygen are different from the atoms of all other elements.

The foil you might use to wrap a sandwich is made of atoms of the element aluminum. Gold, silver, and copper are other elements that are used to make jewelry and other common items.

Natural Elements

Scientists know of about 109 different elements. Of these elements, 92 are called **natural elements.** Natural elements are those that are found in nature. For example, oxygen is an element that you get from the air you breathe. Your body is made of atoms of many different elements. Atoms of the element calcium help keep your bones and teeth strong.

Not all elements are natural elements. Scientists are able to produce a few elements in specialized laboratories. Some of the elements that scientists produce last only a short time—a fraction of a second—before they change into other elements.

The table lists some natural elements and tells what they can be used for. Can you think of other uses for some of these elements?

Some Natural Elements	
Name	**Element Is Used or Found in These Items**
copper	coins, frying pans, electrical wire
silver	jewelry, photography
carbon	pencils, charcoal, diamonds
helium	balloons, airships
nitrogen	air that we breathe, fertilizers
chlorine	bleach, table salt
aluminum	airplanes, cookware, soft-drink cans
neon	"neon" signs
gold	jewelry, seawater, dentistry
mercury	thermometers, medicines, pesticides
iron	steel, eating utensils

Elements in Water

You have learned that a molecule of water is made of three parts like those in the figure below. These parts are elements. The large part of the molecule, shown in blue, is an atom of the element oxygen. The two small parts, shown in green, are atoms of the element hydrogen. The atoms of the element oxygen are different from the atoms of the element hydrogen.

Water molecule

Atom of oxygen

Atoms of hydrogen

Because more than 100 elements are known, scientists need a way to identify them. One way scientists can identify elements is by knowing their **atomic numbers.**

Atomic Number

The table below lists the same ten elements listed in the table on page 44. You can see that an additional column, labeled Atomic number, has been added to the table. The atomic number of an element tells you how many protons are in each atom of the element.

Element	Atomic number	Number of protons	Number of electrons
hydrogen	1	1	1
helium	2	2	2
lithium	3	3	3
beryllium	4	4	4
boron	5	5	5
carbon	6	6	6
nitrogen	7	7	7
oxygen	8	8	8
fluorine	9	9	9
neon	10	10	10

Notice that each element has a different number of protons, and therefore a different atomic number. For example, the element hydrogen has 1 proton. Its atomic number is also 1.

How are elements important to health?

Your body needs many natural elements in order to stay healthy and work properly. There are two groups of elements in your body. The major elements are the elements your body needs in large amounts. Your body needs trace elements in smaller amounts. Your body cannot produce any of these elements. You must get them from food.

The table below lists some of the major elements and tells how they are important for your health. The table also lists some foods that contain these elements. Write a menu for a day. Include healthful foods in your menu that provide a variety of natural elements.

Element	Purpose in the Body	Food That Contains the Element
calcium	builds and maintains teeth and bones; helps blood clot; helps nerves and muscles work properly	cheese, milk, dark green vegetables, sardines, legumes
phosphorus	keeps teeth and bones healthy; helps release energy from the food you eat	meat, poultry, fish, eggs, legumes, milk products
magnesium	aids breaking down of foods; controls body fluids	green vegetables, grains, nuts, beans, yeast
sodium	controls the amount of water in body; helps nerves work properly	most foods, table salt
potassium	controls the fluids in cells; helps nerves work properly	oranges, bananas, meats, bran, potatoes, dried beans
iron	helps move oxygen in the blood and in other cells	liver, red meats, dark green vegetables, shellfish, whole-grain cereals
zinc	helps move carbon dioxide in the body; helps in healing wounds	meats, shellfish, whole grains, milk, legumes

Lesson 4   R E V I E W

Write your answers to these questions in complete sentences on a sheet of paper.

1. What is an element?

2. Give three examples of natural elements.

3. Table salt is made up of one sodium atom and one chlorine atom. Is table salt an element? Explain your answer.

4. Name two elements that we need to build and maintain bones in our body.

5. An element has an atomic number of 33. How many protons does it have?

Achievements in Science

Quarks

A fundamental particle is a particle that is not made up of anything else. An electron is a fundamental particle. Protons and neutrons are made of subnuclear particles called quarks.

There are six types of quarks. Scientists usually discuss them as pairs. The up and down quarks are the first and lightest pair. The strange and charm quarks are the second pair. The last pair is made up of the bottom and top quarks. The existence of the top quark was hypothesized for 20 years before scientists discovered it in 1995. It is the most massive quark and was the last to be discovered.

Quarks are different from protons and electrons. Protons and electrons have a charge that is always a whole number. Quarks have a fractional charge. Protons and neutrons are made of up quarks and down quarks. All of the everyday matter in our world is made of electrons, up quarks, and down quarks. The other quarks usually are found only in particle accelerators.

Objectives

After reading this lesson, you should be able to

◆ explain what a symbol is.

◆ explain how element symbols are alike and different.

◆ identify symbols for common elements.

Symbol

One or two letters that represent the name of an element

Think about addressing an envelope for a letter you write to a friend. You probably use an abbreviation to indicate the state to which the letter should be delivered. What is the abbreviation for your state?

Element Symbols

Scientists also use abbreviations to represent each of the 92 natural elements. The abbreviations for elements are called **symbols.** The tables on this page and page 52 list some symbols for elements. All these symbols are alike in the following ways.

◆ All of the symbols have either one or two letters.

◆ The first letter of each symbol is a capital letter.

◆ If the symbol has a second letter, the second letter is a lowercase letter.

◆ No period appears at the end of a symbol.

Table 1	
Element Name	Element Symbol
hydrogen	H
boron	B
carbon	C
nitrogen	N
oxygen	O
fluorine	F
phosphorus	P
sulfur	S
iodine	I
uranium	U

Table 2	
Element Name	Element Symbol
helium	He
lithium	Li
neon	Ne
aluminum	Al
silicon	Si
argon	Ar
calcium	Ca
cobalt	Co
bromine	Br
barium	Ba
radium	Ra

Notice that the symbols in Table 1 on page 51 use only the first letter of the element name. Look at the symbols in Table 2. This group of symbols uses the first two letters of the element name. The symbols in Table 3 also use two letters. The first letter is the first letter of the element name. The second letter is another letter from the element name.

How do the symbols in Table 4 differ from the other symbols? Most of these symbols come from the Latin names for the elements. For example, the symbol for iron is Fe, which comes from the Latin word *ferrum,* meaning "iron."

In recent years, scientists have made new elements in the laboratory. Some of these elements have symbols with three letters. You can see the symbols for these elements in the table on pages 58 and 59.

Table 3	
Element Name	**Element Symbol**
magnesium	Mg
chlorine	Cl
chromium	Cr
manganese	Mn
plutonium	Pu
zinc	Zn
strontium	Sr
platinum	Pt

Table 4	
Element Name	**Element Symbol**
sodium	Na
potassium	K
iron	Fe
silver	Ag
tin	Sn
tungsten	W
gold	Au
mercury	Hg
lead	Pb
antimony	Sb
copper	Cu

Write your answers to these questions in complete sentences on a sheet of paper.

1. How are all of the element symbols alike?

2. Write the symbol for each of the following elements.
  A helium   **B** silver   **C** carbon   **D** chlorine   **E** calcium

3. Write the element name for each of the following symbols.
  A Hg   **B** Ne   **C** Mn   **D** O   **E** P

4. How are abbreviations and symbols alike?

5. Why is Fe the symbol for iron?

▼◄▲▼◄▲▼◄▲▼◄▲▼◄▲▼◄▲▼◄▲▼◄▲▼◄▲▼◄▲▼◄▲▼◄▲▼◄▲▼◄▲▼◄▲▼◄▲▼◄▲▼

Science at Work

Assayer

Assayers are laboratory technicians who analyze samples of precious metals. Assayers collect and analyze rocks and separate metals from them. Using chemical processes or experiments, an assayer collects information about these metals. This information includes how much and what kind of metals are in the samples.

An assayer must complete a two- to three-year technical program or earn a four-year degree in science.

An assayer must be interested in precious metals and be able to keep track of details. An assayer also must be able to work in a laboratory or at a mine site. Good math, decision-making, and communication skills are very important in an assayer's work.

INVESTIGATION

2

Materials

- safety glasses
- 3 different colored pieces of modeling clay
- craft sticks
- metric ruler

Making Models of Atoms

Purpose

What three things must every atom have? You will make a model of a particular atom in this investigation.

Procedure

1. Copy the data table on a sheet of paper.

Name of Atom:	
Picture of Atom:	

2. Put on your safety glasses.

3. Choose an atom from the table on page 44. Find the numbers of protons, neutrons, and electrons in your atom.

4. Place three different colors of modeling clay on your desk. Choose one color of clay for protons. Pull off a small piece of clay for each of the protons in your element. Roll each piece into a ball about 1 cm in diameter.

5. Use another color of clay for neutrons. Make clay balls the same size as the protons. Be sure to make the same number of balls as there are neutrons in your atom.

6. With the third color of clay, make smaller clay balls to represent electrons. Make the same number of balls as the protons you made.

7. Press the protons and neutrons together gently to make the nucleus of your model atom.

8. Gently put the craft sticks into the nucleus of your model. Put the same number of sticks as there are electrons in your atom.

9. Place the clay electrons on the ends of the craft sticks.

10. Write the name of the atom in your table. Then draw a picture of your model.

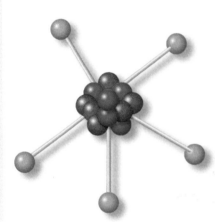

Questions and Conclusions

1. What is the name of your atom?

2. How many protons are in the nucleus?

3. How many neutrons does it have?

4. How many electrons does your atom have?

5. Write at least four things that your model shows about atoms.

Explore Further

Work with other students who have made models of different atoms. Find the mass number of each atom. The mass number is a number equal to the sum of the number of protons and neutrons in an atom. (You will learn more about mass number later in this chapter.) Put the atoms in order from lowest to highest mass number. What happens to the number of protons and neutrons as mass number increases?

Periodic table

An arrangement of elements by increasing atomic number

The **periodic table** is an orderly arrangement of all known elements. Look at the periodic table shown on pages 58 and 59. Notice that elements are arranged from left to right in rows by increasing atomic number. The atomic number of an element tells you the number of protons in its nucleus. The two separate rows at the bottom of the page are too long to fit into the drawing. Arrows show where the rows belong.

Information in the Periodic Table

You can use the periodic table on pages 58 and 59 to learn more about the elements. Each box in the periodic table contains information about one element. The figure below shows the box from the periodic table for the element hydrogen. The symbol for hydrogen, H, is shown in the center of the box. Below the symbol, you can see the name of the element hydrogen.

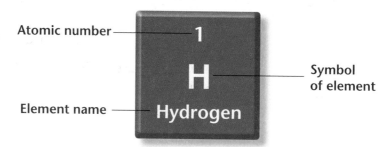

Atomic number — 1

H — Symbol of element

Element name — Hydrogen

Find the atomic number in the box. You can see that the atomic number is shown above the symbol for the element.

The position of an element in the periodic table can tell you many properties of the element. The properties of elements change gradually as you move from left to right across the rows of the table. The properties change because the number of electrons that an atom of an element has increases as you move from left to right. Electrons move around the nucleus of an atom. The number of electrons that surround the nucleus of an atom determines the element's properties.

Isotopes

All atoms of one element have the same atomic number. The atomic number tells the number of protons in the nucleus. However, different atoms of one element may have different masses. The reason for this is that almost every element can be found in slightly different forms. These forms are called **isotopes.** An isotope has the same number of protons and electrons as the original element, but has a different number of neutrons in the nucleus.

The figures below show three isotopes of hydrogen. The first figure shows the most common isotope of hydrogen (H-1). This isotope has one proton and no neutrons. The second figure shows **deuterium** (H-2). Deuterium is an isotope of hydrogen that has one proton and one neutron. The third figure shows **tritium** (H-3). Tritium is an isotope of hydrogen that has one proton and two neutrons. Tritium does not occur naturally on Earth. It is made in a laboratory. Remember that each isotope of hydrogen has the same number of protons and therefore the same atomic number. The labels H-1, H-2, and H-3 refer to the masses of the hydrogen isotopes.

Isotopes have many uses. Scientists use isotopes to follow the path of certain substances in living things. Radioactive isotopes emit particles or rays that can be used to find problems with organs in the human body. Another use of isotopes is to find cracks in underground plumbing pipes.

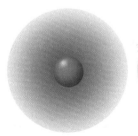

Hydrogen (H-1)
One proton

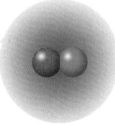

Deuterium (H-2)
One proton and
one neutron

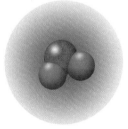

Tritium (H-3)
One proton and
two neutrons

The Periodic Table

1									

1

1
H
Hydrogen
1.01

Metals

Nonmetals

Noble gases

2

	2
1	

3	4
Li	**Be**
Lithium	Beryllium
6.94	9.01

11	12
Na	**Mg**
Sodium	Magnesium
22.99	24.31

		3	4	5	6	7	8	9
4	19 **K** Potassium 39.10	20 **Ca** Calcium 40.08	21 **Sc** Scandium 44.96	22 **Ti** Titanium 47.90	23 **V** Vanadium 50.94	24 **Cr** Chromium 52.00	25 **Mn** Manganese 54.94	26 **Fe** Iron 55.85	27 **Co** Cobalt 58.93
5	37 **Rb** Rubidium 85.47	38 **Sr** Strontium 87.62	39 **Y** Yttrium 88.91	40 **Zr** Zirconium 91.22	41 **Nb** Niobium 92.91	42 **Mo** Molybdenum 95.94	43 **Tc** Technetium (98)	44 **Ru** Ruthenium 101.10	45 **Rh** Rhodium 102.91
6	55 **Cs** Cesium 132.91	56 **Ba** Barium 137.33	57 **La** Lanthanum 138.91	72 **Hf** Hafnium 178.50	73 **Ta** Tantalum 180.95	74 **W** Tungsten 183.90	75 **Re** Rhenium 186.21	76 **Os** Osmium 190.20	77 **Ir** Iridium 192.22
7	87 **Fr** Francium (223)	88 **Ra** Radium 226.02	89 **Ac** Actinium (227)	104 **Rf** Rutherfordium (261)	105 **Db** Dubnium (262)	106 **Sg** Seaborgium (263)	107 **Bh** Bohrium (264)	108 **Hs** Hassium (265)	109 **Mt** Meitnerium (268)

	58	59	60	61	62	63	64
6	**Ce** Cerium 140.12	**Pr** Praseodymium 140.91	**Nd** Neodymium 144.24	**Pm** Promethium 145	**Sm** Samarium 150.40	**Eu** Europium 151.96	**Gd** Gadolinium 157.25
7	90 **Th** Thorium 232.04	91 **Pa** Protactinium (231)	92 **U** Uranium (238)	93 **Np** Neptunium (237)	94 **Pu** Plutonium (244)	95 **Am** Americium (243)	96 **Cm** Curium (247)

# of Elements

			18
			2 **He** Helium 4.00

13	14	15	16	17	
5 **B** Boron 10.81	6 **C** Carbon 12.01	7 **N** Nitrogen 14.01	8 **O** Oxygen 16.00	9 **F** Fluorine 19.00	10 **Ne** Neon 20.18

			13 **Al** Aluminum 26.98	14 **Si** Silicon 28.09	15 **P** Phosphorus 30.97	16 **S** Sulfur 32.07	17 **Cl** Chlorine 35.45	18 **Ar** Argon 39.95

10	11	12						
28 **Ni** Nickel 58.70	29 **Cu** Copper 63.55	30 **Zn** Zinc 65.39	31 **Ga** Gallium 69.72	32 **Ge** Germanium 72.59	33 **As** Arsenic 74.92	34 **Se** Selenium 78.96	35 **Br** Bromine 79.90	36 **Kr** Krypton 83.80
46 **Pd** Palladium 106.42	47 **Ag** Silver 107.90	48 **Cd** Cadmium 112.41	49 **In** Indium 114.82	50 **Sn** Tin 118.69	51 **Sb** Antimony 121.75	52 **Te** Tellurium 127.60	53 **I** Iodine 126.90	54 **Xe** Xenon 131.30
78 **Pt** Platinum 195.09	79 **Au** Gold 196.97	80 **Hg** Mercury 200.59	81 **Tl** Thallium 204.40	82 **Pb** Lead 207.20	83 **Bi** Bismuth 208.98	84 **Po** Polonium 209	85 **At** Astatine (210)	86 **Rn** Radon (222)
110 **Uun** Ununnilium (269)	111 **Uuu** Unununium (272)	112 **Uub** UnFunbium (277)		114 **Uuq** Ununquadium (289)		116 **Uuh** Ununhexium (289)		

65 **Tb** Terbium 158.93	66 **Dy** Dysprosium 162.50	67 **Ho** Holmium 164.93	68 **Er** Erbium 167.26	69 **Tm** Thulium 168.93	70 **Yb** Ytterbium 173.04	71 **Lu** Lutetium 174.97
97 **Bk** Berkelium (247)	98 **Cf** Californium (249)	99 **Es** Einsteinium (254)	100 **Fm** Fermium (257)	101 **Md** Mendelevium (258)	102 **No** Nobelium (259)	103 **Lr** Lawrencium (260)

Note: *The atomic masses listed in the table reflect current measurements.*
The atomic masses listed in parentheses are those of the element's most stable or most common isotope.

Mass number

A number equal to the sum of the numbers of protons and neutrons in an atom of an element

Atomic mass

The average mass of all the isotopes of a particular element

Sometimes an atom's nucleus is unstable. Radioactivity results from the decay of an atom with an unstable nucleus. A radioactive atom sends out small particles and gamma rays. Isotopes that are radioactive are called radioisotopes.

The Mass of an Element

You learned in Chapter 1 that mass is the amount of material in an object. Protons and neutrons have a greater mass than electrons have. In fact, the mass of a proton or a neutron is about 1,800 times the mass of an electron. Yet protons and neutrons are still so small that it would not be possible to measure their mass on a balance scale. Instead, scientists tell about the mass of an element by using its **mass number.** The mass number of an element is equal to the sum of the numbers of protons and neutrons in an atom of the element.

Atomic Mass

The mass number of an element or isotope is the sum of its number of protons and neutrons. The mass numbers are different for hydrogen, deuterium, and tritium. Therefore, each isotope of hydrogen has a different mass number. What is the mass number of each isotope?

The isotopes of most elements do not have names and are identified by their atomic mass. For example, the most common isotope of carbon has a mass number of 12 because it has 6 protons and 6 neutrons. This isotope is called carbon-12. Another isotope of carbon is carbon-13, which has 6 protons and 7 neutrons. Carbon-14 has 6 protons and 8 neutrons.

How does the box shown below differ from the box shown on page 56? An additional number appears at the bottom of the box. Notice that the number is not a whole number. This number is the element's **atomic mass,** the average mass for all the isotopes of the element. The average mass is determined by the masses of an element's isotopes and by the amount of each isotope found in nature.

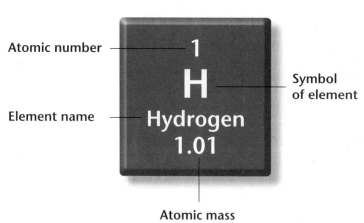

Atomic number

Element name

Symbol of element

Atomic mass

Lesson 6 R E V I E W

Write your answers to these questions in complete sentences on a sheet of paper.

1. How are the elements arranged in the periodic table?

2. Draw the box from the periodic table for hydrogen. Include the symbol for hydrogen as well as its atomic number and atomic mass. Write an explanation of each piece of information in the box.

3. What are isotopes?

4. Explain the differences in hydrogen, deuterium, and tritium.

5. How do you find the mass number of an atom if you know how many protons, neutrons, and electrons that atom has?

Achievements in Science

Helium

Helium (He) is one of the most common elements in the universe. Only hydrogen (H) is more common. Stars are made mostly of helium and hydrogen. Yet helium is very rare on earth.

Helium was first discovered on the sun. Pierre Janssen of France found evidence of helium while studying a solar eclipse in 1868. Helium's name comes from the Greek word *helios,* which means sun.

Chemists discovered helium on earth in 1895. Sir William Ramsay, Nils Langlet, and Per Theodor Cleve found helium in a mineral.

In 1905, Hamilton P. Cady and David E. McFarland made an important discovery about helium. They found that it could be taken out of natural gas wells. Their discovery led to greater use of helium in industry. Helium is largely used in welding. We also use helium to fill different kinds of balloons.

After reading this lesson, you should be able to

◆ explain what a compound is.

◆ give examples of compounds.

Compound

A substance that is formed when atoms of two or more elements join together

All the substances in the figure below are each made of two or more different kinds of atoms. When two or more atoms of different elements join together, the substance that forms is called a **compound.** A compound has properties that are different from the properties of the elements that form the compound.

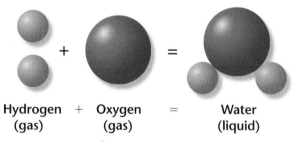

Hydrogen + Oxygen = Water
(gas)   (gas)   (liquid)

Think again about a molecule of water. The drawing to the left shows that an atom of oxygen combines with two atoms of hydrogen to form a molecule of the compound water. Water is different from the elements that form it. Water is a liquid. Both oxygen and hydrogen are gases.

In 1661, Robert Boyle defined an *element* as a material made of only one part. A century later, Antoine Lavoisier defined a *compound*. He defined it as material made of two or more elements.

Another compound that probably is familiar to you is table salt. The chemical name of salt is sodium chloride. It is formed when the element sodium is combined with the element chlorine. Sodium chloride is very different from each of the elements it contains. Sodium is a solid. You might be surprised to learn that chlorine is a poisonous gas. However, when chlorine is combined with sodium to form sodium chloride, chlorine no longer has its poisonous property. Remember that a compound can have completely different properties from the elements that form it.

Most kinds of matter on Earth are compounds. In fact, there are more than 10 million known compounds. The table lists some common compounds and tells the elements that make up each compound.

Some Common Compounds		
Name	Elements in this Compound	How/Where It Is Used
table salt	sodium, chlorine	cooking
water	hydrogen, oxygen	drinking
sugar	carbon, hydrogen, oxygen	cooking
baking soda	sodium, hydrogen, carbon, oxygen	baking
Epsom salts	magnesium, sulfur, oxygen	medicine

You might wonder if you can tell by looking at a substance whether it is an element or a compound. An unknown substance must be tested in a laboratory to determine whether it is an element or a compound.

Lesson 7 R E V I E W

Write your answers to these questions in complete sentences on a sheet of paper.

1. Explain what a compound is.

2. Give two examples of compounds.

3. Suppose you test a gas in the laboratory. You learn that the gas is made up of carbon atoms and oxygen atoms. Is the gas a compound? Explain your answer.

4. Name two common compounds that contain sodium.

5. Name four compounds that contain oxygen.

▼◄▲▼◄▲▼◄▲▼◄▲▼◄▲▼◄▲▼◄▲▼◄▲▼◄▲▼◄▲▼◄▲▼◄▲▼◄▲▼◄▲▼◄▲▼◄▲▼

Science at Work

Accelerator Technician

Accelerator technicians help build, maintain, repair, and operate particle accelerators and related equipment. They are responsible for recording meter readings. Accelerator technicians also keep track of parts and move heavy equipment.

Accelerator technicians need vocational training to learn to make and maintain electrical or mechanical equipment.

Accelerator technicians must be able to follow instructions and keep records. They must be able to use hand tools and electronic instruments. Accelerator technicians also must know how to measure and calculate dimensions, area, volume, and weight.

- A property is a characteristic that helps describe an object.

- A molecule is the smallest particle of a substance that still has the same properties of the substance.

- An atom is the basic building block of matter.

- Molecules move in different ways in each of the three states of matter— solids, liquids, and gases.

- Scientists use models to explain things they cannot see.

- Scientists use models of atoms to show how atoms look and act.

- An atom is made of protons, neutrons, and electrons.

- The number of protons in an atom is equal to the number of electrons.

- An element is matter that is made of only one kind of atom. There are 92 natural elements, which are found in nature.

- Each element has a symbol, an abbreviation for its name.

- Information contained in the periodic table about an element includes its name, its symbol, its atomic number, and its atomic mass.

- The atomic number of an element is equal to the number of protons in its nucleus.

- The mass number of an element is equal to the number of protons plus the number of neutrons.

- A compound is formed from two or more atoms of different elements. A compound has properties that are different from the elements that form the compound.

Science Words

atom, 37	element, 46	natural element, 47	solid, 38
atomic mass, 60	gas, 39	neutron, 43	state of matter, 39
atomic number, 48	isotope, 57	nucleus, 42	symbol, 51
compound, 62	liquid, 38	periodic table, 56	tritium, 57
density, 38	mass number, 60	plasma, 39	
deuterium, 57	model, 41	property, 33	
electron, 42	molecule, 36	proton, 42	

Chapter 2 REVIEW

Word Bank

atom
compound
element
gas
liquid
molecule
natural element
nucleus
plasma
solid

Vocabulary Review

Choose a word or words from the Word Bank that best complete each sentence. Write the answers on a sheet of paper.

1. A(n) _____ is the smallest particle of a substance that can still have the properties of the substance.

2. A form of matter with definite volume but no definite shape is a(n) _____.

3. A form of matter with no definite shape or volume is a(n) _____.

4. A form of matter with definite shape and volume is a(n)_____.

5. A very hot gas made of particles with an electric charge is _____.

6. Matter that has only one kind of atom is a(n) _____.

7. The _____ is the building block of matter.

8. A(n) _____ is the central part of an atom.

9. A(n) _____ is found in nature.

10. A(n) _____ is a substance that is formed when atoms of two or more elements join together.

Concept Review

Choose the answer that best completes each sentence. Write the letter of the answer on your paper.

11. The states of matter are _____.
   A solid, liquid, gas, and plasma
   B elements and natural elements
   C atom, molecule, and compound
   D electrons, protons, and neutrons

12. Models of atoms help describe their _____, although they cannot be seen.
   A mass   **C** appearance and actions
   B state of matter   **D** volume

13. The particles of _____ shake violently at very high temperatures.

 A solids   **B** liquids   **C** gases   **D** plasma

14. Of the following, _____ is not a compound.

 A water   **C** sodium chloride

 B oxygen   **D** epsom salts

15. The particles in an atom are _____.

 A compounds   **C** molecules

 B natural elements   **D** electrons, protons, and neutrons

16. An element's atomic number is the same as the number of _____ it has.

 A electrons   **B** protons   **C** neutrons   **D** nuclei

17. If an element has 4 protons and 5 neutrons, its mass number is _____.

 A 1   **B** 4   **C** 9   **D** 20

Critical Thinking

Write the answer to each of these questions on your paper.

18. How is the movement of a molecule's particles different when it is a solid, a gas, and a liquid?

19. Does the figure at the right show a molecule or an atom? Explain your answer.

20. Look at the figure at the left. Then answer these questions. How many protons and neutrons does the atom have? How many electrons? What is the element's atomic number? What is the mass number?

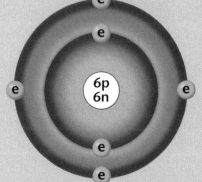

Test-Taking Tip   To remember facts and definitions more easily, write them down on index cards. Practice with a partner using the flash cards.

3

Chemical Reactions

On April 15, 1912, the *RMS Titanic* sank to the bottom of the North Atlantic Ocean after hitting an iceberg. Underwater for more than 90 years, the surface of the *Titanic* has been altered by iron-oxidizing bacteria, or rust. Photos show that chemical change has taken place, and "rusticles" have formed on the prow. Rust covers the shipwreck, and it is slowly wearing away the ship's metal structure.

In Chapter 3, you will learn about chemical and physical changes, and how different elements combine to form compounds. You will also learn what chemical reactions are, and how to write chemical equations.

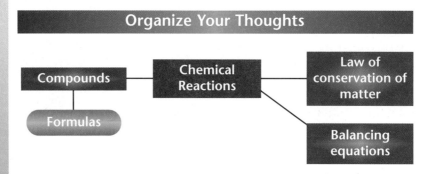

Organize Your Thoughts

Compounds — Chemical Reactions — Law of conservation of matter

Formulas

Balancing equations

Goals for Learning

◆ To describe characteristics of compounds

◆ To explain what the information in a formula means

◆ To explain what a chemical reaction is

◆ To state the law of conservation of matter

◆ To interpret and write balanced chemical equations

Lesson 1 — What Are Some Characteristics of Compounds?

Objectives

After reading this lesson, you should be able to

◆ describe a chemical change.

◆ describe some characteristics of compounds.

Chemical change

A change that produces one or more new substances with new chemical properties

How can you tell when a chemical change has happened? There are several possible signs. Bubbles sometimes appear. A solid may form. Temperature or color may change, or light or energy may be produced.

Only about 90 different elements combine in various ways to form the millions of different compounds you see around you. Do these millions of compounds have any common characteristics? How do these compounds form?

Compounds and Chemical Changes

You learned in Chapter 2 that two or more elements combine to form a compound. For example, hydrogen gas combines with oxygen gas to form the liquid compound water. Water has properties that are different from the elements that form it.

When atoms of elements combine to form a compound, a **chemical change** takes place. A chemical change produces one or more new substances with new chemical properties. A chemical change takes place when hydrogen and oxygen combine to form water.

The photos illustrate a chemical change. As the wood burns, it changes to gases and ash. The ash is a soft, gray powder that cannot burn. Wood and ash are different substances and have different properties.

A chemical change takes place when wood burns.

Did You Know?

Over the years, the Statue of Liberty has changed from a reddish color to a dull green. A chemical change has taken place. The copper in the statue has combined with oxygen in the air to form a new substance— copper oxide. Copper oxide makes the statue green.

Now think about taking a similar piece of wood and chopping it into tiny pieces. Does a chemical change take place when this happens? Ask yourself if the pieces of wood have properties that are different from the original piece of wood. In this case, they do not. Each small piece is still wood. The pieces just have different sizes and shapes. Changes like this are called **physical changes.** In a physical change, the appearance (physical properties) of a substance changes but its chemical properties stay the same. In a physical change, no new substances are formed.

Characteristics of Compounds

Although there are millions of compounds, they all share some basic characteristics. Any particular compound always contains the same elements. For example, the elements that make up water—hydrogen and oxygen—are always the same. The water can be from a faucet, a river, or a puddle in the road.

Another characteristic of compounds is that the atoms in a particular compound always combine in the same numbers. A molecule of water always contains two hydrogen atoms and one oxygen atom. If you change the molecule by adding another oxygen atom, the compound is no longer water. It becomes hydrogen peroxide, the clear liquid that people can use to clean cuts and other skin wounds. Water and hydrogen peroxide are different substances with different properties.

Copy the table on a sheet of paper. Identify each change as a chemical change or a physical change. Tell how you know which kind of change it is. (Remember, a chemical change produces new substances with new chemical properties.)

Change	Chemical or physical?	How do you know?
1. melting ice cream		
2. rusting a nail		
3. chopping onions		
4. baking a cake		
5. coloring hair		

Achievements in Science

Synthetic Dye

Before the 1850s, most dyes were made from vegetables or animals. It took 12,000 shellfish to make 1.5 g of a rare, expensive purple dye. First made in 1600 B.C., this dye— Tyrian purple—became the color of royalty. Because purple dyes were so expensive, only the rich had them.

In 1856, 18-year-old student William Perkin was trying to make artificial quinine, a malaria medication. He combined oxygen and aniline, a compound made from coal tar. The result was not quinine but aniline purple, an intense purple substance. Perkin mixed the substance with alcohol and found it turned silk a beautiful purple color. Named *mauveine,* this solution was the first synthetic, or manmade, dye.

Perkin and his father started a factory to make the dye commercially. Perkin developed the processes for the production and use of the new dye. This was the beginning of the synthetic dye industry. Mauveine made purple clothing available to everyone—not just royalty.

INVESTIGATION 3

Materials

- safety glasses
- 2 small jars with lids
- distilled water
- washing soda
- 2 plastic spoons
- Epsom salts
- clock
- soft-drink bottle
- vinegar
- baking soda
- balloon

Observing a Chemical Change

Purpose

Look at the descriptions of the three changes listed in the data table. Can you predict which will be a physical change and which will be a chemical change? In this investigation, you will observe physical and chemical changes.

Procedure

1. Copy the data table on a sheet of paper.

Change	Appearance
washing soda in water	
Epsom salts in water	
washing soda and Epsom salts in water	

2. Put on your safety glasses.

3. Fill each jar about halfway with distilled water.

4. Add a spoonful of washing soda to one jar. Place the lid on the jar and shake for about 30 seconds. Record your observations in the table.

5. Use a clean spoon to add a spoonful of Epsom salts to the second jar. Place the lid on the jar and shake for about 30 seconds. Record your observations.

6. Carefully pour the contents of one jar into the other jar. Observe for 5 minutes. Record the results.

Questions and Conclusions

1. What happened when you added the washing soda to water?

2. What happened when you added the Epsom salts to water?

3. What did you observe when you mixed the contents of the jars together in step 6?

4. Did a chemical change or a physical change take place in steps 4 and 5? Explain your answer.

5. Did a chemical change or a physical change take place in step 6? Explain your answer.

Explore Further

Place a small amount of vinegar in a soft-drink bottle. Add a small amount of baking soda. Immediately cover the mouth of the bottle with a balloon. What do you observe happening? Does a chemical change take place? Explain your answer.

Objectives

After reading this lesson, you should be able to

◆ describe how electrons in an atom are arranged.

◆ explain how electrons fill the energy levels.

◆ explain how atoms combine to form compounds.

◆ explain how ions form chemical bonds.

Energy level

One of the spaces around the nucleus of an atom in which an electron moves

You now know that compounds form when chemical changes occur. But how do the atoms of elements combine to form compounds? Electrons play an important part when elements combine.

Arrangement of Electrons in an Atom

Electrons in an atom move around the nucleus. Each electron moves in its own space a certain distance from the nucleus. This space is called the **energy level.**

In the model of the atom below, notice that each energy level is labeled with a letter. Level K is closest to the nucleus and is the smallest. Electrons in the outer energy levels have the most effect on the properties of an element.

Each energy level can hold only a certain number of electrons. The table shows the number of electrons each energy level can hold. Notice that the levels farther from the nucleus can hold more electrons than the levels closer to the nucleus.

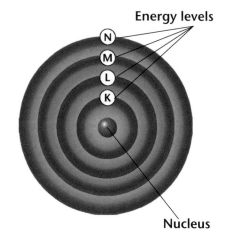

Energy levels

Nucleus

Energy Levels in an Atom	
Name	Number of Electrons When Filled
K	2
L	8
M	18
N	32

An atom has seven
energy levels. They
are named K, L, M,
N, O, P, and Q.
Scientists theorize
that energy level O
can hold 50
electrons, level P
can hold 72, and
level Q can hold 98.

How Electrons Fill Energy Levels

The electrons fill the energy levels in order. Level K is the level closest to the nucleus. It is filled first. Then the second level, level L, is filled. This goes on until all the electrons are in place. For example, the element sodium has 11 electrons. Notice in the figure that two of these electrons fill level K. Eight more electrons fill level L. The remaining electron is in energy level M. Level M is not full because it can hold as many as 18 electrons.

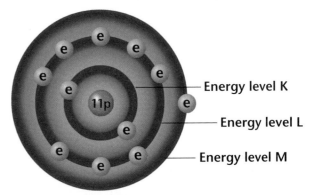

Sodium atom

How Atoms Combine

You learned that compounds form when the atoms of elements combine. Exactly how do the atoms of different elements join together? When atoms form compounds, they share, lend, or borrow electrons that are in their outer energy level.

An atom has a tendency to fill its outer energy level. An atom becomes more stable when its outermost energy level is filled. An atom shares, lends, or borrows electrons to fill its outer energy level.

Look at the model of the sodium atom in the figure above. Notice that only one of its electrons is in the outer energy level. Sodium tends to lose one electron to another atom to become stable. By losing an electron, the outer level— level L—will have 8 electrons. It will have the most electrons it can hold. Some atoms become more stable when they gain or borrow one electron from another atom. Chlorine is one example of this.

Ionic compounds, such as sodium chloride, form a crystal shape. The shape of the crystal is based on the arrangement of the ions that are in it. Sodium chloride forms a cube-shaped crystal.

Science Myth

All chemical bonds form in the same way.

Fact: There are two main types of chemical bonds. A covalent bond forms when two atoms share a pair of electrons. Each atom gives one electron to the electron pair. An ionic bond forms when an atom loses an electron and another atom gains the electron.

Attraction Between Atoms

Table salt is a familiar compound made from one sodium atom and one chlorine atom. The figure below shows how the sodium atom lends its electron to the chlorine atom.

Keep in mind that when sodium loses an electron, the number of protons in the nucleus remains the same. As a result, the atom has more protons than electrons. Protons have a positive charge. Electrons have a negative charge. When an atom has equal numbers of electrons and protons, the atom has no charge. But when an atom has more protons than electrons, it has a positive (+) charge.

Sodium gives an electron to chlorine to form the compound sodium chloride. The chlorine atom now has more electrons than protons. When an atom has more electrons than protons, it has a negative (–) charge.

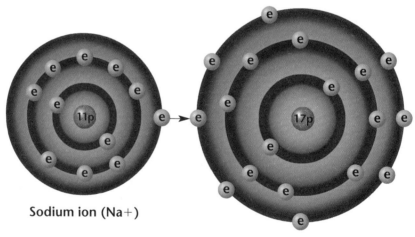

Sodium ion (Na+)

Chloride ion (Cl−)

An atom that has either a positive or a negative charge is called an **ion.** In the sodium chloride example, the chlorine becomes a negative ion. The sodium becomes a positive ion. Positive ions and negative ions strongly attract each other. The attractive force between atoms is called a **chemical bond.** The chemical bond between ions holds the atoms together when they form a compound. For example, a chemical bond keeps sodium and chlorine ions together when they combine to form table salt.

Lesson 2   R E V I E W

Write your answers to these questions in complete sentences on a sheet of paper.

1. How are electrons arranged around the nucleus of an atom?

2. In what order do electrons fill energy levels?

3. Would an atom with 3 electrons in level M tend to gain or lose electrons? Explain your answer. (Hint: Use the table on page 74.)

4. How do atoms of different elements combine?

5. How many electrons can level M hold?

▼◀▲▼◀▲▼◀▲▼◀▲▼◀▲▼◀▲▼◀▲▼◀▲▼◀▲▼◀▲▼◀▲▼

Science at Work

Textile Dye Technologist

Textile dye technologists create and test formulas for different colors of dyes for different fabrics. They have the responsibility of deciding which dye and dyeing process to use. They mix dyes, check the dyeing process at each stage, and take

samples for testing. Textile dye technologists also make sure the machinery used in dyeing fabrics works correctly.

Textile dye technologists must complete a two-year college program in textile dye or textile engineering technology. They also must have two years of on-the-job training.

Textile dye technologists have excellent color perception and a solid understanding of the principles of chemistry.

Objectives

After reading this lesson, you should be able to

◆ explain how to write a chemical formula.

◆ interpret a chemical formula.

◆ explain what a radical is.

◆ give examples of radicals.

Chemical formula

Tells the kinds of atoms and how many of each kind are in a compound

Suppose you want to describe a particular beverage such as the one in the figure. You might tell about its recipe. Notice that the recipe lists all the ingredients. It also tells the amount of each ingredient in the drink.

Recipe

Banana-Strawberry Slush

1 cup sliced bananas
1 cup fresh sliced strawberries
4 mint leaves
1 cup skim milk
1/4 cup crushed ice cubes

Mix all of the ingredients in a blender until slushy. Serve immediately.

You can describe a compound by using the same kind of information you use in a recipe. You can tell what elements form the compound. You can also tell the amount of each element in the compound.

Formulas for Compounds

Scientists use the symbols for the elements to write a **chemical formula** for each compound. A chemical formula tells what kinds of atoms are in a compound and how many atoms of each kind are present. You know that sodium and chlorine combine to form table salt. The symbol for sodium is Na. The symbol for chlorine is Cl. The chemical formula for table salt is NaCl. The formula shows that sodium and chlorine combine to form table salt.

Scientists use a number called a **subscript** to indicate the number of atoms of an element in a compound. For example, the formula for water is H_2O. The number 2 tells that a water molecule contains two atoms of hydrogen. You can see that the subscript number 2 is smaller than the H and written slightly below the letter.

Notice that no subscript is written after the O. If no subscript number is given after the symbol of an element, the compound has only one atom of that element. The formula H_2O shows that one molecule of water contains three atoms—two of hydrogen and one of oxygen.

Look at the tables to learn the chemical formulas for some other compounds. Read carefully to find out what each formula shows about the compound it represents.

CH_4 (methane)			
Symbol	Element	Subscript	Number of Atoms
C	carbon	none	1
H	hydrogen	4	+4
			5 Total atoms

$C_{12}H_{22}O_{11}$ (sucrose)			
Symbol	Element	Subscript	Number of Atoms
C	carbon	12	12
H	hydrogen	22	22
O	oxygen	11	+11
			45 Total atoms

Compounds Containing Radicals

The formulas for some compounds contain groups of two or more atoms that act as if they were one atom. These groups of atoms are called **radicals.** They form compounds by combining with other atoms. During a chemical reaction, the atoms in a radical stay together.

Household lye is one common substance with a formula that contains a radical. This strong chemical is used to clean drains. The formula for lye is NaOH. The OH is an example of a radical. It contains one atom of oxygen and one atom of hydrogen. The chemical name for this radical is the hydroxyl radical. Other examples of radicals and their names are listed in the table.

Some Common Radicals	
Radical	**Name**
SO_4	sulfate
ClO_3	chlorate
NO_3	nitrate
CO_3	carbonate
PO_4	phosphate
OH	hydroxide

Compounds containing more than one radical are written with the radical in parentheses. A subscript outside of the parentheses tells how many units of the radical are in one molecule of the compound.

When formulas contain radicals with subscripts, the subscripts multiply the number of atoms inside the parentheses. The compound $Ba(NO_3)_2$ is barium nitrate. The nitrate radical is made up of one nitrogen atom and three oxygen atoms. But in barium nitrate, the barium atom combines with *two* nitrate radicals. The compound has a total of two nitrogen atoms and six oxygen atoms.

Copy the table on a sheet of paper. Fill in the missing information. Use the periodic table on pages 58 and 59 if you need help naming the elements. The first one is done for you.

Compound	Symbols	Elements	Subscripts	Number of Each Kind of Atom
1. $NaHCO_3$	Na	sodium	none	1
	H	hydrogen	none	1
	C	carbon	none	1
	O	oxygen	3	3
2. $K_2Cr_2O_7$				
3. H_2SO_4				
4. $KClO_3$				
5. HCl				

Write the answers to these questions in complete sentences on your paper. Use the periodic table on pages 58 and 59 if you need help.

6. What does a formula tell about a compound?

7. Write a formula for a compound that contains one atom of aluminum and three atoms of chlorine.

8. What is a radical?

9. In the formula NaOH, _____ is a radical.

    A Na   **C** OH

    B NaO   **D** NaOH

10. From the formula $Al_2(SO_4)_3$, you can see that aluminum sulfate contains _____ atoms of oxygen.

    A 2   **C** 4

    B 3   **D** 12

Chemical reaction

A chemical change in which elements are combined or rearranged

Mixture

A combination of substances in which no reaction takes place

Science Myth

Air and oxygen are the same thing.

Fact: Air is a mixture of a number of substances. Oxygen makes up only 21 percent of air. Air contains mostly nitrogen. Water vapor and a very small amount of other gases are also part of air.

Hundreds of years ago, early scientists known as alchemists tried to change different materials into gold. Imagine being able to change iron or lead into solid gold!

Alchemists were early scientists who tried to turn other materials into gold.

Unfortunately for the alchemists, they never succeeded. Today, scientists know that chemically changing one element into another is not possible. But during a chemical change, elements can be combined to form compounds. The elements in compounds can be rearranged to form new compounds. When elements combine or rearrange, they are said to react. The process is called a **chemical reaction.** For some reactions, it is necessary to heat the substances. And some substances must be mixed with water for a chemical reaction to take place.

Substances do not always react when combined. Many elements and compounds can be mixed together and nothing at all happens. A **mixture** is formed when substances are combined and no reaction takes place. When you stir sugar and cinnamon together, you form a mixture.

Dissolving

Many reactions take place only when the substances have been **dissolved** in other liquids. To dissolve means to break up substances into individual atoms or molecules. An example of dissolving occurs when sugar is placed in water. The sugar mixes with the water and seems to disappear. But the sugar is still there. The pieces of the sugar have been broken down into tiny particles—molecules.

When a substance is thoroughly dissolved in another, the result is a mixture called a **solution.** The substance that dissolves is called the **solute.** When you dissolve sugar in water, the solute is sugar. A substance that is capable of dissolving one or more other substances is a **solvent.** In the sugar-water solution, water is the solvent. Can you think of other examples of solutions, solutes, and solvents?

Types of Solutions		
Substance (solute)	**Dissolved in (solvent)**	**Examples**
liquid	liquid	alcohol in water
	gas	water vapor in air
	solid	ether in rubber
gas	liquid	club soda in water (CO_2 in water)
	gas	air (nitrogen, oxygen, other gases)
	solid	hydrogen in palladium
solid	liquid	salt in water
	gas	iodine vapor in air
	solid	brass (copper and zinc)

A solution does not always have to be a solid dissolved in a liquid. Solutions can also be formed by dissolving substances in solids and gases. The table above gives some examples of solutions.

Dissolve

To break apart

Solution

A mixture in which one substance is dissolved in another

Solute

The substance that is dissolved in a solution

Solvent

A substance capable of dissolving one or more other substances

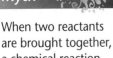

Science Myth

When two reactants are brought together, a chemical reaction automatically starts.

Fact: Most chemical reactions need energy to start. That energy is called activation energy. A catalyst lowers the activation energy that is needed to start the reaction. A catalyst is a substance that enables a chemical reaction to occur faster or under different conditions than is otherwise possible. Catalysts speed up reactions, but are not changed by them. Some substances, called inhibitors, slow down reactions.

Lesson 4   R E V I E W

Write your answers to these questions in complete sentences on a sheet of paper.

1. What element were the alchemists trying to produce? Did they succeed?

2. What are two things a scientist can do to cause some substances that are mixed together to react?

3. Suppose you dissolve salt in water. Name the solvent and the solute.

4. What is a chemical reaction?

5. How is a mixture different from a chemical reaction?

Science in Your Life

How does a permanent wave work?

To understand how a permanent wave works, you need to understand something about hair's biochemistry. Like almost everything in your body, hair is mostly protein. The proteins in hair—called keratin—are long chains of the amino acid cystine. Cystine is made of carbon, hydrogen, oxygen, nitrogen, and sulfur atoms.

In cystine, sulfur atoms can form a disulfide bond. Wherever this bond occurs in the protein chain, hair bends. All hair has some disulfide bonds. Many disulfide bonds in a protein chain make hair curly.

Permanent waves can be added to hair that doesn't have many disulfide bonds. Two chemical reactions take place to make straight hair curly. First, we need to break the existing disulfide bonds in hair. A chemical called a reducing agent breaks the disulfide bonds. This is the first chemical reaction. Next, we use curlers to give the hair a new shape. Then another chemical —a neutralizer—uses oxidation to make new disulfide bonds. This is the second chemical reaction. The longer the neutralizer is left on the hair, the curlier the hair will be when the curlers are removed, and the neutralizer is rinsed away. Now the protein in the hair has many new disulfide bonds—and lots of curls.

Objectives

After reading this lesson, you should be able to

◆ explain how a chemical equation describes a chemical reaction.

◆ balance chemical equations.

You know that chemical symbols and formulas can be used to represent substances. You can also use these symbols to describe reactions. A **chemical equation** is a statement that uses symbols, chemical formulas, and numbers to stand for a chemical reaction. Look at the simple chemical equation below. The symbols and formulas describe the chemicals that are involved. Below the equation, you can see the description in words.

Reactants   Products

$$HCl + NaOH \longrightarrow NaCl + H_2O$$

hydrogen chloride plus sodium hydroxide yields sodium chloride plus water

Chemical equation

A statement that uses symbols, formulas, and numbers to stand for a chemical reaction

Reactant

A substance that is altered in a chemical reaction

Product

A substance that is formed in a chemical reaction

Notice that the arrow symbol ($\longrightarrow$) stands for "yields" or "makes." The chemicals on the left side of the arrow are called **reactants.** They are the substances that are reacting together. A reactant is a substance that is altered in a chemical reaction. The chemicals on the right side of the arrow are called **products.** A product is a substance that is formed in a chemical reaction. The product forms from the reactants. In the above example, HCl and NaOH are the reactants. The products are NaCl and H_2O.

Law of Conservation of Matter

The reactants present *before* a reaction can be quite different from the products present after the reaction. But the kinds of atoms do not change during the reaction.

A chemical equation shows the rearrangement of atoms that happens after a chemical change.

$$Mg \quad + \quad F_2 \longrightarrow MgF_2$$
magnesium   fluorine   magnesium fluoride

Law of conservation of matter

Matter cannot be created or destroyed in chemical and common physical changes

Balance

To keep the number of atoms the same on both sides of the equation

In a balanced equation, a coefficient of 1 usually is not written.

Different substances are formed, but the same atoms are there. The atoms are just rearranged. In the reaction shown on page 85, magnesium and fluorine (the reactants) combine to form a new compound called magnesium fluoride. Notice how the atoms rearrange themselves.

The same numbers and kinds of atoms are present before and after a reaction. Mass does not change during the reaction. The mass of the reactants equals the mass of the products. This fact illustrates the **law of conservation of matter.** The law states that matter cannot be created or destroyed in chemical and common physical changes. This law is sometimes called the law of conservation of mass.

Balancing Equations

To satisfy the law of conservation of matter, a chemical equation must be **balanced.** To balance an equation means to keep the same number of each kind of atom on both sides of the equation.

Look at the following equation. It shows that hydrogen plus oxygen makes water.

$$H_2 + O_2 \longrightarrow H_2O$$

This equation is not balanced. Two oxygen atoms are shown on the left side of the equation. Only 1 oxygen atom is shown on the right. The left side of the equation has a total of 4 atoms, but the right side has only 3 atoms.

$$H_2 + O_2 \longrightarrow H_2O$$

H 2 atoms		H 2 atoms
O 2 atoms		O 1 atom
Total of 4 atoms		Total of 3 atoms

You can see that there are 4 atoms in the reactants and only 3 in the products. The law of conservation of matter says that atoms do not disappear in chemical reactions. You cannot change the formulas for the reactants or products.

To balance the equation, you can place numbers before the formulas. A number that is placed before a formula in a chemical equation is called a **coefficient.** A coefficient shows how many molecules or atoms are involved in the chemical reaction. For example, look at $2H_2O$. The 2 before H_2O means 2 water molecules.

You can change coefficients by changing the numbers of atoms. By writing $2H_2O$, you are saying that 4 atoms of hydrogen and 2 atoms of oxygen are in the products. If you write $3H_2O$, you are saying that 6 atoms of hydrogen and 3 atoms of oxygen are in the products.

By placing a 2 in front of the H_2O, you have made the number of oxygen atoms equal on both sides of the equation. But the number of hydrogen atoms is not equal.

$$\textbf{H}_2 + \textbf{O}_2 \longrightarrow \textbf{2H}_2\textbf{O}$$

$H_2 + O_2$	$2H_2O$
H 2 atoms	H 4 atoms (2 × 2)
O 2 atoms	O 2 atoms (1 × 2)
Total of 4 atoms	Total of 6 atoms

You can see that there are 2 hydrogen atoms in the reactants. There are 4 hydrogen atoms in the product. Therefore, you need 2 more hydrogen atoms in the reactants. Again you can change the number of atoms by using a coefficient. You can balance the equation like this.

$$\textbf{2H}_2 + \textbf{O}_2 \longrightarrow \textbf{2H}_2\textbf{O}$$

$2H_2 + O_2$	$2H_2O$
H 4 atoms	H 4 atoms
O 2 atoms	O 2 atoms
Total of 6 atoms	Total of 6 atoms

The equation is now balanced. The number of each kind of atom is the same before and after the reaction.

1. Copy the table on a sheet of paper. Then complete the table. The first one is done for you.

Reaction	Reactants	Products
A $Fe + S \longrightarrow FeS$	Fe, S	FeS
B $H_2SO_4 + Zn \longrightarrow ZnSO_4 + H_2$		
C $Mg + S \longrightarrow MgS$		
D $AgNO_3 + NaCl \longrightarrow NaNO_3 + AgCl$		

2. Write the following chemical equations in words.

   A $Mg + S \longrightarrow MgS$ **B** $Ba + S \longrightarrow BaS$

Study the following equation. Then write your answers to the questions.

$$2Na + Cl_2 \longrightarrow 2NaCl$$

3. What are the reactants?

4. What is the product?

5. Is the equation balanced? Explain your answer.

Achievements in Science

Nylon

In the late 1920s, Wallace H. Carothers began experimenting with polymers. Polymers are giant molecules made of thousands of smaller molecules. The small molecules are identical to each other and are chemically bonded to each other. The chemically bonded molecules form a chain. Carothers had studied silk, a natural polymer. He understood that the new fiber needed to have the same properties as silk. Carothers began making polymers that were longer than any that had ever been made before.

In 1935, Carothers combined hexamethylenediamine and adipic acid to make a new fiber, Fiber 66. It was stronger and more elastic than silk. Fiber 66 became known as nylon. Nylon is a synthetic, or manmade, polymer. Each molecule has a polymer chain of repeating molecules made of carbon, hydrogen, and oxygen atoms.

The production of nylon began in 1938. The first products made from nylon—toothbrushes—were introduced in 1939. Nylon stockings also appeared on the market in 1939. Today carpets, clothes, parachutes, tires, and thread are among the many products made of nylon.

Chapter 3 SUMMARY

- A compound forms when two or more elements combine. A chemical change takes place when elements combine to form a compound. In a chemical change, new substances with new chemical properties are formed.

- A physical change is a change in which the appearance (physical properties) of a substance changes but its chemical properties stay the same.

- Molecules of the same compound always contain the same elements. The atoms in the molecules of the same compound always combine in the same numbers.

- An electron moves in a certain energy level around the nucleus of an atom. Each energy level can hold only a certain number of electrons. Electrons fill the energy levels in order.

- Different elements have electrons in different numbers of levels. Atoms share, borrow, or lend electrons to other atoms in order to form compounds.

- An atom that has a charge is called an ion. Ions with opposite charges attract each other.

- A chemical formula is used to show what kinds of atoms and how many atoms of each kind are in a compound.

- A radical is a group of elements that behaves as if it were one element.

- A chemical reaction involves a change of substances into other substances.

- A combination of materials in which no reaction takes place is called a mixture.

- Reactions can be represented by chemical equations, which should be balanced for atoms.

- The law of conservation of matter states that matter cannot be created or destroyed in chemical and common physical changes.

Science Words

balance, 86	dissolve, 83	product, 85
chemical bond, 76	energy level, 74	radicals, 80
chemical change, 69	ion, 76	reactant, 85
chemical equation, 85	law of conservation of matter, 86	solute, 83
chemical formula, 78		solution, 83
chemical reaction, 82	mixture, 82	solvent, 83
coefficient, 87	physical change, 70	subscript, 79

Chapter 3 REVIEW

Word Bank

chemical bond

chemical change

chemical equation

chemical formula

ion

law of conservation
   of matter

product

reactant

solute

solution

subscript

Vocabulary Review

Choose the word or words from the Word Bank that best complete each sentence. Write the answers on a sheet of paper.

1. A(n) _____ is an atom that has either a positive or a negative charge.

2. A mixture in which one substance is dissolved in another is a(n) _____.

3. A(n) _____ tells the kinds of atoms and how many are in a compound.

4. A statement that uses symbols, formulas, and numbers to stand for a chemical reaction is a(n) _____.

5. A(n) _____ produces one or more new substances with new chemical properties.

6. A substance that is altered in a chemical reaction is a(n) _____.

7. A(n) _____ tells the number of atoms of an element in a compound.

8. A substance that is formed in a chemical reaction is a(n) _____.

9. A(n) _____ is the attractive force that holds atoms together.

10. A(n) _____ is dissolved in a solution.

11. The _____ states that matter cannot be created or destroyed in chemical and common physical changes.

Concept Review

Choose the best answer to each question. Write the letter of the answer on your paper.

12. Which of the following is *not* a physical change?

   A painting a wall   **C** boiling water

   B developing film   **D** shredding cheese

13. How are radicals shown in chemical formulas?

   A in parentheses   **C** at the beginning

   B at the end   **D** as a subscript

14. When sugar and water are stirred together, _____.

   A water is the solvent   **C** water is the solution

   B sugar is the solvent   **D** water is the solute

15. One molecule of water, H_2O, always contains two hydrogen atoms and _____ oxygen atom(s).

   A one   **C** three

   B two   **D** four

Test-Taking Tip If you have to choose the correct word to complete a sentence, read the sentence using each of the words. Then choose the word that best fits the sentence.

Energy and Motion

Have you ever seen a cheetah run? Cheetahs are the fastest land mammals in the world. How fast can a cheetah run? It can cover approximately 200 meters in 7 seconds. It can accelerate from 0 to 29 meters per second in 3 seconds. But what do these numbers actually tell us about the speed of a cheetah? In Chapter 4, you will find out about the laws of motion. All motion involves energy. In this chapter, you will learn about the different forms of energy and how energy can change from one form to another.

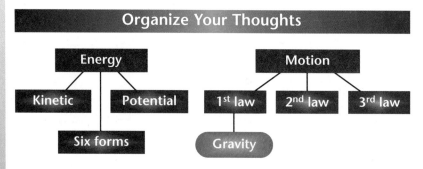

Organize Your Thoughts

Energy — Kinetic — Potential — Six forms

Motion — 1st law — 2nd law — 3rd law — Gravity

Goals for Learning

◆ To explain what energy is

◆ To name six forms of energy

◆ To define and explain motion and speed

◆ To calculate speed

◆ To define and explain force

◆ To explain and apply Newton's three laws of motion

◆ To define and explain gravity

◆ To explain the law of universal gravitation

Energy

The ability to do work

Motion

A change in position

Kinetic energy

Energy of motion

Potential energy

Stored energy

You can see several examples of kinetic energy around you, such as geologic faults and water falls. Can you think of other examples?

Have you ever tried to play a radio with a "dead" battery? The radio would not play because the battery had no more **energy** stored inside. In science, energy is defined as "the ability to do work." Without energy, no work can be done.

Kinetic and Potential Energy

A moving object has the energy of **motion,** called **kinetic energy.** When a car is moving, it can do work. It can overcome road friction and air resistance and keep going forward. The amount of kinetic energy a moving object has depends on the object's mass and speed. The greater the mass or speed, the greater the kinetic energy.

Some objects are not moving, but they have the potential to move because of their position. These objects have stored energy. This stored energy is called **potential energy.** A book sitting on the floor has no potential energy. It cannot do work. But if you set the book so that it hangs over the edge of a table, the book has stored energy. It can do work by falling to the floor. The book's potential energy changes to kinetic energy as it falls. If you place the book over the edge of a higher table, the book has more potential energy because it can fall farther. The spring of a mousetrap is another example of potential energy. It can do work as it snaps shut.

The Forms of Energy

The energy you use to do work exists in six main forms. These six forms of energy can be stored. They can also produce motion. That is, each form of energy can be potential or kinetic.

Chemical energy is stored in the bonds between atoms. When substances react, they can release some of the chemical energy in the substances and warm the surroundings. For example, burning coal produces heat.

Heat energy is associated with the moving particles that make up matter. The faster the particles move, the more heat energy is present. All matter has some heat energy. You will learn more about heat in Chapter 6.

Mechanical energy is the energy in moving objects. Objects, such as a moving bicycle, wind, and a falling rock, have mechanical energy in kinetic form. Sound is a form of mechanical energy that you will learn about in Chapter 7.

Nuclear energy is energy that is stored in the nucleus, or center, of an atom. It can be released in devices such as nuclear power plants and atomic weapons.

Radiant energy is associated with light. Some energy that Earth receives from the sun is in the form of light energy. You will learn more about light in Chapter 7.

Which forms of energy can you find in this photo?

Electrical energy is energy that causes electrons to move. Electrons are the negatively charged particles in atoms. Appliances, such as refrigerators and vacuum cleaners, use electrical energy. You will learn about electricity in Chapter 8.

Energy can be changed from one form to another. For example, at an electric power plant, chemical energy is converted to heat energy when fuel is burned. The heat energy is used to make steam. The steam turns a turbine and produces mechanical energy inside a **generator.** The generator converts mechanical energy to electrical energy by moving coils through a magnetic field.

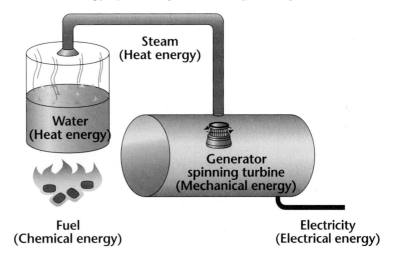

Steam (Heat energy)

Water (Heat energy)

Generator spinning turbine (Mechanical energy)

Fuel (Chemical energy)

Electricity (Electrical energy)

The Law of Conservation of Energy

Energy might change its form, but it does not disappear. You can add energy to an object or take energy away from it, but the total amount of the energy does not change. The **law of conservation of energy** states that energy cannot be created or destroyed. A book falling from a table illustrates the law of conservation of energy.

As the book falls, its potential energy decreases. The kinetic energy increases by the same amount. The total amount of energy (potential plus kinetic) stays the same. Just before the book hits the ground, its potential energy is approaching zero and all the energy has become kinetic. After the book hits the ground, the kinetic energy is changed into heat energy which causes a temperature change in the book and the ground. In this example, the energy has changed form, but the total energy remains the same.

Generator

A device used to convert mechanical energy to electrical energy

Law of conservation of energy

Energy cannot be created or destroyed

Lesson 1   R E V I E W

Write your answers to these questions in complete sentences on a sheet of paper.

1. What is energy?

2. What is the difference between kinetic and potential energy?

3. Explain the law of conservation of energy.

4. Name the six forms of energy.

5. Each figure shows an example of energy changing form. List the energy changes that take place in each example.

A    B    C

Science in Your Life

How can energy change forms?

Have you ever ridden a roller coaster? A roller coaster is a good example of how energy can change from one form to another. When you first climb into the car at the bottom of the hill, the car has no potential energy. A chain must pull you up the first big hill. That chain changes electrical energy into potential energy. When the cars are at the top, they can fall downward. Potential energy changes to kinetic energy as the cars plunge down one hill. Kinetic energy is converted back into potential energy as the cars go up the next hill. The cars slow as they reach the top of the hill. The kinetic energy that pushed them up the hill has changed back to potential energy. That stored energy converts to kinetic energy as the cars zoom down again.

Elapsed time

The length of time that passes from one event to another

Speed

The rate at which the position of an object changes

The motion of an object is always judged with respect to another object or point.

The earth travels in space. A car carries you from place to place. You walk to the store. In each case, objects are changing position in space. We say they are moving. Motion is simply a change in position.

All change, including change in position, takes place over time. To help you understand motion, you will begin by learning how the passage of time is measured.

Elapsed Time

Suppose you have just taken an airplane trip from Miami to New York in the same time zone. Your flight began at 8:00 P.M. It ended at 11:00 P.M. How long did this trip take?

To answer this question, you calculate the **elapsed time.** Elapsed time is the amount of time that passes from one event to another. To calculate elapsed time, just subtract the time of the earlier event from the time of the later event.

In the case of the flight, subtract the departure time from the arrival time.

$$
\begin{array}{rl}
11{:}00 & \text{arrival time} \\
-\ 8{:}00 & \text{departure time} \\
\hline
3\quad & \text{hours travel time} = \text{elapsed time}
\end{array}
$$

Departure time
8:00 P.M.

Arrival time
11:00 P.M.

810 miles

Miami   New York

Speed

Speed tells how fast an object is moving. Notice that speed uses two units—**distance** and time. Distance is the length of the path traveled by the object in motion. You can use the following formula to find the speed of an object.

$$\text{average speed} = \frac{\text{distance}}{\text{time}}$$

Suppose the airplane mentioned on page 97 traveled 810 miles between the two cities. The elapsed time for the trip was 3 hours. You can use the formula to calculate the speed of the airplane.

EXAMPLE

$$\text{average speed} = \frac{810 \text{ miles}}{3 \text{ hours}}$$

$$\text{average speed} = \frac{270 \text{ miles}}{1 \text{ hour}}$$

The speed of the airplane is 270 miles per hour. This means that each hour the plane traveled 270 miles. It is unlikely that the airplane traveled at a constant speed of 270 miles per hour during the entire flight. Between the beginning and the end of the trip, the speed varies. The speed calculated is actually the average speed. The actual speed at any particular moment, called the instantaneous speed, could be more or less than the average speed.

Speed does not have to be measured in miles per hour. Think about a race at a track meet where the distance around the track is 400 meters. Suppose a runner completes the race in 50 seconds. What was the runner's speed?

EXAMPLE

$$\text{average speed} = \frac{\text{distance}}{\text{time}}$$

$$\text{average speed} = \frac{400 \text{ meters}}{50 \text{ seconds}}$$

$$\text{average speed} = \frac{8 \text{ meters}}{1 \text{ second}}$$

The average speed of the runner is 8 meters per second. The runner covers an average distance of 8 meters each second.

Copy the following table. Calculate the average speed for each
of these examples. The first one is completed for you.

Distance traveled	Time	Average speed
30 miles	5 hours	6 miles/hour
100 yards	13 seconds	
10 centimeters	5 seconds	
380 kilometers	2 hours	
3,825 feet	30 minutes	
15 inches	4 hours	
82 miles	10 hours	
10,000 meters	36 minutes	
23 feet	6 minutes	
120 kilometers	2 hours	

Finding Speed

Materials

- safety glasses
- 2 books
- meterstick
- marble
- stopwatch or watch that shows seconds

Purpose

What formula would you use to calculate speed using distance and time? In this investigation, you will calculate speed by measuring distance and time and use a graph to show motion.

Procedure

1. Copy the data table on a sheet of paper.

Length (meters)	Time (seconds)	Speed (distance/time)

2. Put on your safety glasses.

3. Work on a large table, as directed by your teacher. At one end of the table, place one end of the meterstick on the edge of a book. The ruler's groove should be on top.

4. Set a book at the other end of the table. Measure the length from the book to the edge of the ruler on the table. Record the length in your data table.

5. Set the marble at the top of the ruler's groove. Release the marble. Let it roll down the groove. Do not push it. Start the stopwatch when the marble leaves the ruler. Stop timing when the marble reaches the book at the end of the table. Record the time in your data table.

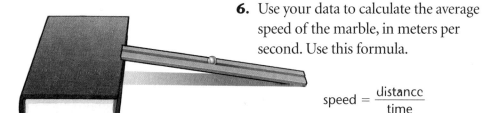

6. Use your data to calculate the average speed of the marble, in meters per second. Use this formula.

$$\text{speed} = \frac{\text{distance}}{\text{time}}$$

Questions and Conclusions

1. Make a graph with distance in meters on the vertical (up-and-down) axis. Place time in seconds on the horizontal (left-to-right) axis. Extend the axes twice as far as you need to in order to graph your data. Plot one point where 0 seconds crosses 0 meters, to show the beginning of the roll. Plot a second point, using the distance and time values you recorded. Connect the two points with a straight line.

2. Use the graph you made to estimate the distance the marble traveled after it had been moving for half the recorded time.

3. Extend the graph. Estimate the distance the marble would have gone if it had traveled for twice the recorded time.

Explore Further

What do you think would happen if you stacked another book on top of the book that is under the ruler? How would the graph for this setup look? How would this graph be different from the graph you made?

Sir Isaac Newton was a scientist who lived about 350 years ago. He studied changes in the motion of objects. From his studies, he was able to propose three laws to explain motion.

The First Law of Motion

If you wanted to move a large box that is resting on the floor, you would have to push or pull it. We call this push or pull a **force.** Whenever any object changes its **velocity** or **accelerates,** a force causes the change in motion. Acceleration refers to the rate of change of velocity.

> Newton's first law of motion states that if no force acts on an object at rest, it will remain at rest. The law also says that if the object is moving, it will continue moving at the same speed and in the same direction if no force acts on it.

Force
A push or a pull

Velocity
The speed and direction in which an object is moving

Acceleration
The rate of change of velocity

Friction
A force that opposes motion and that occurs when things slide or roll over each other

Let's use an example to explain the second part of the law. A car on flat ground will roll to a stop if you take your foot off the gas pedal. The car slows down because an invisible force is at work. This invisible force is called **friction.** Friction is a force that opposes motion and occurs when things slide or roll over each other. Friction resists the movement of one surface past another. The rougher the surfaces are, the greater the friction.

The figure illustrates how friction helps stop a moving car. Notice the air resistance. Air resistance is a form of friction. It occurs when molecules of air touch the surface of the car.

Did You Know?

Automobile designers try to reduce air resistance from friction to make cars more efficient.

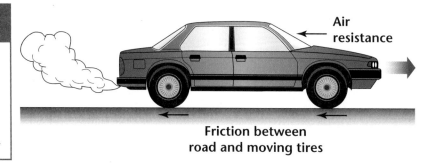

Air resistance

Friction between road and moving tires

An object tends to resist changes in its motion. This tendency to resist changes in motion is called **inertia.** Inertia causes objects at rest to stay at rest. It also causes moving objects to continue moving.

The inertia of an object depends on its mass. The greater the mass of an object, the greater the force needed to cause a given change in its motion. For example, suppose you tried to push two rocks—a large one and a small one—across the ground. You would notice that if you apply the same push (force) to both rocks, the smaller rock will move faster after a certain amount of time. To make both rocks move at the same speed, you would have to push the large rock harder. The large rock has more mass than the small rock. Therefore, it has more inertia.

The Second Law of Motion

Newton's second law of motion says that the amount of force needed to produce a given change in the motion of an object depends on the mass of the object. The larger the mass, the more force is needed to give it a certain acceleration.

Suppose you drive a truck to a brickyard to pick up some bricks. After you load the bricks into the truck, you leave the brickyard. On the drive home, you notice that it takes longer to reach the same speed than it did when the truck was empty. What causes the difference? The truck full of bricks has more mass than the empty truck. So if you apply the same force to the truck both times (push the gas pedal the same amount), the truck with the bricks (more mass) will take longer to reach a given velocity.

Newton's second law can be written as follows.

$$\text{force} = \text{mass} \times \text{acceleration, } or \text{ F} = \text{ma}$$

A small force acting on a large mass will cause very little change in motion. A large force acting on a small mass will cause a much larger change in motion, that is, a greater acceleration.

The Third Law of Motion

Newton's third law of motion says that if an object exerts a force on a second object, the second object will always exert a force on the first object. This force will be equal to the force exerted by the first object. But the force will be in the opposite direction. This law is sometimes stated: For every action, there is an equal and opposite reaction.

A force does not always produce a change in motion. You can push on a car and still not make it move. Why? Friction is another force acting against your push. There will be a change in motion only if there is an unbalanced, or net force.

In the figure, the boy is standing on a skateboard, holding a ball in his hand. When he throws the ball forward, the boy and the skateboard move in the opposite direction from the ball. They move backward. This is an example of action and reaction. The action is throwing the ball. The reaction is the force of the ball on the boy. The boy is standing on the skateboard. Therefore, the skateboard moves backward. The action of throwing the ball causes the equal and opposite reaction of the skateboard moving backward.

Lesson 3   R E V I E W

Write your answers to these questions in complete sentences on a sheet of paper.

1. What are Newton's three laws of motion?

2. When a marble is rolled along a floor, what force or forces cause it to slow down and stop?

3. If an object is at rest, what must happen for it to begin moving?

4. What is the reaction force when a hammer hits a nail?

5. Car A has twice the mass of car B. If the same force is used to push each car separately, how will their acceleration differ?

▼◄▲▼◄▲▼◄▲▼◄▲▼◄▲▼◄▲▼◄▲▼◄▲▼◄▲▼◄▲▼◄▲▼◄▲▼◄▲▼◄▲▼◄▲▼◄▲▼◄▲▼

Science at Work

Wind Tunnel Technician

Wind tunnel technicians help study the effects of wind on airplanes and other objects. In a wind tunnel, air is blown at an object and instruments record the effects. Wind tunnel technicians operate the tunnels and run the computers that collect data. They

also watch tests to be sure that the instruments run smoothly and nothing breaks down.

Wind tunnel technicians usually have a two-year degree in a technical or engineering field. They also have engineering work experience. They often get on-the-job training as well.

Wind tunnel technicians must be observant and good with details. They must also have strong computer skills.

Gravity

The force of attraction between any two objects that have mass

Did You Know?

Friction between an object and liquid or gas is called drag. Sea anemones shrink their bodies to reduce the water current's drag. This keeps them from being pulled off rocks in strong currents.

One force with which you are probably familiar is the force of **gravity.** You might know that gravity keeps you from flying off the earth. If you are like many people, you might think of gravity as the pull exerted by Earth on other objects. But gravity is a force of attraction between any two objects that have mass.

The Law of Universal Gravitation

The gravitational force between two objects depends on the product of the masses of the two objects. Earth and the moon are two objects that have large masses. The gravitational force between them is large. Smaller objects, such as people, trees, and buildings, have much smaller gravitational forces because they have less mass. These forces are so small that they are very difficult to observe.

Mass is not the only thing that affects the pull of gravity. The distance between objects also determines how strong the force is due to gravity. The greater the distance between objects, the smaller the gravitational force is between them.

Think about an astronaut. When the astronaut is on Earth, gravity keeps him or her on the surface. The earth pulls on the astronaut. But the astronaut also pulls on the earth. The earth's gravity is strongest near the earth's surface. As the astronaut travels away from the earth in a spaceship, the pull of Earth's gravity gets weaker. But no matter how far from the earth the astronaut travels, the earth still exerts a force. In fact, Earth's gravity extends millions of kilometers into space.

The gravitational force of the sun, acting on the earth, keeps the earth in its orbit. The gravitational force prevents Earth from traveling away into space. Gravity also keeps the planets in space. And each planet exerts a gravitational force on nearby objects.

Sir Isaac Newton, who stated the three laws of motion, put these ideas about gravity together in the **law of universal gravitation.** That law says two things. First, gravitational force depends on the product of the masses of the two objects involved. Second, the gravitational force depends on the distance between the objects.

Gravity and Acceleration

Have you ever jumped off a low diving board and then a high one? If so, you might have noticed that when you jumped from the higher board, you were moving faster when you struck the water. And you hit the water harder. That is because the force of gravity causes an object to speed up as it falls.

Gravity causes all objects to have the same acceleration as they fall. Acceleration is the rate of change in velocity. But another force—air resistance—also acts on a falling object. Air resistance is a form of friction. It is caused by molecules of air rubbing against a moving object.) Air resistance causes objects to fall at different speeds. The amount of air resistance acting on a moving object depends on the shape of the object. You can see in the figure that a sheet of paper will fall more slowly than a small stone. The reason is because the mass of the paper is spread out over a wider, thinner area than that of the stone. More molecules of air hit the surface of the paper.

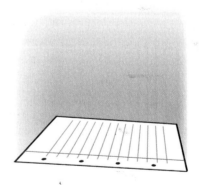

Lesson 4   R E V I E W

Write your answers to these questions in complete sentences on a sheet of paper.

1. What is gravity?

2. What three factors affect the pull of gravity?

3. What is the law of universal gravitation?

4. How does gravity affect acceleration?

5. Why don't all falling objects travel at the same speed?

Achievements in Science

Law of Uniformly Accelerated Motion

Aristotle believed that heavier objects fall faster than lighter ones. He believed that objects that weigh twice as much as others fall twice as fast. For about 1,000 years, scientists generally agreed with Aristotle's thinking.

In the early 1600s, Galileo conducted the first experiment that showed that Aristotle was wrong. Galileo faced challenges in constructing his experiment. He could not simply drop objects from a tall building for two reasons. First, the clocks of his time were not accurate. Second, he had no way to measure the speed when each object hit the earth.

Instead, Galileo tested Aristotle's theory by rolling objects on a slanted ramp. He determined their positions at equal time periods, using his own pulse as a clock.

Galileo's experiments showed that all objects experience constant acceleration when air resistance is not considered. No matter how much they weigh, all objects fall at a steady rate of acceleration. This type of acceleration is known as free fall. Free fall acceleration has its own symbol, g. At sea level, g equals 9.8 m/sec^2.

Chapter 4   S U M M A R Y

- Energy is the ability to do work.

- Kinetic energy is energy of motion. Potential energy is stored energy.

- The six main forms of energy are chemical, heat, mechanical, nuclear, radiant, and electrical. Energy can change from one form to another.

- Energy cannot be created or destroyed.

- Motion is a change in position.

- Elapsed time is the time between events. It is calculated by subtracting the time of the earlier event from the time of the later event.

- Speed is the rate at which the position of an object changes. It is equal to distance divided by time.

- Newton's first law of motion states that an object remains at rest or keeps moving at constant speed unless an outside force acts on it.

- Newton's second law of motion states that the amount of force needed to change the motion of an object depends on the mass of the object.

- Newton's third law of motion states that for every action there is an equal and opposite reaction.

- Gravity is a force of attraction between any two objects that have mass. According to the law of universal gravitation, the greater the masses are, the greater the force is. The greater the distance is, the less the force is.

- Gravity causes all falling objects to have the same acceleration. Air resistance acts on falling objects to slow them down.

Science Words

acceleration, 102	generator, 95	law of universal
distance, 98	gravity, 106	gravitation, 107
elapsed time, 97	inertia, 103	motion, 93
energy, 93	kinetic energy, 93	potential energy, 93
force, 102	law of conservation of	speed, 98
friction, 102	energy, 95	velocity, 102

Chapter 4   R E V I E W

Word Bank

energy

friction

kinetic energy

law of conservation
of energy

law of universal
gravitation

motion

potential energy

Vocabulary Review

Choose a word or words from the Word Bank that best complete each sentence. Write the answer on a sheet of paper.

1. Newton put ideas about gravity together in the _____.

2. A change in position is called _____.

3. When things slide or roll over each other, _____ occurs.

4. Stored energy is _____, and energy of motion is _____.

5. The ability to do work is _____.

6. The _____ states that energy cannot be created or destroyed.

Concept Review

Choose the answer that best completes each sentence. Write the letter of the answer on your paper.

7. To find the speed of an object, you need to know _____ and time.

   A motion   **C** acceleration

   B distance   **D** elapsed time

8. The length of time that passes from one event to another is _____.

   A average speed   **C** elapsed time

   B constant speed   **D** inertia

9. Light is an example of _____ energy.

   A radiant   **C** nuclear

   B mechanical   **D** kinetic

10. The pull of gravity is affected by an object's _____.

   A weight   **C** speed

   B temperature   **D** mass

11. The law that states that if no force acts on an object at rest, it will remain at rest is _____.
    A Newton's first law of motion
    B Newton's second law of motion
    C Newton's third law of motion
    D the law of universal gravitation

12. A generator converts mechanical energy to _____ energy.

    A heat   **C** radiant
    B electrical   **D** chemical

13. _____ energy is stored in the nucleus, or center, of atoms.

    A chemical   **C** potential
    B heat   **D** nuclear

Critical Thinking

Write the answer to each of these questions on your paper.

14. The figure below shows the motion of a bike. Calculate the speed of the bike.

Initial time 3:30 P.M.   7 miles   Final time 5:00 P.M.

15. How does mass affect gravity?

Test-Taking Tip When studying for a test, review any tests or quizzes you took earlier that cover the same information.

Work and Machines

magine what life would be like without machines. There would be no tools, no cars, no appliances. Most tasks would be much harder and take more time. Some would be impossible. In Chapter 5, you will explore the nature of work and how scientists measure work. And you will learn how machines make work easier.

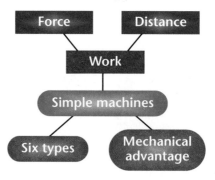

Organize Your Thoughts

Force   Distance

Work

Simple machines

Six types   Mechanical advantage

Goals for Learning

◆ To define and explain work

◆ To describe the classes of levers

◆ To calculate mechanical advantage

◆ To describe six types of simple machines

You probably do some "work" around your home. What things do you consider work? You might think of ironing clothes, washing dishes, taking out the garbage, and sweeping the floors. In everyday language, we use the word *work* as another word for *labor*.

Scientific Meaning of Work

To scientists, however, **work** is what happens when an object changes its position by moving in the direction of the force that is being applied. Remember, a force is a push or a pull.

Suppose you struggled for an hour to lift a very heavy box, but you could not budge it. No work was done in the scientific sense, because the box did not move. If you rolled a ball down a ramp, however, work was done. The reason is the ball changed its direction due to the force of gravity.

Measuring Work

How can you measure work? You can start by measuring how much force is used to do the work. Spring scales, like the one shown on page 114, are used to measure force. In the metric system, force is measured in newtons. The spring scale shows that the apple is exerting a force of 1 newton.

To measure work, you must also measure the distance (in meters) through which the force acted. To find out how much work was done, use this formula.

work = force × distance

When Sarah lifts the box, she is doing work.

Your answer will be in newton-meters. Scientists have a simpler name for a newton-meter. It is called a **joule.** A joule is the metric unit of work. When calculating work, your answer will be in joules.

Suppose a woman is pushing a bike. She uses a force of 2 newtons and pushes the bike a distance of 10 meters. How much work did she do?

Spring scale

> **EXAMPLE**
>
> work = force × distance
> work = 2 newtons × 10 meters
> work = 20 newton-meters
> work = 20 joules

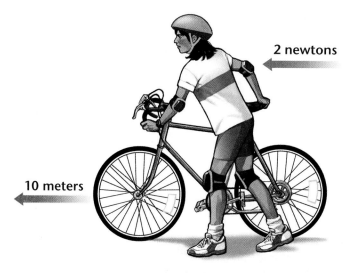

2 newtons

10 meters

Because force, distance, and work are always related, you can calculate any one of them if you know the other two. For example, if you know how much work was done and you know the distance, you can calculate how much force was used. Take the amount of work done and divide it by the distance.

$$force = \frac{work}{distance}$$

If you know how much work was done and how much force was needed, you can calculate the distance. Take the amount of work done and divide it by the amount of force that was used.

$$distance = \frac{work}{force}$$

Lesson 1   R E V I E W

Write your answers to these questions in complete sentences on a sheet of paper.

1. What is the scientific meaning of work?

2. What must you know to find the amount of work done on an object?

3. What is the metric unit of work?

4. A man pushed a table, using a force of 8 newtons. He moved the table 13 meters. How much work did he do?

5. One person solved 40 math problems in her head. Another person picked up a kitten. Which person did more work, in the scientific sense?

Science at Work

Machine Designer

Machine designers work in teams with engineers to design and build machinery. They use computer systems to make designs, drawings, and specifications for machines and their parts. Machine designers make cost and parts estimates and project schedules. As part of their work, they also test and analyze machines and their parts.

Machine designers usually have completed a two- or three-year technical program in mechanical engineering.

Machine designers are natural inventors. They are good at sketching, drawing, mathematics, and mechanical problem solving. Machine designers must know about materials and equipment involved in designing, constructing, and operating machines.

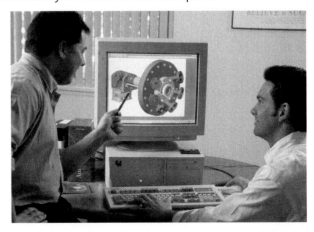

Simple machine

A tool with few parts that makes it easier or possible to do work

Lever

A simple machine containing a bar that can turn around a fixed point

Fulcrum

A fixed point around which a lever rotates

Effort force, F_e

The force applied to a machine by the user

Resistance force, F_r

The force applied to a machine by the object to be moved

Have you ever tried to open a paint can, using only your fingers? It is hard, if not impossible, to do. With a screwdriver, you can easily pry the lid from the can. A screwdriver, used in this way, is an example of a **simple machine.** A simple machine is a tool with few parts that makes it easier or possible to do work. Simple machines change the direction or size of the force you apply. Or, they change the distance through which the force acts.

The Lever

A **lever** is a simple machine. Levers can have many shapes. In its most basic form, the lever is a bar that is free to turn around a fixed point. The fixed point is called a **fulcrum.**

In the figure below, the woman is using a lever to move a boulder. Notice that the lever changes the direction of the force the woman applies. She pushes down, but the boulder moves up. The force the woman applies to the machine is called the **effort force** (F_e).

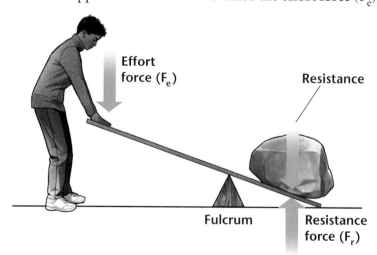

The object to be lifted is called the resistance. In this example, the boulder is the resistance. Gravity is pulling down on the boulder, so the machine must exert a force upward to lift it. The force the machine uses to move the resistance is called the **resistance force** (F_r).

The force the machine exerts is greater than the force the woman exerts. In other words, using the lever makes the woman's job easier. The lever takes the amount of force she exerts and increases that force.

The Three Classes of Levers

Levers can be grouped into three classes. The classes of levers are based on the position of the resistance force, the fulcrum, and the effort force. The figure below illustrates a first-class lever.

In a first-class lever, the fulcrum is positioned between the effort and the resistance. A first-class lever changes the direction of a force and can also increase the force.

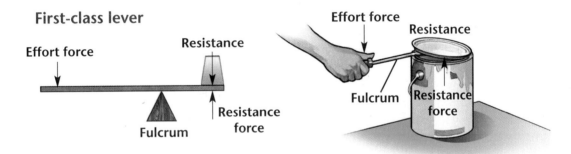

First-class lever

Effort force · Resistance · Fulcrum · Resistance force

Effort force · Resistance · Fulcrum · Resistance force

In a second-class lever, shown below, the resistance is positioned between the effort and the fulcrum. Second-class levers always increase the force applied to them. They do not change the direction of the force. Wheelbarrows, paper cutters, and most nutcrackers are examples of second-class levers.

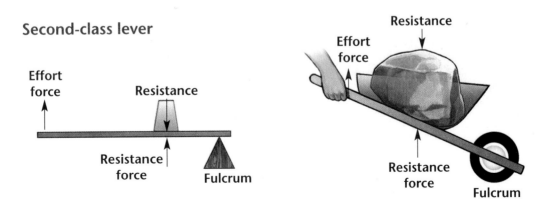

Second-class lever

Effort force · Resistance · Resistance force · Fulcrum

Effort force · Resistance · Resistance force · Fulcrum

Look at the third-class lever in the figure below. Notice that the effort is between the fulcrum and the resistance. Third-class levers increase the distance through which the force moves, which causes the resistance to move farther or faster. A broom is an example of a third-class lever. You use effort force on the handle between the fulcrum and the resistance force. When you move the handle of the broom a short distance, the brush end moves a greater distance.

Third-class lever

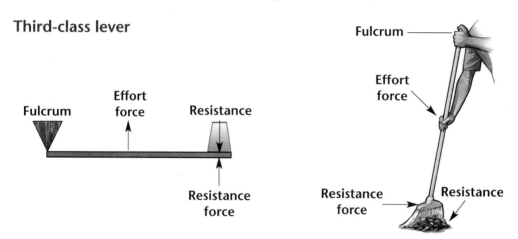

Work and Energy

Energy cannot be created or destroyed. Because energy is the ability to do work, work cannot be created either. No simple machine can do more work than the person using it supplies. What machines can do is increase or change the direction of the force a person exerts.

Science Myth

A machine is something that has been manufactured.

Fact: Our bodies are machines. They contain all three classes of levers. When you lift your head forward or back, you use a first-class lever. When you stand on your toes, you use a second-class lever. When you hold a weight in your hand with your arm extended, you are using a third-class lever.

Mechanical Advantage

Mechanical advantage, MA

Factor by which a machine multiplies the effort force

People often use simple machines to make tasks easier. A simple machine makes a task easier because it multiplies the force a person applies.

The number of times a machine multiplies your effort force is called the **mechanical advantage** of the machine. You can find a machine's mechanical advantage (MA) with this formula.

$$\text{mechanical advantage} = \frac{\text{resistance force}}{\text{effort force}} \quad \text{or} \quad MA = \frac{F_r}{F_e}$$

Look at the figure below. Suppose a machine lifts a resistance that weighs 30 newtons when the woman applies an effort force of only 10 newtons. What is the machine's mechanical advantage?

EXAMPLE

$$MA = \frac{F_r}{F_e}$$

$$MA = \frac{30 \text{ newtons}}{10 \text{ newtons}}$$

$$MA = 3$$

The mechanical advantage is 3. The machine has multiplied the woman's effort force by 3. This makes the object easier for her to lift.

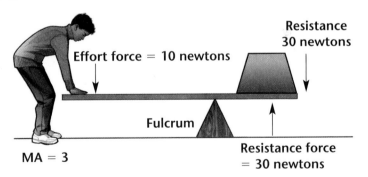

Effort force = 10 newtons
Resistance 30 newtons
Fulcrum
MA = 3
Resistance force = 30 newtons

Some machines are not used to multiply effort force. Instead, people use them to increase the distance or speed the resistance will move, or to change the direction of a force. Rather than increasing a person's effort force, the machine may even reduce it.

Lesson 2 R E V I E W

Write your answers to these questions in complete sentences on a sheet of paper.

1. Draw a first-class lever. Show the fulcrum, effort force, and resistance.

2. Draw a second-class lever. Show the fulcrum, effort force, and resistance.

3. Draw a third-class lever. Show the fulcrum, effort force, and resistance.

4. What is mechanical advantage?

5. How do you find the mechanical advantage of most simple machines?

Achievements in Science

The Law of the Lever

Levers probably were used in prehistoric times. In 260 B.C., Archimedes was the first to prove mathematically how levers work. His proof is known as the law of the lever.

The law of the lever is based on three principles. The first is that equal weights at equal distances from a fulcrum balance. The second is that two weights no longer balance if something is added to one. The side with the increased weight goes down. The third principle is that two weights do not balance if something is taken from one. The side holding the weight that did not change goes down.

Here is the formula for the law of the levers: $F_1 \times l_1 = F_2 \times l_2$. F_1 is the weight of an object on one side of a fulcrum. The length from that object to the fulcrum is l_1. F_2 is the weight on the other side. The length of that object to the fulcrum is l_2.

Archimedes's proof shows that anything, no matter how heavy it is, can be lifted using a lever.

INVESTIGATION 5

Materials

◆ safety glasses
◆ spring scale
◆ 200-g weight
◆ rubber band
◆ stiff meterstick
◆ triangular wooden wedge or other fulcrum

Finding the Mechanical Advantage of a Lever

Purpose

Which fulcrum position would have a greater mechanical advantage—one at 20 cm or one at 80 cm? In this investigation, you will find the mechanical advantage of a lever.

Procedure

1. Copy the data table on a sheet of paper.

Fulcrum Position	Resistance Force	Effort Force	Resistance Arm	Effort Arm
50 cm				
80 cm				
20 cm				

2. Put on your safety glasses.

3. Use a spring scale to hold up a 200-g weight. Record the weight (the resistance force) in newtons.

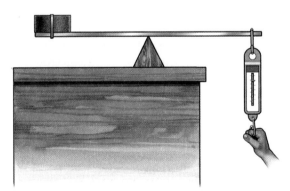

4. Using a rubber band, attach the 200-g weight to the top side of a stiff meterstick, at the 0-cm end.

5. Work at a table or desk. Place the weighted meterstick on a fulcrum so that it is positioned under the stick's 50-cm mark. The end of the stick without the weight should extend beyond the edge of the table, as shown in the diagram.

6. Use a spring scale to gently pull down on the 100-cm end of the stick until it is level at both ends. On the spring scale, read the effort force you apply to make the stick level. Record that force, in newtons, on the 50-cm line of the data table.

7. Record the length of the resistance arm (the distance from the weight to the fulcrum). Then record the effort arm (the distance from the fulcrum to the spring scale).

8. Follow the basic procedure used in steps 4 to 6 except position the fulcrum under the 80-cm mark. Record the values in the data table. Then place the fulcrum under the 20-cm mark. Repeat the basic procedure in steps 4 to 6. Record the values.

Questions and Conclusions

1. Where was the fulcrum placed when you had to apply the most force? Where was it placed when you had to apply the least force?

$$MA = \frac{\text{effort arm}}{\text{resistance arm}}$$

2. Calculate the mechanical advantage of the three levers using the formula at the left.

3. Which setup showed the greatest mechanical advantage? Which setup showed the least?

4. How do the mechanical advantages you calculated in step 3 compare to your answers to question 1?

5. Explain how the position of the fulcrum affects a lever's mechanical advantage.

Explore Further

Repeat the investigation steps, but use a weight with a different mass. Record your observations. Explain how a weight's mass affects mechanical advantage.

There are six types of simple machines, including the lever. In this lesson, you will learn about the other five types.

The Pulley

A **pulley** is a wheel with a rope, chain, or belt around it. Figure A shows a single fixed pulley.

A single fixed pulley changes the direction of the force you apply, but it does not multiply that force. The mechanical advantage equals 1. You can use this type of pulley to lift a heavy object by pulling down instead of lifting up.

The pulley in Figure A is called a fixed pulley because it is fixed or attached at the top. The wheel is free to spin, but it cannot move up and down.

The pulley in Figure B is a movable pulley. As effort is applied to a movable pulley, the entire pulley and the object attached to it will rise. You can use this type of pulley to make a lifting job easier. Because the rope supports the pulley from two directions, you need to apply only half as much force to lift the object. Therefore, the pulley has a mechanical advantage of 2.

Pulley

A simple machine made up of a rope, chain, or belt wrapped around a wheel

Figure A

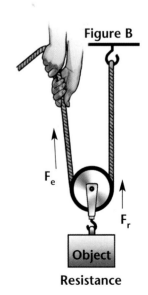

Figure B

There is a price to pay for making the object easier to lift. You must pull twice as far on the rope as the object actually moves. For example, to lift the object 1 meter, you must pull up a distance of 2 meters on the rope. The direction of the force is not reversed. To lift the object, you must pull up on the rope, not down.

Pulleys can be combined in different ways. Look at the figures below. Note the number of supporting ropes pulling up on each object. Note the mechanical advantage (MA) of each pulley system. The MA of a pulley system is usually about equal to the number of ropes that pull upward. In Figure C, two ropes pull up on the object. The mechanical advantage equals 2. In Figure D, three ropes pull up on the object. The MA of this system equals 3.

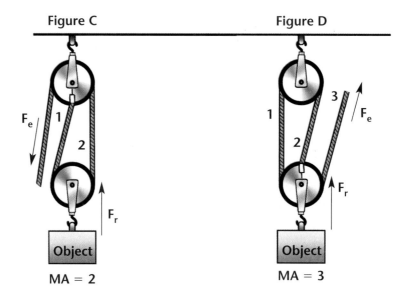

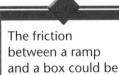
The Inclined Plane

An **inclined plane** is a simple machine made of a ramp. It has no moving parts. You use an inclined plane to lift an object.

Inclined planes, such as the one shown here in Figure E, decrease the force you need to move an object. Once again, you pay for this decrease in effort force by an increase in the distance the object has to be moved.

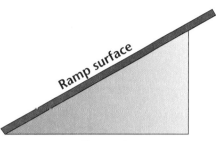

Figure E

For example, if a delivery person needs to put a box on a truck that is 1 meter from the ground, he might use an inclined plane, or ramp, to make his job easier. Rather than lifting the box 1 meter, he can push it up the ramp. It takes less force to push an object than to pick it up. However, he must move the object farther, as shown in Figure F below.

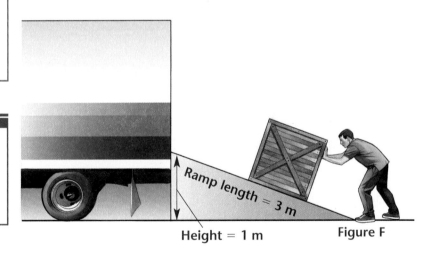

Ramp length = 3 m

Height = 1 m

Figure F

In Figure F, the mechanical advantage is 3. You divide the ramp length, 3 m, by the height, 1 m. The mechanical advantage of an inclined plane is the length of the slanted surface, divided by the vertical (up and down) height. The more gradual the slant, the greater the mechanical advantage, but the farther the object must go.

A speedboat is a simple machine. It is a wedge. In the water, a speedboat puts force on two inclined surfaces and then pushes them apart.

The Screw

Another kind of simple machine, the **screw,** is a form of inclined plane. Think of a screw as a straight piece of metal with an inclined plane wrapped in a spiral around it. The ridges formed by this spiral are called threads.

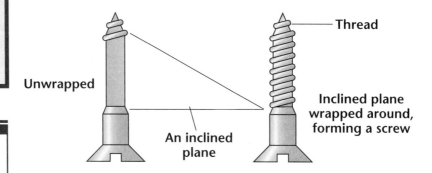

Screws make it easier to fasten objects together. The mechanical advantage of a screw depends on the distance between the threads. The smaller the distance, the more times the inclined plane is wrapped around, making the mechanical advantage greater.

The Wedge

A **wedge** is an inclined plane that moves when it is used. It is thick at one end and thinner at the other. A wedge is often made up of two inclined planes joined together. Both edges are slanted. You can use a wedge for a job like splitting wood. A force applied to the thick end is multiplied and acts at the thin end, piercing the wood. The thinner and more gradual the wedge, the greater the mechanical advantage.

A wedge is useful for splitting wood.

The Wheel and Axle

Wheel and axle

A simple machine made up of a wheel attached to a shaft

An automobile steering wheel and a doorknob are examples of a simple machine called a **wheel and axle.** In this simple machine, a wheel is attached to a shaft called an axle, as shown in the figure.

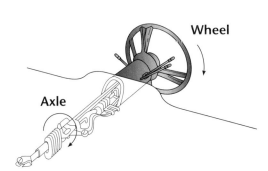

Wheel

Axle

A wheel and axle increases the twisting force you apply to the wheel. The multiplied force can then turn something else attached to the axle. The mechanical advantage of a wheel and axle depends on the size of the wheel compared to the thickness of the axle. The bigger the wheel is in comparison to the thickness of the axle, the greater the mechanical advantage.

Science in Your Life

Do levers make you stronger?

If you wanted to remove a nail from a piece of wood, would you try to pull it out with your fingers? Probably not; you already know how hard that would be. Instead of your fingers, you would use the claw end of a hammer or a crowbar. A crowbar is a steel bar, usually wedge shaped at one end. This end is used as a lever. With one of these tools, you could easily remove a nail. Neither tool makes you stronger, but by using one of them, you can do work that would otherwise be impossible.

A hammer and crowbar are just two of the many levers we use every day. Levers include other tools that can pry something loose, as well as tools like scissors, wheelbarrows, brooms, tweezers, oars, baseball bats, and pliers. Like all simple machines, levers increase the amount of work you can do because they increase the force you are able to apply.

Write your answers to these questions in complete sentences on a sheet of paper.

1. What is a fixed pulley?

2. What is the difference between a fixed pulley and a movable pulley?

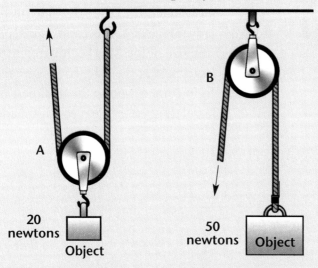

3. What is the mechanical advantage of each of the pulleys in the figure?

4. Explain the mechanical advantage of a movable pulley system that has two ropes that pull upward.

5. What is an inclined plane?

6. How can you find the mechanical advantage of an inclined plane?

7. Screws and wedges are variations of what simple machine?

8. Which will have a greater mechanical advantage: a screw with closely spaced threads or one with widely spaced threads? Explain your answer.

9. Which will have a greater mechanical advantage: a thin, gradual wedge or a thick, greatly sloping one? Explain your answer.

10. Why does a bus usually have a steering wheel that is larger than the one in a car?

- Work is what happens when a force makes something move in the direction of the force.

- To measure work, force and distance must be measured.

- Simple machines make doing work easier by changing the direction or size of a force and the distance through which it acts.

- Resistance force is the force applied by a machine against a resistance. Effort force is the force applied to a machine by the person using it.

- A lever is a bar that turns around a fulcrum.

- Levers are divided into three classes, according to the relationship between the effort, fulcrum, and resistance.

- The mechanical advantage of a machine is the number of times by which the machine multiplies effort force.

- A pulley is made up of a rope, chain, or belt wrapped around a wheel.

- An inclined plane is a ramp.

- A screw and a wedge are special forms of inclined planes.

- A wheel and axle is a wheel attached to a shaft.

Science Words

effort force, 116	lever, 116	resistance force, 116	wheel and axle, 127
fulcrum,116	mechanical	screw, 126	work, 113
inclined plane, 125	advantage, 119	simple machine, 116	
joule, 114	pulley, 123	wedge, 126	

effort force

inclined plane

joule

lever

mechanical
   advantage

pulley

resistance force

simple machine

wedge

wheel and axle

work

Vocabulary Review

Choose a word or words from the Word Bank that best complete each sentence. Write the answer on a sheet of paper.

1. Resistance force divided by effort force equals _____.

2. A(n) _____ is a ramplike simple machine.

3. Force multiplied by distance equals _____.

4. A(n) _____ consists of a rope, chain, or belt wrapped around a wheel.

5. _____ is the force applied by a machine against the resistance.

6. A(n) _____ is a bar that turns around a fixed point.

7. A(n) _____ is a tool with few parts.

8. A(n) _____ is an inclined plane that moves when it is used.

9. _____ is the force applied to a machine by the user.

10. A newton-meter is also called a(n) _____ .

11. A(n) _____ has a wheel attached to a shaft.

Concept Review

Choose the answer that best completes each sentence. Write the letter of the answer on your paper.

12. Work = _____.

    A force + distance   **C** force × distance

    B force − distance   **D** force ÷ distance

13. Machines can be used to _____.

    A multiply effort force

    B increase the distance or speed the resistance will move

    C change the direction of a force

    D all of the above

14. A simple machine containing a bar that can turn about a fixed point is a(n) _____.
   A wheel and axle **C** inclined plane
   B lever **D** wedge

15. A paper cutter is an example of a _____ lever.
   A first-class **B** second class **C** third-class **D** fourth-class

16. A screw contains a(n) _____.
   A axle **B** wheel **C** lever **D** inclined plane

17. A doorknob is an example of a _____.
   A fulcrum **B** wheel and axle **C** pulley **D** wedge

18. To calculate how much work was done, you should _____.
   A multiply force by distance **C** divide resistance force by effort force
   B divide force by distance **D** divide distance by force

Critical Thinking

Write the answer to each of these questions on your paper.

19. What class of lever is shown in the diagram below? How can you tell?

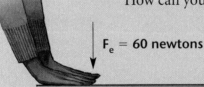

$F_e = 60$ newtons

Object

3.0 m   1.2 m

20. Give examples of three simple machines. Explain how simple machines make it possible or easier to do work.

Test-Taking Tip Before you begin an exam, skim through the whole test to find out what is expected of you.

6 Heat

What words would you use to describe a flame? You might say *fire, bright, hot, glowing,* or *heat.* The flame from a match is a hot gas that will burn if you touch it. It is so hot that it glows. The flame produces heat. But is fire the only way to produce heat? Are there other sources of heat? In Chapter 6, you will learn about heat energy and its sources. You also will learn how heat affects matter and how heat travels.

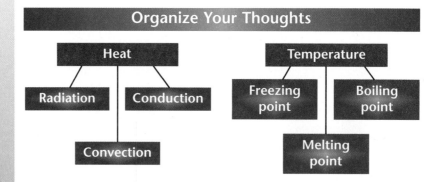

Organize Your Thoughts

Heat
— Radiation
— Conduction
— Convection

Temperature
— Freezing point
— Boiling point
— Melting point

Goals for Learning

◆ To explain how heat energy can be produced

◆ To tell how heat changes matter

◆ To explain how temperature is measured

◆ To identify the difference between temperature and heat

◆ To explain how matter is heated by conduction, convection, and radiation

After reading this lesson, you should be able to

◆ define heat.

◆ explain how heat energy can do work.

◆ explain how heat is produced.

◆ describe some sources of heat.

Heat

A form of energy resulting from the motion of particles in matter

What happens when you hold an ice cube in your hand? Your hand is warmer than the ice cube. The warmth from your hand causes the ice cube to melt. **Heat** causes the ice to melt. Heat is a form of energy that results from the motion of particles in matter. Heat energy flows from a warmer object to a cooler object.

Heat from your hand will cause an ice cube to melt.

You learned in Chapter 4 that heat is a form of energy. Energy can do work. Therefore, heat can do work. Machines can change heat energy into useful mechanical energy. For example, a steam engine uses the heat energy contained in steam to move the parts of the engine. An automobile engine also uses heat energy. Burning fuel produces hot gases that make the engine work.

Heat source

A place from which heat energy comes

Sources of Heat

What produces heat energy? Remember that all matter is made up of atoms and molecules. These tiny particles are always moving. The random motion and vibrations of particles in matter is a measure of the heat energy. The faster the particles move, the more heat energy they have.

Imagine going outside on a summer day. You feel heat from the sun. The sun is the earth's most important **heat source.** A heat source is a place from which heat energy comes. Nuclear reactions in the sun are the source of the heat energy that warms you.

You might recall from Chapter 4 that energy comes in different forms. Other forms of energy can be changed into heat energy. For example, hold your hands together and rub them rapidly. Your hands will begin to feel warm. Friction between your hands is a form of mechanical energy—the energy of motion— that produces heat.

Rubbing your hands together produces heat.

Fusion is the process responsible for the energy of the sun and other stars.

Sometimes the heat produced by mechanical energy can cause harmful effects. For example, the oil well drills used to drill through rock produce a lot of heat. Workers must cool the drills with water to keep them from melting.

Another source of heat is chemical energy. When substances react chemically with each other, they sometimes release heat. For example, when natural gas and other fuels burn, they produce heat.

Electricity is also a heat source. Look at the toaster below. When energy from an electric current passes through the wires of the toaster, the wires become hot. This energy can toast bread. What other appliances can you name that change electricity into heat energy?

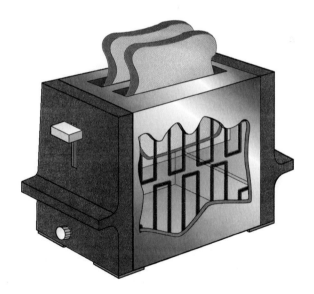

Nuclear energy is another form of energy. It is energy stored in the nucleus of an atom. When the nucleus of an atom is split, the nucleus becomes smaller nuclei. Energy is released as heat and light. This reaction is called **nuclear fission.** Nuclear energy is also released when atoms are joined together. When two nuclei are combined, they form a larger nucleus. This reaction is called **nuclear fusion.** Stars shine because their atoms release nuclear energy. Nuclear energy produces the sun's heat and light.

Lesson 1   R E V I E W

Write your answers to these questions in complete sentences on a sheet of paper.

1. What is heat?

2. What produces heat energy?

3. Give an example of how another form of energy can be changed into heat energy.

4. Does heat energy flow from a warm object to a cooler object or from a cool object to a warmer one?

5. What form of energy produces the sun's heat?

Achievements in Science

Steam Engine

The first steam engine, invented by the Greeks before A.D. 300, was used as a toy. Later steam engines had more practical uses. In 1698, Thomas Savery invented a steam-powered pump to drain water from mines. In 1765, Thomas Newcomen designed a more efficient steam engine pump. James Watt's steam engine, invented in 1763, was the first to do more than pumping. Watt's steam engine could make something turn. Watt's improvements led to machines that could do work that had once been done by hand.

Steam engines use heated water to operate. Most steam engines have a furnace that burns fuel, which produces heat energy. All have a boiler in which heat energy changes water to steam. The pressure from the expanding steam pushes on the engine parts to make them move.

Some early uses of steam engines were in steam locomotives and steamships. Today we continue to use steam engines to convert heat into mechanical work. Steam engines are at work in most electric power plants and all nuclear power plants.

Evaporate

To change from a liquid to a gas

Condensation

A change from a gas to a liquid

Did You Know?

There is no air inside the bubbles of boiling water. The bubbles of boiling water are made up of water vapor, also called steam.

Matter exists in different states. In a gas, the particles (molecules) are generally very far apart. They move freely. In a liquid, the particles are close together, but are still able to move freely. In a solid, the particles are close together and are not able to move past each other. They are constrained to specific positions in the solid. Heat can cause particles to move faster and move farther apart. Heat can change matter from one state to another.

Changing from a Liquid to a Gas

You might have noticed that if you boil water for a period of time, the amount of water gradually decreases. What happens to the water? Heat makes the water molecules move faster. As the molecules move faster, they bump into each other more often and push each other apart. As a result, the water **evaporates,** or changes from a liquid to a gas.

Heat rises

Changing from a Gas to a Liquid

If you have ever seen frost form on a window inside your home, you have seen an example of **condensation.** The temperature outside is cooler than the temperature inside your home. Condensation occurs when water vapor in the air returns to its original liquid state. This happens when the air cools and the temperature of the air drops. The molecules in the air move at a slower speed. Cold air cannot hold as much water vapor as warm air. Some of the water vapor condenses to form tiny drops of liquid water. Water drops that appear on a mirror after you have taken a hot shower are another example of condensation.

Changing from a Solid to a Liquid

What happens to an ice cube (a solid) when it is left in a warm room? It melts. But why does it melt? Heat speeds up the vibrational motion of the molecules in the ice cube. This motion disrupts the structure of the ice crystal. The molecules are free to move around relative to each other. The solid ice cube changes to liquid water.

Expanding and Contracting Matter

Heat causes particles in matter to push farther apart. Then the matter **expands,** or becomes larger in size. It fills up more space. The figure shows a joint in a metal bridge. Summer heat makes the material in the bridge expand. What might happen if the bridge did not have an expansion joint?

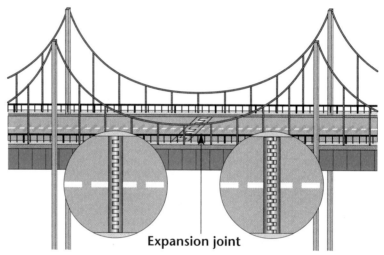

Expansion joint

Bridge in summer   Bridge in winter

Solids, liquids, and gases do not expand equally. In most cases, liquids expand more than solids. Gases usually expand the most.

Sometimes, matter loses heat. Particles in matter move more slowly and stay closer together as they lose heat. The matter **contracts,** or becomes smaller. It takes up less space. In the figure, notice the joint in the bridge in winter. The material in the bridge contracts in cold weather. Water is a material that behaves differently. Cooled water contracts until it reaches 4°C. Below this temperature, water expands until it freezes at 0°C.

Write your answers to these questions in complete sentences on a sheet of paper.

1. What happens to an ice cube when it is heated?
2. What happens when water in a puddle evaporates?
3. How does heat affect the amount of space matter fills?
4. Why does the amount of water decrease when it boils?
5. Is fog an example of condensation? Explain your answer.

▼◄▲▼◄▲▼◄▲▼◄▲▼◄▲▼◄▲▼◄▲▼◄▲▼◄▲▼◄▲▼◄▲▼◄▲▼◄▲▼◄▲▼◄▲▼◄▲▼

Science at Work

Heating, Ventilation, and Air Conditioning (HVAC) Technician

HVAC technicians install, maintain, and repair heating, ventilation, and air conditioning systems. They work in both homes and businesses. They also recharge systems with refrigerants or cooling gases, such as Freon. Their other responsibilities include testing, troubleshooting, and adjusting systems to make sure they work properly.

HVAC technicians receive on-the-job training or they complete an apprenticeship program.

HVAC technicians must work well with their hands and have good vision and hand-eye coordination. They also must be patient and be able to work effectively under stressful conditions.

INVESTIGATION

Observing and Comparing Expansion and Contraction

Materials

- safety glasses
- balloon
- flask
- masking tape or electrical tape
- 2 buckets
- cold water
- hot water
- paper towels

Purpose

What happens when a gas expands and contracts? In this investigation, you will observe and compare expansion and contraction of gases.

Procedure

1. Copy the data table on a sheet of paper.

Environment	Changes in balloon
In hot water	
In cold water	
At room temperature	

2. Put on your safety glasses.

3. Carefully stretch the opening of the balloon over the opening of the flask. Use tape to seal the balloon to the flask.

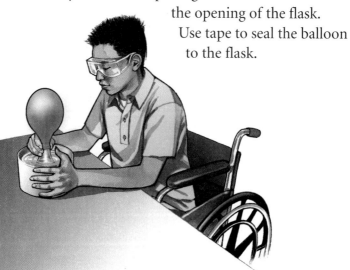

4. Fill one bucket with cold water.

5. Fill the other bucket with hot water. **Safety Alert: Do not use water hot enough to cause a burn.** Place the flask in the bucket of hot water. Keep the flask in the water until the flask becomes hot.

6. Observe the balloon. Record any changes you see in the data table.

7. Remove the flask from the bucket of hot water. Place the flask in the bucket of cold water. Keep the flask in the cold water until the flask becomes cold. Record any changes to the balloon.

8. Take the flask out of the water and dry it. Watch the balloon as the flask returns to room temperature. Record any changes to the balloon.

Questions and Conclusions

1. What happened to the balloon when the flask was heated?

2. What happened to the balloon as the flask cooled?

3. What caused the changes you observed in the balloon?

Explore Further

Explain what would happen to a helium-filled balloon if it was moved to a colder room. Explain what would happen to the balloon if it was moved to a warmer room.

Objectives

After reading this lesson, you should be able to

◆ explain how temperature is measured.

◆ compare and contrast temperature scales.

◆ describe freezing point, melting point, and boiling point.

◆ explain how temperature and heat differ.

Temperature
A measure of how fast an object's particles are moving

Heat energy from Maria's hand heats the water and melts the ice cubes.

What happens when you put your hand in a bowl of cool water? Heat energy from your hand flows into the water and makes the water warmer.

The more your hand heats the water, the faster the water particles move. **Temperature** is a measure of how fast an object's particles are moving. The higher the temperature, the faster an object's particles move.

Touching an object does not always give an accurate measurement of the object's temperature. For example, suppose you place your hand in cold water. Heat energy from your hand moves to the water and your hand becomes cooler. Now move that same hand out of the cold water and into a container of lukewarm water. The water will feel hotter than it actually is because your hand is cool.

Thermometers

You often cannot rely on your sense of touch to accurately tell temperature. So how can you measure temperature accurately? A **thermometer** is a device we use to measure temperature. Two different kinds of thermometers are shown below.

The thermometer in the figure at the right is a glass tube with a small amount of liquid inside. The liquid is usually mercury or alcohol. As the thermometer measures higher temperatures, heat causes the particles of liquid to expand, or move farther apart. As the liquid expands, it moves up the tube. The more heat that passes to the liquid, the more the liquid will expand and the higher it moves in the tube. When the liquid stops expanding, it stops beside a number on the tube. This number tells the temperature of the substance touching the bulb of the thermometer.

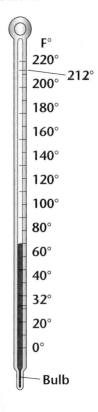

Look at the electronic thermometer in the photo below. Many doctors and medical workers use this kind of thermometer to take people's temperatures. It measures temperatures very quickly.

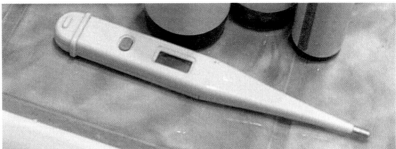

Digital (electronic) thermometers measure temperatures quickly.

Temperature Scales

Farenheit scale

The temperature scale commonly used in the United States, in which water freezes at 32° and boils at 212°

Celsius scale

The temperature scale used by scientists and by people in many countries, in which water freezes at 0° and boils at 100°

Degree

A unit of measurement on a temperature scale

Two common scales are used to measure temperature. People in the United States usually use the **Fahrenheit scale.** Fahrenheit is abbreviated as *F.* People in many other countries use the **Celsius scale.** The abbreviation for Celsius is *C.* Scientists use the Celsius scale.

Look at the thermometers on this page to compare the Fahrenheit scale with the Celsius scale. Find the equally spaced units on each scale. For both temperature scales, temperature is measured in units called **degrees.** The symbol for degree is °. The temperature shown on the Fahrenheit scale is 68 degrees Fahrenheit. It is written as 68°F. The same temperature in the Celsius scale is 20 degrees Celsius. It is written as 20°C.

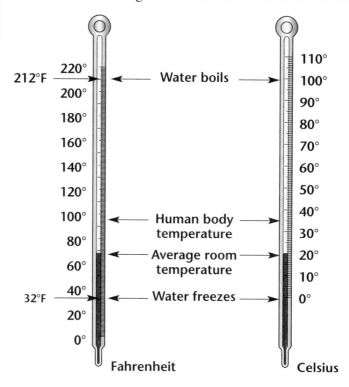

We write any temperature below zero degrees with a minus (–) sign. For example, a temperature of 10 degrees below zero on the Celsius scale is written as –10°C. The table on the next page shows how we write temperatures on the Fahrenheit scale and the Celsius scale.

Temperature Conversion

If you know the temperature of a substance on one scale, you can convert to an equal temperature on the other scale. The table shows how temperatures convert from one scale to the other.

Temperature Conversion Table			
°C	°F	°C	°F
100	212	45	113
95	203	40	104
90	194	35	95
85	185	30	86
80	176	25	77
75	167	20	68
70	158	15	59
65	149	10	50
60	140	5	41
55	131	0	32
50	122		

If you need a conversion that is not listed in the table, you can use a formula to figure it out. You can use this formula to convert a Celsius temperature to Fahrenheit.

$$F = \frac{9}{5} \times C + 32 \text{ or } F = 1.8 \times C + 32 \text{ (the fraction } \frac{9}{5} \text{ is equal to 1.8)}$$

Suppose you want to convert 22° Celsius to Fahrenheit.

EXAMPLE

$F = 1.8 \times C + 32$
$F = 1.8 \times 22 + 32$
$F = 1.8 \times 22 = 39.6 + 32$
$F = 71.6° \text{ or } F = 72°$

We usually round the decimal portion of the number to the nearest whole number. So, you would round 71.6 to 72.

Use this formula to convert a Fahrenheit temperature to Celsius.

$$C = \frac{5}{9} \times (F - 32)$$

Suppose you want to convert 48° Fahrenheit to Celsius.

Freezing point	

Freezing point

The temperature at which a liquid changes to a solid

Melting point

The temperature at which a solid changes to a liquid

EXAMPLE

$$C = \frac{5}{9} \times (F - 32)$$

$$C = \frac{5}{9} \times (48 - 32)$$

$$C = \frac{5 \times 16}{9} = \frac{80}{9}$$

$$C = 8.8° \ or \ C = 9°$$

Notice that $\frac{80}{9}$ is $80 \div 9$ or 8.8888. Round the decimal portion of the number to the nearest whole number to get 9.

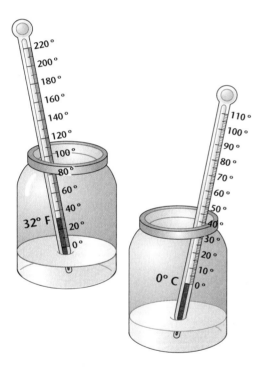

Freezing Point

What happens when you place a container of water in the freezer? The water gradually changes to ice. Suppose you recorded the temperature of the water every five minutes. You would notice that as time passed, the temperature would decrease. As the temperature of the water decreases, the water loses heat. Eventually the liquid water becomes solid.

The temperature at which a liquid changes to a solid is called its **freezing point.** The figure shows the freezing point of water. On the Celsius scale, the temperature at which water freezes is 0°. On the Fahrenheit scale, the temperature at which water freezes is 32°.

Melting Point

The temperature at which a solid changes to a liquid is called its **melting point.** The melting point of a substance is the same as its freezing point. The term *melting point* is used when a substance is being heated. When ice is heated, it changes to a liquid at a temperature of 0°C. Therefore, the melting point of ice is 0°C.

Boiling Point

The **boiling point** of a substance is the temperature at which it changes from a liquid to a gas under normal atmospheric pressure. You can see in the figure that the temperature at which water boils is 100° on the Celsius scale. On the Fahrenheit scale, the boiling point is read as 212°.

Every substance has its own freezing and boiling points. Scientists use the freezing and boiling points of substances to help identify unknown substances. You can see the freezing and boiling points of a few substances in the table.

The Freezing and Boiling Points of Some Substances				
	Freezing/Melting Point		Boiling Point	
Substance	°F	°C	°F	°C
water	32	0	212	100
aluminum	1,220	660	4,473	2,467
iron	1,762	961	4,014	2,212
alcohol	−202	−130	173	78

Changing Freezing Point and Boiling Point

You can change the freezing point and the boiling point of a substance by mixing substances together. For example, if you add alcohol to water, the freezing point of the mixture will be lower than the freezing point of water alone. Antifreeze contains alcohol. Adding antifreeze to an automobile radiator lowers the freezing point of the water in the radiator. This keeps the water from freezing and prevents engine damage. The antifreeze also has a higher boiling point than water. Antifreeze boils more slowly than water in hot weather.

Certain compounds of sodium and calcium are used on icy roads and walkways in winter. These compounds lower the freezing point of water and change the ice back to a liquid.

Temperature and Heat

Temperature and heat are different. Temperature is a measure of how fast the molecules in a substance are moving. The higher the temperature, the greater the atomic or molecular motion. Heat depends on the temperature of a substance and the amount of matter, or mass, the substance has.

As the temperature of an object increases, the amount of heat in the object also increases. If two objects of different mass are at the same temperature, the object with the greater mass will give off more heat. For example, suppose the temperature of a lighted candle is the same as the temperature of a bonfire. The bonfire contains more mass than the candle. Therefore, the bonfire gives off more heat.

Achievements in Science

Temperature Scales

For 2,000 years, people have used temperature scales. But people used different kinds of scales for different purposes. Only in the 1600s did scientists develop temperature scales like those we use today.

The Fahrenheit temperature scale was introduced in 1724. This scale began at 0°, the freezing point of an ice, water, and salt mixture. It ended at 98°, the normal body temperature. Water's freezing point was 32°. Scientists later adjusted Fahrenheit's scale, making the highest point 212°, water's boiling point.

The Celsius temperature scale was introduced in 1742. It made zero the boiling point of water and 100 the melting point of ice. The scale was divided into 100 units called degrees centigrade. Later scientists changed "centigrade" to "Celsius." They also made 0° the freezing point of water and 100° the boiling point.

The Kelvin temperature scale, introduced in 1848, is based on the Celsius scale. On the Kelvin scale, zero is the temperature at which the movement of all atoms stops.

Lesson 3 REVIEW

Write your answers to these questions in complete sentences on a sheet of paper.

1. How does the motion of molecules affect temperature?

2. Explain how a liquid thermometer works.

3. Write the following temperatures:

   A thirty-four degrees Fahrenheit

   B sixty-six degrees Celsius

   C four degrees below zero on the Fahrenheit scale

   D one hundred ten degrees on the Celsius scale

4. What is meant by the freezing point of a substance?

5. What is meant by the melting point of a substance?

6. What is meant by the boiling point of a substance?

7. How can the freezing point of a substance be changed?

8. Which temperature is hotter, 25° Celsius or 68° Fahrenheit?

9. Explain the difference between heat and temperature.

10. Container A contains 10 L of water. Container B contains 2 L of water. The water in both containers is the same temperature. Which container has more heat energy? Explain.

Technology Note

A pop-up timer shows when a turkey is cooked. The timer has an outer case. This case contains a plastic stem within a piece of soft metal and a spring. The soft metal is solid at room temperature. When it reaches its melting point, the metal releases the stem. The spring makes the stem pop up.

Vacuum

Space that contains no matter

Radiation

The movement of energy through a vacuum

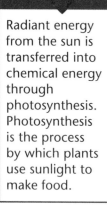

Radiant energy from the sun is transferred into chemical energy through photosynthesis. Photosynthesis is the process by which plants use sunlight to make food.

Think about different ways you can travel, or move, from one place to another. You might walk or run. You might ride a bicycle. You might travel in a car, bus, train, boat, or airplane. Energy also has different ways of moving from warm matter to cool matter.

Radiation

The sun is a very long distance from Earth—150 million kilometers, in fact. Yet the sun heats Earth. How does the sun's energy travel the long distance from its surface to Earth? It must travel through a **vacuum.** A vacuum is a space that has no matter. Energy from the sun reaches us by **radiation.** Radiation is the movement of energy through a vacuum. Radiation can carry energy across space where there is no matter. The energy can heat matter.

Heat from sources other than the sun can also travel by radiation. You can see this illustrated in the figure. Heat energy from the fire moves into the room by radiation and then heats the air.

Conduction

You probably know that if you hold a strip of metal in a flame it will get hot. Why does this happen? The metal gets hot because of **conduction.** Conduction is the movement of heat energy from one molecule to the next. Heat travels by conduction when molecules bump into each other.

Look at the strip of copper in the figure. Heat from the flame makes the copper particles (atoms) near the flame move faster. As the particles move faster, they hit other particles. These particles then bump into the particles farther up on the strip of copper. They transfer energy. As a result, the slower particles move faster. Eventually, all the particles in the copper are moving fast. In other words, the entire piece of copper becomes hot.

Energy moves easily through some kinds of matter. A substance that allows heat energy to flow through it easily is called a **conductor.** Most metals, such as copper, silver, gold, aluminum, and tin, are good conductors.

A material that does not conduct heat well is called an **insulator.** Energy does not move easily through insulators. Insulators are used in the walls of homes to keep heat out in summer and cold out in winter. Some good insulators are glass, wood, sand, soil, Styrofoam, and air.

Convection

Convection is a method of heat movement that happens when the particles of a gas or a liquid rise. As they rise, they carry heat.

Find the heater in the figure. First, conduction heats the air touching the heater. Then the warm air rises. Cool air moves in to take its place. The heater warms the cool air and it rises. The warm air cools as it moves through the room. Then it flows back to the heater and is warmed again. The arrows show how heat energy flows up and around the room. Convection keeps the air moving.

Convection also happens in liquids. Suppose a pot of cold water is placed on the stove. Heat is conducted from the hot burner to the pot and then to the water at the very bottom of the pot. Then convection heats the rest of the water. The warm water rises and the cooler water sinks.

How do different heating systems work?

How can you control the temperature of your home? The chart describes some types of heating systems. People use these types of heating systems to keep their homes at a comfortable temperature.

Heating Systems		
Type of System	Description	How Heat Travels
Hot water	A furnace heats the water. A pump circulates the water through pipes to a radiator in each room.	Convection and radiation circulate heat throughout the room.
Steam	A boiler sends steam to pipes. Steam forces the heat through the pipes to radiators in each room.	Radiation and convection circulate heat throughout the room.
Forced air	Air is heated by a furnace. It is then pumped into rooms through vents at the floor of each room.	Forced convection circulates heat throughout the room.
Passive solar	The sun's rays pass through a large door or window. They heat up a large tile or rock wall. Heat radiates into the room from the wall and sets up convection currents.	Radiation and convection distribute heat.
Radiant electric	Electric current heats up wires in baseboards, walls, and/or ceilings.	Heat radiates from these specific places.

1. Which heating systems heat a home by convection?

2. Which heating systems provide radiant heat?

3. Which type of heating system would be more efficient in a hot, sunny climate? Explain your answer.

4. Which types of heating systems would be more efficient in a cold climate? Explain your answer.

Write your answers to these questions in complete sentences on a sheet of paper.

1. How does the sun's heat travel to the earth?

2. How does heat move by conduction?

3. Explain how convection heats a room.

4. What is a vacuum?

5. Explain the difference between a conductor and an insulator.

Chapter 6 SUMMARY

■ Heat is a form of energy. It results from the motion of the particles in matter. Heat energy flows from a warmer object to a cooler object.

■ Mechanical, solar, electrical, chemical, and nuclear energy are sources of heat.

■ Heat can cause matter to change from one state to another.

■ Generally, heat (a rise in temperature) causes matter to expand; loss of heat (a drop in temperature) causes matter to contract.

■ Temperature measures how fast particles are moving.

■ The Fahrenheit and Celsius scales are used to measure temperature.

■ The freezing point, the melting point, and the boiling point are important temperatures for all substances.

■ Heat depends on the temperature and the mass of the object.

■ Heat travels by radiation, conduction, and convection.

Science Words

boiling point, 147	convection, 152	heat, 133	radiation, 150
Celsius scale, 144	degree, 144	heat source, 134	temperature, 142
condensation, 137	evaporate, 137	insulator, 151	thermometer, 143
conduction, 151	expand, 138	melting point, 146	vacuum, 150
conductor, 151	Fahrenheit scale, 144	nuclear fission, 135	
contract, 138	freezing point, 146	nuclear fusion, 135	

Chapter 6 REVIEW

Word Bank

Celsius scale
condensation
conduction
convection
evaporate
temperature
thermometer
vacuum

Vocabulary Review

Choose a word or words from the Word Bank that best complete each sentence. Write the answer on a sheet of paper.

1. A device that measures temperature is a(n) _____.

2. A measure of how fast an object's particles are moving is _____.

3. The flow of energy that occurs when a warm liquid or gas rises is _____.

4. The movement of heat energy from one molecule to the next is _____.

5. The temperature scale in which water freezes at 0° and boils at 100° is the _____ .

6. To change from a liquid to a gas is to _____.

7. A space that has no matter is a _____.

8. The change of water vapor to liquid water is an example of _____.

Concept Review

Choose the answer that best completes each sentence. Write the letter of the answer on your paper.

9. Heat energy can be produced by _____ energy.
   A nuclear   **C** chemical
   B electrical   **D** all of the above

10. When frozen water melts and then evaporates, heat energy has caused the water molecules to _____.
   A move closer together   **C** move farther apart
   B move faster   **D** both B and C

11. The melting point of a substance is the same as its _____.
A boiling point   **C** both A and B
B freezing point   **D** none of the above

12. As the temperature of an object increases, the amount of heat in the object _____.
A increases   **C** stays the same
B decreases   **D** makes the mass increase

13. A material that keeps heat out of a house in summer and cold out in winter _____.
A is a good conductor   **C** has a low freezing point
B is a good insulator   **D** has a high boiling point

Critical Thinking

Write the answer to each of these questions on your paper.

14. Why does ice cream melt faster in a dish that is room temperature than in a dish that has been in the freezer?

15. The objects shown below have the same temperature. Do they give off the same amount of heat? Explain your answer.

Test-Taking Tip Studying together in small groups and asking questions of one another is one way to review material for tests.

Sound and Light

Almost everyone enjoys watching a fireworks display. Fireworks help us celebrate special holidays and events. What happens when you view fireworks? First, you see an explosion of bright, colorful light. Then, you hear the explosion's crashing boom or sharp whistle. In Chapter 7, you will learn how sound is produced and how light travels. You also will discover how sound and light are alike and how they are different.

Organize Your Thoughts

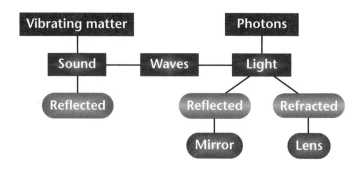

Goals for Learning

◆ To explain how sound is produced

◆ To tell how sound travels

◆ To describe the nature of light

◆ To explain reflection of light

◆ To explain refraction of light

Objectives

After reading this lesson, you should be able to

◆ explain what sound is.

◆ explain how sound is produced.

◆ explain how sound energy moves in waves.

Vibrate

To move rapidly back and forth

You hear many kinds of sounds every minute of every day. But do you know what sound is? Sound is a form of energy. Scientists who study sound also study human hearing and the effect of sound on different objects.

How Sound Is Produced

All the sounds you hear are made when matter **vibrates.** To vibrate means to move quickly back and forth. Look at the figure of the bells. When the clapper hits the bell, energy from the clapper causes the bell to vibrate. When the bell vibrates, it moves back and forth. The bell pushes the air around it. You can see in the figure that as the bell vibrates to the right, it pushes together the air particles to the right of the bell. When it vibrates back to the left, the air particles to the right of the bell move apart. Those particles to the left of the bell are squeezed together. As the bell continues to vibrate, the air particles on each side are squeezed together and spread apart many times.

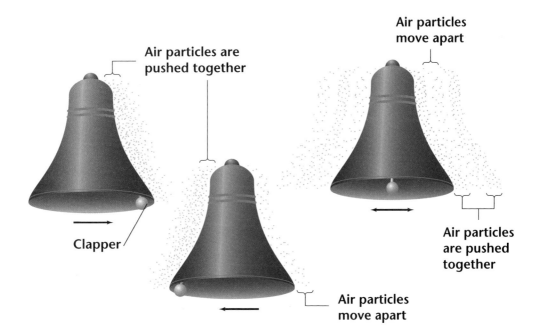

Air particles are pushed together

Air particles move apart

Clapper

Air particles move apart

Air particles are pushed together

How Sound Travels

The strength of a sound is known as its intensity. Scientists measure the intensity of sounds in units called decibels. The sound of rustling leaves would be measured at about 20 decibels. The roar of a jet engine would be approximately 135 decibels.

The movement of the air molecules around a vibrating object is a **sound wave.** You cannot see a sound wave. Sound waves move out from the vibrating object in all directions. As the sound waves travel farther from the object, they become weaker. The figures of the wire spring show how sound energy travels in waves. In Figure A, the wire is pinched together at one end. In Figure B, the "wave" moves across the spring.

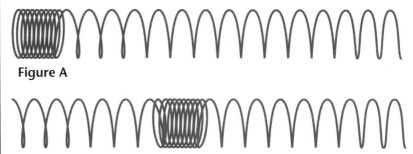

Figure A

Figure B

Some things make sounds even though you cannot see them vibrate. For example, if you strike a tuning fork, you will not see it vibrate. But you will hear the sound it makes. You can see evidence of sound waves by placing the end of a tuning fork that has been struck into a small container filled with water. You will notice water splashing out of the container. The vibrations of the tuning fork cause the water to move about.

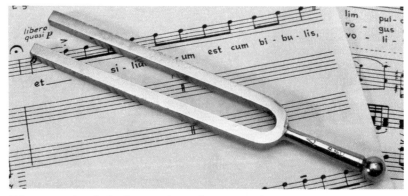

When a tuning fork vibrates, it produces sound waves.

Lesson 1 REVIEW

Write your answers to these questions in complete sentences on a sheet of paper.

1. How is sound produced?

2. How does sound travel?

3. What is a sound wave?

4. What word means "to move quickly back and forth"?

5. What happens to the strength of sound waves as they travel farther from the vibrating object?

Achievements in Science

The Doppler Effect

The Doppler effect, described by Christian Doppler in 1842, is an apparent change in wave frequency. The Doppler effect occurs with all types of waves: sound, light, or radio waves. This effect happens when the sound source is moving or when the observer is moving. The relative motion of the waves' source and the observer causes the frequency change.

As the wave source moves forward, the waves in the front of it get crowded. When the waves move closer together, the frequency of the waves increases. As the source of the waves moves away, the waves spread apart. These waves have a lower frequency.

Scientists use the Doppler effect in many ways. They use it to study the speed and direction of a star. They measure the change that motion causes to the frequency of the star's light. Meteorologists use Doppler radar to track storms by finding changes in wind speed or direction. Police use Doppler radar to measure a car's speed. Edwin Hubble used the Doppler effect to show that the universe is expanding.

INVESTIGATION

Inferring How Sound Waves Travel

Materials

◆ safety glasses
◆ pencil with sharpened point
◆ large plastic-foam cup
◆ 2 rubber bands (one cut)
◆ plastic food wrap
◆ salt
◆ plastic beaker
◆ water
◆ tuning fork

Purpose

Can sound waves travel through matter? This investigation will demonstrate that sound waves are vibrations that travel through matter.

Procedure

1. Copy the data table on a sheet of paper.

How the Rubber Band Was Plucked	Observations

2. Put on your safety glasses.

3. Use the point of the pencil to punch a small hole in the bottom of the cup.

4. Push one end of the cut rubber band through the hole in the cup. Tie a knot in the end of the rubber band so that it cannot be pulled through the hole. The knot should be inside the cup.

5. Stretch a piece of plastic wrap tightly over the top of the cup. Use the other rubber band to hold the plastic wrap in place, as shown in the figure on the next page.

6. Hold the cup with the plastic wrap facing up. Sprinkle a few grains of salt on the plastic wrap.

7. Hold the cup while your partner slowly stretches the rubber band. Gently pluck the stretched rubber band and observe what happens to the salt. Record your observations in the data table.

8. Vary the force used to pluck the rubber band. Notice the difference in sound the rubber band makes as you vary the force.

Questions and Conclusions

1. In Step 7, what happened to the salt when you plucked the rubber band?

2. What do you think caused the salt to move? Explain your answer.

3. In Step 8, how did the force you used to pluck the rubber band affect the sound it made?

4. In Step 8, how did the force you used to pluck the rubber band affect the salt on the plastic wrap?

Explore Further

1. Use a tuning fork and a plastic beaker half-filled with water. Gently tap the tuning fork against the heel of your hand and place the tips of the fork into the beaker of water. What happens to the water?

2. Vary the force used to tap the tuning fork. Notice what happens to the water as you vary the force.

Light

A form of energy that can be seen

Reflect

To bounce back

Photons

Small bundles of energy that make up light

You see **light** everywhere. You see objects because light is **reflected,** or bounced back, from them. But what is light? Light is a form of energy that you can sometimes see. Most visible light is produced by objects that are at high temperatures. The sun is the major source of light on Earth. The sun loses energy by emitting light. The sun's energy arrives as light with a range of wavelengths, consisting of visible light, infrared, and ultraviolet radiation.

Light as a Particle

Scientists have done experiments to gather information about light. Some scientific experiments suggest that light acts like a particle. Evidence tells scientists that light is made up of bundles of energy called **photons.** Photons are like small particles. A single photon is too small to be seen.

Look at the light coming from the flashlight. Streams of photons make up each beam of light. Each photon carries a certain amount of energy.

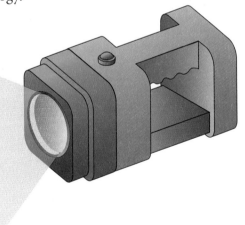

Waves—including waves in water, earthquake waves, sound waves, and light waves—transfer energy when they interact with matter.

Light as a Wave

Other scientific evidence suggests that, like sound, light travels in waves. As a result of their findings, most scientists agree that light seems to have properties of both particles and waves. Scientists agree that light travels as waves in a straight line. Most properties of light can be explained in terms of its wave nature.

Light waves move like water waves.

Light waves move like waves in water. However, light waves travel fastest through empty space. Light waves move more slowly as they pass through matter. In fact, light waves cannot pass through some matter at all.

Light waves travel more quickly than sound waves. Light waves travel about 300,000 kilometers per second. This is the fastest possible speed anything can travel.

Colors in White Light

The light you see from the sun is white light. Did you know that white light is actually made up of many colors of light? If you have ever seen a rainbow, you have actually seen the colors that make up white light.

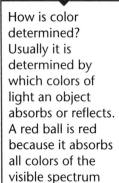

Visible spectrum

The band of colors that make up white light; the colors in a rainbow

Prism

A clear piece of glass or plastic that can be used to separate white light

How is color determined? Usually it is determined by which colors of light an object absorbs or reflects. A red ball is red because it absorbs all colors of the visible spectrum but red.

A rainbow contains all the colors of the visible spectrum.

The band of colors you see in a rainbow is known as the **visible spectrum.** The colors of the visible spectrum always appear in the following order: red, orange, yellow, green, blue, indigo, and violet.

You can use a **prism** like the one in the photo to see the colors in white light. A prism is a piece of glass or plastic that can separate white light into the colors of the visible spectrum.

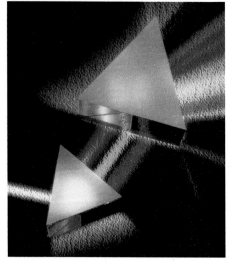

A prism shows the colors in white light.

What are lasers and how do we use them?

A laser is a device that produces a powerful beam of light. Laser light is unique. Wavelengths in ordinary white light differ from one another. They also overlap each other. Wavelengths in laser light are all the same and are in step. The crests, or tops, and the troughs, or bottoms, of the waves are lined up exactly.

Lasers have many uses. We can use lasers to find gas leaks and detect pollutants in the air. Lasers can monitor and identify air pollutants around landfills, factories, and highways. Unlike a flashlight, the concentrated light of a laser can travel miles and miles. So lasers that monitor air pollution do not have to be near the pollution's source. The table shows some other uses for lasers.

Some Other Uses for Lasers	
Communication and entertainment	• transmitting telephone and TV signals • producing and reading compact discs
Business	• identifying bar codes on products • doing sales transactions • making maps • surveying land • printing and scanning
Medicine	• detecting medical problems, diseases, and disorders • doing surgery, such as removing cataracts from eyes, removing cancerous cells, clearing blocked arteries, removing tonsils • treating skin conditions including removal of birthmarks
Scientific research	• collecting data from the moon • studying the atom • studying chemical reactions

Write your answers to these questions in complete sentences on a sheet of paper.

1. What makes up a beam of light?

2. How does light travel?

3. Would light travel faster through space or through a window? Explain your answer.

4. What colors make up white light?

5. Explain what a prism does.

Objectives

After reading this lesson, you should be able to

◆ describe how plane mirrors reflect light.

◆ describe how concave and convex mirrors reflect light.

◆ explain how light is refracted.

◆ describe how concave and convex lenses refract light.

What happens when you look into a mirror? Why can you see yourself? The answers to these questions have to do with the way light waves act.

Light Bounces

When you throw a ball to the floor, it bounces back. Light also bounces back when it hits an object. When light bounces off a surface, we say that the light is reflected. Reflection is the bouncing back of a light wave. Few objects give off their own light. We see most objects only because of the light they reflect.

The figure below illustrates how light is reflected. Like a tennis ball, light waves bounce off a surface at the same angle that they hit the surface.

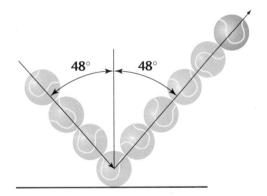

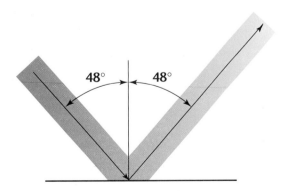

You can see an **image,** a copy or likeness, in a mirror because light waves are reflected. Study the figure below. Notice how light from the cup hits the mirror and is reflected toward the observer's eye. Then the eye forms an image. The cup looks as if it is behind the mirror. The image is the same size as the original cup, but it is reversed. The handle of the cup appears on the opposite side when it is seen in the mirror. The angle at which the light reflects back causes this reversal. Follow the lines of light in the figure to see how this happens.

Types of Mirrors

A mirror with a flat, smooth surface is called a **plane mirror.** The flatter the surface of the mirror, the clearer the image.

Many mirrors have curved surfaces rather than flat surfaces. One kind of curved mirror is called a **concave mirror.** A concave mirror has a reflecting surface that curves inward, like the inside of a spoon. A concave mirror creates an image that looks larger than the real object.

The reflecting surface of some mirrors curves outward like the outside of a spoon. These kinds of mirrors are called **convex mirrors.** A convex mirror creates an image that looks smaller than the real object. However, you can see much more area in a convex mirror. For this reason, rearview and side-view mirrors on vehicles are often convex mirrors.

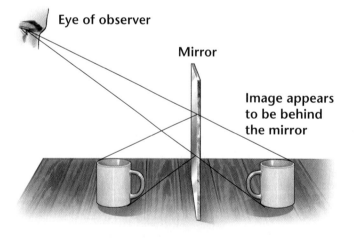

Eye of observer

Mirror

Image appears to be behind the mirror

Bending Light

When light moves from one kind of matter to another, the light waves change speed. As a result, the direction of the light changes. The bending of a light wave as it moves from one material to another is called **refraction.**

Lens

A curved piece of clear material that refracts light waves

Concave lens

A lens that is thin in the middle and thick at the edges

Convex lens

A lens that is thick in the middle and thin at the edges

Notice that the pencil in the photo appears to be bent. Light travels more slowly in water than it does in air. When light passes from the water to the air, the light waves change speed and change direction. As a result, the pencil seems to bend.

Lenses

A **lens** bends light by acting like the water in the container. A lens is a curved piece of glass or other clear material that refracts light waves that pass through it.

A **concave lens** curves inward. Look at Figure A. The lens is thin in the middle and thick at the edges. Light rays that pass through a concave lens are spread apart. When you look through a concave lens, objects appear to be smaller than they really are. Some people say the objects look "sharper." You can see this effect by looking through the glasses of someone who is nearsighted.

A **convex lens** curves outward. Look at Figure B. The lens is thick in the middle and thin at the edges. Light rays that pass through a convex lens are refracted inward. A convex lens focuses light. If you hold a convex lens close to your eye, the lens will magnify an image. If you hold it far from your eye and observe an object at a distance, the image appears upside down. Convex lenses are used in eyeglasses for people who are farsighted.

Refraction causes the pencil to look like it is bent.

Concave lens

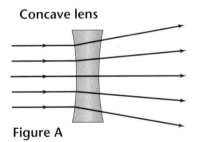

Figure A

Convex lens

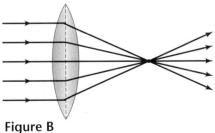

Figure B

Write your answers to these questions in complete sentences on a sheet of paper.

1. How does a concave mirror differ from a convex mirror?

2. Why are side-view and rearview mirrors on vehicles often convex?

3. What is refraction?

4. How does a concave lens refract light?

5. How does a convex lens refract light?

Science at Work

Optician

Opticians fit eyeglasses by following prescriptions written by ophthalmologists or optometrists. They also measure customers' eyes and recommend frames. Opticians write orders to laboratories for grinding and inserting lenses into frames. Some opticians grind and insert lenses themselves. Opticians make sure lenses are correctly ground and frames fit properly. Some opticians specialize in fitting contact lenses.

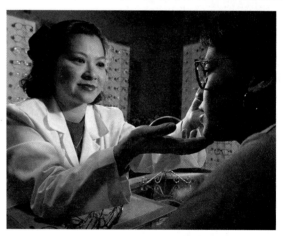

Most opticians complete an apprenticeship or receive on-the-job training. In some states, opticians must be licensed.

Opticians must be courteous, patient, and have good communication skills. They need to work well with their hands and be very detailed. Opticians also must take measurements accurately and have a good understanding of physics.

Chapter 7 SUMMARY

- Sound is caused by vibrations.

- Sound travels in waves.

- People see objects because light is reflected from them.

- Light is made up of bundles of energy called photons.

- Light has properties of both particles and waves.

- Light waves travel fastest through empty space.

- The visible spectrum makes up white light.

- Reflection is the bouncing back of a light wave.

- Refraction is the bending of a light wave.

- A mirror is an object that reflects light.

- Three types of mirrors are plane, concave, and convex.

- Concave and convex lenses refract light and can correct vision.

Science Words

concave lens, 171	image, 170	plane mirror, 170	sound wave, 160
concave mirror, 170	lens, 171	prism, 166	vibrate, 159
convex lens, 171	light, 164	reflect, 164	visible spectrum, 166
convex mirror, 170	photons, 164	refraction, 170	

Chapter 7   R E V I E W

Word Bank

concave lens
concave mirror
convex lens
convex mirror
light
prism
reflection
refraction
sound wave
vibrates

Vocabulary Review

Choose a word or words from the Word Bank that best complete each sentence. Write the answer on a sheet of paper.

1. A _____ separates white light into bands of colors.

2. A _____ is thick in the middle and thin at the edges.

3. Sound is produced when matter _____.

4. The bouncing back of a light wave is called _____.

5. The reflecting surface of a _____ curves inward.

6. A _____ reflects light rays so objects appear smaller than they are.

7. The bending of a light wave is called _____.

8. Light rays that pass through a _____ are spread apart.

9. The movement of air particles around a vibrating object is a _____ .

10. _____ is a form of energy that can be seen.

Concept Review

Choose the answer that best completes each sentence. Write the letter of the answer on your paper.

11. As sound travels farther away from its source, it _____.
    A loses strength   **C** bends
    B gains strength   **D** does not change

12. Sounds are made when matter _____.
    A rotates
    B moves quickly back and forth
    C vibrates
    D both B and C

13. Light is made of tiny bundles of energy called _____.
    A photographs   **C** neurons
    B photons   **D** none of the above

14. A straw sticking out of a glass of lemonade looks bent due to _____.

    A light traveling more slowly in water than in air
    B refraction
    C light waves changing speed and direction
    D all of the above

15. A vibrating object pushes against the _____ around it.

    A sound waves   **C** visible spectrum
    B light waves   **D** air molecules

16. The bands of colors in a rainbow are known as _____.

    A photons   **C** the visible spectrum
    B prisms   **D** waves

17. A lens _____ light waves.

    A reflects   **C** absorbs
    B reverses   **D** refracts

18. Sound travels in _____.

    A waves   **C** images
    B particles   **D** photons

Critical Thinking

Write the answer to each of these questions on your paper.

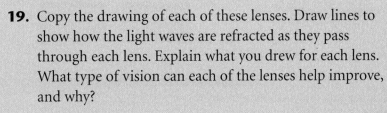

19. Copy the drawing of each of these lenses. Draw lines to show how the light waves are refracted as they pass through each lens. Explain what you drew for each lens. What type of vision can each of the lenses help improve, and why?

20. Explain what is meant when something is called the mirror image of an object.

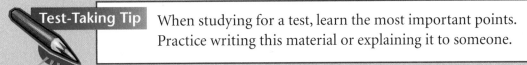

Test-Taking Tip When studying for a test, learn the most important points. Practice writing this material or explaining it to someone.

Electricity and Magnetism

8

Lightning is an example of electricity—static electricity. Electricity is all around us. Every day we use electricity. It lights homes and runs appliances. It starts cars and operates traffic signals. There are even electrical signals in our bodies that make our organs work. Do you know how electricity works and where it comes from? In Chapter 8, you will learn what electricity is, how it works, and how it travels. You will also learn about magnets and how they work.

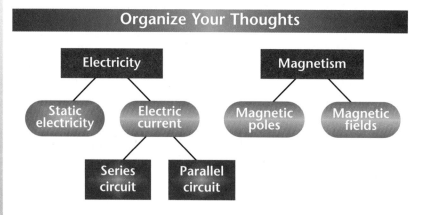

Organize Your Thoughts

Electricity
- Static electricity
- Electric current
  - Series circuit
  - Parallel circuit

Magnetism
- Magnetic poles
- Magnetic fields

Goals for Learning

◆ To explain how electric current flows through a circuit

◆ To describe series circuits

◆ To describe parallel circuits

◆ To describe various kinds of magnets

◆ To explain what a magnetic field is

◆ To explain electromagnetism

In Chapter 2, you read about atoms and the particles that make them. Electrons are negatively charged particles. Under the right conditions, electrons can escape from one atom and move to another one. The atom that loses the electron becomes positively charged. The atom that has picked up the electron becomes negatively charged. In turn, this negatively charged atom can pass the electron on again. This movement, or flow, of electrons is the basis of **electricity.** Electricity is a form of energy.

Static Electricity

Have you ever gotten a shock when you touched metal after walking across a carpet? The shock was caused by a buildup of charge, called **static electricity.** Walking across the carpet caused electrons to leave the carpet and enter your body. When you touched the metal, the extra electrons jumped from your finger to the metal.

When electrons move from one place to another, energy is transferred. Lightning is a discharge of static electricity between clouds or between a cloud and Earth.

Electricity

Flow of electrons

Static electricity

Buildup of electrical charges

Science Myth

Electricity only flows through wires.

Fact: Electrons (electricity) can flow without wires. The transfer of electrons from fingers to a metal doorknob (as shown in the figure on this page) is one example of this.

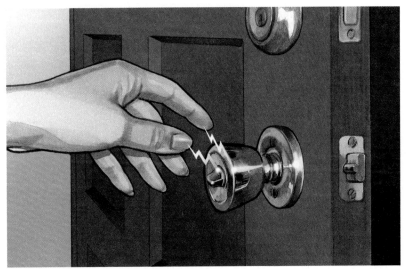

Closed Circuits

The movement of electrons from one place to another is called **electric current.** The rate at which electrons move from one place to another can vary. Electric current is measured in **amperes.** An ampere tells how much current is moving past a point in one second. One ampere is the flow of about 6 billion billion electrons per second! An ampere is often called an amp.

Currents from static electricity are not easy to control. But an electric current produced by a power source can be controlled and is easy to use.

When electrons travel in an electric current, they follow a path. This path is called a **circuit.** Follow the path of current in the figure below. The circuit begins at the power source. It travels through the wire to the light bulb. It lights up the bulb, and then returns to the power source.

Electrons can only follow a complete, unbroken path. You can see that the path in this circuit is unbroken. This path is called a **closed circuit.** As long as the current continues to flow in the circuit, the light will remain lit.

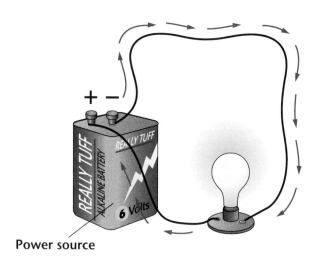

Power source

Open Circuits

Suppose you have a light turned on in your room. You decide you want to turn off the light. What do you do? Most likely you turn off a switch. To turn on the light again, you turn the switch on.

How does a switch work? Look at Figure A. You can see that the wires of the circuit are connected to a switch. When the switch is closed, the electrons can flow in an unbroken path. The light stays lit.

In Figure B, the switch is open. The current cannot pass through it. The bulb does not light. This is an incomplete, or broken, path for electric current. It is called an **open circuit.**

**Figure A
Switch closed**

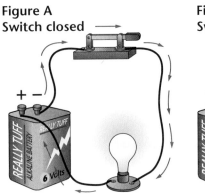

**Figure B
Switch open**

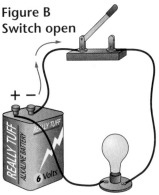

The switches you see in Figures A and B are called knife switches. The switches in your home are different from knife switches, but they work the same way. The switches in your home break the flow of electrons when they are turned off. These three images show some of the switches you might find in your home.

A lamp switch

A doorbell switch

A wall switch

Schematic Diagrams

Schematic diagram

A diagram that uses symbols to show the parts of a circuit

Scientists often use drawings of circuits. To make this job easier, they have developed symbols to show different parts of a circuit. Different symbols represent wires, switches, bulbs, and power sources. You can see some of these symbols in the diagram below.

A diagram that uses such symbols to show the parts of a circuit is called a **schematic diagram.** The schematic diagram below shows a battery in a circuit with a closed switch, wiring, and a bulb.

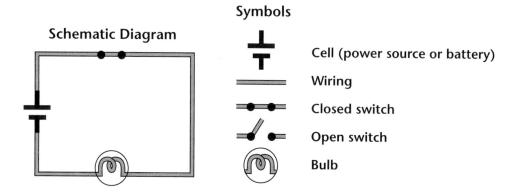

Schematic Diagram

Symbols

Cell (power source or battery)

Wiring

Closed switch

Open switch

Bulb

Achievements in Science

Van de Graaff Generator

In 1931, Robert Van de Graaff invented the electrostatic generator that is named after him. Van de Graaff generators produce high voltage but low currents.

The top of an electrostatic generator is a hollow metal dome. The base is a motor. The motor turns a conveyor-like belt made of insulating material. The belt carries electrons from the base to the dome. When the electrons reach the top, they gather on the dome's outside surface. As more gather, the dome's voltage increases. The result is a source with very high voltage but low current. It is so low that when someone touches the dome, no harm is done.

Van de Graaff generators can be as small as 2 inches high, producing 5,000 volts. They can be several stories high, producing millions of volts. Scientists use Van de Graaff generators to accelerate charged particles for nuclear physics experiments. You may have seen Van de Graaff generators at work in old movies. This is the machine that makes the mad scientist's hair stand on end.

Lesson 1 REVIEW

Write your answers to these questions in complete sentences on a sheet of paper.

1. Explain what happens when you get a shock from a metal doorknob after walking across a carpet.

2. Look at the following schematic diagrams, A and B. Which of the circuits is a closed circuit? Which is an open circuit?

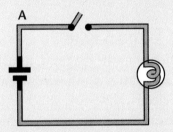
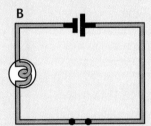

3. In which of the schematic diagrams above would current flow? Explain your answer.

4. What is the name for the path that electrons follow?

5. What unit is used to measure electric current?

Science in Your Life

How do conductors and insulators work?

Look at the electrical cords that carry electric current in your home. You will notice that the metal wire that carries the electricity is covered with a material. This material is often plastic.

The wire in the center of the electrical cord is a conductor. A conductor is a material through which electrons can flow easily. Electricity passes easily through the wire from a power source to the lamp. Metals, such as copper, gold, aluminum, and silver, are good conductors.

The outer covering of the electrical cord is an insulator. An insulator does not conduct electricity well. Electricity does not pass through an insulator easily. Examples of good electrical insulators are glass, rubber, wood, and plastic.

The insulator that covers the electrical cord keeps the electricity flowing in the wire. The covering prevents the current from flowing to places where it might cause fires or electrical shock. For example, if you touch a wire that is carrying an electric current, the electrons are free to travel through your body. You will get a shock. But if the wire is covered with an insulator, the electricity cannot flow through your body.

Electricity and Magnetism Chapter 8 **181**

Have you ever had a string of decorative lights? You might know that with some strings of lights, if one light burns out, all the remaining lights stay lit. But in other strings, all the lights will go out if one burns out. Then you have to change each bulb on the string until you find the one that is burned out. Why do these strings of lights act differently? The answer is in the way the circuit is made.

Devices in Series Circuits

Look at the circuit in the diagram. It includes a source of energy, such as a **battery,** and wire to carry the current. It also has different electrical devices attached to it. This kind of circuit is called a **series circuit.** In a series circuit, current (electrons) flows through only one path around the circuit.

Battery

A source of voltage that changes chemical energy into electrical energy

Series circuit

A circuit in which all current (electrons) flows through a single path

Series Circuit

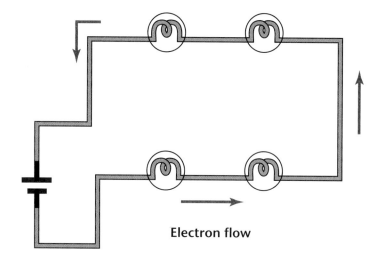

Electron flow

All batteries change chemical energy into electrical energy. Chemical reactions produce electrons that flow between two points on the battery. This produces an electric current.

You can see in the circuit on page 182 that all the electrons must pass through each electrical device. In the example of the decorative lights, each light is a separate device. The electrons must pass through each lightbulb.

Series circuits have a disadvantage. If one light is unscrewed or burns out, all of the other lights will go out. That is because the circuit becomes open, and electrons cannot flow.

When electrical devices are connected in series, the current is the same throughout the circuit. That means that adding electrical devices to the series lowers the voltage through each device. Notice in the diagram below that if only one bulb is connected to a power source, the bulb may shine brightly. If another bulb is added in series, each of the bulbs will be dimmer than the single bulb was.

Batteries in Series Circuits

Batteries in a circuit can be connected in series, too. Batteries in series increase the voltage of the circuit. To find the total voltage, add the voltages of the batteries together.

Series Circuits

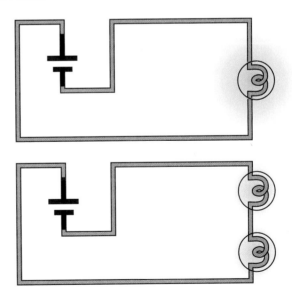

Not all batteries are made of the same materials. One type is called a dry-cell battery. It is an electric power source with a dry or paste-like center. It is used in flashlights and radios. Another type is called a wet-cell. It is an electric power source filled with liquid sulfuric acid. Most cars have wet-cell batteries.

In the figure of the circuit shown to the right, the batteries are in series. A wire connects a positive terminal to a negative terminal. A second wire connects the lamp and switch to the batteries. When batteries are connected in series, they can deliver more energy in the same amount of time. Bulbs in this kind of circuit burn brighter because the voltage is higher.

In a flashlight, dry-cell batteries are usually connected in series. You can see in the figure to the right how the positive terminal of one battery touches the negative terminal (the bottom metal plate) of the next battery.

Cells in Series

6 volts + 6 volts = 12 volts
Total voltage = 12 volts

1.5 volts + 1.5 volts = 3 volts

Fuses and Circuit Breakers

Connecting electrical devices in series can be inconvenient. But there are practical uses for series circuits, too. For example, your home is probably protected by fuses or circuit breakers. Fuses and circuit breakers help prevent fires.

Look at the fuse in the drawing. The piece of metal on the top of the fuse is designed to melt at a certain temperature. When the wires get too hot, the fuse will melt and break the circuit. When a fuse melts, it must be replaced. A circuit breaker, on the other hand, is a switchlike device that can be reset after the circuit has been repaired.

Fuse   **Circuit breaker**

Lesson 2   REVIEW

Write your answers to these questions in complete sentences on a sheet of paper.

1. What is a series circuit?

2. What is one advantage of a series circuit?

3. What happens to the brightness of a bulb when more bulbs are added to the same series circuit?

4. When two cells with the same voltage are connected in series, what happens to the voltage?

5. Compare a fuse and a circuit breaker.

▼◄▲▼◄▲▼◄▲▼◄▲▼◄▲▼◄▲▼◄▲▼◄▲▼◄▲▼◄▲▼◄▲▼◄▲▼◄▲▼◄▲▼◄▲▼◄▲▼

Science at Work

Appliance Service Technician

Appliance service technicians check appliances such as refrigerators, dryers, and ovens for different problems. They perform tests on different parts of appliances, including motors, heating elements, and switches. Because of differences among types of appliances, many appliance service technicians specialize.

Appliance service technicians receive training either through on-the-job experience or a post-high school technical program. Some complete an apprenticeship. Apprenticeships often combine on-the-job training and schooling and may last four to five years.

Appliance service technicians must understand the mechanical workings of machines. They must also be able to work with their hands. In addition, these technicians must enjoy solving problems and managing details.

The lights and appliances in your home are not wired in a series circuit. If they were, every time a bulb burned out, none of the other lights and appliances would work. Instead, most circuits in houses are **parallel circuits.** In a parallel circuit, there is more than one path for the current to follow.

Devices in Parallel Circuits

Look at the following diagram of two lamps connected in parallel. As you can see, there are two paths around this circuit. If one bulb burned out, the other bulb would stay lit. That is because there is more than one path for the electrons.

Parallel Circuit

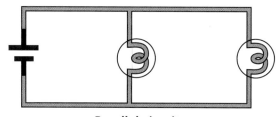

Parallel circuit

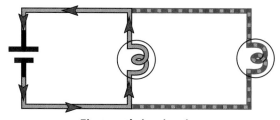

First path in circuit

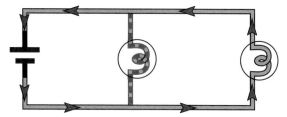

Second path in circuit

Parallel circuit

A circuit in which there is more than one path for current

When we connect several bulbs in parallel, all the bulbs will remain as bright as just one bulb alone would. However, more current must be drawn from the battery to power the extra bulbs.

When more electrical devices are added to the same circuit, more current runs through the circuit. As current in a circuit increases, wires begin to heat up. If they get too hot, the wires can start a fire in the walls. The fuses you read about in Lesson 2 help prevent this problem.

Batteries in Parallel Circuits

Batteries can be connected in parallel. A parallel connection between batteries allows them to keep providing energy longer. A parallel connection does not increase the voltage.

Look at the figures below. Figure A shows a circuit with only one 6-volt battery. The circuit in Figure B has two 6-volt batteries connected in parallel. The bulb in the circuit will stay lit longer. However, it will not burn brighter than the other bulb. The total voltage is still only 6 volts. The voltage is the same for both circuits in the figure. The two bulbs burn equally bright.

Cells in Parallel

Figure A
Total voltage = 6 volts

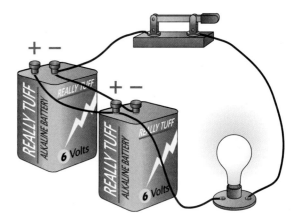

Figure B
Total voltage = 6 volts

Write your answers to these questions in complete sentences.

1. How can you recognize a parallel circuit? What happens to the bulbs in a parallel circuit when one bulb burns out?

2. Determine the number of paths in each of these parallel circuits.

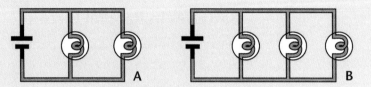

3. What happens to the brightness of bulbs in a parallel circuit when one extra bulb is added?

4. When two batteries with the same voltage are connected in parallel, what happens to the voltage?

5. Identify each of these circuits as either a parallel or series circuit.

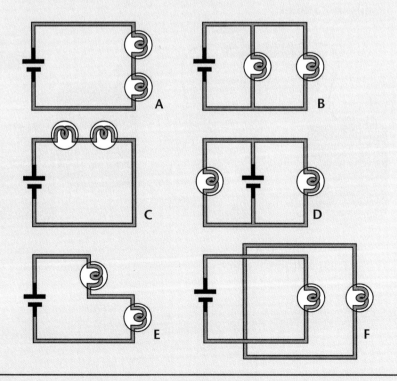

Lesson 4 Magnets

Objectives

After reading this lesson, you should be able to

◆ describe several kinds of magnets.

◆ explain what magnetic poles are.

◆ describe how magnetic poles behave.

Magnet

An object that attracts certain kinds of metals, such as iron

Attract

To pull together

Did You Know?

The ancient Greeks knew about the magnetic properties of lodestone. Lodestone is also called magnetite. The word *magnet* comes from the name Magnesia, the Greek province where the mineral was mined.

You are probably familiar with **magnets.** Magnets **attract,** or pull together, certain kinds of metals. They pick up metal objects, such as paper clips and other things made from iron. Most of the magnets you have seen are made by people. But there are also naturally occurring magnets such as lodestone. Lodestone, one of a variety of magnetite, is made of iron oxide. It is found naturally in the earth and comes in many sizes and shapes.

Most manmade magnets come in several common shapes. These shapes include the horseshoe, bar, cylinder, and doughnut shapes. You may have seen magnets like the ones in the photo.

Magnets come in a variety of different shapes.

Magnetic Poles

Look at the magnets in the figure. The ends of a magnet are called its **magnetic poles.** Whatever the shape, all magnets have two opposite magnetic poles. The magnetic forces are greatest at the poles. You know this because the ends of the magnet will pick up more paper clips than the center of the magnet.

The poles on a magnet are called the north pole and the south pole. On a marked magnet, the north pole is marked with an *N*. The south pole is marked with an *S*.

You cannot tell whether the end of an unmarked magnet is a north pole or a south pole simply by looking at it. But you can find out by placing the magnet close to another magnet whose poles are marked. Observe whether the poles attract or **repel** (push apart). To figure out the poles of the unmarked magnet, use the following rules.

Poles of opposite types attract each other.

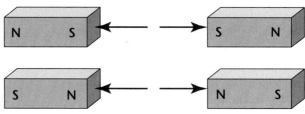

Poles of the same type repel each other.

Write your answers to these questions in complete sentences on a sheet of paper.

1. How can you determine the poles of an unmarked magnet?

2. If two south poles are placed close together, what will happen?

3. If a north and a south pole are placed close together, what will happen?

4. What is lodestone?

5. Name four familiar shapes of magnets.

Achievements in Science

Magnetic Resonance Imaging (MRI)

Scientists first considered using magnetic resonance to make pictures of the human body in 1946. In 1977, the first Magnetic Resonance Imaging (MRI) exam was performed on a human being. Magnetic resonance imaging uses two things to create high-quality cross-sectional images of bodies. Computer-controlled radio waves work with a powerful doughnut-shaped magnet that creates magnetic fields. The magnetic field of an MRI magnet is stronger than an industrial crane magnet.

The protons of hydrogen atoms in the body act like magnetic spinning tops. MRI aligns these hydrogen protons with its magnetic fields. MRI then uses radio waves to move the protons out of alignment temporarily. As the protons return to their original position, they release their own radio waves. These radio waves are used to create a computer image of internal body parts.

MRI shows doctors the difference between healthy and diseased tissues. It lets doctors see into bones and organs without surgery to diagnose illnesses and injuries. MRI is safer than X rays because it has fewer possible side effects.

After reading this lesson, you should be able to

◆ explain what a magnetic field is.

◆ describe Earth as a magnet.

◆ explain how a magnet works.

Magnetic field

Area around a magnet in which magnetic forces can act

Lines of force

Lines that show a magnetic field

A **magnetic field** surrounds all magnets. A magnetic field is an area around a magnet in which magnetic forces can act. The magnetic forces will attract or repel other magnets.

Although you cannot see magnetic fields, you can easily see their effects. Place a bar magnet under a sheet of paper. Sprinkle iron filings on top of the paper. The filings will line up in a pattern of curving lines like those shown in the figure. These lines are called **lines of force.** They are caused by the magnetic field and they show the field. The lines of force reach around the magnet from one pole to another. The lines are closest together near the poles. That is where the field is strongest and the forces are greatest.

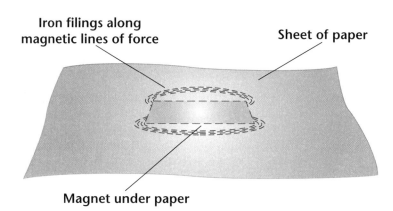

Iron filings along magnetic lines of force

Sheet of paper

Magnet under paper

You can see in the figure below how the lines of force of two magnets affect each other. Notice how they cause the poles of magnets to attract or repel each other.

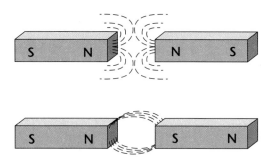

The Earth as a Magnet

You may be surprised to learn that Earth itself is a giant bar magnet. Like other magnets, Earth has magnetic poles. These magnetic poles are located near the geographic north and south poles.

Earth's natural magnetism allows compasses to work. The needle of a compass is a magnet, too. It has a north pole and a south pole. They are located at opposite ends of the needle.

Like magnetic poles repel each other. However, you can see in the figure that the north magnetic pole of Earth attracts the north pole of a compass. This happens because Earth's north magnetic pole is actually like the south pole of a magnet. But it is called the north magnetic pole because it is located near the geographic north pole. Earth's south magnetic pole is really like the north pole of a magnet.

Earth's magnetic field attracts and lines up the compass needle. The north pole of the magnet in a compass is attracted to the earth's magnetic pole. As a result, it points north.

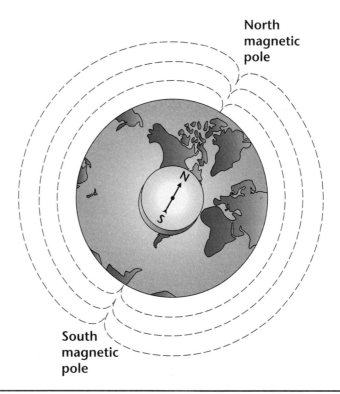

North magnetic pole

South magnetic pole

Lesson 5 R E V I E W

Write your answers to these questions in complete sentences on a sheet of paper.

1. What is a magnetic field?

2. What pattern is made by magnetic lines of force around a bar magnet?

3. How does a compass work?

4. How can you see the lines of force around a magnet?

5. Where are magnetic lines of force closest?

INVESTIGATION

8

Observing Magnetic Lines of Force

Materials

- safety glasses
- 2 bar magnets
- 2 horseshoe magnets
- 2 sheets of paper
- cup of iron filings
- metal bar that attracts a magnet

Purpose

Do the lines of force around a bar magnet look different than the lines of force around a horseshoe magnet? In this investigation, you will observe the lines of force around two magnets.

Procedure

Part A

1. Copy the data table on a sheet of paper.

Parts	Bar Magnet	Horseshoe Magnet
Part A		
Part B		
Part C		

2. Put on your safety glasses.

3. Place one bar magnet and one horseshoe magnet on a flat surface. Cover each magnet with a sheet of paper.

4. Sprinkle some of the iron filings on each of the pieces of paper. Do not pour the filings. It is best to sprinkle them lightly from a height of about 31 cm (about 1 foot).

5. Observe the pattern of iron filings made by the lines of force. Record your observations in the data table.

6. Carefully pour the iron filings from each paper back into the cup.

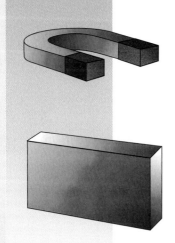

Part B

7. Place the bar magnets end to end with like poles close together.

8. Place a sheet of paper over the magnets and sprinkle with iron filings. Record your observations.

9. Carefully pour the iron filings from the paper back into the cup.

Part C

10. Reverse the poles of one of the bar magnets so that opposite poles are close together. Cover with a sheet of paper.

11. Sprinkle the paper with iron filings. Record your observations.

12. Repeat Part B and Part C with the horseshoe magnets. Record your observations.

Questions and Conclusions

1. Describe the pattern made by the lines of force of the single bar magnet.

2. In Part B, did the poles of the bar magnets attract or repel each other? How did the lines of force show this?

3. In Part C, did the poles of the bar magnets attract or repel each other? How do you know?

4. How were the patterns on the bar magnet similar to those on the horseshoe magnet?

Explore Further

Find a metal bar that is attracted to a magnet. Repeat Parts B and C using the metal bar. Record your observations.

Objectives

After reading this lesson, you should be able to

◆ explain how magnetism and electricity are related.

◆ describe electromagnetism.

◆ list devices that use electromagnetism.

◆ explain how magnetism can be produced from electricity.

Magnets are not the only things that can produce a magnetic field. Electricity can also produce a magnetic field. You can see this when you place a compass near a wire that is carrying electricity. The compass needle will turn until it is at right angles to the wire. The current produces a magnetic field around the wire.

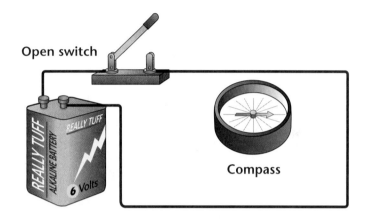

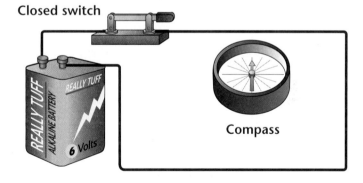

Electromagnetism

The relationship between magnetism and electricity

Electromagnet

A temporary magnet made by passing a current through a wire wrapped around an iron core

The relationship between magnetism and electricity is called **electromagnetism.** Moving electric charges produce magnetic forces and moving magnets produce electric forces.

Electricity can be used to make a type of magnet called an **electromagnet.** An electromagnet is a temporary magnet. It is made by passing a current through a wire wrapped around an iron core. An electromagnet is magnetic as long as an electric current is flowing.

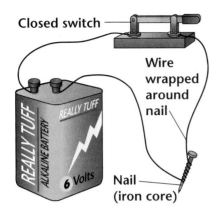

Closed switch

Wire wrapped around nail

REALLY TUFF ALKALINE BATTERY
REALLY TUFF
6 Volts

Nail (iron core)

An electromagnet, like the one in the figure, can be made with a large nail, some common bell wire, and a 6-volt dry-cell battery. The nail serves as the iron core. The flow of current through the wire surrounding the core creates a magnetic field.

The strength of an electromagnet depends on a number of factors. Power sources with higher voltages make more powerful electromagnets. More turns of wire around the core will also increase the strength of a magnet.

Using Electromagnets

The magnetism that electromagnets produce is the same as the magnetism a magnet produces. An electromagnet has a magnetic field and a north and south pole. Unlike a regular magnet, an electromagnet can be switched off and on. This quality makes electromagnets very useful. Many salvage yards have electromagnets like the one in the photo.

When the current is turned on, the electromagnet picks up pieces of metal from piles of scrap. When the current is turned off, the electromagnet loses it magnetism. The metal pieces fall to the ground.

Electromagnets can be turned on and off.

Winding wire into coils makes the wire's magnetic fields stronger. Coiled wire with current flowing through it is called a solenoid. Putting an iron core inside a solenoid creates an electromagnet and even stronger magnetic fields.

You may not be aware that you use electromagnets every day. Many appliances use electromagnets. Speakers, earphones, and telephones use electromagnets to change electric currents into sound waves.

Find the electromagnet in the figure below. Notice the device that provides electric current to the electromagnet. The level of electric current passing to the electromagnet from this device changes. These changes cause the strength of the electromagnet to change, too. As the strength of the electromagnet changes, the plate located in front of the electromagnet vibrates back and forth. The vibration of the plate creates sound waves.

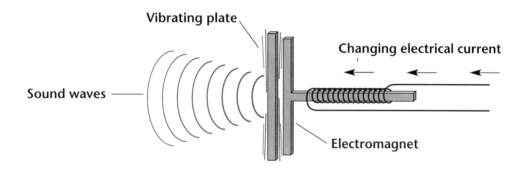

Vibrating plate

Changing electrical current

Sound waves

Electromagnet

Technology Note

Superconducting magnets are electromagnets that produce a very strong magnetic field. Their magnetic field can be 200,000 times greater than the earth's. Superconducting magnets are unique because they are made from materials that have no resistance. The lack of resistance results in greater electric current, which creates a stronger magnetic field.

Motors

Motors also make use of electromagnetism. A motor converts electrical energy to mechanical energy, which is used to do work. The figure illustrates how a motor works.

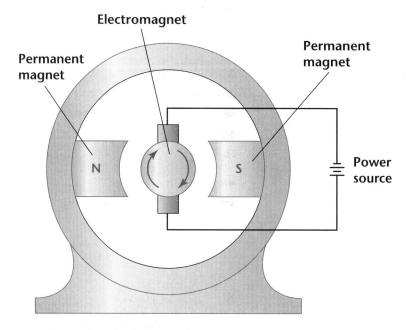

A motor has three basic parts. One part is a permanent magnet that cannot move. A second part is an electromagnet that is free to turn. The electromagnet turns between the opposite poles of the permanent magnet. A third part is a device that supplies electric current to magnetize the electromagnet.

When current is supplied to the electromagnet, each pole of the electromagnet is attracted to the opposite pole of the permanent magnet. This attraction causes the electromagnet to turn so that its poles line up with the opposite poles of the permanent magnet. The constant switch of poles in the electromagnet of a motor causes it to turn.

As the direction of current changes, the electromagnet's poles reverse. As a result, the aligned poles repel each other. And the electromagnet continues to turn. The current in the electromagnet continues to reverse direction after every half turn, causing the electromagnet to continue to turn.

The spinning motion of the electromagnet in a motor can be used to do work or operate other devices. Motors operate cars, refrigerators, electric toys, hair dryers, air conditioners, and many kitchen appliances. Look at the figure below. These items are examples of devices that have motors.

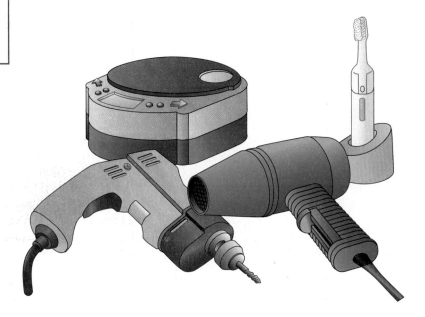

Technology Note

Electric guitars have electromagnetic devices called magnetic pickups. Pickups are bar magnets wrapped with thousands of turns of narrow wire. When the guitar's strings are plucked, they vibrate. Their vibration produces a vibration in the magnet's magnetic field, which creates an electronic signal. An amplifier makes the signal louder. Speakers change the signal into sound waves.

Lesson 6   R E V I E W

Write your answers to these questions in complete sentences on a sheet of paper.

1. What is electromagnetism?

2. Explain how an electromagnet works.

3. Name two devices that use electromagnets.

4. Explain how a motor works.

5. In the following figure, why does the compass needle move when the switch is closed?

Open switch

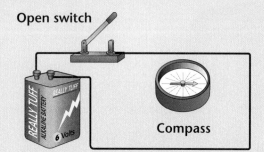

Compass

Closed switch

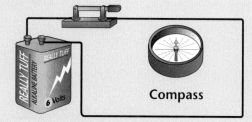

Compass

Achievements in Science

Electromagnetism

Until the 1800s, the only magnetism known came from natural magnets like lodestone and iron. Scientists believed that magnetism and electricity were unrelated.

This belief changed in 1820 after Hans Oersted made a discovery while doing a classroom demonstration. He saw a wire with electricity running through it make a compass needle move. He discovered that every conductor carrying an electric current is surrounded by a magnetic field.

Oersted's discovery of the connection between magnetism and electricity led Andre-Marie Ampere to experiment further. He found that when current flows through coiled wire, the current acts like a magnet. Ampere's law, published in 1827, is one of the basic laws of electromagnetism. It shows the mathematical relationship between electric currents and magnetic fields.

Oersted's and Ampere's discoveries showed that two forces— electric and magnetic—are associated with electricity. Their work led to the development of the electromagnet.

- Electricity is the flow of electrons.

- Static electricity is a buildup of electric charge.

- Current, the rate of flow of electricity, is measured in amperes.

- A closed circuit is a complete, unbroken path for current. An open circuit is an incomplete or broken path for current.

- A schematic diagram uses symbols to show the parts of a circuit.

- Fuses and circuit breakers prevent electrical wires from getting too hot or causing fires.

- In a series circuit, all current flows through a single path. In a parallel circuit, current flows in more than one path.

- Magnets can attract materials such as iron. Magnets may be natural, such as lodestone, or manmade.

- A magnet has a north pole and a south pole. Unlike poles of magnets attract. Like poles of magnets repel.

- A magnetic field surrounds a magnet. Magnetic lines of force extend from pole to pole.

- The earth is a magnet. It has a north magnetic pole and a south magnetic pole.

- Electromagnetism is the relationship between magnetism and electricity.

- Motors make use of electromagnets and permanent magnets to turn electrical energy into mechanical energy.

Science Words

ampere, 178	electromagnetism, 197	open circuit, 179
attract, 189	electromagnet, 197	parallel circuit, 186
battery, 182	lines of force, 192	repel, 190
circuit, 178	magnet, 189	schematic diagram, 180
closed circuit, 178	magnetic field, 192	series circuit, 182
electric current, 178	magnetic pole, 190	static electricity, 177
electricity, 177	motor, 200	

Chapter 8   R E V I E W

Word Bank

ampere

attract

lines of force

magnetic field

magnetic poles

repel

Vocabulary Review

Choose a word or words from the Word Bank that best complete each sentence. Write the answer on a sheet of paper.

1. We use a(n) _____ to describe how much electric current flows through a wire.

2. The area around a magnet in which magnetic forces can act is the _____.

3. The lines that show a magnetic field are the _____.

4. Magnetic poles of opposite types _____ each other.

5. The opposite points or ends of a magnet where magnetic forces are greatest are the _____.

6. Magnetic poles of the same type _____ each other.

Concept Review

Choose the answer that best completes each sentence. Write the letter of the answer on your paper.

7. Lightning is a discharge of _____ between clouds or between a cloud and earth.

   A electric current   **C** static electricity

   B energy   **D** all of the above

8. A magnet's lines of force are closest together near the _____.

   A fields   **B** poles   **C** center   **D** edges

9. The magnetic fields of atoms line up in _____.

   A a nonmagnetized field   **C** iron

   B a magnetized field   **D** both B and C

10. A north pole of one bar magnet is _____ by the north pole of another bar magnet.

    A not affected   **C** attracted

    B affected   **D** repelled

11. Magnetic lines of force of a magnet are closest together _____.

    A midway between the poles

    B near both poles

    C near the north pole only

    D in a metal bar

Critical Thinking

Write the answer to each of these questions on your paper.

12. Explain the circuitry of a string of lights that will not light up if one of the lights is burned out.

13. What is the difference between a closed circuit and an open circuit?

14. Is Earth a magnet? Explain.

15. Explain the difference between a regular magnet and an electromagnet.

Test-Taking Tip   Take time to organize your thoughts before writing answers to short-answer tests.

UNIT 1 S U M M A R Y

- Scientists use the metric system of measurement. It is based on units of ten.

- Area is the amount of space the surface of an object covers. It can be calculated by multiplying the object's length times width.

- Volume is the amount of space an object takes up. The volume of a rectangle can be calculated by multiplying length times width times height.

- A liter is the basic unit of volume in the metric system.

- A gram is the basic unit of mass in the metric system.

- A property is a characteristic that helps describe an object.

- A molecule is the smallest particle of a substance that still has the properties of that substance.

- An atom is the basic building block of matter. It is made of protons, neutrons, and electrons.

- Molecules move in different ways in the three states of matter—solids, liquids, and gases.

- Electrons move around the nucleus of atoms in certain energy levels. Electrons in the outermost energy levels are involved in chemical changes.

- A chemical change creates new substances with new properties. A physical change results in a change in appearance (physical properties) of a substance, but no change in its chemical properties.

- The law of conservation of matter says that matter cannot be created or destroyed in chemical and common physical changes.

■ Energy is the ability to do work.

■ The law of conservation of energy states that energy cannot be created or destroyed, but it can change forms.

■ Motion is a change in position.

■ Gravitational pull is the attractive force between two objects that have mass.

■ Work occurs when a force moves an object in the direction of the force.

■ Simple machines make it easier to do work by changing either the size or direction of a force, or the distance across which a force moves.

■ Heat is a form of energy that speeds up the motion of particles in matter.

■ Temperature is a measure of the motion of molecules.

■ The Fahrenheit and Celsius scales are used to measure temperature.

■ Sound is a form of energy caused by a vibration of matter.

■ Light is a form of energy that can be seen. People can see objects because light is reflected from them.

■ Electricity is a flow of electrons.

■ A magnet is an object that attracts certain kinds of metals. Magnets have north and south poles. Like poles repel each other, and unlike poles attract. The earth is a magnet.

UNIT 1   R E V I E W

Vocabulary Review

Choose the word or words from the Word Bank that best complete each sentence. Write the answer on a sheet of paper.

1. In the metric system, the width of a room can be measured in units called _____.

2. In the metric system, mass is measured in units called _____.

3. A(n) _____ occurs when the appearance of a substances changes, but its properties remain the same.

4. A(n) _____ is the basic building block of matter.

5. A(n) _____ of water is the smallest particle of water that has all of water's properties.

6. Volume is measured in the metric system in units called _____.

7. A(n) _____ is made up of only one kind of atom.

8. A(n) _____ is formed when atoms of two or more different substances chemically combine.

9. A(n) _____ is an attractive force that holds atoms together.

10. A(n) _____ occurs when the properties of a substance are changed.

Concept Review

Choose the answer that best completes each sentence. Write the letter of the answer on your paper.

11. Lightning is a discharge of _____.

   A static electricity   **C** energy

   B electric current   **D** all of the above

12. The _____ states that matter cannot be created or destroyed.
   A law of inertia   **C** law of gravity
   B law of conservation **D** law of motion
      of matter

13. Heat energy can be produced by _____ energy.
   A light   **C** electrical
   B sound   **D** all of the above

14. When matter vibrates, or moves back and forth, _____ is created.
   A sound   **C** electricity
   B light   **D** all of the above

15. Magnetic lines of force are closest together near _____.
   A the equator   **C** the poles
   B the center   **D** the edge

16. Two south magnetic poles _____ each other.
   A pull   **C** attract
   B repel   **D** de-magnetize

17. Machines can be used to _____.
   A make work easier   **C** change the distance
      to do   force moves
   B change the direction **D** all of the above
      of force

Critical Thinking

Write the answer to each of the following questions.

18. What problems might you expect if the basic unit for measuring length was based on the length of a man's foot?

19. How is the movement of particles different in solids, liquids, and gases?

20. A girl rides her bicycle to a friend's house 24 km away. She leaves her own house at 10 A.M. and gets to her friend's house at 12 noon. What was the speed of the bike?

Unit 2

Earth Science

The land, water, and air of the earth are constantly changing and acting upon one another. For example, when rain washes mud off a hillside and into a river, the land and water act upon each other. When a puddle dries up, the water and air act upon each other. A change in one part of the earth affects other parts of the earth. In your local environment, how do land, water, and air affect each other? How do you affect your environment? You'll learn the answers to these questions in Unit 2.

Chapters in Unit 2

Unit

2

What Is Earth Science?

Earth science is the study of the earth's land, water, and air. Earth science also includes the study of outer space and the objects in it.

Fields of Earth Science

Earth science can be divided into many fields of science. The table below describes the main fields, or subject areas, that make up earth science. Which field could answer the question, Why did it rain today? Which field would include scientists who learn about dinosaurs? Compare this table to the Table of Contents for Unit 2 on pages viii–xi. Which chapters in this book deal with which fields of earth science?

Fields of Earth Science	
Field	**What Is Studied**
geology	the earth's land, including the surface of the earth and the inside of the earth; how the earth changes; history of the earth
oceanography	the earth's oceans, including what they contain and how they interact with the air
meteorology	the earth's air, including weather
astronomy	outer space, including planets, stars, and other objects in space

Earth science

Study of the earth's land, water, air, and outer space

Geology

Study of the solid parts of the earth

Oceanography

Study of the earth's oceans

Meteorology

Study of the earth's air and weather

Astronomy

Study of outer space and objects in it

The earth's land, water, air, and living things make up a system. A system is a group of related parts that work together in an ordered way. Each part affects and depends on the other parts.

The Importance of Earth Science

Earth science is important in your life. In fact, you probably use earth science in some way every day. Did you ride in a car or bus today? The fuel was made from oil that geologists located underground. Have you heard a forecast for tomorrow's weather? A meteorologist made this forecast.

The meteorologist in the photo studies climate patterns. By analyzing weather and ocean conditions, he can predict warming systems called El Niños. These systems happen every three to seven years and can cause drought or extra rain.

How is the work of meteorologists important to farmers?

You can use your own knowledge of earth science to make wise decisions. For example, knowledge about soils can help you when planting a garden. Knowing about the earth's underground water table can come in handy when buying a house. Communities often face questions about how to use the land and its resources. An earth science background will help you understand such issues.

Describing the Earth

9

If you looked down on the earth from space, what would you see? From space, the earth looks like a gigantic ball. Most of the earth's surface is covered in oceans that are separated by large masses of land. From space, one side of the earth is dark, and the other side is light. In Chapter 9, you will learn about this and other features of the earth. You will also find out how to determine your position on the earth's surface.

Organize Your Thoughts

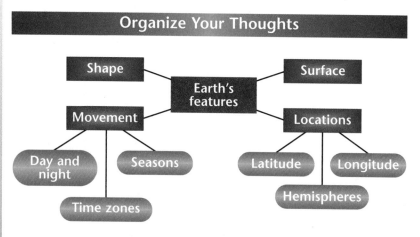

Goals for Learning

◆ To describe the earth's shape, continents, and oceans

◆ To explain what causes day and night

◆ To explain the earth's time zones

◆ To explain how the earth's revolution and the tilt of its axis cause seasons

◆ To use latitude and longitude to locate points on the earth

Objectives

After reading this lesson, you should be able to

◆ describe the earth's shape.

◆ locate the seven continents.

◆ name the four major oceans.

◆ explain rotation.

At one time, many people believed that the earth was flat. They thought that if they walked past its edge, they would fall off the earth! Of course, the earth is not flat and you cannot fall off.

The Earth's Shape

If you could view the earth from the moon, you would see that it has a shape like a ball. Most balls are perfectly round. If you measured the distance around the widest part of a ball in any direction, you would find that all the measurements would be equal. Compare the shape of the earth with the perfect circle below. You can see that the earth is not perfectly round. The distance around the earth in two different directions is given below. How do the measurements compare?

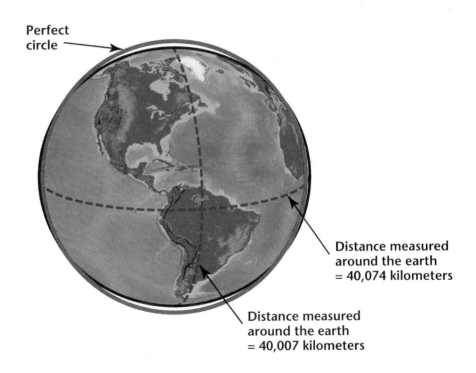

Perfect circle

Distance measured around the earth = 40,074 kilometers

Distance measured around the earth = 40,007 kilometers

The Earth's Surface

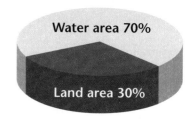

The earth's surface includes areas of land and water. The land areas make up about 30 percent of the earth's surface. Look at the circle graph. How much of the earth's surface is water?

The land on the earth's surface is divided into seven major areas called **continents**. Find the continents of the earth on the map. Which continent do you think is the largest? Which is the smallest? Check your answers in the table below.

> **Continent**
>
> *One of the seven major land areas of the earth*

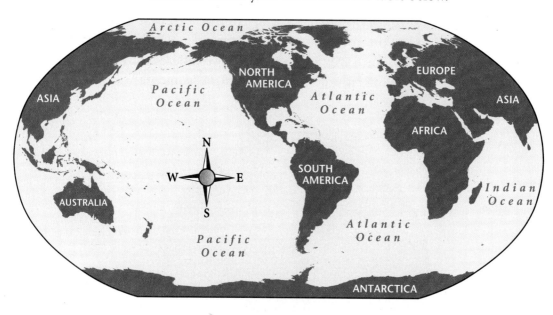

The Seven Continents		
Continent	Area (square kilometers)	Percent of Earth's Land Area
Asia	44,614,000	29.9
Africa	30,355,000	20.3
North America	24,208,000	16.2
South America	17,819,000	11.9
Antarctica	14,200,000	9.5
Europe	10,498,000	7.0
Australia	7,682,000	5.2

Look again at the map on page 216. The major areas of water connect with each other and form one huge, continuous ocean. The earth's ocean, however, is usually divided into four major bodies of water: the Pacific Ocean, Atlantic Ocean, Indian Ocean, and Arctic Ocean. Locate each of these on the map. There are smaller bodies of water, too. Among them are lakes, bays, gulfs, and seas. Oceans are much larger than any of these.

You cannot see across an ocean to land on the other side. The diagram shows why. Just like you cannot see around a ball, the earth's curve keeps you from seeing across an ocean.

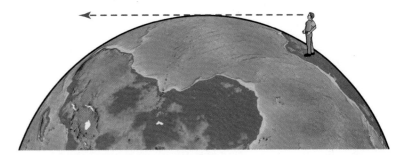

Use the table below to compare the sizes of the four major oceans. Which ocean is the largest? Which is the smallest?

The Four Major Oceans		
Ocean	Area (square kilometers)	Average Depth (kilometers)
Pacific	166,000,000	4.2
Atlantic	82,000,000	3.7
Indian	73,000,000	3.9
Arctic	14,000,000	1.2

Lesson 1   R E V I E W

Write your answers to these questions on a sheet of paper.

1. Describe the earth's shape.

2. What are the seven continents?

3. What are the four major oceans?

4. What percent of the earth's surface is covered with water?

5. Why can't you see across an ocean to land on the other side?

Achievements in Science

A Trip Around the World

In July 2002, Steve Fossett, an athlete and adventurer, achieved what no other human had ever done alone. After four failed attempts, he flew a hot-air balloon completely around the earth. The successful trip took Fossett about 14 days and 20 hours.

Fossett's balloon, the *Spirit of Freedom*, contained about 165,000 cubic meters of helium and 30,000 cubic meters of hot air. The capsule Fossett traveled in during the flight was just big enough for him to stretch out. There was also a special heating system to keep him warm.

Fossett navigated the flight using a global positioning system (GPS). During the trip, he used a laptop computer and satellite e-mail to communicate with his control center in St. Louis, Missouri.

The *Spirit of Freedom* started its flight in Australia. It flew east across the South Pacific Ocean, the tip of South America, across the Atlantic and Indian Oceans, then back to Australia. That's 34,000 kilometers! Trace this trip on the map on page 216. Why was Fossett's trip shorter than the distances shown on page 215?

Rotation

Spinning of the earth

Axis

Imaginary line through the earth that connects the North and South Poles

North Pole

Point farthest north on the earth

South Pole

Point farthest south on the earth

What determines when you go to school, eat lunch, or get ready for bed? More than likely, what you are doing depends on what time of day it is. The time of day depends on the earth's rotation.

The Earth's Rotation

If you spin a top, at first it stands upright, turning around and around. After a while, friction slows down the top. It begins to wobble and stops spinning. Like a top, the earth also spins around. But unlike a top, the earth does not stop—it keeps on spinning. The spinning of the earth is called **rotation**.

As shown below, the earth spins, or rotates, from west to east around an imaginary line that passes through the center of the earth. This line is called the **axis** of the earth. The axis passes through two points called poles. The **North Pole** is the point farthest to the north on the earth. The **South Pole** is the point farthest to the south.

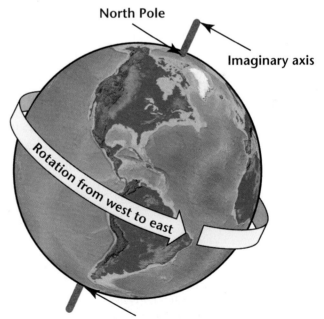

North Pole

Imaginary axis

Rotation from west to east

South Pole (not visible)

You may have heard that the sun "rises" and "sets." This means the sun moves around the earth.

Fact: The sun does not move around the earth "rising" and "setting." Day and night occur because the earth rotates on its axis. As it rotates, one part of the earth moves into the sun's light. As this happens, another part of the earth turns away from the sun's light.

Day and Night

You have learned that the earth rotates on its axis. The earth takes 24 hours, or one day, to rotate once on its axis. Notice in the diagram how the sun shines on the earth as the earth rotates. The sun can shine on only one side at a time. As a result, one side of the earth is light and has daytime. The opposite side is dark and has nighttime.

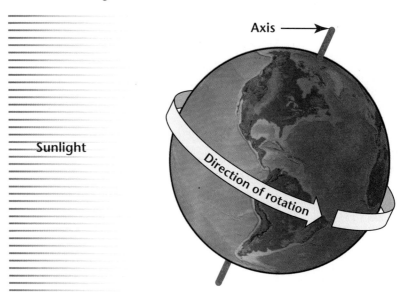

Because the earth continues to rotate, the places on the earth that have daytime keep changing. In other words, the time of day keeps changing everywhere on the earth. The time of day depends on where the sun appears to be in the sky. The sun does not really move across the sky, but the rotating earth makes the sun appear to move. As the earth turns from west to east, the sun appears to rise in the east in the morning. Then it appears to move across the sky and set in the west at night.

Standard Time Zones

Standard time zone

Area that has the same clock time

International date line

Imaginary line that defines the start of a day

Time varies around the earth. When it is noon at one point on the earth, it is midnight at a point that is halfway around the earth. The remaining hours of the day are equally spread around the earth between noon and midnight.

All 24 hours in the day are occurring somewhere on the earth right now. The earth has been divided into 24 **standard time zones**, one for each hour of the day. A standard time zone is an area of the earth that has the same clock time.

The map below shows the world's standard time zones. The boundaries of the time zones do not exactly follow straight lines. Over land areas, the zones usually follow borders of countries, states, counties, and towns. How many time zones are there across North America?

Find the **international date line** on the map. It is an imaginary line that defines the start of a day. When you cross it going west, you move to the next calendar day. When you cross it going east, you move to the previous calendar day.

Did You Know?

Standard time zones were set up in 1883. Until then, most places set their own time zones. For example, Philadelphia's clocks were 5 minutes behind New York's and 19 minutes ahead of Pittsburgh's. Confusing to travelers? You bet.

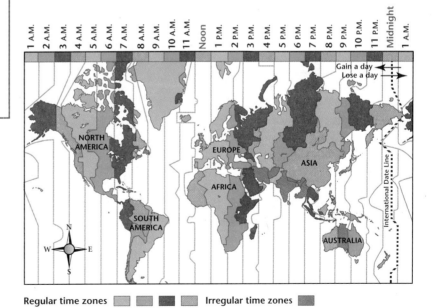

Regular time zones ☐ ☐ ■ ☐   Irregular time zones ■

Use the map below to answer these questions on a sheet of paper.

1. What causes day and night?

2. In what time zone is your home located? What time zone is one hour ahead of yours?

3. If it is 10:00 A.M. in Tulsa, what time would it be in Juneau?

4. If it is noon in New York City, what time would it be in Monterrey?

5. If you were to travel from Toronto to Eugene, would you move your watch forward or backward?

Science in Your Life

Are time zones a part of your daily life?

The map to the right shows the time zones for Hawaii and parts of North America. Notice that the time on the West Coast of the United States is 3 hours earlier than on the East Coast. So the time gets earlier as you travel westward.

If you make long-distance telephone calls, you should know what time it is in other time zones. Suppose you live in California and want to call your friend in New York. If you call when it's 9:00 P.M. where you live (Pacific time), you might wake up your friend. That's because in New York, which is in the Eastern time zone, it's already midnight!

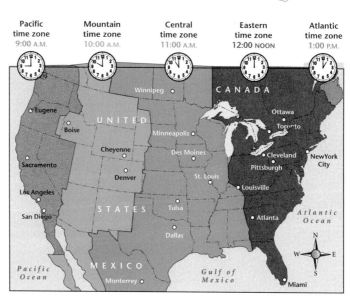

Hawaii-Aleutian time zone
7:00 A.M.

Alaska time zone
8:00 A.M.

INVESTIGATION

9

Materials
◆ globe
◆ masking tape
◆ flashlight

Modeling the Earth's Rotation

Purpose

How would you create a model explaining day and night? In this investigation, you will model the earth's rotation.

Procedure

1. Work with a partner in this investigation. Copy the data table on your paper.

Step 5 Observations	Step 7 Observations

2. On the globe, find the approximate spot where your home is located. Place a piece of masking tape over the spot.

3. On the globe, find the North and South Poles. Imagine that the globe is the earth and that its axis runs through the poles. Place the globe on a table, with the South Pole toward the table. Practice rotating it slowly on its axis. Remember to rotate it from west to east (or counterclockwise, as seen from above the North Pole).

4. Darken the room. Have your partner hold the flashlight and stand at one end of the table. The flashlight represents the sun. Have your partner turn on the flashlight and shine it at the globe. Position the globe so that the masking tape is facing the flashlight. **Safety Alert: Do not shine the flashlight into the eyes of others.**

5. Observe what part of the globe is in light and what part is in shadow. Record your observations in the data table, noting the position of the masking tape.

6. Slowly rotate the globe on its axis from west to east. Stop when the masking tape has moved halfway around the globe.

7. Repeat step 5.

8. Switch places with your partner and repeat steps 4 through 7.

Questions and Conclusions

1. In which step did you model daytime at your home?

2. In which step did you model nighttime at your home?

3. Describe how daytime becomes nighttime at any spot on the earth.

Explore Further

Use the globe and flashlight to model how the earth turns during one 24-hour day. Describe how the position of your home changes during that time. Describe the sunlight you receive during the 24-hour period.

Objectives

After reading this lesson, you should be able to

◆ describe the movement of the earth around the sun.

◆ explain how the earth's revolution and the tilt of its axis cause seasons.

Why is a year about 365 days? Why do seasons change throughout the year? You can answer these questions once you know how the earth moves in space.

Revolution and Rotation

The movement of the earth in its orbit around the sun is the earth's **revolution**. A single revolution of the earth takes about 365 days, which is one year.

While the earth is revolving around the sun, it is also rotating on its axis. As discussed in Lesson 2, the earth rotates once every day, or every 24 hours.

Seasons

As the earth revolves around the sun, the earth's axis always stays tilted at $23\frac{1}{2}°$, as shown below. The tilt causes sunlight to fall more directly on different parts of the earth throughout its orbit. The diagram on the next page shows how this causes seasons. Notice that when it is summer in the Northern Hemisphere, that hemisphere is tilted toward the sun. When it is winter in the Northern Hemisphere, that hemisphere is tilted away from the sun.

Revolution

Movement of one object in its orbit around another object in space

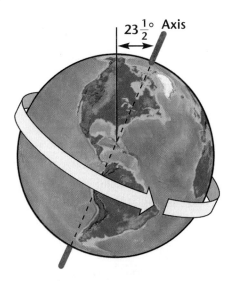

$23\frac{1}{2}°$ **Axis**

When it is summer in the Northern Hemisphere, it is winter in the Southern Hemisphere. For example, July is a summer month in the United States, but it is a winter month in Argentina. In the Northern Hemisphere, October is a fall month. In the Southern Hemisphere, October is in springtime.

No matter where you live, in the summer, the noontime sun appears at its highest in the sky. During the winter, it appears at its lowest. The sun's rays strike the earth more directly in the summer than in the winter. The more direct the sunlight is, the more it heats up the ground. Thus, it is warmer in the summer than it is in the winter, when the earth receives indirect sunlight.

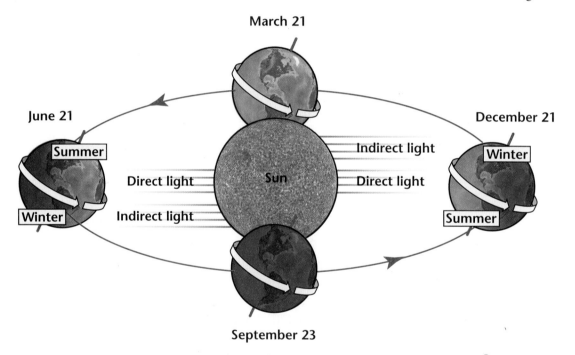

Science Myth

It is warmer in summer because the earth is closer to the sun.

Fact: Actually, in the Northern Hemisphere, the distance between the earth and the sun is slightly greater during the summer months. It is the tilt of the earth toward the sun that causes summer sunlight to hit the earth directly. This results in the warmer temperatures of summer.

Lesson 3 REVIEW

Write your answers to these questions on a sheet of paper.

1. Why is a year about 365 days long?

2. How far is the earth tilted on its axis?

3. When the Northern Hemisphere is tilted toward the sun, what season is it in that hemisphere?

4. When it is spring in the Northern Hemisphere, what season is it in the Southern Hemisphere?

5. Explain the difference between indirect and direct sunlight.

▼◄▲▼◄▲▼◄▲▼◄▲▼◄▲▼◄▲▼◄▲▼◄▲▼◄▲▼◄▲▼◄▲▼◄▲▼◄▲▼◄▲▼◄▲▼

Science at Work

Space Shuttle and International Space Station Crews

The International Space Station (ISS) is a big research laboratory orbiting the earth. Many countries, including the United States, Canada, and Russia, use and contribute to the ISS. Space shuttles are launchable spacecraft designed to shuttle, or go back and forth, between the earth and the ISS.

Space shuttle crew members fly shuttle missions to maintain and supply the ISS. Astronaut and pilot Pamela Ann Melroy was part of a 2002 crew that carried equipment to the ISS and installed it. The entire mission took 11 days.

In addition to space shuttle crews, there are ISS crews. They live and work on the ISS for months at a time.

Space shuttle and ISS crew members help construct, maintain, and repair the ISS. Sometimes crew members go on space walks to perform these tasks. Crew members also perform scientific experiments to test the effects of the space environment on human beings, animals, and diseases. Some experiments test properties of matter in space.

Space shuttle and ISS crew members come from several countries. They must have a bachelor's degree in engineering, biological science, physical science, or mathematics. At least three years of related job experience is also required. An applicant must pass a physical exam that tests vision and blood pressure, among other things. An astronaut must have strong science and math skills and be physically strong and healthy.

Lesson 4 · Latitude and Longitude

Objectives

After reading this lesson, you should be able to

◆ define latitude.

◆ define longitude.

◆ use latitude and longitude to find a point on the earth.

◆ explain what hemispheres are.

Latitude

Angle that describes the distance north or south of the equator

Equator

Line of 0° latitude halfway between the poles

Parallel

Line of latitude

Degree

Unit for measuring angles in a circle or sphere

Lines of **latitude** are imaginary lines that run in an east-west direction around the earth. Latitude describes the distance north or south of the **equator**. The equator is the line of latitude halfway between the North and South Poles. Find the lines of latitude on the map below. Lines of latitude are also called **parallels**. The parallels are numbered in **degrees**. Degrees are used to measure angles in circles and spheres. A complete circle has 360 degrees. The symbol for degrees is a small circle. For example, 90 degrees is written as 90°.

Notice that the latitude numbers begin at 0° at the equator and increase to 90° at the North Pole. All latitude numbers north of the equator are followed by the letter *N*.

The latitude numbers also begin at 0° at the equator and increase to 90° at the South Pole. South of the equator, all latitude numbers are followed by the letter *S*. No line of latitude is greater than 90°.

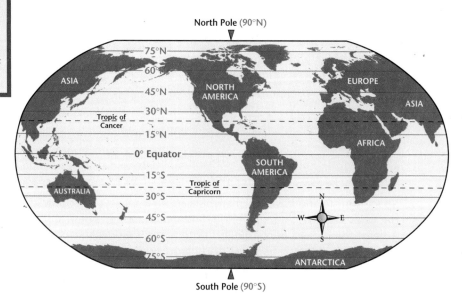

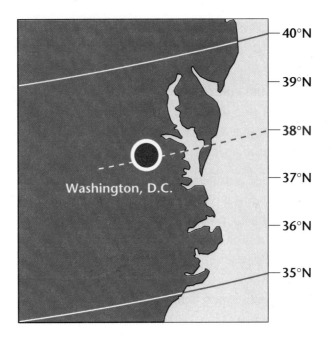

Estimating Latitude

When a map, such as the one above, does not show every parallel, the person using the map must estimate the parallels that are not shown. To do that, the person must divide the space that is between the parallels that are shown. The divisions should be equal.

To find the latitude of Washington, D.C., on the map, use the following procedure.

1. Find the two parallels on either side of Washington, D.C. (35°N and 40°N).

2. In your mind or on paper, put in the latitude lines between 35°N and 40°N that are missing (36°, 37°, 38°, and 39°). Divide the space equally.

3. Use the divisions you added to estimate the latitude of Washington, D.C., to the nearest degree. The correct latitude is 38°N.

Lines of Longitude

Lines of **longitude** are imaginary lines that run in a north-south direction from pole to pole. Longitude lines are also called **meridians**. Longitude describes the distance east or west of the **prime meridian**. The prime meridian is the line of 0° longitude. It is sometimes called the Greenwich meridian because it passes through the town of Greenwich, England.

Like parallels, meridians are numbered in degrees. Numbering begins with 0° at the prime meridian and ends at 180°. The 180° line is on the opposite side of the earth from the prime meridian. Numbers east of the prime meridian are followed by the letter *E*. Numbers west of the prime meridian are followed by a *W*. The line that is 180°W is also 180°E. As you can see on the map below, meridians are not spaced equally at all points. They come together at the poles and are farthest apart at the equator.

Do you remember the steps used to estimate the latitude of Washington, D.C.? Review page 229. To estimate meridians that are not shown on a map, follow a similar procedure.

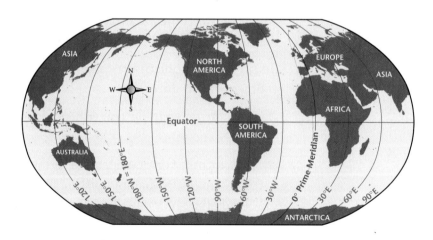

Locating Points by Latitude and Longitude

To locate any point on the surface of the earth, you need to know both the latitude and longitude of that point. When stating any point's location, the latitude is written before the longitude. For example, find point A on the map below. Point A lies on the 45°N parallel and the 30°W meridian. Its location is written as 45°N, 30°W. This means point A is 45° north of the equator and 30° west of the prime meridian.

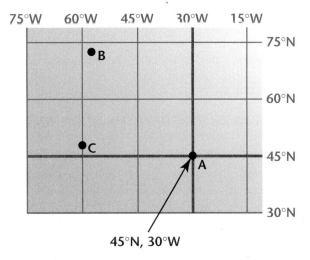

45°N, 30°W

By estimating the position of any missing grid lines, you should be able to locate point C at about 48°N, 60°W. What is the location of point B? It is about 72°N, 57°W.

Hemispheres

The equator is the line of latitude halfway between the North and South Poles. This line divides the earth into two **hemispheres**. A hemisphere is half of the earth. Two equal-sized hemispheres make up the whole earth. The half of the earth north of the equator is called the Northern Hemisphere. The half south of the equator is the Southern Hemisphere. In which of these hemispheres do you live?

If the earth were cut in half through the prime meridian, it would be divided into another set of hemispheres. These two halves are known as the Eastern Hemisphere and the Western Hemisphere. Which hemisphere includes most of Africa?

Lesson 4   R E V I E W

Use the maps on pages 228 and 230 to answer these questions on a sheet of paper.

1. What is the latitude of the equator?

2. What is the latitude of the South Pole?

3. Estimate the latitude where you live.

4. What is the longitude of the prime meridian?

5. Estimate the longitude where you live.

▼◄▲▼◄▲▼◄▲▼◄▲▼◄▲▼◄▲▼◄▲▼◄▲▼◄▲▼◄▲▼◄▲▼◄▲▼◄▲▼◄▲▼◄▲▼

Science at Work

Air-Traffic Controller

Air-traffic controllers are responsible for directing millions of aircraft flights around the world. Their job is to keep the sky safe by preventing aircraft collisions. To do this, they communicate with pilots using a radio. They tell pilots how high to fly and when and where to land or take off. They use special maps to keep track of the positions of aircraft.

To apply for the position of air-traffic controller, a person must have a degree from a 4-year college or at least 3 years of related work experience. The applicant must also pass a written test.

Good air-traffic controllers are calm and able to make snap decisions in emergencies. They must have excellent vision and hearing. For example, in a single glance, they must memorize the positions of several aircraft. Air-traffic controllers must have another special skill. Since their air-traffic maps are flat, they must be able to visualize this information in three dimensions.

Where can you find an air-traffic controller? Every airport that has regularly scheduled flights has an air-traffic control tower where controllers work. From this tower, they can see planes coming in and taking off. Look for the air-traffic control tower the next time you visit an airport.

- The earth has a rounded shape, but it is not perfectly round.

- About 30 percent of the earth's surface is land, which is broken up into seven continents.

- About 70 percent of the earth's surface is water, most of which is divided into four oceans.

- Rotation is the spinning of the earth on its axis. The earth rotates from west to east.

- The turning of the earth on its axis results in day and night.

- The tilt of the earth's axis causes sunlight to fall more directly on different parts of the earth throughout its orbit. This causes seasons.

- Revolution is the earth's movement in an orbit around the sun. One revolution takes about 365 days.

- The earth is divided into 24 standard time zones. Within a given zone, the clock time is the same.

- Latitude lines are imaginary lines that run east and west around the earth. Latitude lines are called parallels.

- Latitude is an angle that describes the distance from the equator.

- Longitude lines are imaginary lines that run north and south from pole to pole. Longitude lines are called meridians.

- Longitude is an angle that describes the distance from the prime meridian.

- Intersecting parallels and meridians make it possible to locate a single point anywhere on the earth.

- A hemisphere is half of the earth.

- The equator divides the earth into the Northern and Southern Hemispheres. The prime meridian divides the earth into the Western and Eastern Hemispheres.

Science Words

axis, 219	international	North Pole, 219	South Pole, 219
continent, 216	date line, 221	parallel, 228	standard time
degree, 228	latitude, 228	prime meridian, 230	zone, 221
equator, 228	longitude, 230	revolution, 225	
hemisphere, 231	meridian, 230	rotation, 219	

Chapter 9   R E V I E W

Word Bank

axis
continents
equator
hemisphere
longitude
parallel
prime meridian
revolution
rotation
standard time zone

Vocabulary Review

Choose the word or phrase from the Word Bank that best completes each sentence. Write the answer on your paper.

1. The movement of the earth in its path around the sun is the earth's _____.

2. One half of the earth is a(n) _____.

3. The line of 0° longitude is the _____.

4. An area that has the same clock time is a(n) _____.

5. The imaginary line through the earth connecting the North and South Poles is the _____.

6. A line of latitude is a(n) _____.

7. The seven major land areas of the earth are _____.

8. The spinning of the earth is _____.

9. The line of latitude halfway between the North and South Poles is the _____.

10. The angle that describes the distance east or west of the prime meridian is _____.

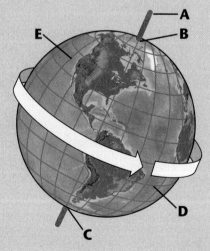

Concept Review

Write the answer to each of the following questions.

11. Name each of the lettered features in the diagram.

12. Describe the shape of the earth.

13. What percentage of the earth's surface do the continents represent?

14. When it is midnight at one point on the earth, what time is it at a point exactly halfway around the earth?

15. What is the measurement unit for latitude and longitude?

16. What is the line of 0° latitude called?

17. On which line of longitude does a point at 31°S, 92°W lie?

18. Which hemispheres lie on either side of the prime meridian?

Choose the word or phrase that best completes each sentence. Write the letter of the answer on your paper.

19. The earth rotates from _____.
    A east to west   **C** west to east
    B north to south   **D** south to north

20. The earth rotates once every _____.
    A day   **B** week   **C** month   **D** year

21. The time in Europe is _____ the time in North America.
    A behind   **C** the same as
    B ahead of   **D** 1 hour different from

20. What is the main cause of the earth's seasons?
    A the earth's tilt
    B the earth's tides
    C the moon's revolution around the earth
    D the gravity between the moon and earth

23. Antarctica is located in the _____ Hemisphere.
    A Northern   **B** Eastern   **C** Western   **D** Southern

Critical Thinking

Write the answer to each of the following questions.

24. How are latitude and longitude alike and different?

25. How would day and night be different if the earth did not rotate?

Test-Taking Tip   Answer all questions you are sure of first, then go back and answer the others.

10 Minerals and Rocks

Suppose you were hiking and found a gleaming chunk of rock. Would you think that you had struck gold? Or would you know that you had found pyrite, sometimes called "fool's gold"? Gold and pyrite are two types of minerals. Minerals combine in a variety of ways to form rocks. Rocks form mountains, islands, valleys, cliffs, and even the ocean floor. The rocks you see around you are thousands of years old. They haven't always looked the same or stayed in the same place. Rocks change. In Chapter 10, you will learn how minerals and rocks are formed. You will also find out how one type of rock can change over time into another rock type.

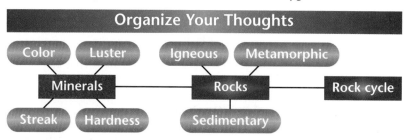

Organize Your Thoughts

Color — Luster — Igneous — Metamorphic

Minerals — **Rocks** — Rock cycle

Streak — Hardness — Sedimentary

Goals for Learning

◆ To explain what a mineral is

◆ To identify basic properties of all minerals

◆ To compare minerals by their properties

◆ To explain what a rock is

◆ To describe igneous, sedimentary, and metamorphic rocks

◆ To explain how each rock type is formed

◆ To describe the rock cycle and the forces involved in it

Mineral

Element or compound found in the earth

The earth around you is a mixture of useful compounds and elements. Scientists classify some of these compounds and elements as **minerals**.

Features of Minerals

What do copper, quartz, and diamond have in common? They are all minerals. Elements or compounds are called minerals if they have these five features:

◆ They are solids.
◆ They are formed naturally in the earth.
◆ They have the same chemical makeup throughout.
◆ They are not alive or made of living things.
◆ They have definite arrangement of atoms.

About 3,000 different minerals are found in the earth. Some are common, but most are rare. In fact, only a small number of minerals make up most of the earth's surface. The most common minerals are aluminum, quartz, feldspar, mica, calcite, dolomite, halite, and gypsum.

Copper deposits often tarnish to a brown or green color.

Some minerals, such as gold (Au) and sulfur (S), are pure elements. Graphite and diamond are different forms of pure carbon. Most minerals, however, are compounds. They are made of two or more kinds of elements. For example, quartz (SiO_2) is made of the elements silicon (Si) and oxygen (O).

Properties Used to Identify Minerals

Pyrite is sometimes called fool's gold because people can easily mistake it for gold. However, no two minerals share the same physical properties. For example, pyrite is almost the same color as gold, but it is harder than gold. In this lesson, you will learn about four properties used for identifying minerals.

Color

Some minerals have a unique color. For example, sulfur is usually bright yellow. However, most minerals can be found in more than one color. For example, quartz might be clear, purple, pink, black, or white. The color varies because the mineral is not usually found in a pure form. It often contains tiny amounts of different minerals called impurities.

Many minerals are similar in color, such as pyrite and gold. Color is one clue to a mineral's identity, but color alone is usually not enough of a clue.

Luster

Some minerals are shiny, but others look dull. Different minerals reflect light differently. The way that a mineral reflects light is called **luster**. There are two main kinds of luster: metallic and nonmetallic. Shiny minerals, such as gold and silver, have a metallic luster.

Minerals with a nonmetallic luster can be described in several ways. For example, if a mineral looks like a pearl, its luster is described as pearly. A mineral that looks like glass is said to have a glassy luster. Compare the luster of the minerals shown here.

Talc has a pearly luster.

Calcite has a glassy luster.

Streak

Streak

Color of the mark a mineral makes on a white tile

Hardness

Ability of a mineral to resist being scratched

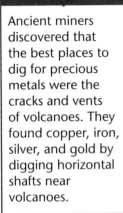

Ancient miners discovered that the best places to dig for precious metals were the cracks and vents of volcanoes. They found copper, iron, silver, and gold by digging horizontal shafts near volcanoes.

When you rub a soft mineral across a tile, it leaves a mark. The color of the mark is the mineral's **streak**. A streak test helps you identify a mineral because all samples of the same kind of mineral make the same kind of streaks. The tile used in a streak test is called a streak plate. It is made of white, unglazed porcelain.

The streak of a mineral may be different from the mineral's color. For example, chunks of gold and pyrite are both gold colored, but you can tell them apart with a streak test. Gold has a yellow streak, but pyrite has a black streak. Some minerals are so hard, however, that they will not leave a streak.

The table below gives the luster and streak of some minerals. Notice that quartz does not leave a streak.

The Luster and Streak of Some Minerals		
Mineral	Luster	Streak
gold	metallic	yellow
silver	metallic	silver-white
pyrite	metallic	gray to black
quartz	glassy	colorless
calcite	glassy	white
talc	pearly	white
hematite	metallic or dull	red to brown

Hardness

Suppose someone offers to sell you a diamond ring. How can you tell if the diamond is real? You could do a simple test. You could see if the diamond can scratch a piece of glass. A diamond will scratch glass because it is harder than the glass. Diamond is the hardest of all minerals. It will scratch any other material. But nothing will scratch diamond.

The **hardness** of a mineral describes how well the mineral resists being scratched. Geologists measure hardness on a scale of 1 to 10, called Mohs' scale of hardness. This scale is described in a table on the next page.

Mohs' Scale of Hardness		
Mineral	**Hardness**	**Quick Test**
talc	1	scratched easily by fingernail
gypsum	2	scratched by fingernail
calcite	3	barely scratched by copper penny
fluorite	4	scratched easily by steel
apatite	5	scratched by steel
feldspar	6	scratches glass easily
quartz	7	scratches both glass and steel easily
topaz	8	scratches quartz
corundum	9	no simple test
diamond	10	no simple test

The higher the number on Mohs' scale, the harder the mineral. A mineral will scratch any other mineral that has a lower number. In the table, the mineral fluorite has a hardness of 4. It scratches calcite but does not scratch apatite. Feldspar will scratch calcite, fluorite, and apatite.

You can use Mohs' scale to find the hardness of an unknown sample. Scratch the sample against each mineral on the scale, starting with the softest mineral. If the unknown sample scratches one mineral, test it with the next. Keep moving up the hardness scale, testing until the sample itself is scratched by one of the minerals. Its hardness is between that of the last two minerals tested. For example, a mineral that scratches feldspar but is scratched by quartz has a hardness of about 6.5.

If you do not have a set of minerals, you can use the "quick test" instead. The quick test in the table above shows how to use common materials to test hardness. For example, suppose you cannot scratch a mineral with your fingernail but you can easily scratch it with a penny. The mineral probably has a hardness between 2 and 3. Geologists working in the field usually use the quick test.

Lesson 1 REVIEW

Write your answers to these questions on a sheet of paper.

1. What are the five features of a mineral?

2. Name two common minerals.

3. How do you determine a mineral's streak?

4. The hardness of quartz is 7. The hardness of topaz is 8. Will quartz scratch topaz? Explain.

5. What is the hardness of a mineral that is scratched by steel but does not scratch glass?

Science in Your Life

Is coal good or bad?

Coal is an organic sedimentary rock that forms from decaying plants and animals. Coal forms very slowly. In fact, it takes millions of years of heat and pressure to turn plant and animal remains into coal. The diagram below shows the stages of coal formation.

Coal is a source of energy. People mine and burn coal to create electricity and to run plants such as steel mills. The energy content of anthracite and bituminous coal is the highest. Some countries, such as Poland, use lignite for energy. In the United States, only Texas and North Dakota use lignite.

Sixty-four percent of the world's coal is used by China, the United States, India, Russia, and Germany. Most of the coal reserves in the world are found in Europe, Asia, Australia, and North America.

Using coal has some disadvantages. First, there is a limited amount of coal in the earth. It won't last forever. Second, coal must be mined by digging deep in the earth or by stripping off a shallow layer of earth. This harms the earth's surface and can be dangerous for miners. Third, burning coal increases air pollution. Find out about other sources of energy that are less harmful in Appendix A.

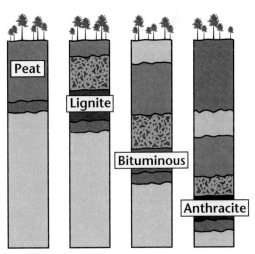

Minerals and Rocks Chapter 10 **241**

10

Materials

◆ labeled samples of minerals
◆ streak plate
◆ copper penny
◆ steel spoon

Observing Color, Streak, and Hardness

Purpose

How could you show that minerals have unique physical properties? In this investigation, you will describe the color, streak, and hardness of known mineral samples.

Procedure

1. Copy the data table on a sheet of paper.

Mineral Name	Color Observations	Streak Observations	Quick Test Observations	Hardness Estimate

2. Write the name of each mineral sample in the first column of the data table.

3. Observe the color of each sample. Record your observations in the data table.

4. Rub each sample across the streak plate, as shown here. Record your observations in the data table.

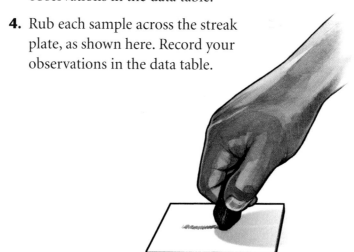

5. Refer to the Quick Test column of Mohs' scale on page 240. Try to scratch each sample with your fingernail, the penny, and the spoon. Record your observations. Wash your hands and fingernails.

6. Using Mohs' scale and your observations from step 5, estimate the hardness number of each sample.

7. Return the samples and equipment.

Questions and Conclusions

1. Which property was the easiest to observe?

2. Which property was the hardest to observe?

3. How did the color of each mineral compare to its streak?

Explore Further

Ask your teacher for an unknown mineral sample. Identify it by finding its hardness. Use the materials and minerals you already have. Explain how you tested the sample.

About 3,000 minerals occur in the earth. Most of them are not found in a pure form. They are mixed together in **rocks**. A rock is a solid, natural material made of one or more minerals. Only about 20 minerals make up 95 percent of the earth's rocks.

Geologists are interested in how rocks are formed and what minerals they contain. This information helps scientists and engineers locate valuable resources, such as oil and metals. Knowledge of rocks is necessary for undertaking construction projects and understanding the environment. Rocks also provide clues about the history of the earth and how the earth changes.

Geologists classify, or group, rocks into three main types, depending on how they form. Some rock forms when hot, melted minerals cool and harden. This rock is **igneous rock**. Igneous rock can form above or below the earth's surface.

Rock

Natural, solid material made of one or more minerals

Igneous rock

Rock formed from melted minerals that have cooled and hardened

Basalt is an example of igneous rock.

Another type of rock forms when bits of other rocks and the remains of living things are pressed and cemented together. The result is **sedimentary rock**. Sedimentary rock can form under a body of water or on the earth's surface.

Sandstone is an example of sedimentary rock.

This metamorphic rock shows the squeezing effect of heat and pressure deep in the earth.

Heat, pressure, and chemical reactions can change sedimentary or igneous rock into another type—**metamorphic rock**. Metamorphic rock always forms below the earth's surface.

The photos show examples of the three rock types. What features do you notice about each one? In this lesson, you will learn more about how each type of rock forms.

Technology Note

Huge blocks or slabs of marble are often needed as building materials. Because of this, explosives are not used to mine marble. Explosives would shatter marble into pieces that are much too small.

Instead, special machines, called channeling machines, are used to mine marble. These machines cut holes in a "dotted line" across a marble rock. More "dotted lines" are cut until a large block shape is outlined. Then wedges are driven into the holes. The marble block is pried away from the surrounding marble and hauled to the surface.

The Rock Cycle

Rocks are always changing. Some melt deep in the earth, then harden. Some are built by layers of sediment. Others twist and bend because of underground heat and pressure. Each type of rock—igneous, sedimentary, and metamorphic—can also change into another type. The series of changes that cause one type of rock to become another type of rock is called the **rock cycle**. This cycle occurs over a long period of time.

Study the rock cycle diagram below. Each arrow is one possible pathway in the cycle. The label by each arrow tells you what force is causing the rock to change.

Follow the arrows as we travel along the cycle, starting with **magma.** As magma rises from deep in the earth, it cools and hardens into igneous rock. Volcanoes quickly deposit lava on the earth's surface as **extrusive** rock. Pressure eventually lifts **intrusive** rock to the surface as well.

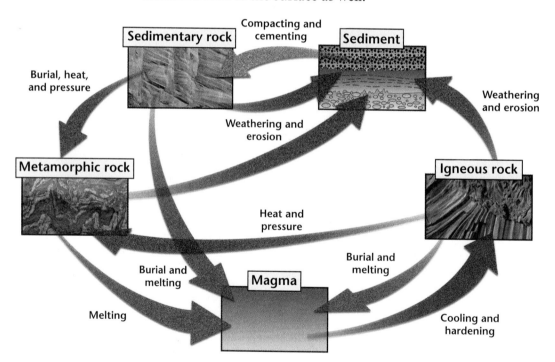

Once on the earth's surface, all rock types begin to slowly break apart into pebbles and then into fine grains like sand. They are easily carried away, often ending up in a large body of water.

At the bottom of a lake or an ocean, sediment forms layers. Over time and under pressure, the layers compact and cement into sedimentary rock. Sometimes sedimentary rock is later brought to the earth's surface, where it begins to break down again.

Other times, sedimentary rock becomes buried deeper in the earth. There the rock is exposed to heat and pressure. These underground forces can bend and twist it into metamorphic rock. In the same way, intrusive rock can become metamorphic rock. Sometimes metamorphic rock is brought to the surface, where it begins to break down again.

In extreme underground heat, all three types of rock can melt. Most rocks melt at temperatures of 800°C or higher. Then they become magma deep in the earth, and the rock cycle continues.

Rocks change by forces inside the earth and by forces on the earth's surface. Look again at the diagram. Below the earth's surface, forces of heat and pressure cause rocks to bend or melt. Above ground, forces such as wind and water cause rocks to break down, move, and settle.

Achievements in Science

The Rock Cycle Theory

The idea of a rock cycle was first proposed in the 1700s. At that time, geology as a formal science did not exist. Most people believed the earth was only about 6,000 years old. Many thought that only major disasters such as earthquakes could change the earth's surface.

James Hutton was a Scottish physician and farmer. He loved to study science and ask questions. In particular, he wanted to find the origin of rocks and minerals.

By studying rocks in Scotland, Hutton noticed streaks of granite among sedimentary rock. He thought this showed that there was heat, even fire, deep in the earth. He also found vertical layers of rock topped with horizontal layers. He concluded that the lower layers had to be very old. They must have been tipped on their side before the new layers were added.

In 1785, Hutton published his theory of rocks in a book. He proposed that one rock type changes into another over time. These changes are caused by pressure and heat deep in the earth. He also stated that erosion, weathering, moving of sediment, and the uprising of rocks from beneath the earth's surface are all part of a cycle. Hutton believed that this cycle has been repeating for millions of years, not for thousands of years. Because of his contributions, James Hutton is called the father of geology.

Lesson 2   R E V I E W

Write your answers to these questions on a sheet of paper.

1. What is a rock?

2. What information about the earth can rocks provide?

3. What are the three main types of rocks?

4. Which type of rock is formed from melted minerals?

5. Name two underground forces that change rocks.

▼◄▲▼◄▲▼◄▲▼◄▲▼◄▲▼◄▲▼◄▲▼◄▲▼◄▲▼◄▲▼◄▲▼◄▲▼◄▲▼◄▲▼◄▲▼

Science at Work

Stonemason

Stonemasons build things out of stone. They build stone walls along shorelines and in landscapes. They lay tiles and paving stones for floors and patios. They cut and polish stone slabs for kitchen countertops and fireplaces. They fix old buildings and carve cemetery statues. They work with either natural stone, such as marble, granite, and limestone, or artificial stone, such as concrete.

A stonemason begins a project by looking at or creating plan drawings. In these drawings, stones may be numbered so they are correctly cut and placed. The stonemason then selects, splits, cuts, and shapes the stones. Stones can be set in different ways. For a wall, stones are first set in a shallow bed of mortar, then aligned and leveled. The wall is built by alternately placing stones and mortar.

Most stonemasons start out as apprentices. Apprentices observe and help experienced workers until the apprentices learn how to do the job alone. Vocational and technical schools also offer stonemason training.

Stonemasons need to be highly skilled at handwork. They need to be precise and creative in solving visual problems. Strength and physical fitness are important because of the tools, machines, and heavy materials involved. Stonemasons should be comfortable working at heights and in noisy environments.

Chapter 10 SUMMARY

- A mineral is an element or a compound that occurs naturally, is a solid, is not alive or made of living things, has the same chemical makeup throughout, and has a definite arrangement of atoms.

- A mineral can be identified by its properties. These include color, luster, streak, and hardness.

- Minerals have either a metallic or nonmetallic luster.

- A mineral's streak is tested by rubbing the mineral across a streak plate.

- Mohs' scale of hardness ranks minerals according to how well they resist being scratched.

- A rock is a solid, natural material made of minerals. The three types of rocks are igneous, sedimentary, and metamorphic.

- Igneous rocks form from magma or lava that hardens.

- Sedimentary rocks form from particles called sediment. The layered sediment gets pressed and cemented into rock.

- Metamorphic rocks form from other rocks that are twisted and bent by heat and pressure.

- Rocks change from one type to another in the rock cycle. This cycle is driven by forces above and below the earth's surface.

Science Words

hardness, 239	luster, 238	mineral, 237	sedimentary
extrusive rock, 246	magma, 246	rock, 244	rock, 245
igneous rock, 244	metamorphic	rock cycle, 246	streak, 239
intrusive rock, 246	rock, 245		

Chapter 10 REVIEW

Word Bank

hardness
igneous rock
luster
magma
metamorphic rock
mineral
rock
rock cycle
sedimentary rock
streak

Vocabulary Review

Choose the word or phrase from the Word Bank that best matches each phrase. Write the answer on your paper.

1. can be tested by scratching

2. solid element or compound that is found in the earth

3. color of the mark left on a tile

4. glassy, pearly, or metallic

5. Rocks change from one type to another in the _____.

6. Hot, liquid rock beneath the earth's surface is _____.

7. _____ forms from rocks that have been changed by heat, pressure, and hot fluids.

8. Layers of sediment that are pressed together and cemented can form _____.

9. Liquid rock that cools on or below the surface forms _____.

10. Natural, solid material made of one or more minerals is called _____.

Concept Review

Choose the word or phrase that best completes each sentence. Write the letter of the answer on your paper.

11. A rock is a mixture of _____.
  A animals **B** minerals **C** plants **D** bands

12. The three main types of rocks are _____.
  A clastic, extrusive, and intrusive
  B sedimentary, organic, and foliated
  C quartz, feldspar, and mica
  D metamorphic, igneous, and sedimentary

13. Not all minerals are _____.
  A solids   **C** shiny
  B found in the earth   **D** formed naturally

14. Mineral A is harder than mineral B if _____.
   A A weighs more than B
   B A scratches B
   C A leaves a bigger streak than B
   D A is more dense than B

15. Gold and pyrite are different in _____.
   A color   **B** luster   **C** feel   **D** streak

16. Two kinds of luster are _____.
   A shiny and dull
   B metallic and nonmetallic
   C yellow and cube-shaped
   D silver and gold

17. You test for streak by _____.
   A rubbing a mineral sample on a white tile
   B breaking a mineral sample
   C weighing a mineral sample in water
   D scratching a mineral with your fingernail

18. On Mohs' scale of hardness, diamond has the _____.
   A lowest hardness   **C** darkest streak
   B brightest luster   **D** highest number

Critical Thinking

Write the answer to each of the following questions.

19. Two unknown mineral samples are different colors. Their other properties are the same. What does this tell you?

20. The wall of a canyon is layered and seems to be made of sand cemented together. In one part of the wall, you see a pattern like the one shown. What rock type is it? How was the rock formed? Where did it form and why?

Test-Taking Tip   When studying for a test, use a marker to highlight important facts and concepts in your notes. For a final review, read what you highlighted.

Weathering and Erosion

Materials on the earth's surface are constantly changing. Rocks and soil break down and move. Sometimes we notice these changes. But most of the time, they happen very gradually. It took millions of years for wind and running water to carve the Grand Canyon. Water and wind continue to shape the canyon today. In fact, water and wind constantly shape the land where you live too. In Chapter 11, you will learn about the processes of weathering and erosion. You also will learn about some landforms caused by erosion.

Organize Your Thoughts

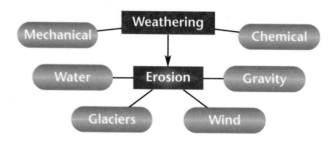

Goals for Learning

◆ To explain weathering and soil formation

◆ To describe how water, glaciers, wind, and gravity cause erosion

◆ To give examples of several eroded landforms

◆ To describe how deposited landforms develop

Objectives

After reading this lesson, you should be able to

◆ define weathering.

◆ give examples of mechanical and chemical weathering.

◆ identify different soil layers.

Weathering

Breaking down of rocks on the earth's surface

Mechanical weathering

Breaking apart of rocks without changing their mineral composition

The earth is constantly changing. Even a hard material like rock changes. Over the years, these carved and polished grave markers have broken down, tilted, and become discolored.

The breaking down of rocks on the earth's surface is known as **weathering**. Weathering occurs when rocks are exposed to air, water, or living things. All these factors help to break rocks apart.

How have these rocks weathered?

Mechanical Weathering

In **mechanical weathering**, rocks break into smaller pieces, but their chemical makeup stays the same. A tree may cause mechanical weathering. A tree can start growing in soil that collects in a small crack of the rock. As the tree grows, its roots push against the rock and split it. You might see this kind of mechanical weathering in a sidewalk near a tree. The growing roots often lift and crumble the sidewalk.

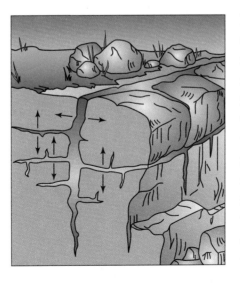

Mechanical weathering also occurs as water freezes in the cracks of rocks. When water freezes, it expands. As the freezing water expands, it pushes the rock apart, as shown in the diagram. The ice may melt, and the water may refreeze. Each time the water freezes, the cracks get bigger. Finally, the rock breaks apart.

Chemical Weathering

In **chemical weathering**, changes occur in the chemical makeup of rocks. New minerals might be added to or taken away from the rock. The minerals might be changed into new substances.

For example, in a process called **oxidation**, oxygen from the air or water combines with the iron in rocks. As a result, a new, softer substance called iron oxide, or rust, forms. Iron oxide stains rocks various shades of yellow, orange, red, or brown. How is the rocky bluff below like the rusty, old can?

A rusting can slowly crumbles.

"Rusting" rock also slowly breaks apart.

Chemical weathering also occurs when water changes minerals in the rocks. For example, the mineral feldspar is part of many rocks. Water changes feldspar to clay and washes it away. Without the feldspar to hold the other minerals together, the rock falls apart.

The limestone cave shown on the next page is the result of chemical weathering. Rain and groundwater combine with carbon dioxide in the air to form carbonic acid. This is the same acid found in carbonated soft drinks. As carbonic acid trickles through the ground, it dissolves calcite—the main mineral in limestone. As more and more limestone is dissolved, small holes become huge caves.

Soil

Mixture of tiny pieces of weathered rock and the remains of plants and animals

Topsoil

Top layer of soil, rich with oxygen and decayed organic matter

Subsoil

Layer of soil directly below the topsoil

Carlsbad Caverns are limestone caves in New Mexico.

How Soil Forms

When rock has weathered for a long time, **soil** may develop. Soil is a mixture of tiny pieces of weathered rock and the remains of plants and animals. The makeup of soil depends on the types of rock particles and remains that are found in it.

As soil develops, it forms layers. Fully developed soil has three layers. Look at the diagram as you read about soil layers.

Topsoil
Subsoil
Weathered rock
Solid rock

Most soil you see is **topsoil**. This layer has the greatest amount of oxygen and decayed organic matter. The organic matter helps the soil hold moisture.

Directly below the topsoil is the **subsoil**. It contains minerals that were washed down from the topsoil. Many of these minerals are forms of iron oxide. They give the subsoil a yellowish or reddish color. Plant roots grow into the subsoil to get minerals and water.

The next layer contains chunks of partially weathered rock. Near the bottom of this layer, rock fragments sit directly on solid rock.

Lesson 1 R E V I E W

Write your answers to these questions on a sheet of paper.

1. What factors in the environment cause weathering?

2. Name two causes of mechanical weathering.

3. Explain how a limestone cave forms.

4. What layer of soil contains the most decayed material?

5. What lies below the three layers of soil?

Technology Note

Many people study and explore caves. Maps help people find their way in unfamiliar caves without getting lost.

Early cave maps were sketched from memory and were not accurate. Today more precise cave maps are made with compasses and measuring tapes. Some maps are made with computers and electronic tools called laser range finders. Maps made with these devices accurately lay out cave features.

Computer programs allow mapmakers to gather data from cave surveys and create three-dimensional cave models. These on-screen models can be rotated to view any angle of the cave. While exploring a cave, people can use a global positioning system device to look at these computer models. These models can be used to find different cave routes and entrances.

Observing Chemical Weathering

Purpose

What will happen when limestone is exposed to acid? In this investigation, you will model and observe chemical weathering.

Procedure

1. Copy the data table on your paper.

Limestone	Observations
before weathering	
after weathering	

2. Use the hand lens to look at the surfaces of the limestone chips. In the data table, describe their appearance.

3. Safety Alert: Put on your safety glasses.

4. Place the chips in the cup. Pour enough vinegar into the cup to cover the chips. Let the chips sit overnight. **Safety Alert: Never taste any substances used in a science investigation. Wipe up any spills immediately.**

5. Pour the vinegar and limestone chips through a strainer over a sink. Run water over the chips to rinse off the vinegar.

6. Place the limestone chips on paper towels. Use the hand lens to look at the limestone surfaces. In the data table, describe any changes you see.

Materlals

- ◆ hand lens
- ◆ safety glasses
- ◆ 5 limestone chips or pieces of chalk
- ◆ clear plastic, 12-ounce cup
- ◆ 1 cup of vinegar
- ◆ strainer
- ◆ water
- ◆ paper towels

Questions and Conclusions

1. How did the surfaces of the limestone change?

2. Vinegar is an acid. What did the vinegar do to change the appearance of the limestone?

Explore Further

Design a similar experiment that varies the soaking time or uses other rocks. For example, you might soak one set of limestone chips for a day, another set for two days, another for three days, and so on. How would each set compare? What would you predict about the mass of each set before and after soaking? Another idea is to repeat the experiment using chips of sandstone, granite, and marble. Which rocks are most resistant to this kind of chemical weathering?

Erosion

Wearing away and moving of weathered rock and soil

Did You Know?

Before water-diversion projects began in the 1950s, Niagara Falls moved upriver about one meter per year. This was caused by eroded limestone tumbling from the top of the falls to the base of the falls.

After rock has been loosened by weathering, it is worn away and moved to another place. The wearing away and moving of weathered rock and soil is called **erosion**. The main agents, or causes, of erosion are rivers, waves, glaciers, wind, and gravity.

River Erosion

Water running downhill is a powerful force. In fact, rivers and their tributaries change more of the landscape than any other agent of erosion. After rain falls to the earth, the water flows downhill. The water pushes soil and rock fragments as it moves. These solid particles are sediment. The water and sediment flow into small gullies, which lead to rivers.

As water flows in a river, it erodes the banks and riverbed, which is the bottom of the river. Compare the eroding power of a river to a hose. The force of water from the hose can easily dig up soil and move it across a lawn. A jet of water may even chip away at a sidewalk. Similarly, river water erodes the land. Sand and stones in the river scrape against the banks and riverbed, causing more erosion. The boulders in the photo below have been worn smooth by fast-moving water and sediment.

Water and sediment act like sandpaper on these rocks in the Madison River in Wyoming.

River Deposits

Deposition

Dropping of eroded sediment

Mouth

Place where a river flows into a larger body of water

Delta

Fan-shaped area of land formed when sediment is deposited where a river empties into a lake or an ocean

Alluvial fan

Fan-shaped area of land deposited where a mountain stream moves onto flat land

Sediment carried by the agents of erosion is eventually dropped in a process called **deposition**. For example, when a river slows down, it may drop, or deposit, its sediment. Heavy particles, such as stones, drop out first. As the river slows down further, lighter sediment, such as sand and clay, drops out.

A river slows down considerably as it empties into a lake or an ocean. The place where a river flows into a larger body of water is called the **mouth** of the river. Sediment settles out at the river's mouth. Eventually, the sediment builds up above the water level and forms a fan-shaped area of land called a **delta**. As the diagram below shows, a river usually branches off as it winds through the delta and empties. A delta provides rich farmland. Much of Egypt's farmland, for example, is located on the fertile Nile River delta.

An **alluvial fan** is similar to a delta. It forms at the base of a mountain where a mountain stream meets level land.

Wave Erosion

Waves in an ocean or a large lake change the shoreline through erosion and deposition. As waves pound the shoreline, they hurl not only water but also bits of rock and sand against the coast. These materials chip away at the rocky shore. Waves also force water into cracks in rocks along the shoreline. With each wave, the water presses against the sides of the cracks. The cracks get bigger, and pieces of rock split off.

This type of erosion formed the cliffs, towers, and other rocky shapes shown in the photo below. During storms, waves reach higher on cliffs and carve steep sides. Arches form when waves erode through a cliff. If the top of an arch collapses, a tower of rock called a sea stack is left standing.

How has wave erosion shaped this shoreline in Australia?

Wave Deposits

Beaches are areas where waves have deposited sand, pebbles, or shells. Some of this beach material is sediment from nearby eroded rocks. Other beach material is sediment carried to the lake or ocean by rivers. Currents near the shore carry sediment to different parts of the shoreline. As waves break on shore, the sediment is pushed onto the beach.

Currents along the shore can change the shape of a beach. One result is a spit, or curved finger of sand, sticking out into the water. Waves and currents can also carry sand away from the beach and deposit a long, underwater sandbar offshore.

Lesson 2   R E V I E W

Write your answers to these questions on a sheet of paper.

1. What is erosion?

2. How does river water change the features of the river?

3. How does a delta differ from an alluvial fan?

4. How does erosion change the shoreline?

5. From where does the sand on a beach come?

Science in Your Life

How do people cause erosion?

People's actions sometimes increase the normal rate of erosion. This can be harmful to the environment and to people. One way that people increase erosion is by using off-road vehicles (ORVs) such as dirt bikes, dune buggies, and all-terrain vehicles. Their overuse has damaged land and threatened the survival of plants and animals.

The photo below illustrates this problem. This hillside used to be covered with grass. The roots of grass and other plants hold soil in place and catch water runoff. Animals use the plants and the areas around them as habitats. Many of the plants are food for animals.

Within weeks, ORVs dug up the vegetation and created ruts. When it rained, the rainwater followed these ruts and formed deep gullies. The exposed soil now erodes quickly from the hill. Areas have been set aside for ORVs, but some people go into closed areas.

Are there areas around your home where people are causing erosion? Go for a walk and take your own survey. Look for evidence of erosion from human activity. Can you think of ways to prevent this erosion?

Glacier

Thick mass of ice that covers a large area

In cold climates, water falls as snow. This snow can build up into thick layers. If the snow does not melt, increasing pressure causes the snow below to form solid ice. Year after year, more ice builds up. Eventually, a **glacier** may form. A glacier is a thick mass of ice that covers a large area. Glaciers may be as small as a football field or hundreds of kilometers long. The weight of snow and ice and the pull of gravity can cause a glacier to move slowly downhill.

The Muldrow Glacier in Alaska flows down the north side of Mount McKinley. It is a popular climbing route.

As glaciers move, they pick up loose sediment. Because of their great size, glaciers move huge boulders and soil. These materials freeze onto the bottom and sides of the glacier. They act like grinding and cutting tools as the glacier continues to move. The photo shows how large rocks in the bottom of a glacier cut long grooves in the surface rock. Small rocks in a glacier act like sandpaper, smoothing and shaping the land beneath.

This limestone cliff on Kelleys Island in Lake Erie was carved by a glacier.

Moraine

Ridge of sediment deposited by a glacier

Did You Know?

The majestic fjords of Norway and Alaska are U-shaped glacial valleys that are partly filled by ocean water.

Two conditions are needed for glaciers to form: year-round cold temperatures and heavy snowfall. Siberia in northern Russia has constant cold weather. But because it receives little snowfall, no glaciers form there.

Deposition by Glaciers

Glaciers continue to move downhill until they reach temperatures warm enough to melt. As the ice melts, it deposits sediment. The sediment forms ridges called **moraines.** Moraines are the "footprints," or evidence, of glaciers, telling us they were here.

The last ice age ended about 10,000 years ago. When the glaciers began to melt, huge blocks of ice broke off. As shown below, these blocks became partly buried in sediment. When an ice block melted, it left a hole in the ground. The hole filled with water. Many of the small lakes in Wisconsin and Minnesota formed this way.

Large lakes formed from glaciers, too. Some glaciers carved wide, deep basins. As they melted, the glaciers filled the basins with water. Moraines dammed parts of the lakes. This process created the Great Lakes, the Finger Lakes in New York, and Lake Winnipeg in Canada.

1. **An ice block breaks off a glacier.**

2. **The ice block gets partly buried in sediment.**

3. **The ice block melts to form a lake.**

Lesson 3   R E V I E W

Write your answers to these questions on a sheet of paper.

1. What two conditions are necessary for the formation of glaciers?

2. What causes glaciers to move?

3. How does a glacier erode the land as the glacier moves?

4. How does a moraine form?

5. Describe how the Great Lakes formed.

Achievements in Science

Artificial Glaciers

A new process is being developed to capture and hold water needed for crops. This process creates artificial glaciers. Some scientists think artificial glaciers may someday help many water-starved villages around the world.

Chewang Norphel, an engineer from Ladakh, India, has experimented with artificial glaciers. Norphel wanted to solve the water shortage in Ladakh. This farming village is located high in the Himalayas. It gets very little rain.

In the 1990s, Norphel helped Ladakh build five artificial glaciers. The new glaciers increased the village's water supply and improved farming.

Creating the glaciers was simple. Before winter set in, water from an existing stream was piped to valley areas. Then this water was forced to flow downhill. Along the way, stone walls were built to stop the water flow and form pools. As temperatures fell, the pools froze. The process of flowing, pooling, and freezing was repeated for many weeks. The pools became thick sheets of ice—artificial glaciers.

It cost only $2,000 to build Ladakh's glaciers. Because of the success of Norphel's experiment, interest in artificial glaciers is growing. A major project to create glaciers in Pakistan has already begun.

Did You Know?

Some sand dunes in the Sahara, a desert in Africa, grow to be hundreds of meters tall.

Science Myth

Deserts are hot, sandy places.

Fact: Deserts are harsh environments with little rainfall and extreme temperatures. Parts of frozen Antarctica are considered deserts.

Wind Erosion and Deposits

Wind is another cause of erosion. Like water, wind picks up and carries materials from one place to another. Wind also erodes by blowing sand against rock. This action is similar to a sandblaster used to clean buildings discolored by pollution. If you have ever been stung in the face by windblown sand, you know wind can be an effective agent of erosion. Much rock in desert areas is pitted with tiny holes from windblown sand.

You are probably familiar with wind deposits called sand dunes. These are mounds formed as the wind blows sand from one place to another. Sand dunes are most common in deserts, but they also occur around beaches.

Wind may bounce sand along the ground until it hits an obstacle, such as a small rock. A small sand pile forms behind the rock. The pile blocks other sand grains, and a larger mound forms. The mound continues to grow, forming a sand dune. The dune moves as wind blows sand up the gentle slope and deposits it on the steeper back slope, as shown below.

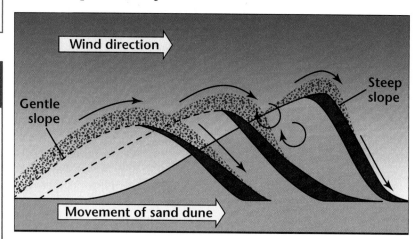

Wind direction

Gentle slope

Steep slope

Movement of sand dune

Landslides can occur because of earthquakes, floods, and volcanic eruptions. These events loosen soil and rock. Human activities, such as cutting down trees or overdeveloping areas, can increase the likelihood of landslides.

The Role of Gravity in Erosion

Gravity plays a part in all erosion. For example, rivers and alpine glaciers flow because of gravity. Gravity can move only material that has been loosened in some way. One way rock and soil are loosened is by freezing and thawing. Another way this happens is by heavy rains. A great deal of water can make soil smooth and slippery. Soil in this condition flows easily. When material on a hillside is loosened, gravity can cause rapid erosion. Mudflows and landslides are examples of this.

The photo below shows how gravity can make erosion happen rapidly. This hillside was loosened until it gave way to gravity's downward pull. In this case, the result was a landslide that damaged a Colorado road. Have you ever seen a sign that reads Caution: Falling Rock? Then you know about another result of erosion by gravity.

Gravity works slowly, too. You may have noticed old telephone poles or grave markers that tilt downhill. Loose soil and rocks move slowly downhill, tilting objects along the way.

This road in the Rocky Mountains crosses an area of landslide activity.

Write your answers to these questions on a sheet of paper.

1. What are two ways that wind erodes the land?

2. How does a sand dune form?

3. Where do sand dunes form?

4. Give examples of erosion caused by gravity.

5. How are rocks and soil loosened?

Science at Work

Floodplain Manager

Flooding can cause great loss, damage, and danger to people and the environment. Rebuilding after a flood is costly. Floodplain managers help prevent floods and reduce flood damage. They also protect water and soil resources.

Floodplain managers inspect systems that hold storm water. Floodplain managers make sure that builders follow rules for excavating, or digging, at construction sites. They also meet with government officials and city planners.

Many floodplain managers have a bachelor's degree in civil engineering. Some local governments offer floodplain management training programs. These training programs focus on storm water runoff, erosion control, and rules to prevent water pollution.

Floodplain managers should have a strong math and science background. They should be able to understand blueprints and maps. Computer and communication skills are also important. A good floodplain manager cares about the environment and safety.

Chapter 11 SUMMARY

- All rock exposed at the surface begins to break apart.

- Mechanical weathering is the process of breaking up rocks without changing their mineral makeup.

- Chemical weathering is the process of breaking up rocks by changing the minerals in them.

- Soil is a mixture of weathered rock and the remains of plants and animals.

- Fully developed soil includes a topsoil, a subsoil, and a layer of partially weathered rock.

- The process by which weathered rock bits and soil are moved is called erosion.

- Erosion is caused by water, glaciers, wind, and gravity.

- A river deposits sediment where it flows into a lake or an ocean, forming a delta.

- Waves wear away the shoreline in some places and build it up in others.

- Glaciers are moving masses of ice.

- Glaciers leave ridges of sediment called moraines. Glaciers have formed many lakes.

- Wind causes erosion by carrying sediment and by blowing it against rock.

- Sand dunes form as sand collects into a huge mound.

- Gravity moves rock and soil downhill. This process can occur quickly or slowly.

Science Words

alluvial fan, 260	erosion, 259	moraine, 264	subsoil, 255
chemical	glacier, 263	mouth, 260	topsoil, 255
weathering, 254	mechanical	oxidation, 254	weathering, 253
delta, 260	weathering, 253	soil, 255	
deposition, 260			

Chapter 11 R E V I E W

Word Bank

delta

deposition

erosion

glaciers

gravity

moraine

mouth

rock

soil

weathering

Vocabulary Review

Choose the word or phrase from the Word Bank that best completes each sentence. Write the answer on your paper.

1. The process of wearing away and moving weathered rock and soil is _____.

2. Sediment settles out where a river empties into an ocean, forming a(n) _____.

3. The breaking down of rocks on the earth's surface is _____.

4. Moving bodies of ice are _____.

5. Rivers and glaciers flow downhill because of _____.

6. A mixture of bits of weathered rock and decayed material is _____.

7. Sediments carried by wind and water are dropped in the process of _____.

8. Rock and sediment that drop from a glacier form a ridge called a _____.

9. The place where a river meets the ocean is the _____ of the river.

10. Below the three layers of soil is _____.

Concept Review

Choose the word or phrase that best completes each sentence. Write the letter of the answer on your paper.

11. Limestone caves form as a result of _____.
    A deposition
    B chemical weathering
    C mechanical weathering
    D wave erosion

12. During oxidation, oxygen combines with iron to form iron oxide, or _____.

    A clay   **B** carbonic acid   **C** feldspar   **D** rust

13. The _____ is the layer that contains the most oxygen and organic matter.

    A subsoil   **C** delta

    B moraine   **D** topsoil

14. Water freezing in the cracks of rocks is an example of _____.

    A deposition   **C** mechanical weathering

    B chemical weathering   **D** erosion

15. The main process that forms a beach is _____.

    A weathering   **C** deposition

    B erosion   **D** oxidation

16. An alluvial fan forms at the base of a mountain and is similar to a _____.

    A sand dune   **B** valley   **C** glacier   **D** delta

Critical Thinking

Write the answer to each of the following questions.

17. Name each lettered layer shown in the diagram.

18. Why would a farmer plow across a hillside instead of plowing straight down the slope?

19. Once a rock breaks into pieces, weathering occurs faster. Explain why.

20. Sand dunes near a beach are being blown toward a neighborhood. Residents want to keep the dunes, but they don't want the blowing sand. What can they do?

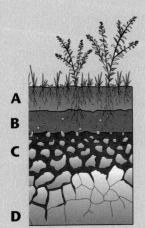

Test-Taking Tip   When studying for a test, use the titles and subtitles within a chapter to help you recall information.

Chapter

12 Forces in the Earth

Red hot lava bursts forth when a volcano erupts. What forces deep inside the earth cause such an awesome event? Why do volcanoes occur only in some locations? The answers to these questions begin with the ground on which we stand. It is moving, even though we usually don't notice it. But a fiery volcano or a shattering earthquake reminds us that the earth's surface and the material beneath it are moving. In Chapter 12, you will discover how parts of the earth move and what happens when they do.

Organize Your Thoughts

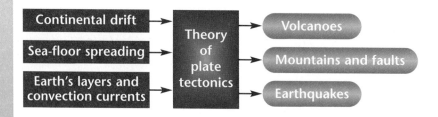

Goals for Learning

◆ To describe the structure of the earth

◆ To explain the theory of plate tectonics

◆ To relate volcanoes to plate tectonics

◆ To explain how mountains and faults form

◆ To relate earthquakes to plate tectonics

Objectives

After reading this lesson, you should be able to

◆ identify the earth's layers.

◆ explain continental drift, sea-floor spreading, and plate tectonics.

Core

Dense center of the earth made of solid and melted metals

Mantle

Layer of the earth that surrounds the core

Crust

Outer layer of the earth

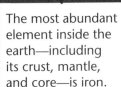

The most abundant element inside the earth—including its crust, mantle, and core—is iron.

The Earth's Layers

Although we cannot directly see the interior of the earth, scientists use instruments to collect data about it. These data are used to make a model of what the inside of the earth is like.

The earth is made up of three main layers. At the center is a dense **core**. The core is solid iron and nickel, surrounded by melted iron and nickel. The core is about 3,500 kilometers thick. Outside the core is the **mantle**. The mantle is made of liquid and solid rock that moves and churns. The entire mantle is about 2,900 kilometers thick. The outermost layer of the earth is the **crust**. Compared to the other layers, the crust is very thin and cold. It is between eight and 70 kilometers thick. The continents and ocean floor are part of the crust. The thickest part of the crust is found below large mountain ranges.

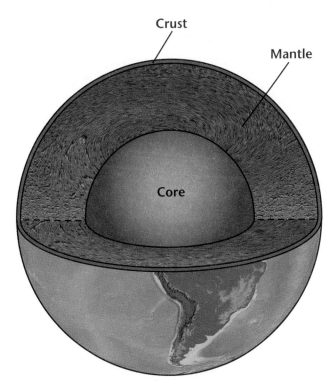

Crust

Mantle

Core

Continental drift

Theory that the major landmasses of the earth move

Pangaea

Single landmass from which Alfred Wegener thought the continents separated millions of years ago

A theory, such as Wegener's theory of continental drift, is a possible explanation for many related observations.

Continental Drift

Have you ever noticed that some continents, such as Africa and South America, look as if they might fit together? In 1912, a German scientist named Alfred Wegener proposed the theory of **continental drift** to explain why.

According to this theory, the earth's continents used to be joined as a single, large landmass called **Pangaea**. Wegener believed Pangaea started breaking up millions of years ago. The continents slowly moved to their present positions.

225 million years ago

180 million years ago

Present day

Besides the puzzle fit of the continents, Wegener had other evidence to support his theory. For example, fossils found on one continent were similar to those found on other continents. Mountain ranges and rock layers seemed to continue from one continent to another. In addition, glacial deposits were found at the equator where no glaciers could exist. Could the glacial deposits have formed when the continents were in a different place? Wegener thought so.

Sea-Floor Spreading

After World War II, new instruments allowed scientists to map the ocean floor. Here is what scientists discovered about the long, underwater mountain ranges called mid-ocean ridges:

◆ A rift valley splits these ridges in half.
◆ The amount of heat coming from a mid-ocean ridge is almost eight times greater than the heat from other parts of the ocean floor.
◆ Magma rises from beneath the ocean floor through cracks in the rift.
◆ The age of the ocean floor increases with distance from a ridge.

Sea-floor spreading

Theory that the ocean floor spreads apart as new crust is formed at mid-ocean ridges

Plate tectonics

Theory that the earth's surface is made of large sections of crust that move

Plate

Large section of the earth's crust that moves

The theory of **sea-floor spreading** explains these observations. This theory states that hot magma from the mantle rises and pours out onto the ocean floor through cracks in a rift. The magma cools, hardens, and forms new crust. This new crust piles up around the rift, forming a mid-ocean ridge. More rising magma pushes the new crust away on both sides of the ridge. This process widens the oceans and pushes the continents apart.

Plate Tectonics

The ideas of sea-floor spreading and continental drift have led to one of the most important theories in science—**plate tectonics**. This theory states that the earth's crust is made of large sections, or **plates**. As shown on the map, most plates include ocean crust and continental crust.

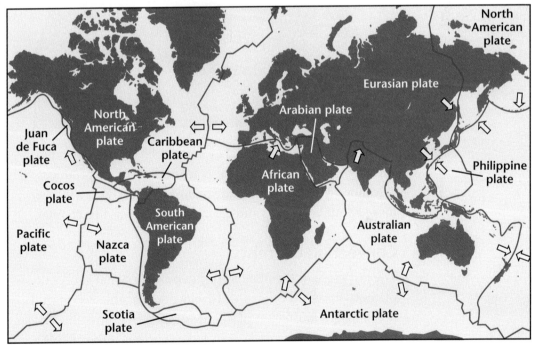

⇨ Plate movement

— Plate boundary

Convection current

Circular motion of a gas or liquid as it heats

Did You Know?

Plates usually move slowly, about 4 to 10 centimeters per year. That's about as fast as your hair grows.

Plates move in three different ways: they move apart, collide, or slide past each other. How they move determines what happens where they meet.

Look at the diagram below. The South American and African plates are moving apart. Where plates move apart, a rift forms. The Nazca and South American plates are moving toward each other. Here the Nazca plate is forced under the South American plate, forming a deep trench. The Nazca plate melts as it sinks into the mantle. Some plates slide past each other. The map on page 275 shows the Pacific plate sliding northwest past the North American plate.

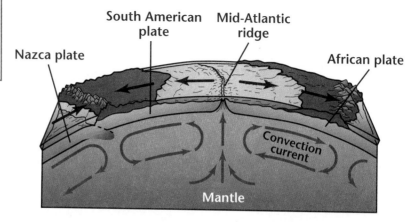

The pushing, pulling, and grinding of plates cause volcanoes and earthquakes. Magma that reaches the surface produces volcanoes where plates collide or spread apart. You will learn more about volcanoes and earthquakes later in this chapter.

Convection Currents

The last piece in the plate tectonics puzzle is what causes the plates to move. In other words, why does magma rise at mid-ocean ridges in the first place? Most scientists think the answer is **convection currents**. A convection current is the circular movement of a liquid or gas as it heats. Convection currents in the partly melted upper mantle can push the plates along as if on a conveyor belt. Look at the convection currents shown in the diagram above. Compare their movement to the movement of the plates.

The diagram shows cross-section labels:
Nazca plate · South American plate · Mid-Atlantic ridge · African plate · Convection current · Mantle

Lesson 1 REVIEW

Write the answers to these questions on a sheet of paper.

1. Describe the layers of the earth.

2. What is the theory of continental drift?

3. Explain how mid-ocean ridges probably formed.

4. What is the theory of plate tectonics?

5. Why do the earth's plates move?

Achievements in Science

The Theory of Sea-Floor Spreading

How did scientists discover the underwater mountain ranges known as mid-ocean ridges? They used a tool called sonar. Sonar is a device that bounces sound waves off underwater objects. The echoes of these sound waves are recorded. The time it takes for the echo to reach the sonar device tells how far away the object is. This information allowed scientists to map mid-ocean ridges.

How did scientists connect mid-ocean ridges to sea-floor spreading? They took a dive to the ocean floor in *Alvin*, a deep-sea submersible. *Alvin* can stand up to the crushing water pressure at the ocean bottom. *Alvin*'s crew took pictures of rocks that looked like toothpaste squeezed from a giant tube. These strange rocks were igneous rocks. They form when liquid rock erupts from deep in the earth and quickly cools. The rocks showed evidence of many eruptions. Scientists think these eruptions from mid-ocean ridges pushed the ocean floor to the sides. This pushing is sea-floor spreading.

More evidence of sea-floor spreading came from rock samples. Scientists on a ship drilled through six kilometers of water. The drills took samples of the ocean floor around a ridge. The scientists determined the ages of the rock samples. They discovered that samples taken farthest from the ridge were the oldest. The youngest rocks were at the center of the ridge. This was more evidence of sea-floor spreading.

Volcano

Mountain that develops where magma pushes up through the earth's surface

Vent

Round opening through which magma reaches the surface of the earth

Did You Know?

The rock particles that create cinder cones are called cinders. Shield volcanoes are so named because they are shaped like a warrior's shield.

How Volcanoes Form

A **volcano** is a mountain that builds around a **vent**, or opening, where magma pushes up through the surface of the earth. The mountain is shaped like a cone. It is built up by rock particles, ash, and hardened lava that erupt from the volcano.

Most volcanoes form where two plates meet. For example, Mount St. Helens in Washington formed where the Juan de Fuca plate sinks beneath the North American plate. The sinking Juan de Fuca plate melts into magma, which then rises to the surface. Where plates collide beneath the oceans, the volcanoes may rise above sea level to form islands. The Aleutian Islands of Alaska and the islands of Japan formed this way.

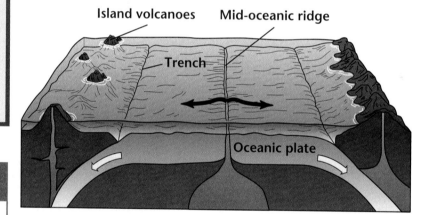

Types of Volcanoes

Volcanoes are grouped into three types. This grouping is based on how the volcano erupts, the material that comes out, and the shape of the volcano. Compare the photos to the following descriptions.

Kilauea Volcano on the island of Hawaii is a shield volcano. It has been erupting constantly since 1983.

Cinder cones are small volcanoes with steep sides and narrow bases. Their eruptions are explosive, shooting ash and igneous rock high into the air. Most cinder cones are less than 500 meters high. These small volcanoes are found in western North America and in other parts of the world.

Shield volcanoes are low and broad with wide craters. They are not very explosive. Thin basalt lava flows from their quiet eruptions. Shield volcanoes are built up by layer after layer of lava that has spread out and hardened.

Composite volcanoes form when gentle eruptions of lava alternate with explosive eruptions of ash and rock. The gentle eruptions add thin layers of lava to the mountain. The explosive eruptions add rocky layers. Composite volcanoes grow to be very tall.

Sunset Crater Volcano in Arizona is a cinder cone.

Mauna Loa Volcano in Hawaii is the largest volcano in the world. This shield volcano extends down to the ocean floor.

Mount Fuji in Japan is a composite volcano.

Lesson 2   REVIEW

Write the answers to these questions on a sheet of paper.

1. What is a volcano?

2. How do volcanoes relate to plate tectonics?

3. What are the characteristics of a cinder cone?

4. Describe a shield volcano.

5. How do composite volcanoes form?

Science in Your Life

What does it mean to live on a tectonic plate?

Earthquakes and volcanoes usually occur where two tectonic plates come together. If you live on or near a plate boundary, you may know people who have experienced an earthquake or volcano. Perhaps you have experienced one yourself. What is the best way to prepare for these events? What should you do in such an emergency?

Many cities lie close to or on plate boundaries. Builders design structures in these cities to withstand the force of earthquakes. The worker in the photo is strengthening a freeway support in a city affected by earthquakes.

A new product may help to reduce earthquake damage to buildings. It is called magnetorheological (MR) fluid. It is a mixture of oil and metal particles. When exposed to a magnetic force, MR fluid thickens into a material like cold peanut butter. It changes back to a liquid when the magnetic force is gone.

Since earthquakes cause strong magnetic forces, scientists are testing MR fluid as a possible shock absorber for buildings. The fluid can be put in special containers controlled by a computer. Hundreds of these devices can be placed within a building's structure. When an earthquake hits, these devices can respond by cushioning and supporting the building.

Objectives

After reading this lesson, you should be able to

◆ describe two ways that mountains form (in addition to volcanoes).

◆ identify forces that cause mountains to form.

◆ name three types of movement along faults.

Folding

Bending of rock layers that are squeezed together

You may have heard the expression "as old as the hills." In fact, mountains and hills are still being built. The process is usually so slow, however, that you don't notice it. Movements of the earth's crust cause these landforms to rise above the surrounding landscape.

Folding Plates

Mountains can form when plates collide. You have already read about how volcanic mountains form when one plate sinks beneath another. This usually happens when a dense ocean plate collides with a continental plate. The Cascade Range in northwestern United States and the Andes in Peru were built this way.

When a continental plate collides with another continental plate, the plates usually crumple like a rug. The rock layers of the plates bend without breaking, as shown in the diagram. This process is called **folding**. Folding can occur either where the two plates meet or somewhere in the middle of a plate. The Himalayas in Asia were formed where two plates met and folded.

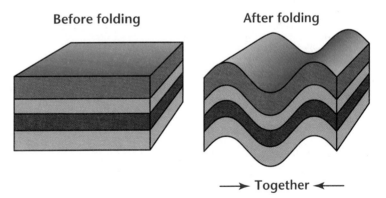

Before folding   **After folding**

⟶ **Together** ⟵

Faults

When pressed together, some rocks break rather than bend. A **fault** is a break in the earth's crust along which movement occurs. Some faults are visible on the earth's surface. Most faults, however, are deep underground. Rock movement along faults can cause mountains to form.

There are three types of faults shown in the diagram below. In a **normal fault**, the two sides of the fault pull apart. The overhanging rock on one side drops down. In a **reverse fault**, the two sides push together. The overhanging rock on one side is pushed up. In a **strike-slip fault**, blocks of rock slide against each other horizontally. The San Andreas fault in California is a strike-slip fault.

Blocks of rock along a fault usually move short distances at a time. When enough pressure builds up, the rocks move and the pressure is released. When the pressure builds up again, more movement occurs.

Over time, movement along faults can raise large blocks of rock, forming mountains. Rock movement along faults built the Grand Tetons of Wyoming and the Wasatch Range of Utah.

Fault

Break in the earth's crust along which movement occurs

Normal fault

Break in the crust in which the overhanging block of rock has slid down

Reverse fault

Break in the crust in which the overhanging block of rock has been raised

Strike-slip fault

Break in the crust in which the blocks of rock move horizontally past each other

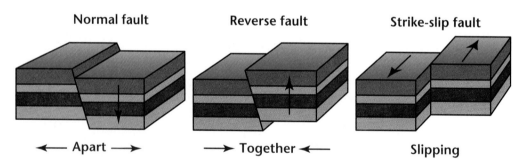

Normal fault — Apart

Reverse fault — Together

Strike-slip fault — Slipping

Science Myth

A fault is a single crack on the earth's surface.

Fact: A fault is a deep break in the earth's crust. Most faults are very long and travel far underground. Because of this, many smaller faults actually make up a large fault.

Lesson 3 R E V I E W

Write the answers to these questions on a sheet of paper.

1. What are two ways that mountains form?

2. Define folding.

3. What is a fault?

4. Compare the direction of movement in a reverse fault and in a strike-slip fault.

5. How do normal faults differ from reverse faults?

Technology Note

Earthquakes are best known for causing destruction. But the data collected by studying earthquakes can be useful. In the next lesson, you will learn that earthquakes cause energy waves to travel through the earth. Scientists use these waves to learn about the interior of the earth. With a technique called seismic tomography, they can even create images of the earth's flowing mantle.

To understand this technique, think of turning on a lamp in a dark room. The lamp sends out light waves. These waves light up things so you can see them. Seismic tomography uses earthquake waves to "light up" the earth's interior.

The process is not an easy one. First, a computer processes wave data from thousands of recent earthquakes. Then this information is used to make a series of images. Each image represents a slice of the earth's interior. When the slices are put together, a three-dimensional picture of the earth is produced. This picture provides information about convection currents within the earth's mantle.

12

Making Models of Folding and Faults

Purpose

How could you model the formation of mountains? In this investigation, you will model the movement of rock layers where folding and faults occur.

Materials

◆ 2 thick telephone books or catalogs

Procedure

1. Copy the data table on your paper.

Type of Rock Movement	Sketch of Model

2. Work with a partner to model folding rock layers. Have your partner hold a telephone book as shown below. Your partner should grasp it firmly with both hands.

3. Have your partner slowly push both hands together, squeezing the book. In the data table, sketch the folds that appear and record the type of rock movement you modeled.

4. Switch places and repeat step 3 so your partner has a turn to sketch.

5. Use two telephone books to model rock layers along a fault. With your partner, hold the books together as shown above. Be sure to place the book spines at an angle.

6. Slowly move the books to model rock movement at a normal fault. If needed, refer to the diagram on page 282.

7. Sketch what happens to the books and record the type of movement you modeled.

8. Repeat steps 6 and 7 two more times, modeling rock movement along a reverse fault and then along a strike-slip fault.

Questions and Conclusions

1. What kind of plate motion might produce the change you saw in step 3?

2. Compare and contrast the motion of the rock layers you modeled for a normal fault and a reverse fault.

3. How did you move the books to model a strike-slip fault?

4. How do the models demonstrate mountain building?

Explore Further

Use modeling clay to create a model of a normal fault, a reverse fault, and a strike-slip fault. Use arrow labels to show the direction of movement in each model. What other ways can you model faults?

Objectives

After reading this lesson, you should be able to

◆ explain what causes earthquakes.

◆ describe earthquake waves and explain what a seismograph does.

◆ explain how an earthquake is located and how its strength is measured.

Earthquake

Shaking of the earth's crust

What does it feel like when you sit in the bleachers at a sporting event? When someone stands up, sits down, or walks nearby, you probably feel the bleachers shake. Shaking also occurs in the rocks of the earth's crust. This shaking is called an **earthquake**.

Causes of Earthquakes

An earthquake is a shaking of the earth's crust that occurs when energy is suddenly released. An erupting volcano releases energy and causes some earthquakes. But most earthquakes occur when rocks break or move suddenly along a fault. For example, two blocks of rock that are sliding past each other may get snagged on the jagged rocky sides. Friction holds the blocks together, but they are still being pushed. Energy builds up. When the pushing overcomes the friction, the blocks move suddenly and a lot of energy is released, causing an earthquake.

Like volcanoes, most earthquakes occur near plate boundaries. This is where most fault movements occur. In fact, the boundary between two plates that are sliding past each other is a large fault. Smaller faults occur near such large faults. An example of this is the San Andreas fault along the coast of California. This large fault is where the Pacific plate meets the North American plate. When these plates suddenly slip, an earthquake occurs. Many smaller faults branch off this large fault.

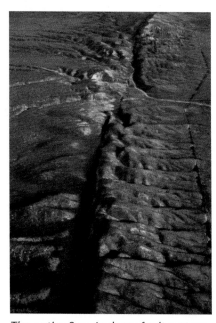

The entire San Andreas fault system is about 1,300 kilometers long. In some places, it cuts deeper than 16 kilometers into the earth.

Did You Know?

Astronauts have placed seismographs on the moon to detect moonquakes caused by meteorite impacts and forces within the moon.

Earthquake Waves

The energy from an earthquake travels through rock in waves. There are three different types of earthquake waves. Primary waves, or P-waves, cause rock particles to vibrate back and forth. Secondary waves, or S-waves, cause rocks to vibrate up and down or side to side. Both P-waves and S-waves travel inside the earth. When P-waves or S-waves reach the earth's surface, they cause long waves, or L-waves. L-waves travel along the surface of the earth. L-waves are the most destructive of earthquake waves because they cause the ground to bend and twist.

Earthquake waves are detected by an instrument called a **seismograph**, shown below. A seismograph uses a suspended pen that does not move and a roll of paper that does move. When the earth shakes, the paper chart also shakes. This makes the pen record a jagged line instead of a straight one. A seismograph records all three kinds of earthquake waves. P-waves are recorded first. They move the fastest and are the first to arrive at the recording station. P-waves also make the shortest lines on the chart. S-waves follow the P-waves. S-waves make longer lines. The L-waves arrive last. They make the longest lines. In the diagram below, you can see how the recordings of the different waves look.

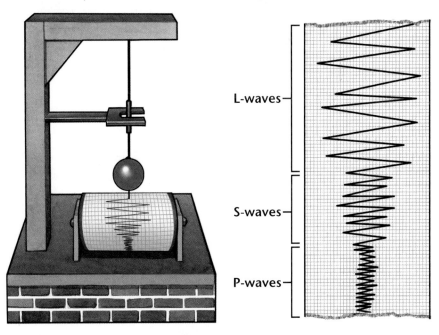

Locating the Epicenter

Focus

Point inside the earth where rock first moves, starting an earthquake

Epicenter

Point on the earth's surface directly over the focus of an earthquake

Richter scale

Scale used to measure the strength of an earthquake

The point inside the earth where the earthquake starts is called the **focus**. The point on the earth's surface directly above the focus is called the **epicenter**. Scientists can pinpoint the epicenter of an earthquake. To do this, they compare the arrival times of the P-waves and the S-waves.

To locate the epicenter, scientists compare seismograph readings from at least three locations. For example, suppose Station A detects waves that show an earthquake started 100 kilometers away. On a map, a circle with a 100-kilometer radius is drawn around Station A. Readings at Station B put the earthquake at 200 kilometers away. So, a 200-kilometer-radius circle is drawn around Station B. Readings at Station C show the earthquake to be 50 kilometers away. A circle with a 50-kilometer radius is drawn around Station C. The point where the three circles meet is the earthquake's epicenter.

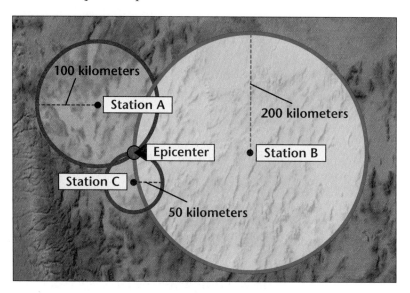

Earthquake Strength and Its Effect

The strength of an earthquake is measured on the **Richter scale**. This scale is based on seismograph wave measurements. The Richter scale assigns every earthquake a number from 1 to 9. Each number represents an earthquake that is 10 times stronger than the next lowest number. The strongest earthquake ever recorded had a measurement of 8.9 on this scale.

Tsunami

Large sea wave caused by vibrations of the earth

The effect of an earthquake on a given region depends on the strength of the earthquake and the distance from the epicenter. Earthquakes can cause great damage and loss of life. Most injuries result from the collapse of buildings, bridges, and other structures in heavily populated areas.

An earthquake damaged this Los Angeles, California, highway in 1994.

Even earthquakes on the ocean floor can cause much damage. They may trigger **tsunamis**, or large sea waves. A tsunami may reach a height of 35 meters, as tall as a 10-story building. Large tsunamis can destroy coastal towns.

Predicting Earthquakes

Scientists hope to learn how to predict where and when an earthquake will occur. They watch for several signs. For example, a sudden drop in the level of well water often precedes an earthquake. Bulges in the earth's surface near a fault could indicate the buildup of stress. Near a fault, seismic activity produces an almost constant occurrence of P-waves and S-waves. A change in the speed of the P-waves may signal a coming earthquake. Scientists use these clues to predict earthquakes. If earthquakes could be accurately predicted, many lives could be saved.

Lesson 4   R E V I E W

Write the answers to these questions on a sheet of paper.

1. What is an earthquake?

2. What instrument is used to measure earthquake waves?

3. Compare and contrast the three kinds of earthquake waves.

4. Describe how the Richter scale is used to identify an earthquake's strength.

5. What two factors determine the effect of an earthquake?

▼◄▲▼◄▲▼◄▲▼◄▲▼◄▲▼◄▲▼◄▲▼◄▲▼◄▲▼◄▲▼◄▲▼◄▲▼◄▲▼◄▲▼◄▲▼◄▲▼◄▲▼

Science at Work

Seismologist

Seismologists study earthquakes and the seismic waves caused by earthquakes. Their job is to detect earthquakes and earthquake-related faults.

Seismologists use many instruments to collect data. Seismographs and seismometers are instruments that receive and record seismic waves. Magnetometers detect and measure magnetic fields. Seismologists interpret data from these instruments to detect the coming of an earthquake. They also determine the location and strength of earthquakes. Much of their job involves managing data on a computer.

A bachelor's degree in geology is needed for a beginning job in seismology. Research positions require a master's or doctoral degree.

Seismologists must have strong science, math, and computer skills. Good communication skills are important for writing reports and working on a team. Seismologists need to be willing to travel to faraway survey sites. Some seismologists may perform their jobs from a ship.

Chapter 12 S U M M A R Y

- The earth has three main layers: the core, the mantle, and the crust.

- The theory of continental drift states that the continents were once joined as a single landmass that slowly separated and moved apart over time.

- The theory of sea-floor spreading states that the ocean floor spreads as new crust is formed at mid-ocean ridges.

- The theory of plate tectonics states that the earth's crust is made of several large plates that move.

- Convection currents in the mantle push the crust, causing the plates to move.

- Volcanoes occur where magma pushes up through the earth's surface. This happens most often at plate boundaries.

- Volcanoes are grouped into three types: cinder cones, shield volcanoes, and composite volcanoes.

- Mountains can form from volcanic eruptions, from folding, and from movement at faults.

- An earthquake is a shaking of the earth's crust. Most earthquakes occur near plate boundaries.

- Earthquake energy travels through the earth as waves. A seismograph detects and records these waves.

- The epicenter of an earthquake can be located by using the arrival times of earthquake waves at different locations.

- The strength of an earthquake is measured on the Richter scale.

Science Words

cinder cone, 279	crust, 273	Pangaea, 274	shield volcano, 279
composite volcano, 279	earthquake, 286	plate tectonics, 275	strike-slip fault, 282
	epicenter, 288	plate, 275	tsunami, 289
continental drift, 274	fault, 282	reverse fault, 282	vent, 278
	focus, 288	Richter scale, 288	volcano, 278
convection current, 276	folding, 281	sea-floor spreading, 275	
core, 273	mantle, 273	seismograph, 287	
	normal fault, 282		

Chapter 12 REVIEW

Vocabulary Review

Choose the word or phrase from the Word Bank that best completes each sentence. Write the answer on your paper.

1. The earth's crust shakes during a(n) _____.

2. The bending of rock layers is _____.

3. An instrument used to record earthquake waves is a(n) _____.

4. The idea that new crust forms along rifts in the ocean floor is called _____.

5. The point on the earth's surface above the focus of an earthquake is its _____.

6. The idea that the earth's landmasses move is the _____ theory.

7. The circular movement of a gas or liquid as it heats is a(n) _____.

8. The idea that the earth's crust is made of moving sections is the theory of _____.

9. The layer of the earth between the core and the crust is the _____.

10. A break in the earth's crust where the earth moves in different directions is a(n) _____.

Concept Review

Choose the word or phrase that best completes each sentence. Write the letter of the answer on your paper.

11. The earth's surface is part of the _____.

   A core

   B atmosphere

   C crust

   D mantle

12. Continental drift, sea-floor spreading, and plate tectonics all help explain _____.
  A how the earth's surface changes
  B where convection currents come from
  C why the earth has layers
  D the age of the earth

13. Where two plates meet, they usually _____.
  A explode
  B scrape or squeeze each other
  C stop moving
  D become attached

Write the answer to each of the following questions.

14. Name the three types of volcanos and one unique feature of each.

15. Describe two of the three ways that mountains form.

16. Explain what the Richter scale measures.

17. Look at the lettered diagrams. Name the type of fault each diagram represents.

Critical Thinking

Write the answer to each of the following questions.

18. Tell how mountains, volcanoes, and earthquakes are related to the earth's plates.

19. Review the factors that determine the effect of an earthquake. What factors might determine the effect of a tsunami?

20. A string of active volcanoes rings the Pacific Ocean basin. In fact, the circle is called the Ring of Fire. What conclusion might you draw about the earth's crust under this ring? Why?

A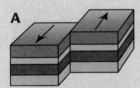

B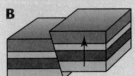

C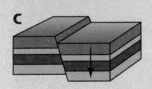

Test-Taking Tip Decide which questions you will do first and last. Limit your time on each question accordingly.

13

A Record of the Earth's History

Imagine a quiet forest. All is still. Suddenly, a blurry shape flies by close to the ground. Landing on a low branch, the shape shows itself to be a bird about the size of a crow. At least it *looks* like a bird. It has wings and feathers. But it also has a head like a lizard. Sharp teeth line its mouth, and its wings end in claws. Is this a creature from a movie? No, this kind of animal really existed in the past. Its features have been preserved in rock. Evidence like this provides clues to what life on the earth was like long ago. In Chapter 13, you will learn about geologic time. You also will find out about the kinds of evidence scientists use to reconstruct the earth's history.

Organize Your Thoughts

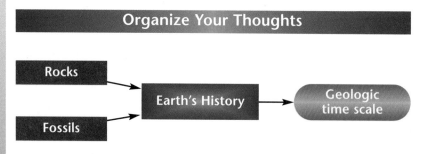

Goals for Learning

◆ To define geologic time

◆ To explain how fossils form

◆ To explain relative and absolute dating of rocks

◆ To define half-life

◆ To outline major events in the earth's history

Objectives

After reading this lesson, you should be able to

◆ define geologic time.

◆ explain what a fossil is.

◆ describe three ways fossils form.

Geologic time

All the time that has passed since the earth formed

Does a year seem like a long time to you? Your idea of time depends on what you compare it to. Compared to events in your life, a year probably is a long time. Compared to the history of most nations, a year is not very long at all. Scientists who study the earth describe a long time in terms of millions or billions of years. For example, the carving of the Grand Canyon took about 6 million years. Compared to that amount of time, a year is not even noticeable.

Geologic Time

Most events in earth science are compared to **geologic time**— all the time that has passed since the earth formed. Scientists estimate that the earth is about 4.6 billion years old. Compared to this amount of time, even the Grand Canyon is fairly young.

When an event, such as a hurricane, happens today, it is recorded. Newspaper reports, videotapes, and photographs record the event. No such records exist for most of the earth's events. Yet much has happened in the earth's long history. Mountains have built up, continents have moved, living things have come and gone. These events left records in the rock of the earth's crust. As you will see, scientists study rock layers to learn what happened in the past and the order in which events took place.

The Colorado River has carved the Grand Canyon over millions of years.

Fossils

Fossils are evidence that living things on the earth have changed over time. Fossils also show that the earth's climates haven't always been the same.

Among the most important records of the earth's history are **fossils**. Fossils are the traces or remains of organisms preserved in the earth's crust. Organisms are living things and include plants and animals. Fossils are evidence that certain kinds of life existed. Other living things may have been present on the earth in the past. However, unless these living things left fossils, scientists have no evidence of their existence.

It's not easy to become a fossil. When an organism dies, its soft parts usually decay. They might also be eaten by other creatures. The parts most likely to become fossils are the hard parts, such as wood, teeth, bones, and shells. Usually, these parts must be buried quickly in some way in order to become fossils. Most organisms that become fossils are buried by sediment on the ocean floor. Burial might also occur during sandstorms, volcanic eruptions, floods, or avalanches.

Types of Fossils

Most fossils preserve the shape of the organism but not the actual body matter. For example, some fossils form when minerals replace the original parts of a buried organism. This process is called **petrification**. The photo shows petrified wood. Over thousands of years, the wood was dissolved by groundwater and replaced by the minerals in the water.

What details can you see preserved in this petrified wood?

Mold

Type of fossil that forms when the shape of a plant or an animal is left in a rock

Cast

Type of fossil that forms when minerals fill a mold; a model of an organism

Another type of fossil forms when an organism leaves an imprint behind. For example, a plant or an animal may become buried in sediment that later forms rock. Eventually, the organism decays or dissolves. The space left in the rock, called a **mold**, has the shape of the plant or animal. If minerals fill the mold, a **cast** forms. The cast becomes a model of the original plant or animal. In the photo below, find both a mold and a cast of a trilobite. This sea animal lived 500 million years ago.

Many buried trilobites created the molds and casts in this rock.

Fossils, such as this amber, offer a glimpse of life from the past.

Sometimes, the actual body matter of an organism is preserved as a fossil. For example, remains of woolly mammoths, ancient ancestors of elephants, have been found preserved in ice and frozen soil. The remains of saber-toothed tigers have been discovered trapped in petroleum deposits called tar pits. The insects in the photo on the left were trapped in tree sap. The sap hardened into a material called amber, preserving the actual body of each insect.

Write the answers to these questions on a sheet of paper.

1. What is geologic time?

2. What is a fossil?

3. What are three ways that fossils form?

4. Describe the process of petrification.

5. Explain how a cast forms from a buried organism.

Achievements in Science

Uncovering the History of Life

Fossils are keys to understanding the past. Paleontologists are scientists who uncover and study fossils. These scientists have learned much about the history of plant and animal life on the earth.

Fossils show what past climates were like. For example, fossils of palm and magnolia leaves have been found in Greenland. This shows that Greenland, an icy region today, had a warm, wet climate about 80 million years ago.

Fossils tell about an area's history. For example, paleontologists have found fossil shellfish in the Rocky Mountains. Since fossil shellfish are found in rocks formed under an ocean, this indicates that the Rocky Mountains were once underwater.

Fossils reveal past forms of life that are now extinct. Richard Owen was a British paleontologist who examined fossil teeth discovered in the 1820s. Other scientists thought the teeth belonged to a large lizard. Owen had a different idea. He thought the teeth belonged to a huge reptile that was unlike any known reptiles. In 1841, he proposed a name for this new group of animals—Dinosauria. The term *dinosaur* soon became part of scientific language.

How do paleontologists uncover fossils? When these scientists find part of a fossil in a rock, they dig the rock away from it. They start with large tools or even explosives. As they get closer to the fossil, they use smaller tools to carefully free the fossil. Then they use delicate tools and tiny brushes to clean the fossil.

Relative dating

Method that compares two rock layers to find out which is older

To find the age of a fossil, scientists find the age of the rock in which the fossil was found. How is this done? It's not as difficult as you might think.

Principles of Relative Dating

One way to find the age of a rock is to compare it to other rocks. In this method, called **relative dating**, you place rock layers in order from oldest to youngest without using actual dates. Some basic principles can guide you when using relative dating.

If you are unpacking a box of books, you can be fairly certain that the book on the bottom was put in before the books on top. You can apply this simple idea to relative dating. Look at the layers of sedimentary rock shown in the diagram below. The oldest layer is at the bottom. The principle of superpostion states that if sedimentary rock layers have not been overturned, the oldest rock layer is on the bottom and the youngest rock layer is on the top. Based on this principle, a fossil found in one layer of rock is older than a fossil found in a layer above it.

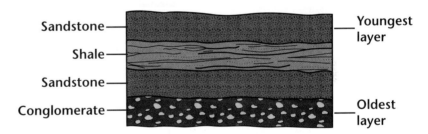

Principle of superposition

Suppose you saw a nail stuck in a tree trunk. You would realize that the tree grew first and the nail was later pounded into it. A similar principle is used to determine the relative ages of some rocks. According to the principle of crosscutting relationships, a rock that cuts through another rock must be younger than the rock it cuts. The diagram on the next page illustrates this principle. The rock features in the diagram are numbered from oldest (1) to youngest (6).

The igneous rock pocket (5) formed when magma forced its way up through cracks in the existing rock layers. According to the principle of crosscutting relationships, this section of igneous rock is younger than the sedimentary rock layers (1 to 4).

The diagram also shows a fault cutting through layers of rock. Using the principle of crosscutting relationships, you can see that the fault (6) occurred after the pocket of igneous rock formed. So the fault is the youngest rock feature.

Some fossils, called **index fossils**, can be used to establish the relative ages of rocks that contain these fossils. Index fossils are useful because they are widespread and lived for a relatively short period of time. Therefore, when scientists find an index fossil anywhere in the world, they know the relative age of the rock in which the fossil was found.

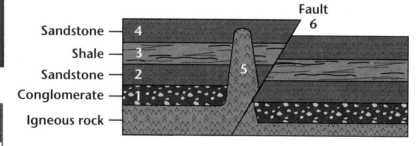

Principle of crosscutting relationships

Absolute Dating Using Half-Life

Relative dating is useful, but **absolute dating** is more specific. Scientists use absolute dating to estimate the absolute age, or actual age, of a rock or fossil. Absolute dates are measured in years, just as your age is.

Scientists find the absolute age of a rock by studying certain **radioactive elements** the rock contains. Radioactive elements break apart, or decay, to form other elements. This decay happens at a constant rate. The length of time it takes for half of the atoms of a radioactive element to decay is the element's **half-life**. By comparing the amounts of different elements in a rock, scientists can estimate the absolute age of the rock.

Index fossil

Fossil that can be used to establish the relative age of the rock in which the fossil occurs

Absolute dating

Method that estimates the actual age of a rock or fossil

Radioactive element

Element that breaks apart, or decays, to form another element

Half-life

Length of time it takes for half of the atoms of a radioactive element to decay

Did You Know?

Scientists estimate that only about 1 percent of all past organisms became fossils.

For example, the radioactive element carbon-14, a form of carbon, is used in absolute dating of some fossils. All living things contain carbon-14. When an organism dies, the carbon-14 starts to decay, forming nitrogen-14. The diagram below shows the rate of decay. The half-life of carbon-14 is 5,730 years. After 5,730 years, half of the carbon-14 is decayed. Every 5,730 years after that, half of the remaining carbon-14 decays. By measuring the amount of carbon-14 and nitrogen-14 in a sample, scientists can determine about how many years ago the organism died.

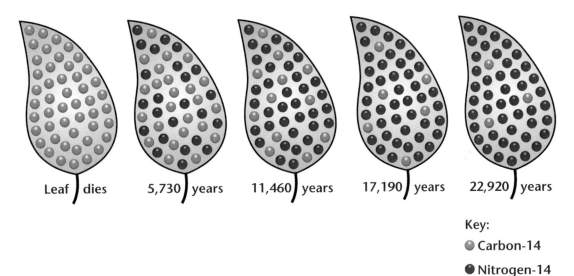

Leaf dies   5,730 years   11,460 years   17,190 years   22,920 years

Key:
- Carbon-14
- Nitrogen-14

After about 50,000 years, almost all carbon-14 in an organism has decayed to nitrogen-14. Therefore, carbon-14 cannot be used to date fossils older than 50,000 years. Other radioactive elements with longer half-lives are used to determine the absolute age of older fossils and rocks.

For example, uranium-238 occurs in some igneous rocks and decays to form lead-206. The half-life of uranium-238 is about 4.5 billion years. Scientists can compare the uranium-238 content of a rock to its lead-206 content. From such a comparison, they can determine the absolute age of the rock. Using this method on meteorites, scientists have estimated the age of the earth to be 4.6 billion years old.

Lesson 2   REVIEW

Write the answers to these questions on a sheet of paper.

1. How does relative dating differ from absolute dating?

2. Define the principles of superposition and crosscutting relationships. Give an example of each.

3. How can a rock's absolute age be determined?

4. What is a radioactive element's half-life?

5. For what kind of fossils would uranium-238 be used to determine absolute age?

▼◄▲▼◄▲▼◄▲▼◄▲▼◄▲▼◄▲▼◄▲▼◄▲▼◄▲▼◄▲▼◄▲▼◄▲▼◄▲▼◄▲▼◄▲▼◄▲▼

Science at Work

Petroleum Engineer

Petroleum engineers travel the world searching for underground deposits of oil or natural gas. Once these deposits are located, petroleum engineers decide on the best way to recover, or get at, the oil or gas. To do this, they often use computer models and other technology. Then petroleum engineers work with geologists to set up drilling equipment and manage drilling operations. An important part of this job is making sure that people and the environment are not in danger.

Petroleum engineers work for petroleum companies, exploration companies, or governments. Petroleum engineers often work where oil or gas is being recovered or processed. These places include Alaska, Texas, Louisiana, Oklahoma, California, western and northern Canada, and countries overseas. Petroleum engineers also work on oil rigs, drilling for oil that is located under oceans.

Petroleum engineers must have at least a bachelor's degree in petroleum engineering. Strong computer and technology skills are also required for their work. These engineers need to be good problem-solvers and careful planners. Because of the likelihood of travel, a petroleum engineer should be willing to learn about other cultures and languages.

13

INVESTIGATION

Making a Half-Life Model

Purpose

How does a radioactive element show age? In this investigation, you will model and graph the decay of a radioactive element.

Procedure

1. Copy the data table on a sheet of paper.

Time	Mass (grams)	
	Radioactive Element	New Element
0		
1 half-life		
2 half-lives		
3 half-lives		

2. Label one sheet of paper *radioactive element* and another sheet of paper *new element*.

3. Place all of the beans on the sheet marked *radioactive element*. Each bean represents 1 gram of a radioactive element in a rock sample. At time 0, before any decay has occurred, record the mass in grams of the radioactive element.

4. Assume that the half-life of the beans is 1 minute. Note your starting time on the clock as time 0.

5. Wait 1 minute. Then remove half of the beans from the *radioactive element* paper and place them on the *new element* paper. Record the mass of each element at 1 half-life.

6. Repeat step 5 two times: at 2 half-lives and at 3 half-lives.

7. Draw a graph like the one shown here. Place the time in half-lives along the bottom axis and the mass of the radioactive element in grams along the side axis. Plot your data and connect the points.

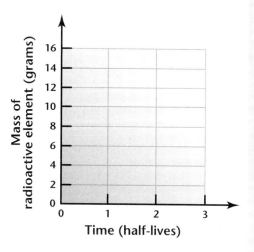

Questions and Conclusions

1. What do the beans that did not get moved represent?

2. What do the beans that did get moved represent?

3. How much of the radioactive element was left after 2 half-lives? After 3 half-lives?

4. How much of the radioactive element would be left after 4 half-lives?

Explore Further

This investigation shows only one of many different ways to make a half-life model. Design a half-life model yourself. You might shake pennies in a box and remove the "heads" or "tails" after each shake, or half-life. You might also use beans of different colors. Graph your data as you proceed. After a couple of half-lives are graphed, extend the graph to predict how many "radioactive atoms" will remain after additional half-lives. Check your predictions.

Using evidence from the rock record and fossil record, scientists have developed the **geologic time scale**, shown on page 306. The geologic time scale is an outline of major events in the earth's history. Find the four major units, or eras, of geologic time. Notice how eras are divided into smaller units called periods. Some periods are divided into even smaller units called epochs. Refer to this table as you read about each era.

The Precambrian Era

The **Precambrian Era** is the oldest and longest era. It accounts for about 85 percent of all geologic time. The Precambrian Era began with the formation of the earth and ended about 540 million years ago.

Most Precambrian rocks are igneous or metamorphic. They form the foundation of the continents. These ancient rocks are exposed in some areas where the earth's crust has lifted and eroded. Precambrian rocks can be seen in the Black Hills of South Dakota, the Appalachian Mountains in the eastern United States, and the Ozark Mountains of Missouri.

Simple organisms probably first appeared at least 3.5 billion years ago, early in the Precambrian Era. These organisms may have included relatives of algae, fungi, and bacteria. The fossil record contains limited evidence of Precambrian organisms.

Objectives

After reading this lesson, you should be able to

◆ describe the geologic time scale.

◆ summarize events that occurred during each era of geologic time.

Geologic time scale

Outline of the events of the earth's history

Precambrian Era

Oldest and longest era of the earth's history; began about 4.6 billion years ago and ended about 540 million years ago

We know the earth has changed over time. But how the earth actually began is still a big question. Scientists use the evidence they have to suggest theories about the earth's origin.

The Geologic Time Scale						
			Years Before the Present (approximate)			
Era	Period	Epoch	Began	Ended	Forms of Life	Physical Events
Cenozoic	Quaternary	Recent	11,000		Humans dominate	West Coast uplift continues in U.S.; Great Lakes form
		Pleistocene	2,000,000	11,000	Primitive humans appear; mammoths	Ice age
	Tertiary	Pliocene	7,000,000	2,000,000	Modern horse, camel, elephant develop	North America joined to South America
		Miocene	23,000,000	7,000,000	Grasses; grazing animals thrive	North America joined to Asia; Columbia Plateau
		Oligocene	38,000,000	23,000,000	Mammals progress; elephants in Africa	Himalayas start forming; Alps continue rising
		Eocene	53,000,000	38,000,000	Ancestors of modern horse, other mammals	Coal forming in western U.S.
		Paleocene	65,000,000	53,000,000	Many new mammals appear	Uplift in western U.S. continues; Alps rising
Mesozoic	Cretaceous		145,000,000	65,000,000	Dinosaurs die out; flowering plants	Uplift of Rockies and Colorado Plateau begins
	Jurassic		208,000,000	145,000,000	First birds appear; giant dinosaurs	Rise of Sierra Nevadas and Coast Ranges
	Triassic		245,000,000	208,000,000	First dinosaurs and mammals appear	Palisades of Hudson River form
Paleozoic	Permian		280,000,000	245,000,000	Trilobites die out	Ice age in South America; deserts in western U.S.
	Pennsylvanian		310,000,000	280,000,000	First reptiles, giant insects; ferns, conifers	Coal-forming swamps in North America and Europe
	Mississippian		345,000,000	310,000,000	Early insects	Limestone formation
	Devonian		395,000,000	345,000,000	First amphibians appear	Mountain building in New England
	Silurian		435,000,000	395,000,000	First land animals (spiders, scorpions)	Deserts in eastern U.S.
	Ordovician		500,000,000	435,000,000	First vertebrates (fish)	Half of North America submerged
	Cambrian		540,000,000	500,000,000	Trilobites, snails; seaweed	Extensive deposition of sediment in inland seas
Precambrian			4,600,000,000	540,000,000	First jellyfish, bacteria, algae	Great volcanic activity, lava flows, metamorphism of rocks; evolution of crust, mantle, core

Science Myth

People and dinosaurs lived at the same time.

Fact: Most scientists believe that dinosaurs existed from the Triassic Period through the Cretaceous Period. This was between 245 and 65 million years ago. People appeared about 2 million years ago, which was long after the dinosaurs disappeared.

The Paleozoic Era

The **Paleozoic Era** began about 540 million years ago and ended about 245 million years ago. It was a time of great development of life in the oceans. At times, oceans covered large portions of the continents. Paleozoic rocks contain fossils of trilobites, sponges, and shellfish. The first land plants and animals also developed during this era. In the geologic time scale on page 306, note the progression of life from amphibians to insects to reptiles. Many ancient insects were huge. Some dragonflies had the wingspan of eagles!

During the Paleozoic Era, the earth's crust underwent many changes. For example, the Appalachian Mountains formed during this time as the crust buckled over millions of years. Much of the coal, oil, and natural gas we use today for energy formed from the organisms that lived in large swamps and shallow seas during this era. Many rock layers built up over the dead organic matter. Heat and pressure slowly turned the organic matter into coal, oil, and natural gas.

Compare the trilobite model above with the fossils shown on page 297.

The Mesozoic Era

The **Mesozoic Era** began about 245 million years ago and ended 65 million years ago. Life on land flourished during this time. Trees similar to our palm and pine trees were common. Small mammals and birds first appeared. But this era is often called the Age of Reptiles because they were the major form of life on land. The most dominant of the reptiles were the dinosaurs.

In many ways, the kinds of dinosaurs were like the kinds of animals today. Some ate meat and some ate plants. Some were larger than an elephant, while others were as small as a chicken. Some were fierce and others were gentle. Some traveled in herds and some were loners. Even their color probably varied, though we cannot tell this from the fossil record.

The end of the Mesozoic Era is marked by the end of the dinosaurs. Why the dinosaurs died out, or became extinct, during this time is still a mystery.

This is a fossil model of the largest Tyrannosaurus rex *skeleton ever discovered. It is displayed at The Field Museum in Chicago.*

The Cenozoic Era

We are living in the **Cenozoic Era**. It began about 65 million years ago. During this era, the Alps and the Himalayas formed as the earth's plates continued to collide. Late in the era, several ice ages occurred. An ice age is a period of time when glaciers cover large portions of the land. About 2 million years ago, glaciers carved out huge basins and formed the Great Lakes.

Although dinosaurs became extinct at the close of the Mesozoic Era, mammals survived and flourished. The Cenozoic Era is known as the Age of Mammals. In this era, mammals, including humans, became the dominant form of life. The variety of mammals grew. The population, or total number, of each kind of mammal grew as well. At the same time, the kinds and numbers of birds, reptiles, fish, insects, and plants also increased.

Scientists estimate that about 30 million kinds of animals and plants live on the earth today. This is a small percent of all the kinds of organisms that have ever existed. Scientists also believe that about 100 kinds of organisms become extinct each day. Two factors that threaten the survival of plants and animals are pollution and the destruction of the natural environment. Many people are working to save animals and plants from extinction.

As time continues, living things and the earth that supports them will continue to change.

Technology Note

Scientists use fossils to find the ages of rocks. Scientists also use fossils to find deposits of oil. Some fossils, called conodonts, were formed in a variety of colors. The colors are related to how hot the rock was when the fossil formed. This is important because oil forms underground only at certain temperatures. The colors of the conodonts, then, help scientists locate rock layers that might contain oil.

Lesson 3   R E V I E W

Write the answers to these questions on a sheet of paper.

1. What is the geologic time scale?

2. Describe the Precambrian Era.

3. Name two forms of life that first appeared during each of the Paleozoic, Mesozoic, and Cenozoic Eras.

4. What time periods were spanned by the Paleozoic, Mesozoic, and Cenozoic Eras?

5. For each era of geologic time, name a major change that occurred in the earth's crust during that era.

Science in Your Life

How can you cut down on fossil fuels?

Petroleum, coal, and natural gas are fossil fuels. Deposits of fossil fuels are found in layers of underground rock. They formed there long ago from decayed plants and animals. Today fossil fuels are burned to create energy. They currently supply at least 60 percent of the world's electrical needs. They also are used to make cosmetics, paints, dry-cleaning chemicals, asphalt, and many other products.

Fossil fuels are nonrenewable. This means there is a limited supply of fossil fuels. They won't last forever, and we are using them up quickly. Because of this, scientists are improving ways to use renewable sources of energy. Renewable energy includes wind, hydroelectric, solar, geothermal, and nuclear energy. You can read about these forms of energy in Appendix B.

Make a list of ways you use gasoline, electricity, motor oil, coal, and natural gas. Then list other products you use that are made from fossil fuels. What can you do to reduce your use of fossil fuels?

Chapter 13 SUMMARY

- Geologic time is all the time that has passed since the earth formed—about 4.6 billion years.

- Rocks contain clues about events that happened in the earth's past.

- Fossils are evidence that certain organisms existed.

- Fossils form when plant or animal remains become replaced with minerals, leave an imprint, or become preserved.

- Relative dating is a method used to find the relative age of a rock layer by comparing it to other layers.

- The principle of superposition states that the youngest layer in sedimentary rock is the top layer.

- The principle of crosscutting relationships states that a rock feature that cuts through other rock layers is younger than those layers.

- Absolute dating is a method used to determine the actual age of a rock layer.

- Absolute dating relies on the decay of radioactive elements in a rock or fossil. How fast a radioactive element decays depends on its half-life.

- The events in the earth's history occurred over geologic time and are outlined on the geologic time scale.

- Earth's history is divided into four eras: Precambrian, Paleozoic, Mesozoic, and Cenozoic. Each era is unique in terms of the living things that developed and the changes that took place in the earth's crust.

Science Words

absolute dating, 300	geologic time	Mesozoic Era, 308	Precambrian
cast, 297	scale, 305	mold, 297	Era, 305
Cenozoic Era, 309	geologic time, 295	Paleozoic Era, 307	radioactive
fossil, 296	half-life, 300	petrification, 296	element, 300
	index fossil, 300		relative dating, 299

Chapter 13 REVIEW

Word Bank

absolute dating

cast

fossil

geologic time

half-life

index fossil

mold

petrification

radioactive element

relative dating

Vocabulary Review

Choose the word or phrase from the Word Bank that best matches each definition. Write the answer on your paper.

1. trace or remains of an organism preserved in the earth's crust

2. impression left in a rock by an organism

3. process by which original plant or animal parts are replaced with minerals

4. model of an organism

5. total amount of time since the earth was formed

6. method used to determine how old a rock layer is by comparing it to another rock layer

7. method that determine the actual age of a rock or fossil

8. fossil that provides clues to the age of the rock in which the fossil appears

9. length of time it takes for half of the atoms of a radioactive element to decay

10. an element that breaks apart, or decays, to form other elements

Concept Review

Choose the word or phrase that best completes each sentence. Write the letter of the answer on your paper.

11. The geologic time scale divides the history of the earth into four _____.

    A epochs   **B** eras   **C** periods   **D** events

12. Scientists study _____ to learn about the history of life on the earth.

    A mammals   **C** radioactive elements

    B reptiles   **D** fossils

13. To find the absolute age of a rock, scientists use _____.
  A radioactive uranium   **C** the principle of superposition
  B relative dating   **D** crosscutting relationships

14. To find the relative age of a rock, scientists use _____.
  A carbon-14   **C** the principle of superposition
  B radioactive uranium   **D** half-lives

15. During the _____ Era, dinosaurs and other reptiles were the major forms of life on the earth.
  A Mesozoic   **C** Precambrian
  B Paleozoic   **D** Cenozoic

16. A radioactive element decays to form _____.
  A an index fossil   **C** carbon-14
  B petrified wood   **D** another element

17. According to the principle of crosscutting relationships, a rock feature that cuts across other rock layers is _____ than the rock layers.
  A older   **B** younger   **C** harder   **D** sharper

18. During the Cenozoic Era, the Great Lakes basins were carved out by _____.
  A glaciers   **B** rivers   **C** wind   **D** mudslides

Critical Thinking

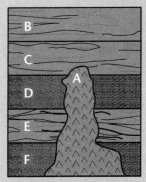

Write the answer to each of the following questions.

19. In the diagram, which lettered rocks are younger than rock D? Explain your answer in terms of two scientific principles.

20. An organism dies and becomes a fossil. Later scientists discover the fossil and find it contains 100 units of carbon-14 and 300 units of nitrogen-14. How many half-lives have occurred? How many years ago did the organism die?

Test-Taking Tip | Before you begin a test, look it over quickly. Try to set aside enough time to complete each section.

The Earth's Water

Earth is called the water planet for a good reason. More than 70 percent of the earth's surface is covered with water. Water is also in the atmosphere and under the ground. All of this water is continuously moving. For example, ocean water evaporates into the air. Clouds gather and carry this moisture. Eventually, water droplets in clouds fall back to the earth. In Chapter 14, you will learn how water moves and changes. You will also learn about different bodies of water, such as rivers, lakes, and oceans.

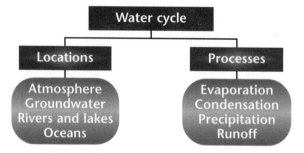

Organize Your Thoughts

Water cycle

Locations — Processes

Atmosphere
Groundwater
Rivers and lakes
Oceans

Evaporation
Condensation
Precipitation
Runoff

Goals for Learning

◆ To explain the water cycle

◆ To compare fresh water and salt water

◆ To describe the sources and movement of fresh water

◆ To explain the water table

◆ To describe ocean water, waves, currents, and the ocean floor

◆ To identify three major groups of ocean life

Objectives

After reading this lesson, you should be able to

◆ describe the movement of water through the water cycle.

◆ explain how groundwater moves and forms the water table.

◆ describe springs, geysers, and caves.

◆ describe how runoff creates rivers, drainage basins, and lakes.

◆ identify three purposes of reservoirs.

Water cycle
_____

Movement of water between the atmosphere and the earth's surface

Groundwater
_____

Water that sinks into the ground

Runoff
_____

Water that runs over the earth's surface and flows into streams

Water is everywhere. Almost all of the earth's water is in the oceans. But it is also in rivers and lakes, under the ground, in the air, and even in your own body.

Earth's water is in continuous motion. It moves from the atmosphere to the earth's surface and back to the atmosphere. This movement of water is called the **water cycle**. Study the diagram below and notice the different forms that water takes as it goes through a complete cycle.

The water cycle is powered by the sun. Heat from the sun evaporates surface water, and the water vapor rises into the atmosphere. The rising water vapor cools and condenses into clouds. Water droplets or ice crystals in the clouds grow larger, then fall to the earth as precipitation.

What happens after precipitation falls? Some of it sinks into the ground and becomes **groundwater**. This water collects in the spaces between rocks and moves slowly underground. Precipitation that does not sink into the ground is called surface water. Some surface water evaporates. But most of it becomes **runoff**—surface water that flows over the land and into streams and rivers.

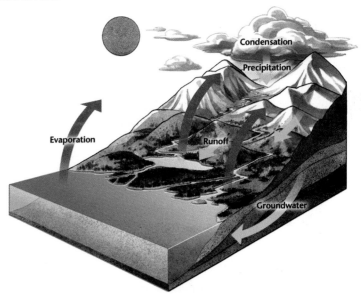

As water travels through the water cycle, it carries dissolved gases and minerals. For example, lake and ocean water contains dissolved oxygen gas. That is what fish "breathe" through their gills.

Why doesn't all precipitation sink into the ground? There are three main reasons.

1. The ground may be saturated, or completely soaked, and unable to hold any more water. It is like pouring water on a sponge. Eventually, the sponge fills and water runs off it.

2. On a slope, the water may run off too quickly to sink in.

3. The ground may not have enough vegetation to stop the water from flowing elsewhere. Plants and their roots soak up water.

Eventually, surface water evaporates or rivers carry it to the oceans. If you have ever tasted ocean water, you know it is much too salty to drink. Salt water also cannot be used for farms and industry. Salt water kills most land plants and ruins machinery. In Lesson 3, you will learn more about the properties of salt water.

Like the water on land, ocean water evaporates and moves back into the atmosphere. Dissolved salts are left behind, however. So the water that condenses in the atmosphere and falls onto the land contains no salt. It is fresh water.

Science in Your Life

How much water do you use?

Probably more than you think. The table lists the average amount of water used for different tasks. Estimate how much water you have used so far today. Think about ways to cut down on the water you use. Then make a water budget by planning the amount of water you will "spend" each week.

Water Uses	
Task	**Average Amount Used**
drinking water	2 liters per person per day
flushing a toilet	11 to 19 liters per flush
taking a shower	19 liters per minute
taking a bath	133 to 152 liters per bath
washing hands	1 liter
watering a lawn	912 liters per half hour

Sources of Fresh Water

Fresh water is an important resource. Think of the many ways you use it every day, such as for drinking, washing, and cooking. Farms and industry, however, use 90 percent of the fresh water consumed in the United States. Fresh water can be found in many places, both above and below the ground.

Groundwater

Groundwater starts as precipitation or runoff that soaks into the earth. The water can sink into the ground because most soil is **porous**, or has spaces between its particles. Loose soil, such as sandy soil or soil with a lot of decayed plant material, is very porous. The rocks beneath the soil may also be porous. Water trickles around broken rock pieces and through cracks.

As water continues downward, it comes to a solid rock layer through which it cannot move. Groundwater collects on top of the rock layer, filling the spaces above it. The top of this wet earth layer is the **water table**. If you drill a well down past the water table, water flows into the well and can be pumped to the surface. About half the drinking water in the United States comes from groundwater.

Springs, Geysers, and Caves

The water under the ground is moving. Groundwater flows out of the ground as a natural **spring**. Certain springs, called **geysers**, shoot water and steam into the air. Geysers occur where groundwater lies close to hot rock or magma. Pockets of groundwater are heated and turned to steam. The steam rises, pushing the hot water above it. The steam and water erupt as a geyser.

Moving groundwater may seep through cracks in limestone, dissolving the rock and forming caves. If the roof of a cave collapses, a funnel-shaped **sinkhole** forms. Sinkholes may fill with groundwater and rain to become ponds.

Rivers and Drainage Basins

Rivers are important sources of fresh water. They provide much of the water that people use every day. Yet rivers make up a tiny percent of the earth's water. Only 3 percent of the earth's water is fresh water. Only 1 percent of all fresh water is not frozen or underground. Of this available fresh water, less than 1 percent is in rivers.

Rivers begin as runoff that moves over the land, carving small paths in the ground. These paths get wider and deeper as water continues to flow through them. The paths become streams. They always flow downhill because of gravity. The streams join and become rivers. These rivers then join and form even larger rivers. Rivers that join other rivers are called **tributaries**. Notice the rivers on the map below. You can see how water and sediment in the most distant tributaries end up in the main river.

The land area in which runoff drains into a river and its tributaries is a **drainage basin**. The map shows five drainage basins. The Mississippi-Missouri River basin covers about 40 percent of the United States. Notice how rain that falls in Montana can eventually reach the Gulf of Mexico. Ridges that separate drainage basins are called **divides**. One divide runs along the Rocky Mountains. Rivers east of this divide flow into the Gulf of Mexico. Rivers west of this divide flow into the Pacific Ocean. What other divide is shown?

Tributary
River that joins another river of equal or greater size

Drainage basin
Land area that is drained by a river and its tributaries

Divide
Ridge that separates drainage basins

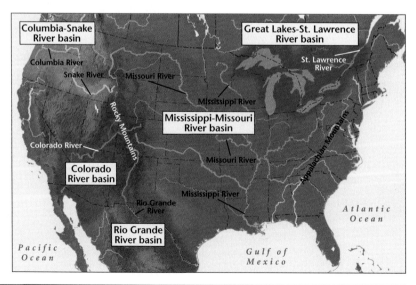

Lakes

Surface water does not always flow along a path. Some of it collects in depressions, or low areas. Water eventually fills the depressions, forming lakes. Even though some of the water evaporates, lakes continue to be fed by precipitation, runoff, springs, and rivers. Many lakes also lose water through outflowing streams or moving groundwater.

Lakes are many different sizes. For example, some lakes in Wisconsin are only a few meters deep. You can hear people talking from the opposite shore. The Great Lakes, on the other hand, are so wide that you cannot see across them. Lake Superior is the largest freshwater lake in the world. Its deepest point is about 400 meters. Many of the lakes in the northern United States and Canada formed when huge sheets of moving ice carved out depressions.

Reservoirs

Many cities store large supplies of fresh water in artificial lakes called **reservoirs**. Reservoirs are made by constructing dams along rivers. Water backs up behind the dam, turning part of the river into a lake. Reservoirs serve several purposes.

Reservoirs store water for home use, farming, and industry. This water can be piped to dry areas. Much of southern California's water, for example, comes through a canal from Lake Havasu, a reservoir behind Parker Dam on the Colorado River.

Reservoirs control flooding. During periods of heavy rain and runoff, a reservoir may fill up. This water can be released slowly and safely downstream through gates in the dam.

Reservoirs produce electricity. In a hydroelectric dam, the water moves through generators near the bottom of the dam. The rushing water turns the blades of a turbine, which makes electricity.

Write your answers to these questions on a sheet of paper.

1. How does water move between the atmosphere, the land, and bodies of water?

2. What is the difference between groundwater and surface water?

3. What is a water table?

4. How can runoff on a mountain end up in an ocean 2,000 kilometers away?

5. How are reservoirs useful?

▼◄▲▼◄▲▼◄▲▼◄▲▼◄▲▼◄▲▼◄▲▼◄▲▼◄▲▼◄▲▼◄▲▼◄▲▼◄▲▼◄▲▼◄▲▼◄▲▼

Science at Work

Hydroelectric Power Plant Operator

Hydroelectric power plant operators manage an entire plant and supervise many people. They control the water flow in the dam and the machinery that generates electricity. This includes gates, valves, turbines, and generators.

Plant operators adjust the plant's power output to meet changing electricity demands. They check water, voltage, and electricity flows. Plant operators maintain and repair equipment. They prepare reports about equipment or performance.

Hydroelectric power plant operators must have at least a high-school diploma. College-level courses in mechanical or technical fields are helpful. Computer, math, and science skills are important. A good plant operator has mechanical ability, is responsible, and understands equipment and safety procedures.

Plant operators must be willing to work under tiring conditions. Their job requires constant attention. They may spend hours sitting or standing at control stations. They also may maintain buildings, grounds, and access roads.

INVESTIGATION

14

Materials

◆ 3 plastic petri dishes

◆ plastic eye dropper

◆ small container of water

◆ petri dish cover

◆ lamp with at least a 60-watt bulb

◆ clock or stopwatch

◆ paper towels

Exploring Evaporation

Purpose

How does heat affect evaporation? In this investigation, you will discover factors that cause evaporation.

Procedure

1. Copy the data table on your paper.

Time	Uncovered Dish	Covered Dish	Uncovered Dish with Lamp
start			
time of evaporation			

2. Place the petri dishes on a tabletop. Use the dropper to place one drop of water in the center of each dish.

3. Place a cover over one of the dishes.

4. Move one of the uncovered dishes at least 50 centimeters away from the other two. Position the lamp directly over this dish, as shown.

5. Turn on the lamp. If you have a clock, record the time. If you have a stopwatch, start the watch. **Safety Alert: The lamp will become very hot. Do not touch the bulb or the lamp.**

6. Observe the three dishes every two minutes. Record the time when each drop evaporates.

7. Clean your work area and return the equipment.

Questions and Conclusions

1. Which drop of water took the longest time to evaporate?

2. Which drop took the shortest time to evaporate?

3. What conclusions can you make about the factors that affect evaporation?

4. What predictions can you make about the evaporation rate on a hot, sunny day and on a cool, cloudy day?

Explore Further

Design an experiment to find out how wind affects evaporation. How could you model wind blowing over a petri dish? How could you vary the amount of wind modeled?

Properties of Ocean Water

Objectives

After reading this lesson, you should be able to

◆ identify two properties of ocean water.

◆ explain what causes ocean waves and currents.

◆ describe several features of the ocean floor.

◆ identify three major groups of ocean life.

The water in the oceans is salt water. The circle graph shows why. Notice that 96.5 percent of ocean water is pure water. But 3.5 percent is dissolved salt. That amount of salt makes a mouthful of ocean water saltier than a mouthful of potato chips. Most of the salt is sodium chloride—common table salt. This salt comes from rocks in the ocean floor. Salt also washes into oceans from rivers.

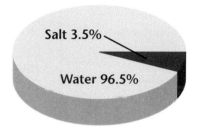

Not all parts of oceans are equally salty. The saltiness, or **salinity**, of ocean water varies. In warm, dry climates, ocean water evaporates quickly. Since salt doesn't evaporate, the salt that remains makes the salinity greater than average. In some oceans, the salinity is less than average. This happens in rainy climates or where rivers and melting ice add fresh water to oceans.

Salinity

Saltiness of water

Ocean water is warmest at the surface where the sun heats it. Near the equator, the surface temperature can reach 30°C. Near the poles, the ocean surface is frozen. The diagram shows average ocean temperatures in a tropical or temperate zone. Notice how the water temperature decreases with depth.

Did You Know?

On average, one cubic meter of ocean water contains about 35 kilograms of salt.

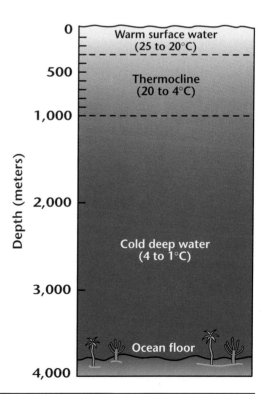

Thermocline

Ocean layer between about 300 and 1,000 meters below the surface, where the temperature drops sharply

Wave

Up-and-down motion of water caused by wind energy moving through the water

Along the edges of oceans are smaller bodies of salt water. They are called gulfs, seas, or bays. The Gulf of Alaska is part of the Pacific Ocean. The Mediterranean Sea is part of the Atlantic Ocean. The word *sea* can also be used in a general sense to mean "ocean."

The temperature is fairly constant near the surface because winds and waves keep the water well-mixed. However, in the **thermocline**, between 300 and 1,000 meters below the surface, the temperature drops sharply. Below the thermocline, the temperature decreases slowly. The bottoms of oceans are near freezing.

Ocean Waves

When you think of oceans, you probably picture **waves**. A wave is the regular up-and-down motion of water caused by energy traveling through the water. A wave gets its energy from wind. When the wind blows, it pushes up the water to start small waves. The waves become larger as the wind blows longer and harder. Most ocean waves are less than three meters high. However, storms can produce waves as high as 30 meters—the height of a 10-story building. No matter what the size, all waves have the parts shown below.

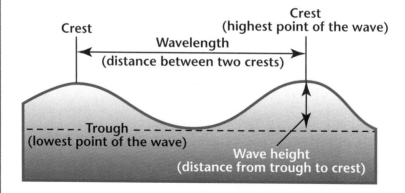

Have you ever seen a leaf bob up and down on passing waves? The waves move forward, but the leaf does not. Although it looks like waves constantly push water forward, the water generally stays in the same place. Only the waves move forward.

As a wave approaches shallow water and a shore, the wave rubs against the ocean floor. Friction slows the bottom of the wave, but the crest keeps moving at the same speed. Therefore, the crest moves ahead of the rest of the wave. The wave tilts forward and tumbles over, or breaks. After a wave breaks on a shore, the water can actually move quite a distance. It may be hurled against rocks or pushed up the slope of a beach.

Ocean Currents

Although waves do not move water, **currents** do. Ocean currents are large streams of water flowing in oceans. Winds cause currents near the ocean surface. Therefore, currents tend to follow the major wind belts. On the map below, trade winds and prevailing westerlies are shown as wide arrows. Major ocean currents are shown as thin arrows. Compare the trade winds with the currents near the equator. Both move westward.

Currents carry warm water from the equator toward the poles and bring cold water back toward the equator. In so doing, currents affect climates on land by warming or cooling the coasts of continents. Both wind and land absorb heat from warm ocean currents.

The Gulf Stream and the North Atlantic Drift are currents that have a warming effect. Find these currents on the map. The Gulf Stream carries warm water from the tropics up along the east coast of North America. The North Atlantic Drift carries this warm water across the Atlantic. It gives western Europe mild summers and winters.

Now locate the California Current on the map. This current carries cold water from high latitudes. It has an "air-conditioned" effect along the west coast of the United States and Mexico.

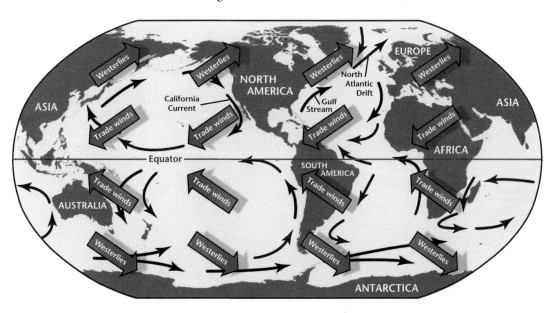

The Ocean Floor

Continental shelf

Part of a continent that extends from a shoreline out into an ocean

Continental slope

Steep slope between the continental shelf and the deep ocean floor

Mid-ocean ridge

Mountain chain on the ocean floor

Seamount

Underwater mountain that is usually a volcano

Trench

Deep valley on the ocean floor

Until the late 1800s, the ocean floor was a great mystery. Today oceanographers use complex technology to measure distances and take pictures underwater. They also travel to the ocean floor. The main features of the ocean floor are listed below and shown in the diagram.

◆ A **continental shelf** is the part of a continent that extends underwater. A continental shelf slopes gently. The average water depth is 130 meters. The average width is 75 kilometers.

◆ A **continental slope** dips sharply from a continental shelf to the deeper ocean floor.

◆ Plains are wide, flat areas where sediment constantly settles. About half of the ocean floor consists of plains. Their average depth is about 4,000 meters.

◆ A **mid-ocean ridge** is an underwater mountain chain. Such a chain may extend for thousands of kilometers along the ocean floor.

◆ A **seamount** is an underwater mountain. Many of these are active or extinct volcanoes. A seamount that rises above sea level forms an island.

◆ A **trench** is a long, deep valley. Trenches are the deepest places on the earth. Some are 10 kilometers deep.

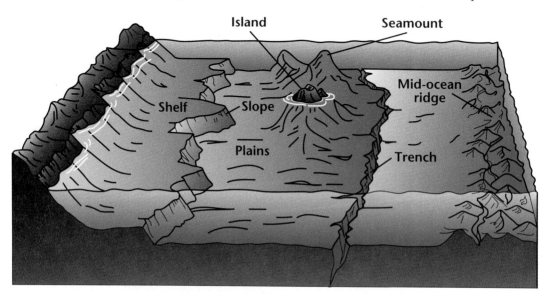

Island   Seamount   Mid-ocean ridge   Shelf   Slope   Plains   Trench

Ocean Life

Ocean environments support a rich variety of living things. Scientists divide these forms of life into three groups, based on how and where they live. Look at the cross section of ocean life below. Which group provides most of the seafood people eat?

Plankton are one form of life in oceans. This group includes tiny plants and animals that float at or near the ocean surface. Plankton are a source of food for larger animals.

Animals that swim freely are classified as **nekton**. This group includes the widest variety of sea creatures, from the tiniest fish to the largest whale.

Organisms that live on the ocean floor are called **benthos**. They do not swim. Some, such as corals, remain in one place their whole lives. Others, such as snails and crabs, crawl along the ocean floor.

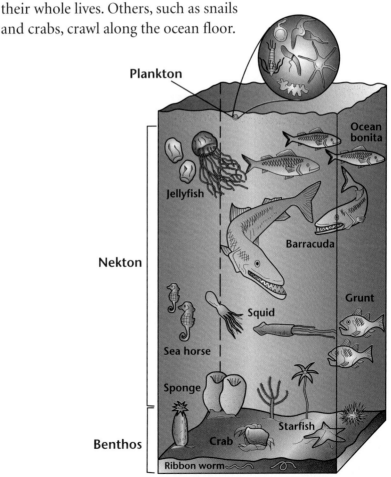

Lesson 2   R E V I E W

Write your answers to these questions on a sheet of paper.

1. What are two sources of salt in ocean water?

2. Describe how water temperature changes with ocean depth.

3. What causes most ocean waves and currents?

4. How do currents affect climate?

5. What are several features of the ocean floor?

Achievements in Science

Protecting the Environment

Today most people know the importance of clean water, land, and air. However, protecting the environment has not always been a popular concern. Before 1960, there were few laws about what people could dump in rivers, on land, or into the air. Thousands of people died from smog, or polluted air, given off by factories in London and in U.S. cities. The Cuyahoga River in Cleveland often caught on fire because of the oil floating in it. Many fish in Lake Erie died because of pollution.

By 1960 the public began to understand how chemicals and other wastes could affect their health and the environment. Rachel Carson was a biologist who helped promote this awareness. In 1962 she wrote a book that warned about the dangers of pest-killing chemicals, or pesticides, on the environment. Her book, *Silent Spring*, had a strong impact on its readers. In fact it led to the banning of DDT and other pesticides.

In 1970 the U.S. Environmental Protection Agency was created to protect people and the environment. Now federal and state laws exist to preserve and improve the quality of our water, land, and air.

Chapter 14 SUMMARY

- Water moves between the land, the atmosphere, and bodies of water in the water cycle.

- The earth's water includes salt water, which is too salty to drink, and fresh water, which does not contain salt. Most of the earth's water is salt water.

- Water under the earth's surface is called groundwater.

- Springs, geysers, and caves are evidence of moving groundwater.

- Groundwater moves downward in the ground and collects to form a soaked layer, the top of which is called the water table.

- Rivers and their tributaries drain runoff from large areas of land called drainage basins.

- Lakes form when water collects in a depression on land.

- Reservoirs are lakes made when people dam a river. Reservoirs store water, control flooding, and produce electricity.

- Ocean water is salt water because it contains dissolved salt.

- The temperature of ocean water decreases with depth.

- A wave is the up-and-down motion of water caused by energy from the wind.

- Currents move ocean water. Currents are caused by winds and follow the same general pattern as global winds.

- Features of the ocean floor include continental shelves and slopes, mid-ocean ridges, trenches, seamounts, and plains.

- Ocean life includes floating plankton, free-swimming nekton, and ocean floor-dwelling benthos.

Science Words

benthos, 327	drainage basin, 318	porous, 317	thermocline, 324
continental shelf, 326	geyser, 317	reservoir, 319	trench, 326
continental slope, 326	groundwater, 315	runoff, 315	tributary, 318
current, 325	mid-ocean ridge, 326	salinity, 323	water cycle, 315
divide, 318	nekton, 327	seamount, 326	water table, 317
	plankton, 327	sinkhole, 317	wave, 324
		spring, 317	

Chapter 14 R E V I E W

Word Bank

continental shelf

drainage basin

geyser

mid-ocean ridge

salinity

trench

tributary

water table

Vocabulary Review

Choose the word or phrase from the Word Bank that best completes each sentence. Write the answer on your paper.

1. A river that flows into another river is a _____.

2. The land area in which runoff flows into a river and its tributaries is a _____.

3. Underground water forms a soaked layer, the top of which is the _____.

4. Heated groundwater blasts out of the ground at a _____.

5. A deep valley on the ocean floor is called a _____.

6. A mountain chain on the ocean floor is called a _____.

7. Water with more salt has greater _____ than water with less salt.

8. A _____ extends from a shoreline out into an ocean.

Concept Review

Choose the word or phrase that best completes each sentence. Write the letter of the answer on your paper.

9. In the water cycle, water moves from oceans to the atmosphere by _____.

   A evaporation   **C** precipitation

   B condensation   **D** runoff

10. The water cycle is powered by _____.

   A oceans and rivers   **C** the water table

   B precipitation   **D** the sun's heat

11. Precipitation that doesn't evaporate or sink into the ground _____.

   A is not part of the water cycle

   B becomes groundwater

   C flows out of the ground as a spring

   D flows into streams as runoff

12. As ocean water deepens, its temperature _____.
    A gets warmer   **C** stays the same
    B gets colder   **D** varies

13. Artificial lakes that supply fresh water, control flooding, and produce electricity are called _____.
    A water tables   **C** drainage basins
    B reservoirs   **D** tributaries

14. The top of a wave is the _____.
    A trough   **B** wave height   **C** crest   **D** seamount

15. Ocean currents are caused by _____.
    A waves   **B** tides   **C** winds   **D** runoff

16. Underwater mountains, or _____, may rise above the ocean's surface to form islands.
    A seamounts   **B** trenches   **C** ridges   **D** plains

17. Moisture that sinks into the ground is called _____.
    A plankton   **C** surface water
    B groundwater   **D** a reservoir

Critical Thinking

Write the answer to each of the following questions.

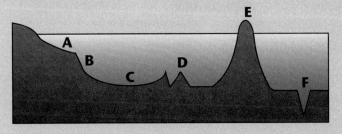

18. Refer to the diagram. Name each lettered feature of the ocean floor.

19. After a dry summer, water no longer comes up through a well. What has happened?

20. One way to make salt water fit to drink is to heat it and collect the water vapor. How is this like the water cycle?

Test-Taking Tip Before writing out an answer on a test, read the question twice to make sure you understand what it is asking.

15

The Earth's Atmosphere

The earth's atmosphere is all around us. The air we breathe is part of the atmosphere. The clouds in the sky are part of the atmosphere. Rainbows remind us that the atmosphere contains moisture. When sunlight passes through water droplets in the air, the different colors that make up the light separate. We see this separation of light as a rainbow. In Chapter 15, you will learn about the gases and layers that make up our atmosphere. You will also learn about clouds, precipitation, and wind patterns.

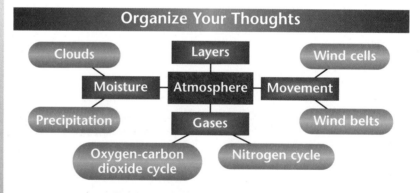

Organize Your Thoughts

Clouds

Layers

Wind cells

Moisture — Atmosphere — Movement

Precipitation

Gases

Wind belts

Oxygen-carbon dioxide cycle

Nitrogen cycle

Goals for Learning

◆ To explain what the earth's atmosphere is

◆ To explain how gases in the air cycle through the environment

◆ To describe the structure of the atmosphere

◆ To classify clouds

◆ To explain how precipitation forms

◆ To describe the earth's wind patterns

Objectives

After reading this lesson, you should be able to

◆ identify the gases in the atmosphere.

◆ describe the oxygen-carbon dioxide cycle.

◆ describe the nitrogen cycle.

◆ identify the four layers of the atmosphere.

◆ name one characteristic of each layer.

Atmosphere

Layer of gases that surrounds the earth

What basic things do you need in order to live? At the top of the list is the air you breathe. When you breathe in (inhale), you take in gases that your body needs to work. When you breathe out (exhale), you release gases that are needed by other living things.

The layer of gases that surrounds the earth is called the **atmosphere**. Most people simply refer to the atmosphere as the air. Although some other planets have atmospheres, ours is the only one known to support life.

The earth's atmosphere contains many different gases. Some of these gases are elements. Others are compounds. From the circle graph, you can see that oxygen and nitrogen make up most of the earth's atmosphere. What other gases are in the air you breathe?

Oxygen and nitrogen are needed by all living things. Plants and animals take these gases from the atmosphere, use them, and then return them to the atmosphere. Oxygen and nitrogen go through these natural cycles over and over.

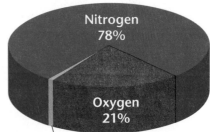

Nitrogen 78%

Oxygen 21%

Argon, carbon dioxide, water vapor, neon, helium, krypton, xenon, methane, hydrogen, ozone 1%

The Oxygen-Carbon Dioxide Cycle

Oxygen and carbon dioxide circulate between living things and the atmosphere. When animals and people breathe in air, their bodies use the oxygen to change the food they eat into energy. When they breathe out, they release carbon dioxide into the air. Plants take in this carbon dioxide. They use carbon dioxide, water, and the sun's energy to make sugar and oxygen. Plants use or store the sugar, but release the oxygen into the air. Animals and people take in this oxygen, and the cycle continues.

The Nitrogen Cycle

Nitrogen also cycles through the environment, as shown below. All living things need nitrogen. Most living things cannot use nitrogen gas directly from the air. However, bacteria in the soil can use this form of nitrogen. These organisms change nitrogen gas into chemical compounds that plants use. Animals take in nitrogen when they feed on plants or on plant-eating animals. Nitrogen is returned to the soil in animal waste. Nitrogen is also returned to the soil when plants and animals die. Bacteria in the soil break down these wastes, releasing nitrogen into the air and into the soil. The return of nitrogen gas to the atmosphere allows the cycle to continue.

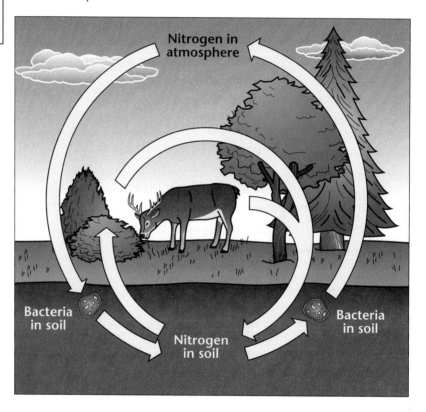

Layers of the Atmosphere

Imagine four glass balls, one inside the other. Now picture the earth at the very center of the glass balls. You've just imagined a model of the earth and its atmosphere. The atmosphere consists of four layers. Refer to the diagram below as you read about each one.

You live in the **troposphere**, the bottom layer of the atmosphere. The troposphere extends from the earth's surface upward to about 16 kilometers. Air particles are packed more tightly in this layer than in other layers because of the weight of the air above. Therefore, even though the troposphere is the smallest of the four layers, it contains 75 percent of the air particles in the entire atmosphere.

Air gets colder and thinner, or less dense, as you go higher in the troposphere. That's why mountain climbers often need extra clothing and oxygen tanks when they climb. The troposphere is characterized by up-and-down as well as side-to-side air movements, or air currents. Most of the clouds you see in the sky are in the troposphere.

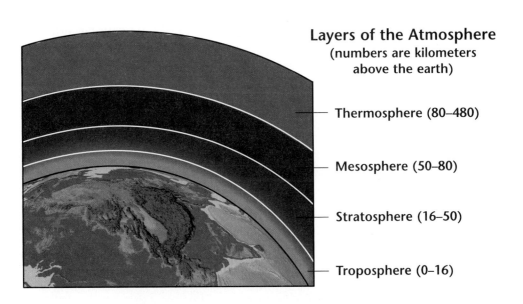

Layers of the Atmosphere
(numbers are kilometers above the earth)

Thermosphere (80–480)

Mesosphere (50–80)

Stratosphere (16–50)

Troposphere (0–16)

Clouds and weather activity occur in the troposphere. Airplanes, especially jets, usually fly in the stratosphere. Satellites orbit well above the ionosphere.

The **stratosphere** is above the troposphere. It extends from about 16 to 50 kilometers above the earth's surface. The stratosphere is clear and dry. Temperature increases with increasing height in the stratosphere. The ozone layer is in the lower half of the stratosphere. The ozone layer is important because it absorbs harmful radiation from the sun.

Above the stratosphere is the **mesosphere**. Here, temperature decreases with increasing height. The mesosphere is the coldest layer of the atmosphere. It is located from about 50 to 80 kilometers above the earth's surface.

The outermost layer is called the **thermosphere**. The air is the thinnest here. Temperature increases with height. It can reach 2,000°C because nitrogen and oxygen atoms absorb the sun's energy. This energy strips electrons from these atoms, making them electrically charged particles, or ions. Most of these ions are found between 60 and 300 kilometers above the earth. Therefore, this section of the atmosphere is called the **ionosphere**.

If you have ever wondered how you are able to pick up a radio station hundreds of kilometers away, the answer is the ionosphere. AM radio waves bounce off the ions in the ionosphere and travel back to the earth. As the diagram shows, this reflection of waves can carry radio messages great distances. This is especially true at night, when the sun's energy does not cause interference.

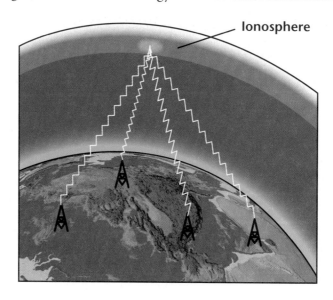

Ionosphere

Lesson 1   R E V I E W

Write your answers to these questions on a sheet of paper.

1. What are the two main gases in the atmosphere?

2. What living things in soil are needed to change nitrogen into a form plants can use?

3. Describe the four layers of the atmosphere.

4. Where is the ozone layer?

5. Why is part of the atmosphere called the ionosphere?

Science in Your Life

Is ozone a protector or a pollutant?

Ozone makes up a tiny but important part of the atmosphere. Ozone is a form of oxygen. A thin layer of ozone high in the atmosphere absorbs ultraviolet radiation from the sun. This prevents most of the radiation from reaching the earth. This radiation can cause sunburn and skin cancer.

People have damaged this protective ozone layer. For example, certain gases from spray cans and refrigeration equipment drift high into the atmosphere and break down ozone. Laws now limit the use of such gases.

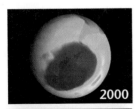
2000

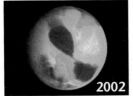
2002

Scientists have been monitoring a hole that has appeared in the ozone layer over Antarctica. In 2000, this hole reached a size of 17.6 million square kilometers. But in 2002, the Antarctic ozone hole decreased to 9.6 million square kilometers. It also split into two separate holes.

Ozone holes in the atmosphere are harmful. But too much ozone at the earth's surface is also harmful. Ozone is one of the ingredients of smog. This hazy mixture of gases damages people's lungs and worsens heart disease. How does ozone collect at ground level? It is made by people. Factories make and use ozone for cleaning flour, oil, fabrics, and water. Car exhaust also releases ozone.

Evaporate

Change from a liquid to a gas

Water vapor

Water in the form of a gas

Condense

Change from a gas to a liquid

Have you ever seen your breath on a cold day? You are seeing a cloud. It forms the same way as a cloud in the sky.

How Clouds Form

Much of the earth's surface is covered with water. The sun's heat causes some of this liquid water to **evaporate**, or change into a gas. This gas, called **water vapor**, becomes part of the air. When this air is heated, it becomes less dense than the surrounding air. Therefore, the heated air rises, taking the water vapor with it. As the air continues to rise, it cools. Then the water vapor **condenses**, or changes back to liquid water. The droplets of water are so tiny that they stay afloat in the air. Billions of tiny droplets form a cloud, as shown in the left diagram.

The right diagram below shows that clouds also form when air containing water vapor is forced up a mountainside. As the air rises, it cools. The water vapor condenses into tiny droplets of water to form clouds. The tops of some mountains are often hidden in clouds.

So how is a cloud like the breath you can see? Air in your lungs contains water vapor. When you breathe out, the vapor meets the cold air outside and condenses into tiny droplets—a cloud.

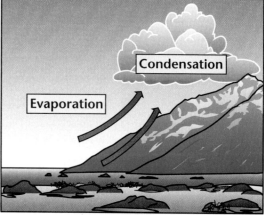

Types of Clouds

Clouds are grouped according to their shape and **altitude**, or height above the earth's surface. There are three basic types of clouds.

Stratus clouds are low, flat clouds that form in layers. Their altitude is less than 2,000 meters. These clouds are wider than they are high, often covering the entire sky like a blanket. Often, you can see only their gray bottoms because they block out much of the sunlight. Stratus clouds often bring rain.

The droplets of most clouds are small enough to stay in the air, suspended by air currents. But if the droplets grow large enough, they fall to the earth. Any moisture that falls from the atmosphere to the earth's surface is called **precipitation**. There are several kinds of precipitation, including rain, sleet, snow, and hail.

A stratus cloud near the ground is **fog**. How does this kind of cloud form? Without sunlight, the ground cools quickly at night. The cold ground cools the air directly above it. If the water vapor in this air condenses, a cloud forms. Fog usually develops in the early morning after a clear, calm, cold night. Fog settles in low areas. Sometimes fog forms over warm bodies of water.

Stratus clouds are flat and low in the sky.

Cumulus cloud

Puffy, white cloud occurring at medium altitudes

Cirrus cloud

High, wispy cloud made of ice crystals

Cumulus clouds are puffy, white clouds at altitudes from 2,000 to 7,000 meters. They look like piles of cotton balls. You can usually see their sides and tops shining brilliant white in sunlight. Their shaded bottoms are flat and may look gray. Cumulus clouds are often seen in fair weather.

When you think of clouds, you probably picture white, puffy cumulus clouds like these.

Cirrus clouds look like thin, wispy streaks high in the sky. Their altitude ranges from 7,000 to 13,000 meters. They are made of ice crystals instead of water droplets because the air at that altitude is below freezing. Cirrus clouds often accompany fair weather, but they may mean rain or snow is on the way.

Thin, wispy cirrus clouds are made of ice crystals.

Lesson 2 REVIEW

Write your answers to these questions on a sheet of paper.

1. What is a cloud?

2. Describe two ways that clouds form.

3. Explain how fog forms.

4. Compare cumulus and cirrus clouds.

5. Name and describe the type of cloud that may indicate rain.

Achievements in Science

Balloon Pilots

Aeronauts, or balloon pilots, have been challenging the atmosphere for hundreds of years. In 1783, the first hot-air balloon to fly with passengers was built by the Montgolfier brothers in France. The passengers included a duck, a rooster, and a sheep. Following the historic 8-minute flight, all three landed safely.

To launch their cloth-and-paper balloon, the brothers placed it over a fire. They thought the balloon flew because it was filled with smoke. They didn't understand that the key to flight was hot air. Hot air is less dense than cool air. Because hot air in a balloon is lighter than the air outside it, the balloon rises.

Since then, aeronauts have also piloted gas balloons. These are balloons filled with a light gas such as hydrogen. The record holders for the highest gas-balloon flight are two United States Navy officers. In 1961, they reached the middle of the stratosphere, more than 34 kilometers above the earth.

The Earth's Atmosphere   *Chapter 15*   **341**

Making a Model of Rain

Purpose

How does a raindrop form? In this investigation, you will make a model of water droplets and observe how they combine.

Procedure

1. Copy the data table on your paper.

Spray Number	Description of Mist on Surface	Number of Running Droplets
1		
2		
3		
4		
5		

2. Cover your work surface with newspaper. Use the books to prop open the binder cover as shown in the figure on page 343. The plastic surface should make a slope.

3. Adjust the mister nozzle to produce a fine mist. Hold the mister about 30 centimeters from the plastic surface. Then gently spray the surface just once with the mister. **Safety Alert: Wipe up any spills immediately.**

4. Using a magnifying glass, look closely at the mist on the surface. Notice the different sizes of water droplets. In your data table, describe the mist. Count any water droplets running down the slope. Record this in your data table.

5. Repeat steps 3 and 4 at least four more times.

6. Use the paper towels to dry all wet surfaces. Clean your work area and return the equipment.

Materials

- newspaper
- books
- plastic binder (or other flat, plastic surface)
- spray mister containing water
- magnifying glass
- paper towels

Questions and Conclusions

1. How many times did you spray before one droplet ran down the surface?

2. How did the size of the mist droplets on the plastic surface change?

3. How does this activity model raindrops forming?

Explore Further

Use a mister to repeat this investigation on an inside wall of a freezer. Compare your observations with the observations made at room temperature.

Objectives

After reading this lesson, you should be able to

◆ explain what causes air to move.

◆ recognize how air moves in wind cells.

◆ identify three wind belts.

Wind cell

Continuous cycle of rising warm air and falling cold air

When you see a flag waving or leaves blowing, you know that moving air is moving these objects. But what do you think starts the air moving?

Wind Cells

The earth's atmosphere is constantly in motion. Moving air is known as wind. The motion of air is caused by unequal heating of the earth's surface by the sun. When the sun's energy heats air, the air expands because the air particles are moving farther apart. This makes the warmed air lighter, or less dense, than the cold air around it. The lighter air begins to rise. Then cold air moves in to take the place of the rising air. The new air is then warmed. This cycle of air flow is called a **wind cell**. As the diagram shows, a wind cell is a continuous cycle of rising warm air and falling cold air.

On the earth, some of the warmest air is near the equator. Warm air near the equator rises. It moves toward the North Pole and the South Pole. As the air gets closer to the poles, it becomes colder. The cold air falls back to the earth and moves back toward the equator. As this air warms up, the cycle repeats.

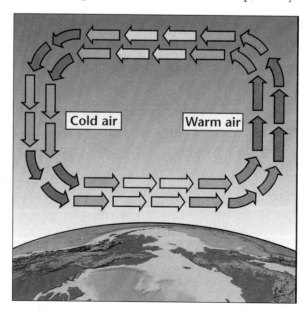

Cold air   Warm air

Global Winds

Wind belt

Pattern of wind movement around the earth

Trade wind

Strong, reliable wind just north or south of the equator; blows from the east

Prevailing westerly

Wind generally between 30°N and 60°N latitudes (or 30°S and 60°S); blows from the west

Polar easterly

Wind near a pole; blows from the east

Winds move around the earth in patterns called **wind belts**. The two wind belts just north and south of the equator are known as **trade winds**. These winds blow from the northeast in the Northern Hemisphere and from the southeast in the Southern Hemisphere. Trade winds are strong and reliable. They have been called trade winds since the days when trading ships were powered by wind alone. The captains of those sailing ships sought out the steady trade winds to help them on their way. Hawaii lies within this wind belt.

Most of the United States and southern Canada are affected by the northern belt of the **prevailing westerlies**. They usually blow from west to east, the opposite direction of trade winds. Prevailing westerlies are not as predictable as the winds in other belts.

Wind belts also blow from the poles toward warmer latitudes. Winds in these belts are called **polar easterlies**. They move from east to west, like trade winds. Polar easterlies bring cold, stormy weather. Most of Alaska lies within this wind belt.

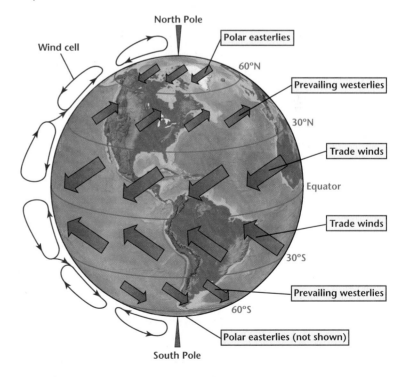

Write your answers to these questions on a sheet of paper.

1. What causes air to move?

2. What is a wind cell?

3. Where is the earth's warmest air?

4. Where are trade winds found? From what direction do they blow?

5. Does the weather in the United States and southern Canada usually move to the east or to the west? Why?

▼◄▲▼◄▲▼◄▲▼◄▲▼◄▲▼◄▲▼◄▲▼◄▲▼◄▲▼◄▲▼◄▲▼◄▲▼

Science at Work

Environmental Science Technician

Environmental science technicians perform tests to identify and measure pollution in air, water, or soil. They collect samples to test. They look for ways to reduce or prevent pollution. Environmental science technicians also manage and control hazardous wastes. They make sure pollution laws are carefully followed.

Environmental science technicians use science and mathematics to solve problems. They use laboratory equipment to perform tests or analyze samples. They often use computers. They keep detailed reports and interpret data.

Some environmental science technicians have a bachelor's degree in chemistry, biology, or environmental science. Others have two years of specialized training or an associate degree in a field of applied science. Successful environmental science technicians are organized, enjoy detailed tasks, and can interpret and communicate scientific results. They are often very concerned about protecting the environment.

Chapter 15 SUMMARY

- The atmosphere is the layer of gases that surrounds the earth.

- The earth's atmosphere consists mostly of the elements nitrogen and oxygen.

- Oxygen and nitrogen move between the atmosphere and living things through the oxygen-carbon dioxide cycle and the nitrogen cycle.

- The four layers of the atmosphere are the troposphere, stratosphere, mesosphere, and thermosphere.

- The ozone layer is in the stratosphere.

- The ionosphere is located in the upper mesosphere and lower thermosphere. It contains ions, which are positively charged particles.

- Clouds are masses of water droplets or ice crystals in the atmosphere.

- Clouds form in the atmosphere when water evaporates into the air and then cools and condenses.

- Three main types of clouds are stratus, cumulus, and cirrus. Fog is a stratus cloud near the ground.

- Precipitation is moisture that falls to the earth from the atmosphere. It may fall as rain, snow, sleet, or hail.

- The sun's unequal heating of the earth's surface causes wind.

- Continuous cycles of rising warm air and falling cold air occur in the atmosphere and are known as wind cells.

- Trade winds, prevailing westerlies, and polar easterlies make up the earth's major wind belts.

- Prevailing westerlies carry weather from west to east.

Science Words

altitude, 339	fog, 339	prevailing westerly, 345	trade wind, 345
atmosphere, 333	ionosphere, 336	stratosphere, 336	troposphere, 335
cirrus cloud, 340	mesosphere, 336	stratus cloud, 339	water vapor, 338
condense, 338	polar easterly, 345	thermosphere, 336	wind belt, 345
cumulus cloud, 340	precipitation, 339	troposphere, 335	wind cell, 344
evaporate, 338			

Vocabulary Review

Choose the word or phrase from the Word Bank that best matches each phrase. Write the answer on your paper.

Word Bank

altitude

cirrus clouds

condenses

evaporates

polar easterlies

precipitation

stratus clouds

trade winds

water vapor

wind belt

1. steady winds north and south of the equator

2. height above the earth's surface

3. water that falls from the atmosphere

4. what water vapor does to become cloud droplets

5. what liquid water does to become water vapor

6. gas form of water

7. winds near the poles that blow from the east

8. pattern of wind movement around the earth

9. low, flat, gray clouds

10. high, wispy clouds

Concept Review

11. Refer to the diagram. Name each lettered layer of the atmosphere. Write your answers on your paper.

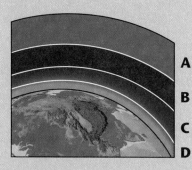

Choose the word or phrase that best completes each sentence. Write the letter of the answer of your paper.

12. Gases that cycle between the atmosphere and living things include _____.
    A oxygen, carbon dioxide, and nitrogen
    B methane, hydrogen, and helium
    C argon, neon, and ozone
    D nitrogen, xenon, and oxygen

13. The _____ reflects radio signals.
    A troposphere   C mesosphere
    B stratosphere   D ionosphere

14. The _____ is important because it absorbs most of the harmful ultraviolet radiation from the sun.
   A troposphere   **C** mesosphere
   B ozone layer   **D** ionosphere

15. Fluffy, white clouds are called _____.
   A cirrus clouds   **C** cumulus clouds
   B stratus clouds   **D** rain clouds

16. Unequal heating of the earth's surface by the sun causes _____.
   A formation of cumulus clouds
   B wind
   C rain
   D condensation of water vapor

17. A continuous cycle of rising warm air and falling cold air is called _____.
   A water vapor   **C** the nitrogen cycle
   B a thunderstorm   **D** a wind cell

18. The prevailing westerlies are _____.
   A winds coming from the west
   B the wind belts nearest the equator
   C trade winds
   D winds blowing to the west

Critical Thinking

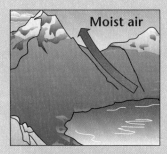

Moist air

Write the answer to each of the following questions.

19. When a rain forest is destroyed, how does this affect the composition of the atmosphere?

20. Moist air is pushed up a mountainside, as shown. How might the weather on the right side of the mountain be different from that on the left side?

Test-Taking Tip   Do not wait until the night before a test to study. Plan your study time so that you can get a good night's sleep before a test.

Weather and Climate

W eather takes many different forms. One form of severe weather begins as a tropical storm over an ocean. As the storm gains energy, it becomes a spinning hurricane. The center, or eye, of a hurricane is surrounded by swirling white masses of clouds. In Chapter 16, you will learn about different weather conditions and how they are measured. You also will explore weather patterns and climate zones.

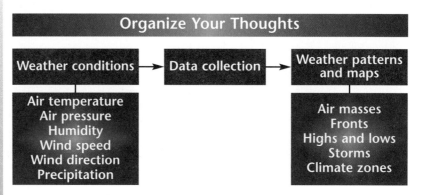

Organize Your Thoughts

Weather conditions → Data collection → Weather patterns and maps

Air temperature
Air pressure
Humidity
Wind speed
Wind direction
Precipitation

Air masses
Fronts
Highs and lows
Storms
Climate zones

Goals for Learning

◆ To describe weather conditions

◆ To identify instruments that measure weather conditions

◆ To explain how fronts, highs, and lows affect weather

◆ To read a weather map

◆ To describe various kinds of storms

◆ To describe the earth's major climates

Weather

State of the atmosphere at a given time and place

Look out the window. Is it a cloudy day? Is it windy? *Cloudy* and *windy* refer to conditions of the atmosphere. **Weather** is the state of the atmosphere at a given time and place.

The weather is always changing because conditions in the atmosphere are always changing. A meteorologist measures these conditions, looks for patterns, and uses this information to predict the weather.

Air Temperature

One of the first weather conditions you hear on a weather report is the temperature of the air. Air temperature is measured with a thermometer. Most thermometers are made of a thin tube filled with colored alcohol. Heat causes a liquid to expand, or take up more space. So when the air gets warmer, the liquid in the thermometer expands and moves up the tube. If the air gets cooler, the liquid contracts, or takes up less space. Then the liquid moves down the tube.

The unit of measure for temperature is the degree (°). Two scales for measuring temperature are shown in the diagram. People in the United States usually use the Fahrenheit scale. People in most other countries use the Celsius scale. All scientists use the Celsius scale. Compare the common temperatures shown on both scales.

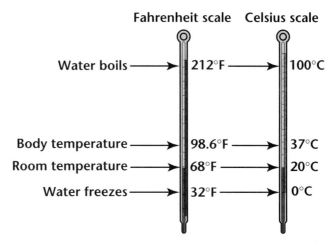

	Fahrenheit scale	Celsius scale
Water boils	212°F	100°C
Body temperature	98.6°F	37°C
Room temperature	68°F	20°C
Water freezes	32°F	0°C

Air Pressure

Think about what happens when you blow air into a balloon. The balloon gets bigger because the air particles push against the inside wall of the balloon. The push, or force, of air against an area is called **air pressure**.

Air in the atmosphere exerts pressure, too. The air above you and around you constantly pushes against your body. You don't feel this pressure because air in your body pushes out with the same amount of force. But what happens if air pressure suddenly changes? For example, while riding upward in an elevator, you may have felt your ears "pop." Your ears pop because they are adjusting to a drop in air pressure. As you move higher in the atmosphere, there is less air present to push on you, so air pressure drops.

Air pressure is measured with an instrument called a **barometer**. Two kinds of barometers are shown here. In a mercury barometer, air pushes down on a dish of mercury, forcing the mercury to rise in a tube. In an aneroid barometer, air pushes on a short metal can. A pointer connected to the can shows the amount of air pressure. Aneroid barometers are lightweight and portable.

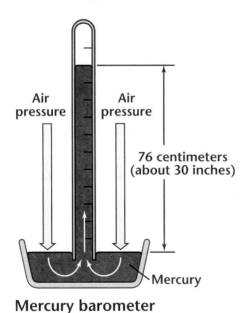

Mercury barometer

Air pressure · Air pressure · 76 centimeters (about 30 inches) · Mercury

Aneroid barometer

Different scales are used to measure air pressure. Most weather reports give the air pressure in inches. Air pressure usually ranges from 29 to 31 inches (74 to 79 centimeters), which is the height of mercury in a mercury barometer.

A change in air pressure indicates a change in weather. A rise in air pressure usually means drier weather is on the way. A drop in air pressure often means precipitation is coming.

Humidity

Have you ever described a hot day as sticky or muggy? Such days are uncomfortable because of high **humidity**. Humidity is the amount of water vapor in the air. When the air contains a lot of water vapor, the humidity is high. The maximum amount of water vapor that the air can hold, or its capacity, depends on the air temperature. Warmer air can hold more water vapor than colder air can.

The amount of water vapor in the air compared to its capacity is called **relative humidity**. It is calculated as a percent. A relative humidity of 50 percent means that the air contains half, or 50 percent, of its water vapor capacity. When the air is completely filled with water vapor and cannot hold more, the relative humidity is 100 percent.

A **psychrometer** is an instrument used to measure relative humidity. It is actually made up of two thermometers. The bulb of one thermometer is covered with a damp cloth. As water evaporates from the cloth, it cools. The temperature of this thermometer is lower than the temperature of the dry thermometer. The lower the humidity, the faster the water evaporates and the lower the temperature drops. The relative humidity is then found by comparing the temperatures of the two thermometers to a special chart.

Wind Speed and Direction

The speed of the wind is an important weather condition. It helps meteorologists predict how fast an approaching storm will arrive. Wind speed is measured with an **anemometer**. An anemometer has three or four arms, with a cup attached to the end of each arm. These cups catch the wind and cause the arms to rotate. When the wind speed increases, the arms rotate faster. This spinning rate may be indicated on a dial or digital display.

The photo below shows a simple anemometer with three arms. It also shows another important weather instrument: a **wind vane**.

A wind vane shows the direction from which the wind is blowing. It is often shaped like an arrow. Wind hits the larger back section of the vane. The vane turns so that it points into the wind.

Wind is named by the direction from which it comes. A wind that moves from north to south is called a north wind. A north wind causes a wind vane to point north.

A quick glance at this anemometer and wind vane will tell you both wind speed and direction.

Rain gauge

Instrument used to measure the amount of rainfall

Did You Know?

The wettest place on the earth is Mount Waialeale. This soggy mountain is on the island of Kauai in Hawaii. It receives about 12 meters of rain a year. This rain comes from trade winds carrying rain clouds up the side of the mountain.

Precipitation

Chapter 15 introduced four kinds of precipitation: rain, snow, sleet, and hail. If any precipitation falls, a weather report usually tells you how much. A **rain gauge** measures the amount of rainfall. As you can see, a rain gauge is a container that collects rain. A scale along the side shows the amount in centimeters or inches. Snow depth is usually measured simply by inserting a meterstick in a flat area of snow. Hail can be measured in two ways: by its depth on the ground and by the diameter of the hailstones.

Rain gauges come in different shapes and sizes. To accurately measure rainfall, rain gauges should be placed in open areas.

Lesson 1 **R E V I E W**

Write your answers to these questions on a sheet of paper.

1. What is weather?

2. How does a thermometer work?

3. What does a change in air pressure tell you about the weather?

4. Why does air pressure drop as you go higher in the atmosphere?

5. What weather condition does each of these instruments measure: barometer, thermometer, rain gauge, anemometer, psychrometer?

▼◄▲▼◄▲▼◄▲▼◄▲▼◄▲▼◄▲▼◄▲▼◄▲▼◄▲▼◄▲▼◄▲▼◄▲▼◄▲▼◄▲▼◄▲▼

Science at Work

Atmospheric Scientist

A scientist who studies the atmosphere is called an atmospheric scientist. These specialists study the atmosphere's properties and patterns. They also study how weather affects the environment and how people affect the atmosphere.

Atmospheric scientists collect air samples and gather data from weather satellites, Doppler radar, and weather balloons. They use this information to create computer models of the atmosphere and to design experiments.

Atmospheric scientists predict long-term weather changes. They research the effect of pollution on clouds. They study how processes in the ocean and on the sun change weather. They design better instruments and give advice to government and industry leaders.

Atmospheric scientists must have at least a bachelor's degree in meteorology, atmospheric science, or a related science field. A graduate degree is often helpful.

People who want to work in this field should have strong computer and mathematics skills. A good atmospheric scientist is creative, patient, organized, and stays up-to-date on research methods.

After reading this lesson, you should be able to

◆ explain how fronts, highs, and lows affect weather.

◆ read the information on a weather map.

◆ describe types of storms

Air mass

Large section of the atmosphere with the same temperature and humidity throughout

Front

Moving boundary line between two air masses

Warm front

Boundary ahead of a warm air mass that is pushing out and riding over a cold air mass

Cold front

Boundary ahead of a cold air mass that is pushing out and wedging under a warm air mass

To predict the weather, meteorologists need data from many places. At about 10,000 weather stations worldwide, measurements are taken at the exact same time several times a day. In the United States, the National Weather Service (NWS) collects these data for meteorologists to use.

Air Masses and Fronts

Weather data from a large area of the earth show meteorologists where **air masses** are located. An air mass is a huge body of the lower atmosphere that has similar temperature and humidity throughout. An air mass can be warm or cold. It can have a lot of water vapor or very little. Air masses are so large that two or three of them can cover the United States. As air masses move, they bring their weather to new places.

A **front** is a moving boundary line between two air masses. A **warm front** occurs where a warm air mass glides up and over a cooler air mass. As the warm air rises, it cools and water vapor condenses. Typically, high cirrus clouds appear. Low stratus clouds follow. The barometer falls continuously, and a period of steady precipitation begins. When the front passes, skies clear and the barometer rises. The temperature rises as warm air replaces the cooler air.

A **cold front** occurs where a cold air mass pushes out and wedges under a warmer air mass. The warm air mass rises quickly. If the warm air mass has a lot of water vapor, towering storm clouds form quickly. Heavy precipitation follows, but only for a short period of time. Several hours after the front passes, the weather becomes clear and cool.

Highs and Lows

High

Cold area of high air pressure

Low

Warm area of low air pressure

Isobar

Line on a weather map connecting areas of equal air pressure

Cold air is more dense than warm air. Therefore, cold air exerts more pressure on the earth's surface than does warm air. A cold air mass, then, is usually an area of high pressure, or a **high**. Highs often have fair weather. Look at the map below. You can see that air moves outward from a high in a clockwise rotation. However, air moves into an area of low pressure, or a **low**. The air coming into a low is warm and rotates counterclockwise. Lows often have clouds and precipitation. On a map, lines called **isobars** connect areas of equal pressure. Isobars form a circular pattern around highs and lows.

In most of the United States and Canada, weather moves from west to east. Therefore, a high passing through Oklahoma may soon pass through Arkansas. The high will likely bring similar weather to both places.

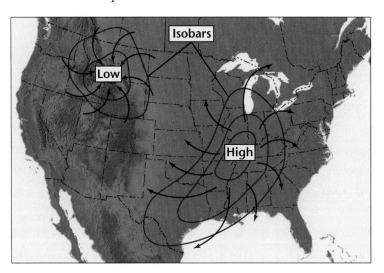

Weather Maps

As you can see, meteorologists must consider a lot of data to develop a weather forecast. They organize these data on weather maps, like the one above. Weather maps generally include information about precipitation, cloud cover, air masses, highs, lows, and fronts. Weather maps may also include isobars, temperatures, wind speeds, and wind directions.

Science Myth

Heat lightning is the result of high temperatures.

Fact: Heat lightning has nothing to do with heat. It is simply lightning from thunderstorms far away. Heat lightning is usually seen close to the horizon. This explains why it appears orange or red. When you look at the horizon, you are looking through the troposphere. The particles in the troposphere scatter the light you see.

Storms

Storms are violent kinds of weather. They are caused by rapid changes in the movement of air masses. Storms usually include precipitation and high winds.

Thunderstorms occur when warm air is forced upward by a cold front. Large, dark, cumulus clouds form. Such clouds are also called thunderheads. These clouds produce heavy rain and sometimes hail. They also produce lightning and thunder. The diagram above shows how lightning forms.

+ = positive electrical charge
− = negative electrical charge

A **tornado** is a small but powerful wind storm with a whirling, funnel-shaped cloud. Tornadoes sometimes form in thunderstorms when warm, humid air rushes up to meet cool, dry air. Tornadoes have very low air pressure and can rotate at speeds up to 450 kilometers per hour. When they touch the ground, they can uproot trees, toss cars, and destroy houses. Tornadoes last for a very short time.

A **hurricane** is a large tropical storm that often covers thousands of square kilometers. Winds spiral toward the center of the storm, with speeds up to 320 kilometers per hour. At the center of a hurricane is an area of calm air called the eye that is surrounded by spiraling clouds.

All hurricanes form over the ocean near the equator. They collect warm, moist air and begin to spin. They grow stronger over the warm tropical water. As hurricanes approach land, their wind pushes the water of the ocean against the shore, and flooding occurs. Hurricanes may drop tremendous amounts of rain as they move inland, causing further damage. Hurricanes lose their force as they continue to move over land because they are no longer fed by the heat and moisture of tropical seas. Friction with the land also slows the winds of the storm.

Lesson 2   R E V I E W

Write your answers to these questions on a sheet of paper.

1. What organization collects and analyzes weather data?

2. How is a cold front different from a warm front?

3. What is the difference between a high and a low?

4. What are isobars?

5. Name three kinds of information found on a weather map.

6. How does a thunderstorm form?

7. What is lightning?

8. What is a tornado?

9. Under what conditions does a hurricane form?

10. What causes a hurricane to lose its force?

Achievements in Science

Doppler Radar

The ability to predict weather events has improved greatly in the last century. Even as recently as 15 years ago, meteorologists could provide only a two-day forecast. Today, improved technology helps them provide a mostly accurate four-day forecast.

One of the tools that meteorologists use is a Doppler radar system. This type of radar uses a high-powered antenna that rotates and sends out radio waves. Some of these waves bounce off raindrops or snowflakes in the air and return to the antenna. A computer detects and measures how these waves have changed. It also measures the time it took for the waves to return. From this information, the computer calculates the distance and direction of the precipitation. Wind speed and direction also can be calculated.

This information is used to create a Doppler map. The map shows the locations and amounts of precipitation. You have probably seen a Doppler map on television weather reports. Meteorologists are trained to use these maps and other resources to understand and predict weather.

Using a Weather Map

Purpose

How can you show weather conditions on a map? In this investigation, you will make and interpret a weather map.

Procedure

1. On your map, copy the weather information from the weather map on page 362. Copy the legend of symbols, too.

2. Show that it is raining across southern Florida.

3. Show that snow is falling in Minnesota and Ontario behind the cold front.

4. Show that a warm front is occurring across Alabama, Georgia, and South Carolina and heading toward Florida.

5. Show that it is now cloudy in Honolulu, Hawaii, and partly cloudy in Juneau, Alaska.

Questions and Conclusions

1. Which cities have clear skies?

2. Which kind of front is heading toward Dallas and Chicago? What kind of weather will these cities have after the front passes them?

3. From your map, predict what will happen to temperatures in Florida tomorrow. Explain your answer.

4. Suggest two more symbols that could be added to your map. Explain the symbols. How do they make the map more useful?

Materials

◆ map without weather symbols

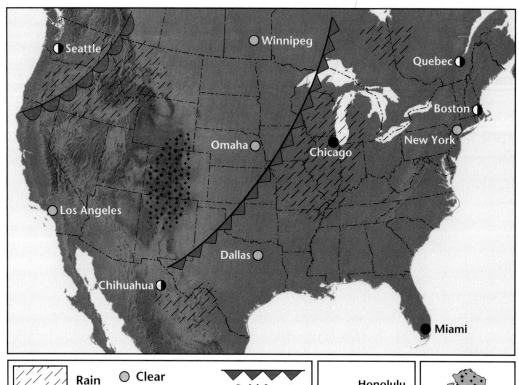

///// Rain	◐ Clear	Cold front	
Snow	◑ Partly cloudy	Warm front	
	● Cloudy		

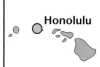

Explore Further

Compare local weather maps for two days in a row. How accurate was the first day's forecast? Did the fronts move as expected? Are there any new fronts? From which direction did they arrive?

Objectives

After reading this lesson, you should be able to

◆ compare and contrast the three world climate zones.

◆ identify factors that affect climate.

What kind of weather do people have on the other side of the world? It may be similar to yours. Scientists have identified global patterns in weather.

Climate Zones

Like weather, **climate** describes conditions of the atmosphere. Weather is the state of the atmosphere at a given time and place. Climate is the average weather of a region over a long period of time. A region's climate depends on two kinds of measurements:

◆ The average temperature pattern during a year
◆ The average amount of precipitation in a year

The climates of the world are divided into three major groups, called climate zones. Find each zone on the map. Refer to this map as you learn more about these zones.

Climate

Average weather of a region over a long period of time

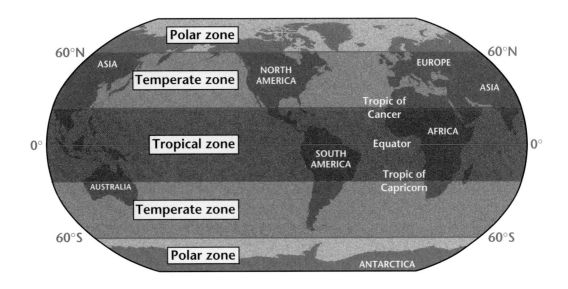

Polar climates are marked by generally cold temperatures. There is little precipitation in these climates, and it is usually in the form of snow. The temperatures are so low that very little snow melts. Polar climates generally extend from the poles to about 60° latitude. They also exist at very high elevations on mountains.

Temperate climates generally extend from 60°N latitude to the tropic of Cancer and from 60°S latitude to the tropic of Capricorn. These climates feature the greatest changes in weather. There are four different weather seasons in these climates, where winters are cold and summers are warm.

Tropical climates occur near the equator between the tropic of Capricorn and the tropic of Cancer. These climates are marked by the highest average temperatures on the earth. Tropical climates are also the most humid regions. There is little variation in the kind of weather from one month to the next.

Each of the three major climate zones are further divided into climate regions. The table on the page 365 provides some information about these regions.

Factors That Affect Climate

Why is one climate different from another? The main factor is the angle at which sunlight hits the earth. Because the earth is a sphere, sunlight hits the tropics more directly than areas toward the poles. The more direct sunlight provides warmer temperatures.

Climate is also affected by how high a place is above sea level. The temperatures in a mountain region are cooler than the temperatures in a nearby valley. In general, higher places tend to be cooler. This is why you can find snow-capped mountains near the equator.

The nearness of large bodies of water also affects climate. In general, areas that are close to an ocean or a large lake get more precipitation than areas farther from water. Water heats up and cools off more slowly than land. As a result, areas near large bodies of water have more mild temperatures than areas far from water.

Polar Climates

Ice cap climate

| Temperatures below freezing | Precipitation less than 25 centimeters per year | No visible plant life |

Tundra climate

| Temperatures slightly higher than ice cap | Precipitation less than 25 centimeters per year | Mosses and small shrubs |

Subarctic climate

| Short summer, cold winter | Precipitation 25–30 centimeters per year | Small pines, spruce, and fir |

Temperate Climates

Marine west coast climate

| Temperatures generally above freezing | Precipitation 50–76 centimeters per year | Thick evergreen forests |

Deserts and steppes

| Warm to hot summer, cold winter | Precipitation less than 25 centimeters per year | Cactus in deserts, grasses in steppes |

Mediterranean climate

| Warm summer, mild and wet winter | Precipitation 25 centimeters per year | Scattered trees, low shrubs |

Humid subtropical climate

| Warm and humid summer, mild winter | Precipitation 76–165 centimeters per year | Heavy plant growth and forests |

Humid continental climate

| Warm and humid summer, cold winter | Precipitation 76 centimeters per year | Hardwood and softwood forests, grass prairies |

Tropical Climates

Tropical rain forest

| Always hot and humid | Precipitation 254 centimeters per year | Very thick forests and plant growth |

Tropical desert

| Dry and relatively hot | Precipitation less than 25 centimeters per year | Almost no plant life |

Savannah

| Humid and warm summer, dry and cool winter | Precipitation 76–152 centimeters per year | Scattered trees and shrubs, tall grasses |

Lesson 3 REVIEW

Write your answers to these questions on a sheet of paper.

1. Where do polar climates occur?

2. Where do tropical climates occur?

3. Which climate zone has warm summers and cold winters?

4. How does height above sea level affect climate?

5. What effect does a large body of water have on climate?

Science in Your Life

What is your climate zone?

Now that you have learned about climate zones, identify the zone you live in. How would you describe the climate in your zone? If you have friends or family who live in other climate zones, compare your zone with theirs. Do you think you'd rather live in their climate zone?

What kinds of severe weather occurs in your climate zone? How would you know if severe weather was predicted for your area? Local newspapers provide important weather information. They may also show radar and satellite images of weather patterns that could affect your area. Radio stations regularly broadcast weather reports.

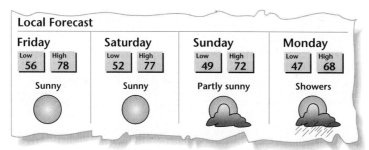

Local Forecast

Friday	Saturday	Sunday	Monday
Low 56 High 78	Low 52 High 77	Low 49 High 72	Low 47 High 68
Sunny	Sunny	Partly sunny	Showers

Are you prepared for severe weather? In your class or at home, discuss what you should do in a weather emergency. How can you prepare now for severe weather?

The Federal Emergency Management Agency recommends that you have a disaster supply kit ready in case of a weather emergency. The kit should include water, a first-aid kit, a flashlight, a radio, a few basic tools, extra clothes, canned food, and a can opener.

Chapter 16 SUMMARY

- Weather is the state of the atmosphere at a given time and place.

- To study weather, meteorologists gather information about air temperature, air pressure, humidity, wind speed, wind direction, type of precipitation, and amount of precipitation.

- A barometer measures air pressure. A psychrometer measures relative humidity. An anemometer measures wind speed. A wind vane shows wind direction.

- An air mass is a large body of air near the earth's surface. It has the same temperature and humidity throughout.

- Fronts are the moving boundaries of air masses.

- At a warm front, warm air glides up and over cooler air. Steady precipitation often results.

- At a cold front, cold air pushes under warmer air. A short storm often results.

- Data about fronts, air masses, highs, and lows are recorded on weather maps and used to predict weather.

- Storms are severe weather conditions and include thunderstorms, tornadoes, and hurricanes.

- Climate is the average weather of a region over a long period of time.

- The major world climates are divided into three zones: polar, temperate, and tropical.

- Climate is affected by the angle of sunlight, height above sea level, and nearness of large bodies of water.

Science Words

air mass, 353	cold front, 357	isobar, 358	tornado, 359
air pressure, 352	front, 357	low, 358	warm front, 357
anemometer, 354	high, 358	psychrometer, 353	weather, 351
barometer, 352	humidity, 353	rain gauge, 355	wind vane, 354
climate, 363	hurricane, 359	relative humidity, 353	

Chapter 16 R E V I E W

Word Bank

air mass

anemometer

barometer

climate

humidity

hurricane

isobar

psychrometer

tornado

weather

Vocabulary Review

Choose the word or phrase from the Word Bank that best matches each phrase. Write the answer on your paper.

1. tropical storm that forms over an ocean

2. instrument for measuring air pressure

3. state of the atmosphere at a given time and place

4. large section of the atmosphere having the same humidity and temperature throughout

5. storm with a dangerous funnel cloud

6. instrument for measuring wind speed

7. instrument for measuring relative humidity

8. average weather over a long period of time

9. line on a weather map connecting areas of equal air pressure

10. amount of water vapor in the air

Concept Review

Choose the word or phrase that best completes each sentence. Write the letter of the answer on your paper.

11. In an area of low pressure, the air coming in is _____.

    A cold   **C** rotating clockwise

    B warm   **D** dense

12. The force of the atmosphere against the earth's surface is _____.

    A air pressure   **C** wind

    B air temperature   **D** precipitation

13. A wind vane shows _____.

    A altitude   **C** air pressure

    B wind speed   **D** wind direction

14. Thunderstorms occur when _____.
   A warm air is pushed up by a cold front
   B cold air is pushed up by a warm front
   C moist air over the ocean begins to spin
   D an air mass stalls

15. A moving boundary between two air masses is called a(n) _____.
   A eye **B** front **C** isobar **D** storm

16. A hurricane forms over a(n) _____.
   A ocean **C** forest
   B prairie **D** mountain

17. The _____ climate zone has warm summers and cold winters.
   A polar **B** tropical **C** temperate **D** tundra

18. A warm front often brings _____.
   A cirrus clouds **C** fair conditions
   B cool weather **D** steady rain

Critical Thinking

Write the answer to each of the following questions.

19. Two cities are located in the temperate climate zone. One city is located on the coast at sea level. The other city is located in the mountains, high above sea level. How would you expect the climates of the two cities to be the same and different? Explain your answer.

20. If a high pushes out a low in your area today, what weather changes would you expect?

Test-Taking Tip To prepare for a test, study in short sessions rather than in one long session. During the week before the test, spend time each evening reviewing your notes.

17

The Solar System

The center of the solar system is the sun. Even though it is 150 million kilometers away, the sun affects us in many ways. For example, huge explosions, called solar flares, sometimes move outward from the sun's surface. Solar flares send electrically charged particles into space. Some of these particles reach the earth and cause static on radios. The particles can also change the amount of power in electric lines. In Chapter 17, you will learn more about the sun, planets, and other objects in the solar system.

Organize Your Thoughts

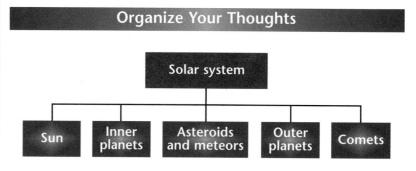

Goals for Learning

◆ To explain what the solar system is

◆ To identify the four inner planets

◆ To identify the five outer planets

◆ To tell something about each planet

◆ To describe the motions and positions of the planets

◆ To compare comets and asteroids

Objectives

After reading this lesson, you should be able to

◆ explain the difference between stars, planets, and moons.

◆ identify objects of the solar system.

◆ describe the sun.

Star

Glowing ball of hot gas that makes its own energy and light

Planet

Large object in space that orbits a star such as the sun

Moon

Natural satellite that orbits a planet

Stars, Planets, and Moons

If you stand outside on a clear night, away from bright city lights, you should be able to see hundreds of shining objects in the sky. Most of the objects are **stars**. These glowing balls of hot gas shine because they make their own light. A few of the objects you might see are **planets**. Planets are large objects in space that orbit the sun. You will likely see the earth's **moon**, although there are other moons in space. A moon is an object that orbits a planet. It takes the earth's moon about 29 days to complete its revolution around the earth. From the earth, we can see only one side of the moon as it travels around us. The moon always keeps the same side toward the earth.

Planets and moons do not make their own light. They shine because they reflect the light of the sun, our closest star. Stars are the source of light for all objects in space. The diagram below shows how a star like the sun can cause a planet to shine. You can see the ball because it reflects light from the flashlight. You can see a planet or moon because it reflects light from the sun.

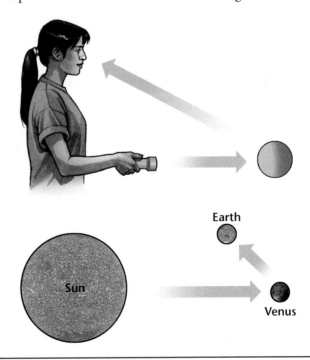

Earth

Sun

Venus

The motion of the solar system has a regular pattern to it. This means you can predict where in space a planet will be on your next birthday! You can even predict where it will be several years from now.

The word *planet* comes from a Greek word meaning "wanderer." Because planets change their position in the sky from day to day, ancient stargazers thought of planets as wandering stars. Planets, with their moons, revolve around the sun in what is known as the **solar system**. *Solar* refers to the star in the center of the system: the sun.

The stars in the night sky are not part of the solar system. But they do move. Planets seem to move across the sky faster than stars do. Why? Think about riding in a car and looking out the window. Have you ever noticed that objects closer to the car seem to go by faster than objects farther away? The more distant something is, the more slowly it seems to move. Stars are much, much farther away from the earth than the planets are. Therefore, stars appear to move very slowly in the sky.

A star is made mostly of hydrogen and helium gas particles. Deep inside the star, temperatures of 15,000,000°C make these particles move at incredible speeds. When moving at high speeds, the particles collide and combine, or fuse. This process is called **fusion**. Continuous fusion produces a constant supply of energy. This energy makes its way to the star's surface. Gas particles on the surface become very hot and radiate light. We see this as a shining star.

At first glance, you might think that all stars are white. Many of them are. But if you observe stars carefully, you will see that some are red, some are yellow, and others are blue-white. The color of a star depends on its temperature. The following table shows the temperature of stars of each color.

The sun's surface temperature is about 5,500°C. Looking at the table, you can see that the sun is a yellow star.

Star Color and Temperature	
Color	**Average Surface Temperature (°C)**
blue-white	35,000
white	10,000
yellow	5,500
red	3,000

Since astronauts float
in outer space, this
means that there is
no gravity there.

Fact: Gravity is
everywhere. It holds
our solar system
together. Astronauts
appear to float
because they are in
orbit. The orbital
force pulling them
away from the earth
is balanced by the
force of gravity
pulling them toward
the earth. Because of
this, astronauts
weigh less in space
than at home.

Objects in the Solar System

The solar system contains many objects. Nine of these objects
are planets. Each planet travels in a fixed orbit around the
sun. Look at the diagram below to find the name and path of
each planet. Most of the planets do not orbit in an exact circle,
but in an ellipse.

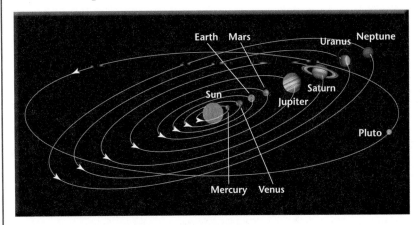

Imagine tracing the paths of these nine planets in space. You
would see that most of the orbits could be traced on a flat plane
or on a giant piece of paper. One planet orbits a little outside
of this flat plane. Look at the diagram again to see which one it is.

All of the planets move around the sun in the same direction.
However, the planets don't orbit together as a group. Each
planet moves along its path at its own speed. Mercury orbits
the fastest. In general, the farther away a planet is from the sun,
the bigger its orbit and the slower its speed. Besides planets,
smaller objects in space orbit the sun, too.

The entire solar system holds together because of gravity. There
is gravity between every object in the solar system, attracting
these objects to each other. Because the sun has much more
mass than the objects orbiting it, the objects are pulled toward
the sun. This pull of gravity is balanced by the speed and motion
of the objects. This balance keeps the objects in orbit. Without
this perfect balance, an orbiting planet could fly off in a straight
line or fall toward the sun.

Galaxy

Group of billions of stars

? Did You Know?

It takes about eight minutes for sunlight to reach the earth.

The Sun

The largest object in the solar system is the sun. In fact, the sun is larger than all of the planets put together. Its mass, the amount of matter it contains, is 99 percent of the entire solar system. So 99 percent of the "stuff" in the solar system is in the sun! The diagram compares the size of the earth and the sun.

The sun is made mostly of two gases: hydrogen and helium. The sun also contains very small amounts of the elements found on the earth. Because the sun is mostly gas, it has no solid surface.

The sun is not fixed in space. It rotates on an axis like a planet. Because it is mostly gas, parts of the sun rotate at different rates. On average, the sun rotates once a month.

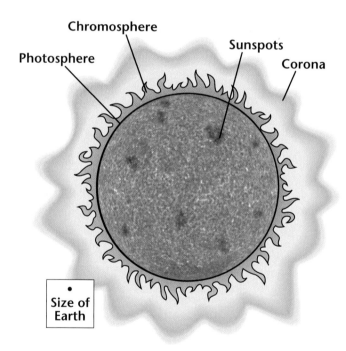

The sun is a star in the Milky Way **galaxy.** A galaxy is a group of billions of stars. Galaxies are grouped by their shapes. The Milky Way galaxy is shaped like a spiral.

Atmosphere

Envelope of gas surrounding an object in space

Sunspot

Dark area on the sun's surface that gives off less energy than the rest of the sun

The outer temperature of the sun is about 5,500°C. This high temperature is caused by nuclear reactions inside the sun. In the sun's center, temperatures of 15,000,000°C cause hydrogen particles to fuse and form helium. These nuclear reactions produce energy that we see as light and feel as heat. Later you will learn how the sun's energy is important for many processes on the earth, such as wind and rainfall.

The only part of the sun that can be seen is its **atmosphere**. An atmosphere is an envelope of gas surrounding an object in space. The sun's atmosphere consists of three layers, as shown in the diagram on page 374. The inner layer is called the photosphere. This is the layer of gas that gives off light. Just outside of this layer is another layer of gas called the chromosphere. The gas of the chromosphere can sometimes be seen during a total solar eclipse, when the photosphere is blocked. The outer layer of the sun's atmosphere is the corona. It is a layer of gas thicker than the chromosphere. The corona can also be seen during a solar eclipse.

Notice in the diagram that the photosphere contains dark areas called **sunspots**. Sunspots give off less energy and are, therefore, cooler than the rest of the sun. But they are still about 4,000°C. Sunspots move in groups across the face of the sun. This shows that the sun rotates.

Many spacecraft and satellites have photographed the sun and measured its surface activity. The satellite SOHO was launched in 1995 to study the sun. It contains 12 instruments. Besides taking photos, it measures corona activity, vibrations in the sun, and space conditions. SOHO stands for Solar and Heliospheric Observatory.

Lesson 1   R E V I E W

Write your answers to these questions on a sheet of paper.

1. What is the difference between a star and a planet?

2. Why do the moon and planets shine in the night sky?

3. What makes up our solar system? What holds it together?

4. Compare the sun and the earth in terms of size, makeup, and temperature.

5. Describe the layers of the sun's atmosphere.

Science in Your Life

What is a solar house?

The sun not only warms our planet, but it also provides us with energy. Solar energy is energy that comes from the sun.

Solar energy can be used in many ways. For example, a solar house is specially built to capture solar energy. Solar panels are mounted on the roof of the house. The panels collect radiant energy from the sun and change it to heat energy. This heat energy is used to run electric appliances and heat water.

The main benefit of using solar energy is that it saves our natural resources. Oil, gas, and coal are natural resources that are burned for energy. These resources are limited and will run out someday. But the sun's energy is unlimited. The sun will keep producing energy for about another 5 billion years.

Are there any solar houses or solar panels in your neighborhood? To learn about other ways to save our natural resources, read Appendix B: Alternative Energy Sources.

Objectives

After reading this lesson, you should be able to

◆ identify the four inner planets.

◆ describe the four inner planets.

◆ explain what the greenhouse effect is and how it affects Venus.

The planets of the solar system are divided into two groups: the inner planets and the outer planets. The inner planets are the ones that are closest to the sun. They are Mercury, Venus, Earth, and Mars. All of the inner planets are solid and similar in size. But these rocky worlds are also very different from one another. Read about each one below. Then look at Appendix D to learn more facts about the planets.

Mercury

The planet closest to the sun is Mercury. Because it is so close to the sun, Mercury is not easy to see in the sky. Named after the Roman god of speed, Mercury is the fastest-moving planet. Its average speed as it orbits the sun is about 50 kilometers per second. Mercury completes an entire revolution of the sun in 88 Earth days. It rotates slowly though. One day on Mercury lasts about 59 Earth days.

In 1974 and 1975, a spacecraft called *Mariner 10* passed close by Mercury three times. It photographed about half of its surface. These photos show that Mercury is covered with craters and flat areas, like those on the moon.

Of all the planets, Mercury's surface temperature changes the most. This is because Mercury has almost no atmosphere to hold in or keep out the sun's heat. The side of Mercury facing the sun reaches 427°C. The side away from the sun drops to −183°C.

This image is actually many small photos put together. The smooth band and patches are areas that Mariner 10 *did not photograph.*

Venus

The planet that is next closest to the sun is Venus. It was named after the Roman goddess of love and beauty. Venus is the hottest planet at 460°C. It is also the brightest planet in the sky. Like the moon, you can sometimes see Venus during the day. Depending on the time of year, Venus is known as the "morning star" or the "evening star."

Venus is different from most of the other planets because it rotates in the opposite direction. Earth and the other inner planets rotate from west to east. Venus rotates from east to west. That means the sun rises in the west on Venus. Also, it takes a long time for Venus to rotate. A day on Venus is 243 Earth days.

This radar image of Venus shows surface features that are visibly hidden by clouds.

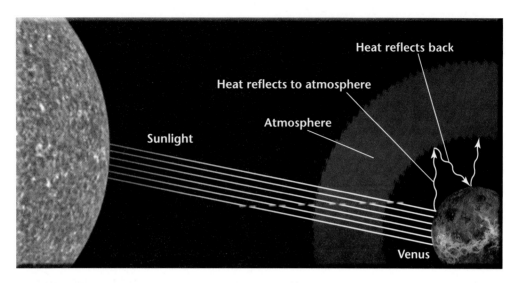

Heat reflects back

Heat reflects to atmosphere

Atmosphere

Sunlight

Venus

Greenhouse effect

Warming of the atmosphere because of trapped heat energy from the sun

The average temperature on Earth's surface is 15°C (59°F). The coldest temperature on record is −89°C (−128°F). The hottest temperature on record is 58°C (136°F). Earth is the only planet that has the right temperature range for life.

Unlike Mercury, Venus has an atmosphere. It contains great amounts of the gas carbon dioxide. Carbon dioxide in the atmosphere traps heat energy from the sun. As a result, the atmosphere heats up. This warming, shown above, is called the **greenhouse effect**. The clouds of Venus's atmosphere are made of tiny drops of sulfuric acid. These clouds trap heat and add to the greenhouse effect. Because of the greenhouse effect, the surface temperature of Venus is very high. The surface of the planet would be much cooler without this effect.

We cannot see through Venus's thick clouds with our eyes. However, in the 1990s, a spacecraft called *Magellan* used radar to penetrate the clouds and make images of the planet's surface. These images show areas of rolling plains, towering highlands, and craters.

Earth

Our own planet, Earth, is the third planet from the sun. It is about the same size as Venus. But Earth has several differences from the other inner planets:

◆ Earth has a mild surface temperature that changes very little.
◆ It has a dense, protective atmosphere.
◆ It is the only planet to have liquid water on its surface.

People are concerned that the burning of oil and coal is adding too much carbon dioxide to the atmosphere. This activity strengthens the natural greenhouse effect and could raise temperatures on Earth. Droughts and crop losses may result.

Because of these unique features, Earth can support life. There is no evidence of life on the other planets. Earth is also the closest planet to the sun that has a moon.

The greenhouse effect occurs on Earth as well as on Venus. Without an atmosphere that traps heat, Earth would be an icy planet with temperatures no warmer than $-10°C$.

Mars

Mars, the fourth planet from the sun, is named for the Roman god of war. Its reddish color in the night sky may have reminded ancient people of blood. Mars has two small moons.

The rotation period of Mars is about the same as that of Earth. Mars rotates once every 24 hours and 38 minutes. It takes the planet 687 Earth days to complete one revolution around the sun. So, a Martian day is similar to an Earth day, but its year is almost twice as long as ours.

The atmosphere on Mars is much less dense than on Earth. The atmosphere is mostly carbon dioxide. Mars is colder than Earth because it is farther from the sun and has a thinner atmosphere. Little heat can be trapped by a thin atmosphere.

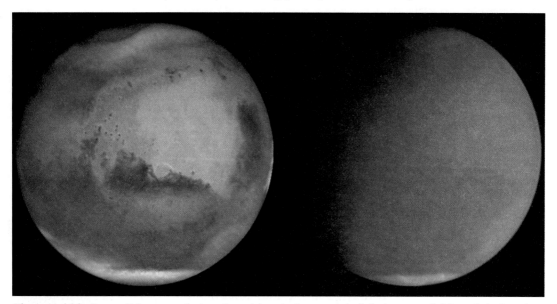

These Hubble Space Telescope photos show Mars before a global dust storm (left) and during the storm (right).

Lesson 2   R E V I E W

Write your answers to these questions on a sheet of paper.

1. What are the names of the inner planets?

2. How would you describe Mercury?

3. Which planet has a reddish surface?

4. What does the greenhouse effect do to the temperature on a planet's surface?

5. How is Earth unique?

Achievements in Science

The Struggle to Accept the Solar System

In the early 1500s, a Polish astronomer named Nicolaus Copernicus had a new idea. Using careful observations and mathematics, he concluded that the sun must be at the center of all the planets. In such a system, Earth and the other planets revolve around the sun. Other astronomers at the time thought that Earth was at the center of everything. They believed Earth didn't move. They rejected Copernicus's idea of a sun-centered, or solar, system.

Copernicus's idea was not picked up again until almost 100 years later. In the early 1600s, an Italian astronomer named Galileo Galilei concluded that not all objects in space revolve around Earth. Galileo was one of the first astronomers to use a telescope. The more he observed the moon and the planets, the more convinced he became that Copernicus's idea was correct. Galileo published a book explaining the idea of a solar system. Still, this idea was very unpopular.

In the late 1600s, Isaac Newton, an English scientist, took a serious look at Galileo's idea. He was able to prove that Copernicus and Galileo were right. People finally accepted the fact that Earth revolves around the sun. Newton became a hero and was knighted by the queen of England.

Objectives

After reading this lesson, you should be able to

◆ identify the five outer planets.

◆ describe the five outer planets.

Except for Pluto, the outer planets have rings and are much larger than the inner planets. The outer planets are mostly frozen gas and liquid, with a small, solid core. Over the last 25 years, *Voyager* and *Galileo* spacecraft have collected much information about these planets. Look at Appendix E to learn more about space exploration.

Jupiter

Jupiter is the largest planet in the solar system. In fact, all of the other planets in the solar system could fit inside Jupiter. The diameter of Jupiter is more than 11 times larger than Earth's. It's no wonder Jupiter was named for the Roman king of the gods.

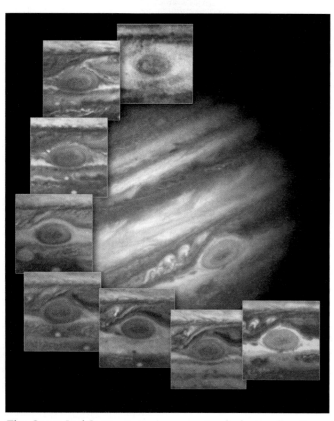

The Great Red Spot rotates in a counterclockwise direction. Wind speeds inside this storm reach 400 kilometers per hour.

Among the most noticeable features of Jupiter are its colorful bands. These bands are clouds of gases where storms are taking place. The bands change shape every few days but generally run in the same direction. Jupiter's fast rotation might cause these bands. It takes Jupiter only 10 hours to rotate once.

A large red oval appears on the surface of Jupiter. This area is called the Great Red Spot. It is more than twice as wide as Earth. This spot is actually a spinning windstorm. It is the largest known storm in the solar system, and it has lasted at least 300 years! The Great Red Spot changes its shape and color, as shown in the photo.

When two Voyager spacecraft flew by Jupiter in 1979, astronomers discovered faint rings around the planet. Astronomers also discovered more moons than they had thought existed. At least 60 moons orbit this giant planet.

Shown below is one of Jupiter's moons, Io. This moon has active volcanoes that erupt constantly. Io's volcanoes spew out sulfur, which colors the surface yellow, orange, and green.

The largest of Jupiter's moons is Ganymede. It is bigger than the planet Mercury. The smallest moon is only about two kilometers in diameter. A moon called Europa is an icy world with a smooth, cracked surface. It has been described as a giant, cracked cue ball.

The spacecraft Galileo *flew close to Io in 1999 and photographed its colorful surface.*

Saturn

You are probably familiar with the rings of Saturn. Saturn, the sixth planet from the sun, was named for the Roman god of agriculture. Saturn is the second largest planet in the solar system. It revolves around the sun once every 29 years.

About 1,000 individual rings orbit Saturn's equator. They are mostly ice particles and dust. When you look at Saturn through a telescope, you can see the rings only at certain times during Saturn's orbit. That is because the rings are very thin, and Saturn rotates on a tilted axis. When the edge of the ring system is pointed toward Earth, the rings disappear from view. The images below were taken between 1996 and 2000. They show how Saturn nods as it revolves.

Like Jupiter, Saturn is a giant planet of gases with stormy bands of clouds running along its surface. Winds in these storms reach speeds of 1,800 kilometers per hour. Also like Jupiter, Saturn spins very fast. One day is about 11 hours.

Saturn has at least 31 moons, the largest of which is Titan. Titan is the only moon in the solar system that is known to have an atmosphere of its own. This atmosphere is mostly nitrogen. Titan may also have active volcanoes.

The *Cassini* spacecraft, launched in 1997, is scheduled to put a probe on Titan in 2004. Then the spacecraft will orbit Saturn for four years, studying its atmosphere, rings, and moons.

We see Saturn's rings at different angles during its revolution around the sun.

Uranus

The seventh planet from the sun is Uranus. This greenish-blue planet was named for the Greek god of the sky. One unusual thing about Uranus is the tilt of its axis. Uranus rotates on its side. During some parts of its revolution, one pole of Uranus points directly at the sun. Because of this, astronomers disagree about which of Uranus's poles is its north pole.

In 1977, astronomers discovered that Uranus has a faint, dark ring system. They were using a telescope to observe Uranus as it passed in front of a star. They noticed that the star dimmed briefly many times. Each dimming occurred as another ring passed in front of the star. In 1986, the *Voyager 2* spacecraft studied the rings and moons of Uranus up close. Since then, more rings and moons have been discovered. Uranus has at least 11 rings and 22 moons.

Because Uranus is so far out in the solar system, it takes 84 Earth years to complete a single orbit of the sun. Uranus rotates on its axis once every 17 hours.

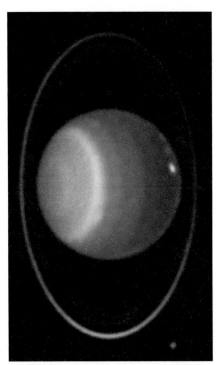

The outer planets are very cold. The cloud tops of Uranus are −200°C.

Neptune

Neptune is the eighth planet from the sun. Named after the Roman god of the sea, Neptune cannot be seen without a telescope. Like Uranus, Neptune appears greenish blue because of methane gas in its atmosphere. Neptune has four rings: two thin and two thick. Like Jupiter, Neptune has a big spot in its atmosphere. The Great Dark Spot seen at the center of the photo is about as wide as Earth. The wispy, white streaks are clouds.

It takes Neptune 164 Earth years to complete a revolution around the sun. The planet rotates once on its axis every 16 hours.

The Great Dark Spot is a storm system spinning counterclockwise.

Until 1989, astronomers thought Neptune had two moons. Later, nine more moons were found. One of Neptune's 11 moons is unusual. It rotates in the opposite direction from Neptune's rotation. This moon, named Triton, also has active volcanoes.

Pluto

Pluto is the coldest, outermost planet of the solar system, but it is not always the farthest from the sun. It has a tilted, stretched-out orbit that sometimes falls inside the orbit of Neptune, as shown below. Even so, if you were to stand on Pluto, the sun would appear only as a bright star in the sky. Pluto has not yet been visited by a spacecraft.

Pluto is the smallest planet. It is the only outer planet without a ring system and a thick atmosphere. Pluto has one known moon, Charon. Even with powerful telescopes, Pluto and Charon are hard to see. At an average distance from the sun of almost 6 billion kilometers, Pluto takes 248 Earth years to make one revolution. Pluto seems to rotate about once every six days.

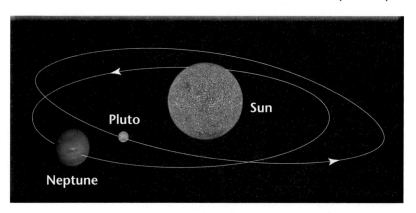

Write your answers to these questions on a sheet of paper.

1. What are the five outer planets of the solar system?

2. What are the large outer planets made of?

3. Which outer planets have rings?

4. Besides on Earth, where could you find active volcanoes?

5. How is Pluto different from the other outer planets?

▼◄▲▼◄▲▼◄▲▼◄▲▼◄▲▼◄▲▼◄▲▼◄▲▼◄▲▼◄▲▼◄▲▼◄▲▼◄▲▼◄▲▼◄▲▼◄▲▼

Science at Work

Astronomer

Astronomers study stars, planets, and other objects in space. Most astronomers do research by analyzing large amounts of data. The data are collected from satellites and powerful telescopes. Some astronomers try to solve problems with space flight or satellite communications.

The usual education needed to be an astronomer is a doctoral degree, or Ph.D. An astronomer needs to have a strong background in physics and mathematics.

Besides science skills, a successful astronomer needs to be a problem-solver. A curious mind and an active imagination are also helpful.

Many astronomers teach at colleges or universities. Other astronomers are planetarium directors. They may also be members of a research team that operates large telescopes on Earth or in space.

Modeling Distances in the Solar System

Purpose

What kind of model might show how far the planets are from the sun? In this investigation, you will use a scale to show distances in the solar system.

Procedure

1. Tape the strip of adding machine paper to the floor. Draw a circle at one end of the paper. The circle represents the sun.

2. The table on the next page shows the relative distances of the planets from the sun. Use this table and a meterstick to mark the location of each of the planets on the adding machine paper. Label the position of each planet with its name.

Materials

◆ one 12-meter length of adding machine paper

◆ meterstick

◆ tape

Planet	Distance from Sun in Model (centimeters)*
Mercury	12
Venus	22
Earth	30
Mars	46
Jupiter	156
Saturn	286
Uranus	574
Neptune	900
Pluto	1,180

*1 centimeter in model = 5,000,000 kilometers in space

3. Each centimeter on the strip of paper represents 5 million kilometers in space. Next to each planet on the paper, record its actual distance in kilometers from the sun.

Questions and Conclusions

1. What is the scale of this model?

2. Which four planets are closest together?

3. Which two planets have the greatest distance between their orbits?

Explore Further

Make a model that shows the diameters of all nine planets. Appendix D lists the actual diameters. What scale will you use? Use your model to compare the sizes of the planets.

Asteroid

Rocky object, smaller than a planet, that orbits a star

Asteroid belt

Region between Mars and Jupiter where most asteroids orbit the sun

Meteor

Brief streak of light seen when an asteroid enters the earth's atmosphere and burns up

Asteroids

The solar system has other objects besides the sun, the planets, and their moons. Some of these objects are **asteroids**. An asteroid is a rocky object smaller than a planet that has its own orbit around the sun. Most asteroids are smaller than a kilometer in diameter, but a few are 1,000 kilometers across.

As the diagram shows, a large number of asteroids lie between the orbits of Mars and Jupiter. This area is known as the **asteroid belt**. As many as a million asteroids make up this belt, orbiting the sun. The belt may have formed as Jupiter's gravity pulled matter toward this region of space.

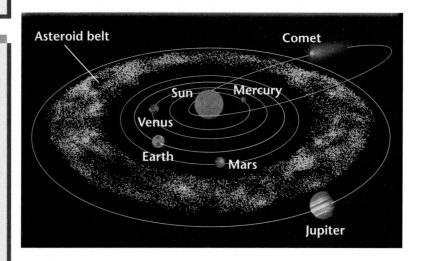

Not all of these asteroids stay in their orbits. Sometimes they are pulled out of orbit by the gravity of other planets. Asteroids may also be pulled in toward the sun.

A few asteroids come close to Earth and, at times, are captured by Earth's gravity. If an asteroid enters Earth's atmosphere, it heats up and becomes a ball of glowing gases. This brief streak of light seen in the sky is called a **meteor**. You probably know meteors as "shooting stars" or "falling stars." When many shooting stars occur, they are referred to as a "meteor shower."

One of the best-known comets is Hale-Bopp. It was discovered in 1995 by two astronomers named Alan Hale and Thomas Bopp. The comet's closest approach to Earth was on March 22, 1997.

Did You Know?

When comets come close to Earth, they can be seen for days or weeks. They do not streak across the sky like meteors.

If an asteroid is big enough and does not completely burn up, it may hit Earth. The part that actually strikes Earth is called a **meteorite**. Large meteorites can leave craters. About 50,000 years ago, a meteorite created Meteor Crater in Arizona, shown in the photo.

Meteor Crater in Arizona is more than a kilometer across.

Comets

Other objects of the solar system include **comets**. Most of these objects follow large orbits. Most comets are not on the same orbital plane as the planets. A comet's orbit may take it far beyond the orbit of Pluto.

Scientists have found that comets are made of ice, rock, frozen gases, and dust. When a comet approaches the sun, the comet begins to warm up. Some of the ice turns to gas, and dust is also released. The gas and dust reflect sunlight, making the comet visible. A stream of particles from the sun, called the solar wind, pushes the gas and dust away from the head of the comet. This gas and dust form a tail that points away from the sun.

Comet Hale-Bopp, seen in 1997, has a very long orbit. It will not be seen again until the year 4377!

Lesson 4   R E V I E W

Write your answers to these questions on a sheet of paper.

1. What is an asteroid?

2. Where is the asteroid belt located?

3. What is the difference between a meteor and a meteorite?

4. What are comets made of?

5. How does the tail of a comet form?

Technology Note

A photovoltaic (PV) cell, or solar cell, uses the sun's energy to produce electricity. The biggest advantage to this kind of energy is that it's free. Since PV cells have no moving parts, they require very little maintenance and are clean and quiet.

The basic idea of a PV cell was discovered in 1839. But the details of the technology were not worked out until about 100 years later. PV cells were first used in space. In fact, PV cells are still used to power most of the satellites orbiting Earth. PV cells are especially useful in remote places where regular power lines are not available.

PV cells also have more common applications. Simple PV systems power wristwatches and solar calculators. More complicated PV systems produce electricity for water pumps and communications equipment. PV systems even provide electricity for some homes and appliances.

- Stars shine because they give off their own light. Planets and moons shine because they reflect light from the sun.

- The solar system is made of the sun, the planets and their moons, and other objects that revolve around the sun.

- The sun is a star. It is mostly hydrogen and helium gas. The sun's atmosphere has three layers: the photosphere, the chromosphere, and the corona.

- The inner planets are Mercury, Venus, Earth, and Mars. They are all solid, rocky worlds.

- Mercury has craters and almost no atmosphere.

- Venus rotates in the opposite direction from most other planets, has an atmosphere of carbon dioxide, and is very hot.

- Earth has one moon, moderate temperatures, a dense atmosphere, and much water. It is the only planet known to have life on it.

- Mars has a thin atmosphere, a reddish surface, and two moons.

- The outer planets are Jupiter, Saturn, Uranus, Neptune, and Pluto. Pluto is small and solid. The others are large and mostly gas.

- Jupiter is the largest planet and has 60 moons. A giant storm, called the Great Red Spot, can be seen in its atmosphere.

- Saturn has a big ring system and 31 moons.

- Uranus rotates on its side. It has a ring system and 22 moons.

- Neptune has a ring system and 11 moons.

- Pluto has a tilted, stretched-out orbit and one moon.

- Asteroids are small objects that orbit the sun between Mars and Jupiter. A meteor is the streak of light seen when an asteroid enters Earth's atmosphere.

- Comets are made of ice, rock, frozen gases, and dust.

Science Words

asteroid, 390	fusion, 372	meteor, 390	solar system, 372
asteroid belt, 390	galaxy, 374	meteorite, 391	star, 371
atmosphere, 375	greenhouse	moon, 371	sunspot, 375
comet, 391	effect, 379	planet, 371	

Chapter 17 REVIEW

Vocabulary Review

Word Bank

asteroid

asteroid belt

atmosphere

comet

greenhouse effect

meteor

moon

planet

solar system

star

sunspot

Choose the word or phrase from the Word Bank that best completes each sentence. Write the answer on your paper.

1. The planets, moons, and sun are part of the _____.

2. The sun is the _____ that the planets orbit.

3. The gases around a planet make up its _____.

4. A dark area that appears on the sun is called a(n) _____.

5. Venus has a hot surface temperature because of the _____.

6. The _____ is between Mars and Jupiter.

7. A(n) _____ is a large object that orbits a star.

8. A shooting star is a(n) _____.

9. A(n) _____ is made of ice, rock, frozen gases, and dust.

10. Another name for a natural satellite is a(n) _____.

11. A rocky object smaller than a planet is called a(n) _____.

Concept Review

Write the answer to each of the following questions.

12. Identify each member of the solar system shown in the diagram below. On your paper, write the name after each letter.

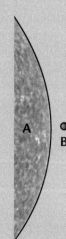
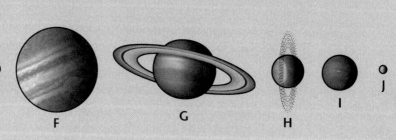

13. Name five different kinds of objects that make up the solar system.

14. What makes Earth unique compared to other planets?

15. Four of the outer planets are very similar. Give two features that they share.

Choose the word or phrase that best completes each sentence. Write the letter of the answer on your paper.

16. The sun is mostly _____.
    A helium and oxygen
    B helium and hydrogen
    C hydrogen and nitrogen
    D hydrogen and oxygen

17. The solar system is held together by _____.
    A gravity   C energy
    B mass   D gases

18. The moon shines in the sky because _____.
    A the moon is very hot
    B the moon produces its own light
    C it reflects the light of the sun
    D the moon is a close star

Critical Thinking

Write the answer to each of the following questions.

19. What is the difference between a star and a planet?

20. One of Jupiter's moons is as big as the planet Mercury. If this moon is so big, why is it a moon and not a planet?

Test-Taking Tip Don't get stuck on a hard question. Keep moving and go back to it later.

UNIT 2   SUMMARY

- About 30 percent of the earth's surface is land and about 70 percent is water.

- Rotation is the spinning of the earth on its axis. Earth's rotation causes day and night.

- Revolution is Earth's movement in an orbit around the sun. One revolution takes about 365 days.

- Intersecting lines of latitude and longitude make it possible to locate a single point anywhere on Earth's surface.

- A mineral can be identified by its properties, including color, luster, streak, and hardness.

- The three main types of rocks are igneous, sedimentary, and metamorphic. Rocks change from one type to another in the rock cycle.

- Mechanical weathering is the process of breaking up rocks without changing their minerals. Chemical weathering is the process of breaking up rocks by changing the minerals in them.

- Soil is a mixture of weathered rock and the remains of plants and animals.

- Erosion is caused by water, glaciers, wind, and gravity.

- Earth has three main layers: the core, the mantle, and the crust.

- The theory of plate tectonics states that Earth's crust is made up of several large plates that move about over the mantle.

- Mountains can form from volcanic eruptions, from folding, and from movement along faults.

- Rocks contain clues about events that happened in Earth's past.

- The events in Earth's history occurred over geologic time and are outlined on the geologic time scale.

- Water moves between the land, the atmosphere, and the ocean in the water cycle.

- Features of the ocean floor include continental shelves, continental slopes, mid-ocean ridges, trenches, plains, and seamounts.

- The atmosphere is the layer of gases that surrounds Earth. It consists mostly of the elements nitrogen and oxygen.

- The sun's unequal heating of Earth's surface causes wind.

- Weather is the state of the atmosphere at a given time and place.

- Precipitation is moisture that falls to Earth from the atmosphere as rain, snow, sleet, or hail.

- Climate is the average weather of a region over a long period of time.

- The solar system is made of the sun, the planets and their moons, and other bodies that revolve around the sun.

- The sun is a star made primarily of hydrogen and helium.

- The entire solar system is held together by gravity.

Word Bank

atmosphere

axis

fossil

humidity

mantle

oxidation

precipitation

rock cycle

water table

Vocabulary Review

Choose the word or phrase from the Word Bank that best completes each sentence. Write the answer on your own paper.

1. The imaginary line around which the earth rotates is called the _____.

2. Rocks change from one type to another as they go through the _____.

3. An example of chemical weathering is _____.

4. The layer of Earth between the core and the crust is the _____.

5. A(n) _____ is a trace or remains of an organism preserved in Earth's crust.

6. Underground water forms a soaked layer, the top of which is the _____.

7. Solid or liquid water that falls from the atmosphere is _____.

8. The amount of water vapor in the air is called _____.

9. The gases around a planet make up its _____.

Concept Review

Write the answer to each of the following questions.

10. Earth rotates from _____.
    A east to west   **C** west to east
    B north to south   **D** south to north

11. Rocks that have been changed by heat, pressure, and chemical reactions form _____ rocks.
    A metamorphic   **C** sedimentary
    B igneous   **D** organic

12. The main process that creates a beach is _____.
    A erosion   **C** weathering
    B luster   **D** deposition

13. Earth's surface is part of the _____.

    A core   **B** mantle   **C** epicenter   **D** crust

14. The _____ Era is known as the Age of Mammals.

    A Cenozoic   **C** Mesozoic

    B Paleozoic   **D** Precambrian

15. Fluffy white clouds are called _____ clouds.

    A stratus   **B** cumulus   **C** cirrus   **D** polar

16. The boundary between two air masses is called a(n) _____.

    A eye   **B** front   **C** isobar   **D** hurricane

17. Between Mars and Jupiter is a zone called the _____.

    A atmosphere   **C** asteroid belt

    B greenhouse effect   **D** meteor belt

Match each ocean feature below with a letter in the diagram. Write the letter of each answer on your paper.

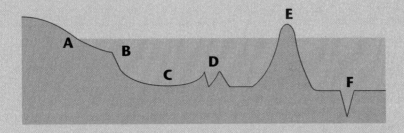

18. mid-ocean ridge

19. continental shelf

20. island

21. plain

22. continental slope

23. trench

Critical Thinking

Write the answer to each of the following questions.

24. One way to make salt water safe to drink is to heat it, collect the water vapor, and condense it. How is this method like the water cycle? Suggest a way to collect the water vapor.

25. Suppose you are going to a picnic today. Fluffy white clouds are floating across the sky. Do you think it will rain at the picnic? Explain.

Review   U

Unit 3

Life Science

Everything in the world can be grouped into two big categories: living things or nonliving things. Wolves, earthworms, bacteria, clams, and pine trees are examples of living things. Nonliving things include water, air, and rocks. In Units 1 and 2 you learned about nonliving things.

In this unit, you will learn about living things. You will see how all living things are alike and how they are different. You will find out how living things reproduce, develop, and change. You will see that living things depend on the nonliving and the living parts of their surroundings. Nonliving things like water, oxygen, and light are necessary for living things. Living things also act upon one another. The study of the living and nonliving parts of the world is called ecology.

Unit 3

What Is Life Science?

The Study of Living Things

The study of living things is called **life science.** Another word for life science is biology. Scientists who study living things are called biologists. Many biologists specialize in one field of life science. The table below lists just a few of those fields.

Some of the fields in the table can be broken down into even more specialized branches. For example, zoology, the study of animals, has many branches. Ornithology, the study of birds, is one branch. Another branch is herpetology, the study of amphibians and reptiles. Entomology is the study of insects.

Fields of Life Science	
Field	**What Is Studied**
Zoology	Animals
Botany	Plants
Anatomy	The structure of living things—what body parts are made of
Physiology	The functioning of living things—how their body parts work
Cytology	Cells and how they work
Microbiology	Tiny living things that can be seen only with a microscope
Ecology	The interactions among different kinds of living things and their environment
Genetics	How characteristics are passed from parents to offspring
Taxonomy	How living things can be classified into groups

How Biologists Work

When you hear the word biologist, do you think of someone wearing a white coat and working in a laboratory? Many biologists do work in a laboratory, at least part of the time.

A biologist who studies genetics, for example, might do lab experiments with fruit flies or other living things that reproduce quickly. A microbiologist studying bacteria or a cytologist studying cancer cells would need to work with powerful microscopes in a lab.

The mushroom Amanita muscaria *is poisonous.*

In contrast, other biologists work mostly outdoors. They observe living things in their natural environments and collect information to be analyzed later. For example, a zoologist might study the family life of wolves, elephants, or chimpanzees. An ecologist might analyze how cutting down a forest to create farmland affects different kinds of animals living in the area. Biologists sometimes do experiments outdoors, too.

You can see that biologists study many different things and work in different ways. But all biologists are similar in one major way: they study living things.

Marsupials complete their development in their mother's pouch.

Chapter

18

Living Things Are Alike

Did you ever wonder what kinds of things live in an ocean or a lake? You might see fish, snakes, turtles, coral, or seaweed under the water. But many other things live in the water that are too tiny to see. These tiny living things and the larger ones you can see are alike in many ways. For one thing, they are all made up of the basic unit of life—the cell. In this chapter, you will learn about the parts of cells and how cells are organized in living things. You will find out how living things are different from nonliving things and how living things are divided into groups.

Organize Your Thoughts

Living things
— Similarities
— Cells — Plant
— Life activities — Animal
— Differences
— Important chemicals
— Five kingdoms

Goals for Learning

◆ To explain what a cell is and describe the organization of cells in living things

◆ To compare and contrast plant and animal cells

◆ To identify chemicals that are important for life and explain how living things use these chemicals

◆ To describe some basic life activities

◆ To describe the similarities and differences between living things in different kingdoms

Objectives

After reading this lesson, you should be able to

◆ describe a cell and explain some of its functions.

◆ explain what tissues are.

◆ explain what organs are.

◆ identify ways that plant and animal cells are alike and different.

◆ describe the functions of the parts of cells.

Cell
The basic unit of life

Organism
A living thing that can carry out all the basic life activities

Bacteria
The simplest organisms that carry out all basic life activities

Microscope
An instrument used to magnify things

All living things are made of **cells**. A cell is the basic unit of life. It is the smallest thing that can be called "alive." Most living things that you have seen are made of many cells. Depending on their size, plants and animals are made of thousands, millions, billions, or even trillions of cells. Cells are found in all parts of an animal: they make up blood, bone, skin, nerves, and muscle. Cells also are found in all parts of a plant: they make up roots, stems, leaves, and flowers.

Cells carry out many functions, or jobs. Some cells are specialized. Some of the functions of the specialized cells in your body are listed below.

◆ Skin cells: cover and protect
◆ Muscle cells: allow for movement
◆ Bone cells: support and protect
◆ Nerve cells: send and receive messages
◆ Blood cells: transport materials and fight diseases

Another word for a living thing is an **organism**. An organism is a complete, individual living thing. It can carry out all the basic life activities. Large living things such as an elephant or a redwood tree are organisms. But so are some tiny living things that have only one cell. The **bacteria** that cause sore throats are organisms. Bacteria are the simplest organisms that carry out all basic life activities.

Observing Cells

Cells come in different sizes. However, most cells are so small that they are invisible to the unaided eye. They can be seen only with a **microscope**. A microscope is an instrument that scientists use to magnify small things in order to make them appear larger. Some microscopes are similar to a magnifying glass. Without the magnifying glass, an insect might look like just a black dot. With the magnifying glass, you can see the insect's tiny parts, such as legs. The same thing happens when scientists use a microscope. Tiny things that were not visible before can be seen through the microscope.

When you look at cells through a microscope, the different shapes of the cells become visible. Cells may be long, short, wide, or narrow.

When a cell is viewed under a light microscope, some of its tiny parts can be seen. A cell is surrounded by a thin membrane that encloses its contents. Inside the cell are tiny structures called **organelles.** They perform specific functions such as storing material or producing energy.

Tissues

Groups of cells that are alike and act together to do a certain job are called **tissues**. For example, muscle cells in animals are joined together to make muscle tissues. These tissues include leg muscles, arm muscles, stomach muscles, and heart muscles. The cells in muscle tissues work together to make the body move. Other examples of tissues in animals are nerve tissue, bone tissue, and skin tissue.

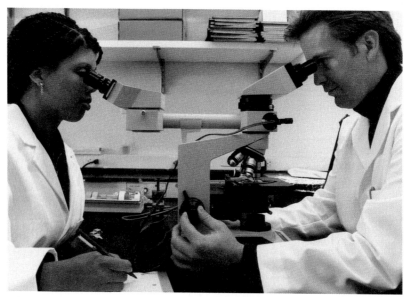

These technicians use a microscope to enlarge the cells they are studying.

Plants also have different kinds of cells, such as root cells, stem cells, and leaf cells. Similar cells are organized together into tissues. Different tissues carry out different functions necessary for plant growth. These functions include covering the plant and moving water and other substances in the plant.

Organs

An **organ** is a group of different tissues that work together. Organs are the main working parts of animals and plants. They do special jobs. Your heart is an organ. It pumps blood through your body. Your lungs are organs. They allow you to breathe. Other organs in your body include your stomach, liver, kidneys, and eyes.

You can see in the diagram below that the main organs of plants are roots, leaves, and stems. Roots take in water from the soil. Leaves make food for the plant. Stems support the plant and carry water and food to different parts of the plant.

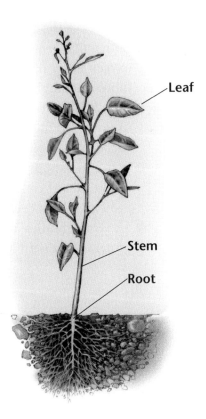

Leaf

Stem

Root

Comparing Plant and Animal Cells

Plants have different kinds of cells than animals have. For example, plants have stem cells and you have muscle cells. If you look at a single plant cell, you can see that some parts are the same as the parts of an animal cell. You can also see that a plant cell has certain parts that make it different from an animal cell. Some of these similarities and differences are listed below.

Similarities

- Both animal and plant cells have **cell membranes** that enclose the cell.
- Both animal and plant cells are filled with **cytoplasm**, a gel-like substance containing chemicals needed by the cell.
- Both animal and plant cells have a **nucleus**, where **DNA** is stored. DNA controls many of the characteristics of living things. Inside the nucleus is the nucleolus.
- Both animal and plant cells have **ribosomes**, protein builders of the cell.
- Both animal and plant cells have **mitochondria** that use oxygen to break down food and release the energy in food's chemical bonds.
- Both kinds of cells have **vacuoles** that contain food, water, or waste products. Animal cells usually have many more vacuoles than plant cells do.
- The cells of both plants and animals have **endoplasmic reticulum**, where a system of tubes process and transport proteins within cells.
- The **Golgi bodies** in both plant and animal cells package proteins for distribution outside the cell.

Cell membrane

A thin layer that surrounds and holds a cell together

Cytoplasm

A gel-like substance containing chemicals needed by the cell

Nucleus

Information and control center of the cell

DNA

The chemical inside cells that stores information about an organism

Ribosome

A protein builder of the cell

Mitochondrion

An organelle that uses oxygen to break down food and release the energy in food's chemical bonds (plural is mitochondria)

Vacuole

Stores substances such as food, water, and waste products

Endoplasmic reticulum

A system of tubes that process and transport proteins within the cell

Golgi body

Packages and distributes proteins outside the cell

Differences

Cell wall
The outer part of a plant cell that provides shape to the cell

Chloroplast

Captures the light energy from the sun to make food

Photosynthesis

The process in which a plant makes food

Lysosome

Contains chemicals that break down materials

◆ Plant cells have **cell walls** that provide structure, but animal cells do not.
◆ A few large animal cells have more than one nucleus, but plant cells always have just one.
◆ Plant cells have **chloroplasts** for **photosynthesis.** Animal cells do not.
◆ Animal cells tend to have many small vacuoles. Mature plant cells may have only one large vacuole.
◆ Animals cells have **lysosomes,** but plant cells do not.

Examine the animal cell and the plant cell in the diagram below. Identify the parts you just read about and review the function of each part.

Animal and Plant Cells

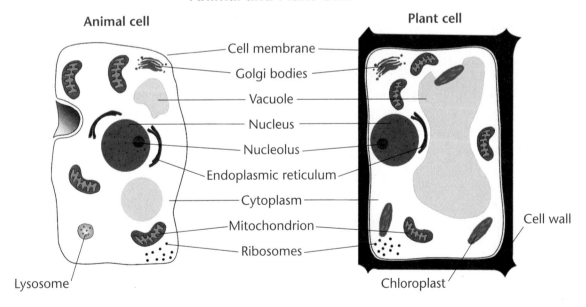

When the bonds
of larger molecules
are broken down,
smaller molecules
are formed. Energy
is released when
the bonds are
broken. These
new molecules
have chemical
bonds that have
less energy.

Cells Store and Use Energy

The energy that cells need comes originally from the sun. Chloroplasts in plant cells trap light energy from the sun and change it into chemical energy. This chemical energy is stored in chemical bonds between atoms of carbon, hydrogen, and oxygen. An atom is the smallest particle of an element that still has the properties of that element. Chemical bonds hold the atoms of carbon, hydrogen, and oxygen together to form molecules. A molecule is two or more atoms joined together. Cells can combine these molecules with other atoms to make larger molecules.

Both plant and animal cells break down these molecules by breaking their chemical bonds. Remember that energy is stored in these bonds. Energy is released when the bonds are broken. Cells can either use the energy or store it.

The mitochondria in plant and animal cells use oxygen to release the energy in chemical bonds. Cells store the chemical energy from food in high-energy **ATP** molecules. ATP stores energy in a form the cells can easily use. When the cell needs energy, the ATP is broken down to release energy.

Cells Store and Use Information

The nucleus of plant and animal cells is the control center of the cell. The nucleus contains DNA, a molecule that has instructions for all of a cell's activities. One of these activities is putting together protein molecules. Cells require thousands of proteins in order to work well. DNA and **RNA** molecules work together in the cell to make the proteins.

DNA in a cell's nucleus determines what kind of cell it is. When a cell divides and becomes two cells, the information needs to be passed on. To make certain that each cell has the information, the DNA doubles when a cell divides. Each of the two new cells contains the needed information to carry out all the cell's activities.

Write your answers to these questions on a separate sheet of paper. Write complete sentences.

1. What are cells?

2. What are three functions of cells?

3. What are tissues made of?

4. What are organs made of?

5. Name four organs.

6. What are five things that plant cells and animal cells have in common?

7. What are three ways that a plant cell is different from an animal cell?

8. What is the function of mitochondria?

9. What is the function of a cell's nucleus?

10. What is the function of chloroplasts?

▼◄▲▼◄▲▼◄▲▼◄▲▼◄▲▼◄▲▼◄▲▼◄▲▼◄▲▼◄▲▼◄▲▼◄▲▼◄▲▼◄▲▼

Science at Work

Microbiologist

A microbiologist needs good observation and communication skills. Microbiologists use microscopes and other equipment such as computers. They need a minimum of a two-year technical training degree. Most have at least a four-year college degree, and others have a master's degree or Ph.D.

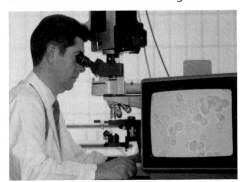

A microbiologist is a scientist who studies living things that are too small to be seen without a microscope. Because of the variety of cells and tiny living things, microbiologists often specialize in a certain area. For example, some become cell biologists and study how cells function. Some study bacteria or other living things. Microbiologists often work as a part of a team. They might work in a laboratory at a hospital or in other industries. They might travel and study living things that cause disease. Microbiologists sometimes discover living things that have not been seen before.

INVESTIGATION

18

Comparing Cells

Purpose

Do all cells look the same? In this investigation, you will observe differences and similarities among different types of cells.

Procedure

1. Choose one of the prepared slides. On a sheet of paper, record the type of cells you selected. Look at the slide without using the microscope. What can you see? **Safety Alert: Handle glass microscope slides with care. Dispose of broken glass properly.**

2. Place the slide on the stage of the microscope. Refer to the instructions for the microscope you are using. Focus and adjust the microscope so that you can see the cells on the slide clearly. Look at the cells under different levels of magnification. How does what you see now differ from what you saw without the microscope?

3. Observe one of the cells on the slide. What is its shape? Do you see any organelles inside the cell? If so, what do they look like? Make a drawing of the cell on your paper.

4. Repeat the procedure, observing at least one type of animal cell, one type of plant cell, and one type of bacterial cell.

Materials

- prepared slides of animal, plant, and bacterial cells
- light microscope

Questions and Conclusions

1. What were some similarities between the plant cells and the animal cells? What were some differences?

2. How did the plant cells and animal cells differ from the bacterial cells?

Explore Further

Observe prepared slides of other cells or find out how to make your own slides of cells. Then draw the individual cells you observe and compare them.

Objectives

After reading this lesson, you should be able to

◆ explain why water is important to life.

◆ describe how living things use carbohydrates, fats, and proteins.

◆ discuss the importance of eating a variety of foods.

Carbohydrate

A sugar or starch, which living things use for energy

Fat

A chemical that stores large amounts of energy

Protein

A chemical used by living things to build and repair body parts and control body activities

Besides being made of cells, living things are alike because they have similar chemicals. Living things use these chemicals to stay alive. Water is one of the chemicals all living things use.

Importance of Water

Life cannot exist without water. It is the most plentiful chemical in living things. Water is found in each of the approximately 100 trillion cells in the adult human body. It makes up about two-thirds of the weight of the cell.

Water is a useful chemical. Have you ever put sugar in a cup of tea? When you put sugar in tea, you stir the liquid until the sugar dissolves in the liquid. As the sugar dissolves, it breaks apart into tiny pieces that you can no longer see. The water in the tea is the chemical that does the dissolving. Special properties of water allow it to break things apart into tiny particles. When the water, sugar, and tea particles become equally mixed, they form a solution.

The ability to dissolve other chemicals is one of the most important properties of water for life. Cells are so small that the materials that go in and out of them must be very tiny. When a material dissolves into tiny pieces, it can move more easily from cell to cell.

Have you ever accidentally bitten your tongue so hard that it bled? Blood tastes salty. Your body fluids and the liquid in your cells are not pure water. They are a solution of many things, including salts. One example of a salt is sodium chloride. Another name for sodium chloride is table salt. The liquid found in living things is a solution of salts, water, and other chemicals.

Other important chemicals found in living things are **carbohydrates, fats,** and **proteins.** Each of these common chemicals has a job to do in the body of a living thing.

Carbohydrates are divided into two groups: simple and complex. Simple carbohydrates include several types of sugars. Complex carbohydrates are also made up of sugars but include fiber and starches.

Did You Know?

Humans can survive up to several weeks without food. However, they can survive only a few days without water.

Carbohydrates

Carbohydrates are sugars and starches. Sugar is a carbohydrate that is used to sweeten drinks and many foods. Fruits and vegetables, such as oranges and potatoes, contain sugar too. Starches are found in foods such as bread, cereal, pasta, rice, and potatoes. Plants use the energy from sunlight to make carbohydrates from carbon dioxide and water. Carbon dioxide is a gas found in air. Animals get energy from the carbohydrates that plants make.

Energy is needed to carry on various life activities. Energy comes from fuel. You can think of carbohydrates as fuel chemicals. Carbohydrates in your body work like gasoline in a car. Gasoline from the fuel tank gets to the engine, where it is broken down and energy is released. This released energy runs the engine. When carbohydrates are broken down in your body, energy is released. This energy powers your body. The same thing happens in other animals. Plants and other living things use carbohydrates for energy too.

Fats

Fats also can be thought of as fuel chemicals. Fats store large amounts of energy that are released when they are broken down. Of all the chemicals important for life, fats contain the most energy. They are found in foods such as meat, butter, cheese, and peanut butter. Fats are related to oils. Fats are solid at room temperature. Oils, such as corn oil used for frying foods, are liquid at room temperature.

Foods contain water, carbohydrates, fats, and other chemicals important for life.

Proteins that are not formed correctly are found in the brains of people who have Alzheimer's and mad cow disease.

Proteins

Proteins are another kind of chemical important for life. Meats, such as beef, chicken, and fish, contain large amounts of proteins. Beans, nuts, eggs, and cheese also contain large amounts of proteins.

Like carbohydrates and fats, proteins provide energy for living things. But they have other important functions too. Proteins help to repair damaged cells and build new ones. Hair, muscles, and skin are made mostly of proteins. Proteins also help control body activities such as heart rate and the breaking down of food in the body.

Proteins are basic parts of living cells. The cell assembles molecules—mainly proteins—to carry out cellular functions. Proteins are made up of long chains of smaller molecules called amino acids. There are 20 different amino acids that can be arranged in different ways to make different proteins. This means that there can be many different kinds of proteins. For this reason, proteins have a wide range of jobs in the body. These include digesting food, fighting infections, controlling body chemistry, and keeping the body working smoothly.

Protein chains fold into a particular shape to carry out a particular function. Proteins with different shapes carry out different functions. If a protein twists into the wrong shape or has a missing part, it may not be able to do its job.

Technology Note

Scientists use computers to help them predict the structure of a protein. Computer models identify a protein's shape based on the arrangement of its amino acids. A computer image shows the physical and chemical properties of the protein. It also provides clues about its role in the body. This information helps scientists understand a protein's role in health and disease. Scientists can then work to develop ways to treat disease.

The DNA in a cell nucleus contains the code that's needed to produce a protein. When a cell receives a signal that a certain protein is needed, the DNA inside the nucleus reproduces the code. The code is then carried by RNA out into the cell. There, ribosomes read the RNA. The ribosomes join together the long chains of amino acids using the RNA code. A change in even one atom in the DNA molecule can change the protein that is produced.

Importance of Nutrients

Keeping your body working properly is not a simple job. You must get a regular supply of carbohydrates, proteins, and fats from the foods you eat. Each kind of food provides different chemicals your body needs. Therefore, it is important to eat a variety of foods every day.

In addition to water, carbohydrates, proteins, and fats, your body also needs **minerals** and **vitamins**. Minerals are natural substances that your body needs to work properly. Vitamins are used by your body for growth and activity. Your body needs these in small amounts only. Different foods contain different minerals, such as zinc, and vitamins, such as vitamin B_{12}. The chemicals that are needed for life and that come from foods are called **nutrients**. To be healthy, living things need to take in the right amounts of nutrients every day.

Lesson 2 **REVIEW**

Write your answers to these questions on a separate sheet of paper. Write complete sentences.

1. What is one of the most important properties of water for life?

2. How does your body use carbohydrates and fats?

3. What do proteins do in your body?

4. What are vitamins and minerals?

5. How can you get all the nutrients you need?

Achievements in Science

Plant Cells Observed

Before the microscope was invented, scientists could observe only what they could see with the unaided eye. Using a microscope, the world of tiny living organisms was revealed. Imagine how exciting it would be to see these organisms for the first time!

It is believed that the earliest microscope used drops of water to make things look larger. A later microscope was a tube that had a place for the object to be observed on one end. On the other end there was a lens that made something look about 10 times its actual size.

One English scientist, Robert Hooke, used a microscope to observe a slice of a cork. He saw that the cork was made up of tiny units that he called "cells." He thought that these cells existed only in plants. He believed that they were just containers, not the basic unit of life that we now know they are.

After reading this lesson, you should be able to

◆ identify some basic life activities.

◆ compare how plants and animals get food, move, and respond.

◆ explain the difference between growth and development.

Digestion

The process by which living things break down food

Respiration

The process by which living things release energy from food

Excretion

The process by which living things get rid of wastes

Most living things carry on the same kinds of activities. These activities allow living things to stay alive. Some examples of basic life activities are described below.

Getting Food

A familiar example of a life activity is getting food. Animals get food by eating plants or other animals. Plants make their own food. They use the energy from sunlight to make carbohydrates from carbon dioxide and water.

Using Food and Removing Wastes

Digestion is a life activity that breaks down food into chemicals that cells can use. **Respiration** is another basic life activity. During respiration, cells release the energy that is stored in the chemicals. Oxygen is used to release the stored energy. Cells use the energy to do work. Respiration also produces wastes. **Excretion** is the process that removes wastes from living things.

Movement

Movement is another activity that is common to living things. Plants do not move from one place to another, but they still move. Plants have roots that hold them in place, but their parts bend and move. For example, leaves may move to face sunlight. Animal movement is easier to see. Most animals move freely from place to place.

The movements of most animals are obvious.

Besides outward movement, there is constant movement inside living things. The material inside plants and animals is always changing. Liquids are flowing, food is being digested, and materials are moving into and out of cells.

Sensing and Responding

Living things sense and respond. Animals and plants have tissues and organs that pick up, or sense, signals from their surroundings. These signals include light, sound, chemicals, and touch. Plants and animals change something, or respond, based on the kinds of signals they pick up. For example, some moths fly around lights at night. Fish swim to the top of a tank for food. Dogs respond to the sound of a human voice. Many flowers open in the morning light and close with night's darkness.

Homeostasis

Organisms have the ability to maintain their internal conditions. This ability is called **homeostasis**. An example of this is your body's ability to keep your temperature within a normal range.

Growth

Growing is part of being alive. You were once a baby, but you have grown into a larger person. You may still be growing. You will continue to grow until you reach your adult size. Most living things go through a similar pattern of growth.

Reproduction

Living things produce offspring, or children, through the basic life activity of **reproduction**. Some living things reproduce by themselves. For example, bacteria reproduce by dividing in two. For other living things, such as humans, reproduction involves two parents. The offspring of all living things resemble their parent or parents.

Development

Development

The changes that occur as a living thing grows

Many living things develop as they grow. **Development** means becoming different, or changing, over time. Tadpoles hatch from eggs and develop by stages into frogs or toads. Notice in the photos below that tadpoles look more like fish than like frogs. Unlike frogs, tadpoles have a tail and no legs. Tadpoles also have no mouth when they first hatch. As a tadpole develops, a mouth forms and changes in shape. The legs form, and the tail is absorbed into the body.

Lesson 3   R E V I E W

Write your answers to these questions on a separate sheet of paper. Write complete sentences.

1. List three basic activities of living things.

2. How do animals and plants get food?

3. What is the difference in the way animals and plants move?

4. Contrast growth and development.

5. What does "sensing and responding" mean?

Science in Your Life

Can you identify life activities?

Living things around you carry out basic life activities all the time. Animals move around much of the time. A flowering plant being pollinated by a bee is involved in reproduction. Even when living things seem to be just sitting there not doing anything, they are carrying out basic life activities. A plant is constantly making food with energy from the sun by using carbon dioxide and water. The cells of a dog resting in the shade are carrying out respiration. If the dog just finished eating, it is also carrying out the basic life activity of digestion.

Can you recognize basic life activities? Take pictures of living things around you or look for photos in magazines. Nature magazines may be easiest to use. Try to find at least one example of each basic life activity. Some examples like those above may not be seen directly in the photos. Cut out the photos and arrange them as a collage on a large sheet of paper. Then number the images. On a separate sheet of paper, list the basic life activities that you can identify in each photo. Most photos will show more than one basic life activity.

Kingdom

One of the five groups into which living things are classified

While most scientists follow the five kingdom classifications, some want to add a sixth kingdom for viruses. A virus is a type of germ. A virus can reproduce only inside a living cell. It cannot carry out life processes outside the cell. As new information becomes known, the five groupings may change.

Living things are more like one another than they are like nonliving things. For example, living things all carry out the basic life activities. However, living things can be very different from one another. A cat is different from a dog. A bird and a tree are even more different from each other.

Scientists divide the world of living things into five groups, or **kingdoms.** These kingdoms are plant, animal, protist, fungi, and monera. Biological classifications, or groupings, are based on how organisms are related. The study of living things is called biology. The science of classifying organisms based on the features they share is called taxonomy. Most of the living things you know are either in the plant kingdom or the animal kingdom. There are three other kingdoms that you may not know very well.

The Plant Kingdom

Most plants are easy to recognize. Examples of plants are trees, grasses, ferns, and mosses. Plants don't move from place to place like animals. They don't need to do so. Plants make their own food, using sunlight and other substances around them. All plants have many cells. These cells are organized into tissues. Many plants also have organs.

The Animal Kingdom

Animals have many different sizes and shapes. You probably recognize dogs, turtles, and fish as animals. Corals, sponges, and insects are animals too.

Animals get their food by eating plants or by eating other animals that eat plants.

Animals cannot make their own food. They get their food from other living things. They eat plants, or they eat other animals that eat plants. Most animals move around to capture or gather their food. Moving also helps them to find shelter, escape danger, and find mates. All animals have many cells. These cells form tissues in all animals except the sponge. In most animals, the tissues form organs.

The Protist Kingdom

At one time, biologists divided the living world into only two kingdoms, plant and animal. Then the microscope was invented. When biologists used the microscope, they discovered tiny organisms. They called them **microorganisms** because biologists could see these organisms only under a microscope. These organisms did not fit into either the plant or the animal kingdom. Biologists placed them in a separate kingdom. They called the organisms **protists**.

Most protists have only one cell. A few have many cells. Some protists make their own food. Others absorb food from other sources. **Algae** are plantlike protists. **Protozoans** are animal-like protists. Some protozoans have properties of plants and animals. All protists can carry out the basic life activities.

Algae live in lakes, streams, rivers, ponds, and oceans. You have probably seen the algae that grow as a green scum on a pond. The green scum is thousands of tiny algae. Like plants, algae can make their own food. Algae are food for the organisms that live in waters around the world. Many larger algae are called seaweeds. Some seaweeds can become as long as a football field. Algae also produce oxygen that other organisms use. At one time, biologists classified algae as plants. Algae, however, are simpler than plants and have more in common with protists.

Did You Know?

Athlete's foot is a disease caused by a fungus.

Protozoans live in water, soil, and the bodies of animals. Most protozoans are harmless. But a few, such as *Giardia*, cause disease. This protozoan infects the small intestine of humans and other animals. It causes tiredness, weight loss, and stomach pain.

Protozoans behave like animals by getting food and moving. Different kinds of protozoans have different methods of moving. Protozoans can use **flagella**, **cilia**, or **pseudopods** to move. **Amoebas** push out a part of their cell. This part is called a pseudopod. It looks like a foot and pulls the amoeba along. Some protozoans have tails, or flagella, that move them back and forth. Others, such as **paramecia**, use cilia to move. Cilia are tiny hairlike structures that beat like boat paddles.

Euglenas are protozoans that behave like both plants and animals. Like plants, they make their own food when sunlight is present. Like animals, they can absorb food from the environment. They absorb food when sunlight is not present.

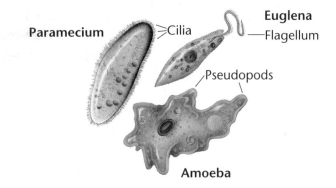

The Fungi Kingdom

You are probably more familiar with organisms in the fourth kingdom, **fungi**. Mushrooms and the mold that grows on bread are fungi. Most fungi have many cells. At one time, fungi were classified as plants. Like plants, fungi do not move around by themselves. But unlike plants, fungi do not make their own food. They absorb food from other organisms.

Decompose

To break down or decay matter into simpler substances

Parasite

An organism that absorbs food from a living organism and harms it

Moneran

An organism, usually one-celled, that does not have organelles

Because of the way fungi get food, they are important to other organisms. Fungi release special chemicals on dead plant and animal matter. The chemicals break down, or **decompose**, the matter. The fungi then absorb the decomposed material. But some of the decomposed matter also gets into the soil. Other organisms, such as plants, can then use it.

Some fungi are **parasites**. They absorb food from a living organism. Some fungi harm plants. For example, Dutch elm disease kills elm trees. Other fungi harm animals. A fungus causes ringworm, a human skin disease.

The Monera Kingdom

The last of the kingdoms contains **monerans**. *Monera* means "alone." This kingdom has only one kind of organism, which is bacteria. Monerans are usually one-celled organisms. Like animals, some can move and get food. Like plants, some stay put and make their own food. You may wonder why bacteria are not placed in the protist kingdom. The cells of bacteria are different from the cells of all other organisms. Bacteria do not have organelles in their cells. Organelles are tiny structures in cells that do certain jobs. The cells of all other organisms have organelles.

Some bacteria cause disease. For example, bacteria cause strep throat. Most bacteria, though, are harmless. Many are even helpful. Like fungi, bacteria help to decompose the remains of plants and animals. People also use bacteria to make foods such as cheese and yogurt.

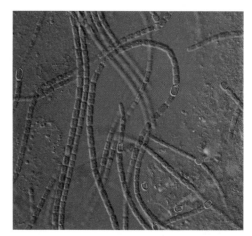

Some bacteria are green like plants and make their own food.

Lesson 4 REVIEW

Write your answers to these questions on a separate sheet of paper. Write complete sentences.

1. Name the five kingdoms of living things.

2. List two differences between plants and animals.

3. How are protists similar to plants and animals?

4. What is an important function of fungi?

5. Why are bacteria placed in a kingdom by themselves?

▼◀▲▼◀▲▼◀▲▼◀▲▼◀▲▼◀▲▼◀▲▼◀▲▼◀▲▼◀▲▼◀▲▼

Science at Work

Taxonomist

Taxonomists should have good organization and research skills and be able to classify data. A college degree in botany, zoology, or biology is needed. Some taxonomists may need a master's degree or a Ph.D.

A taxonomist is a scientist who studies organisms and classifies them into groups. Taxonomists not only classify the organisms into groups, they study all the information about a specific group. They label thousands of species and collect various data. Because so many different kinds of organisms exist, taxonomists usually specialize by choosing which organisms to study. Taxonomists need to keep up with new technologies. New information could lead to changes in the way organisms are classified.

Some taxonomists travel around the world to study organisms. They may even discover a kind of organism no one else has identified before. Some taxonomists work in museums, zoos, or botanical gardens. They study plants and animals that have been collected. Other taxonomists study organisms in laboratories or teach at universities.

Are bacteria helpful or harmful?

Bacteria live everywhere. They are in the ocean, on top of mountains, in polar ice, on your hands, and even inside you. You cannot go anywhere without coming in contact with bacteria.

Most bacteria are helpful. Bacteria in soil break down plant and animal material and release nutrients. They also take in gases from the air, such as nitrogen. They change nitrogen into a form that plants and animals can use. Bacteria in your intestines make vitamin K. This vitamin helps your blood clot when you are cut.

Bacteria can also be harmful. Many bacteria cause diseases in people. Bacteria cause diseases such as tuberculosis, tetanus, and cholera. Food that is contaminated by certain kinds of bacteria can cause illness.

Microbiologists are scientists who work with bacteria and other microorganisms. Some microbiologists help to identify bacteria that cause disease. They grow the bacteria on special plates. Each cell multiplies until it forms millions of bacteria cells, called a colony. It is impossible to see a single bacterium without a microscope. But it is easy to see colonies of bacteria.

There are ways to get rid of most harmful bacteria. Antibiotics are drugs that kill bacteria in people and animals. Pasteurization, or rapid heating, kills harmful bacteria in milk. Drinking water is purified to remove bacteria and other microorganisms. Sewage is treated so that it will not pollute water supplies. Sometimes bacteria help to clean up sewage. Helpful bacteria break down material in the sewage so that it does not harm people.

Science Words

- Living things are made of cells. Cells come in different shapes and sizes and carry out many different functions.

- Cells are organized into tissues, which are organized into organs.

- Plant cells and animal cells have many of the same parts. Plant cells have cell walls and chloroplasts. Animal cells do not.

- Each organelle has a different function in the cell.

- An important property of water is its ability to dissolve things.

- Cells use carbohydrates, fats, and proteins for energy. Sugars and starches are carbohydrates.

- Plants use energy from sunlight to make carbohydrates from carbon dioxide and water.

- Fats store large amounts of energy. Fats are solid at room temperature. Oils are liquid at room temperature.

- Proteins provide energy, help to build and repair body parts, and control body activities.

- Minerals and vitamins are chemicals in foods. Your body needs them only in small amounts.

- All living things have basic life activities: getting and using food, removing wastes, moving, sensing and responding, growing, developing, and reproducing.

- Living things are divided into five kingdoms based on how they are related: plant, animal, protist, fungi, and monera.

- Plants make their own food.

- Animals eat other organisms for food.

- Protists include algae, seaweeds, and protozoans. Most are one-celled. They have properties of both animals and plants.

- At one time, fungi were classified as plants. But fungi do not make their own food. They absorb their food from other organisms.

- Monerans are bacteria. They are usually one-celled organisms that do not have organelles. Some make their own food and others absorb it.

Chapter 18 R E V I E W

Word Bank

carbohydrates

development

digestion

excretion

fats

microscopes

nutrients

organelles

organs

proteins

reproduction

respiration

tissues

vitamins

Vocabulary Review

Choose the word from the Word Bank that best completes each sentence. Write the answer on a sheet of paper.

1. Sugars and starches are _____.

2. Living things get rid of wastes by the process of _____.

3. Large amounts of energy are stored in _____.

4. _____ help control body activities.

5. Scientists observe the shapes and sizes of cells by using _____.

6. _____ produces offspring.

7. During _____, cells release energy stored in food.

8. Nutrients that living things need in small amounts are _____.

9. During _____, food is broken down into chemicals that cells can use.

10. Groups of different kinds of tissues form _____.

11. _____ is the change that occurs as a living thing grows.

12. Tiny structures found inside cells are called _____.

13. _____ are made of groups of similar cells that work together to do a certain job.

14. Water, carbohydrates, proteins, fats, vitamins, and minerals are _____.

Concept Review

Choose the answer that best completes each sentence. Write the letter of the answer on your paper.

15. Plants can make their own _____.
   A minerals   **C** flagella
   B water   **D** food

16. Another word for a living thing is _____.
   A biology   **C** organism
   B protist   **D** multicellular

17. Organisms made of many cells that break down dead plants and animals for food are _____.
   A protozoans   **C** parasites
   B fungi   **D** monerans

18. An organism that is too small to be seen without a microscope is a(n) _____.
   A microorganism   **C** moss
   B fungus   **D** pseudopod

19. An organism that lives on a living organism and harms it is a(n) _____.
   A organelle   **C** moneran
   B ciliate   **D** parasite

Critical Thinking

Write the answer to the following question.

20. What are some of the properties that are used to divide living things into kingdoms? Give some examples.

Test-Taking Tip Read test questions carefully to identify questions that ask for more than one answer.

Classifying Animals

In Chapter 18, you learned that biologists use similarities and differences to classify organisms into five kingdoms. The organisms are further classified into smaller groups. In this chapter, you will learn how biologists classify animals into groups. You will also learn about the body systems that help animals stay alive.

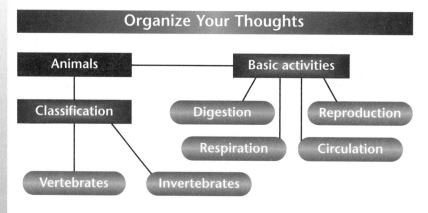

Organize Your Thoughts

Animals ——— Basic activities

Classification

Digestion

Reproduction

Respiration

Circulation

Vertebrates — Invertebrates

Goals for Learning

◆ To learn how biologists classify and name animals
◆ To identify the features of different groups of vertebrates
◆ To identify the features of different groups of invertebrates
◆ To understand how animals obtain and digest food
◆ To explore respiration and circulation in animals

After reading this lesson, you should be able to

◆ explain how biologists classify animals.

◆ name the seven levels in the classification system of organisms.

◆ identify the two parts of a scientific name.

Biologists have identified more than one million different kinds of animals in the world. More kinds of animals are added to the list every day. To deal with such a large list, biologists need a way to divide it into smaller groups.

Biologists divide animals into groups based on their similarities. For example, falcons, sparrows, and geese are classified as birds because they all have feathers. All birds have feathers, but no other type of animal does.

The Seven Levels of Classification

Biologists use a system to classify living things. The diagram below shows that there are seven levels in the classification system of organisms: kingdom, **phylum**, class, order, family, **genus**, and **species**.

Phylum

Subdivision of a kingdom (plural is phyla)

Genus

A group of living things that includes separate species

Species

A group of organisms that can breed with each other to produce offspring like themselves

Levels of Classification

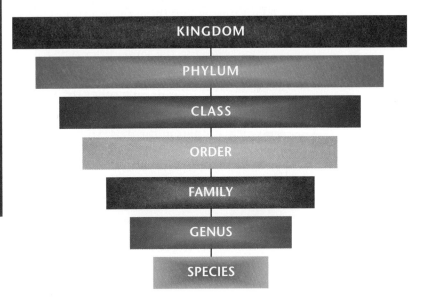

KINGDOM

PHYLUM

CLASS

ORDER

FAMILY

GENUS

SPECIES

You learned in Chapter 18 that biologists classify all organisms into five kingdoms. Kingdoms represent the highest level in the classification system. The animal kingdom is one of the five kingdoms. Each kingdom is divided into groups called phyla. The phyla represent the second-highest level of classification. More organisms are included in a kingdom than in any one of its phyla. Each phylum is divided into classes, each class is divided into orders, and so on.

The lowest level in the classification system is the species. Each species represents a single type of organism. Members of the same species can breed and produce offspring like themselves. A group of separate but related species belongs to the same genus.

A Place for Every Organism

Every organism that has been identified has its own place in the classification system. The diagram on the next page shows how biologists classify four species of animals. Notice that the African elephant, the red tree mouse, and the heather mouse belong to the same phylum. The boll weevil belongs to a different phylum. This means that these three animals are more similar to each other than they are to the boll weevil. Notice also that the two mice belong to the same order. The elephant belongs to a different order. Thus, the red tree mouse and the heather mouse are more similar to each other than they are to the elephant. Organisms that are very similar belong to the same genus. Which animals in the diagram belong to the same genus?

Some classification groups contain a large number of species. For example, the order Coleoptera contains over 360,000 species, including the boll weevil. Other orders may have just a few species. For example, the African elephant and the Asian elephant are the only two species in the order Proboscidea.

Kingdom	**Animalia**			
Phylum	**Arthropoda**	**Chordata**		
Class	**Insecta**	**Mammalia**		
Order	**Coleoptera**	**Proboscidea**	**Rodentia**	
Family	**Curculionidae**	**Elephantidae**	**Cricetidae**	
Genus	*Anthonomus*	*Loxodonta*	*Phenacomys*	
Species	*grandis*	*africana*	*longicaudus*	*intermedius*
	Boll weevil	African elephant	Red tree mouse	Heather mouse

Scientific Names

Most people call animals by their common names, such as mockingbird and mountain lion. However, using common names can be confusing. The mountain lion in the photo below has at least four other common names: puma, cougar, catamount, and American panther. All five names refer to the same species. People who use one of these names may not know that the other names refer to the same species. The opposite problem occurs with the common name "June bug." At least a dozen different beetle species have that name. When someone says "June bug," you have no way of knowing which species that is. The same animal may have different names in different languages too. For example, an owl is called *gufo* in Italian, *hibou* in French, and *búho* in Spanish.

The mountain lion has several common names but only one scientific name: Felis concolor.

To overcome these problems, biologists give each species a **scientific name**. An organism's scientific name consists of two words. The first word is the organism's genus, and the second word is its species label. For example, the scientific name of the mountain lion is *Felis concolor*. Thus, the mountain lion belongs to the genus *Felis* and the species *concolor*. Look again at the diagram on page 435. What is the scientific name of the African elephant?

The scientific name given to each species is unique. This means that different species have different scientific names, even if they have the same common name. Scientific names are in Latin, so they are recognized by biologists around the world. For example, *Felis concolor* means the same thing in France, the United States, and Mexico. As you may have noticed, scientific names are always printed in *italics* or are underlined. The first word in the name is capitalized, but the second word is not.

Science in Your Life

Has everything been classified?

You may think that every kind of organism on Earth has already been studied, classified, and named. In fact, biologists continue to discover species that no one has identified before. Many of the newly found species are insects. Some biologists think there could be millions of insect species that still have not been identified.

Some new species may be useful in finding new medicines. Others may help control pests that damage crops. To learn how a new species might be useful, biologists must study the organism closely. They must learn how it carries out its life activities. Then they can classify the organism.

Write your answers to these questions on a separate sheet of paper. Write complete sentences.

1. On what do biologists base their classification of organisms?

2. List the seven levels of classification of organisms, from highest to lowest.

3. What is a species?

4. The banana slug and the cuttlefish belong to the same phylum. The clownfish belongs to a different phylum. Is the banana slug or the clownfish more similar to the cuttlefish?

5. The barn owl belongs to the genus *Tyto* and the species *alba*. What is the barn owl's scientific name?

Technology Note

As scientists continue to research new and existing species of animals, they use computers to store and study their data. Computers also allow scientists to share information with each other. Large amounts of information about animal species are available to you on the Internet. You can get this information by using an Internet search engine. Search for words such as *vertebrates*, *invertebrates*, *mammals*, and *birds*. Also search for *zoos*, *aquariums*, and *universities*. These places often have Web sites that provide interesting information about animal groups.

Classifying Objects

Purpose

How are objects classified? In this investigation, you will make a classification system for objects found in your classroom.

Procedure

1. Form a team with two or three other students. On a sheet of paper, make a list of objects in your classroom. Include objects that may be on shelves or in drawers and cabinets.

2. Divide the objects on your list into groups based on their similarities. Name each group.

3. Make up a classification system for the objects on your list. Your system should have several levels. Each level should include all of the groups in the next-lower level.

4. Write your classification system on a sheet of paper. List the objects that belong in each group. Show how the different levels are related to each other.

5. Compare your classification system with the system made up by other student teams.

Materials

◆ assortment of objects found in a classroom

Questions and Conclusions

1. What were the names of the groups your team came up with?

2. How many levels did your classification system have?

3. How did your classification system differ from the systems of other student teams?

4. How does this investigation show the value of having a single system for classifying organisms?

Explore Further

Work with two other teams to combine your classification systems into one system. Write the combined system on a sheet of paper. Describe how your classification system changed.

Vertebrate

An animal with a backbone

Cartilage

A soft material found in vertebrate skeletons

Vertebra

One of the bones or blocks of cartilage that make up a backbone

The animals that are probably most familiar to you are animals with backbones. These animals are called **vertebrates**. Vertebrates include tiny hummingbirds and enormous blue whales. Humans also are vertebrates. Altogether, there are nearly 50,000 species of vertebrates in the world.

Features of Vertebrates

Vertebrates have three features that set them apart from other animals. First, all vertebrates have an internal skeleton, which is inside their body. The skeleton of vertebrates is made of bone or a softer material called **cartilage**. Some other animals also have an internal skeleton, but it is made of different materials.

The second feature of vertebrates is their backbone. A backbone is made up of many small bones or blocks of cartilage. For example, the human backbone contains 26 bones. Each bone or block of cartilage in the backbone is called a **vertebra**. That is why animals with backbones are known as vertebrates.

The third feature of vertebrates is the skull. The skull surrounds and protects the brain. Look for the backbone and skull in the skeleton of this cow.

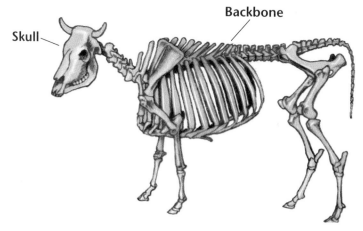

Vertebrate Skeleton

Vertebrates are divided into seven classes. Three of the classes consist of different types of fish. The other four classes are amphibians, reptiles, birds, and mammals.

Fish

Biologists have identified about 24,000 species of fish. There are more species of fish than of any other kind of vertebrate. All fish live in water and breathe with structures called **gills**.

A bony fish is covered with scales.

Most fish have a skeleton made of bone and are called bony fish. This first type includes bass, trout, salmon, and many others. You can see in the photo that the body of a bony fish is covered with scales that overlap like roof shingles. The scales protect the fish and give it a smooth surface. Many bony fish have an organ called a **swim bladder** that is filled with gas. By changing the amount of gas in its swim bladder, the fish can move up or down in water.

Sharks, rays, and skates make up the second type of vertebrate. They have a skeleton made of cartilage instead of bone. Many of these fish have powerful jaws and rows of sharp teeth. Their tiny, toothlike scales make their skin feel like sandpaper. Lampreys and hagfish, the third type, are jawless fish. They also have a skeleton made of cartilage, but they have no jaws or scales.

Amphibians

Amphibians include about 5,000 species of frogs, toads, and salamanders. The word *amphibian* comes from two Greek words meaning "double life." This refers to the fact that many amphibians spend part of their life in water and part on land. Recall from Chapter 18 that frogs begin their life as tadpoles that live in water. After a while, a tadpole grows legs, loses its gills and tail, and develops into an adult frog. This change is called **metamorphosis**. The frog may spend much of its life on land.

Science Myth

Whales, dolphins, and porpoises are classified as fish.

Fact: Whales, dolphins, and porpoises are mammals. They do look similar to fish and live in the ocean. However, they have lungs instead of gills and must swim to the surface to breathe air. They also have hair and feed their young with milk.

Reptile

An egg-laying vertebrate that breathes with lungs

Cold-blooded

Having a body temperature that changes with temperature of surroundings

Adult amphibians breathe with lungs or through their skin. The skin is thin and moist. To keep from drying out, amphibians must stay near water or in damp places. Since amphibian eggs do not have shells, they must be laid in water or where the ground is wet.

Reptiles

Snakes, lizards, turtles, alligators, and crocodiles are **reptiles**. There are about 7,000 species of reptiles. Some reptiles, such as sea turtles, live mostly in water. Others, such as tortoises, live on land. The skin of reptiles is scaly and watertight, so reptiles can live in dry places without drying out. Some tortoises, for example, live in deserts where water is scarce. Most reptiles lay eggs on land. The eggs have a soft shell that keeps the young inside from drying out. All reptiles breathe with lungs. Reptiles that live in water must come to the surface to breathe.

Dinosaurs were reptiles. The first dinosaurs appeared about 235 million years ago. Some dinosaurs were taller than a four-story building and heavier than ten elephants. However, many dinosaurs were no bigger than a house cat. All dinosaurs became extinct about 65 million years ago.

Fish, amphibians, and reptiles are **cold-blooded** animals. Their body temperature changes with the temperature of their surroundings.

Amphibians have smooth, moist skin. The skin of reptiles is dry and scaly.

Penguins, ostriches, and emus are classified as birds, but they do not fly. Like other birds, they have lungs, feathers, beaks, and lay eggs covered by a hard shell. Ostriches and emus have strong legs and can run quickly. Penguins are good swimmers.

Birds

There are more than 9,000 species of birds, and almost all of them can fly. Feathers make flight possible by providing lift and smoothing the lines of the body. Birds also have hollow bones, which keep their skeleton light. Flying requires a lot of energy, so birds cannot go long without eating. Feathers act like a warm coat that keeps heat inside the bird's body. All birds breathe with lungs and have a horny beak. Birds lay eggs that are covered by a hard shell. As **warm-blooded** animals, birds and mammals have a body temperature that stays the same.

Mammals

Mammals are named for their **mammary glands**, which are milk-producing structures on the chest or abdomen. As shown in the photo, female mammals nurse their young with milk from these glands. Mammals also have hair covering most of their body. Hair helps keep in body heat. Most mammals live on land, but some, such as whales and porpoises, live in water. All mammals have lungs.

More than 4,000 species of mammals have young that develop inside the mother. These mammals include bears, elephants, mice, and humans. About 300 species of mammals, including opossums and kangaroos, have young that develop in a pouch on the mother. The duck-billed platypus and the spiny anteater are the only mammals that lay eggs.

Mammals feed their young with milk produced by mammary glands.

Lesson 2   R E V I E W

Write your answers to these questions on a separate sheet of paper. Write complete sentences.

1. What three features do all vertebrates have?

2. How does a trout's skeleton differ from a shark's skeleton?

3. What happens during metamorphosis in a frog?

4. Why are a reptile's eggs able to survive in dry places?

5. What two features do mammals have that other vertebrates do not have?

▼◀▲▼◀▲▼◀▲▼◀▲▼◀▲▼◀▲▼◀▲▼◀▲▼◀▲▼◀▲▼◀▲▼◀▲▼◀▲▼

Science at Work

Zookeeper

Zookeepers should have good observation skills and strong communication skills. They should be able to deal with emergencies and solve problems. Usually a college degree in zoology, biology, or an animal-related field is needed.

Because of the variety of animals in a zoo, a zookeeper might take care of mammals, birds, fish, amphibians, or reptiles. The job may include making sure the animals are clean and that they get enough food and exercise. The zookeeper may have to keep the animals' living area clean. Zookeepers must also notice any changes in the appearance or behavior of the animals. Changes could mean the animal is sick or has another problem.

Zookeepers talk to people who visit the zoo. They answer questions and help teach visitors about the animals.

Invertebrate

An animal that does not have a backbone

Radial symmetry

An arrangement of body parts that resembles the arrangement of spokes on a wheel

Tentacle

An armlike body part in invertebrates that is used for capturing prey

Every animal that is not a vertebrate is called an **invertebrate**. An invertebrate is an animal that does not have a backbone. Invertebrates make up about 97 percent of all animal species and belong to more than 30 phyla. You will learn about eight of those phyla in this lesson.

Sponges

Sponges are the simplest animals. Their bodies consist of two layers of cells without any tissues or organs. All 10,000 species of sponges live in water. Sponges strain food particles out of the water as the water moves through their body. The water enters through pores in the body wall. If you use a natural bath sponge, you are using the skeleton of a dead sponge.

Cnidarians

Cnidarians include animals such as jellyfish, corals, and hydras. There are about 10,000 species of cnidarians. All live in water. Cnidarians have body parts that are arranged like spokes on a wheel. This type of arrangement of body parts is known as **radial symmetry**. You can see the radial symmetry of a sea anemone in the photo. Cnidarians have armlike **tentacles** with stinging cells. The tentacles capture small prey and push them into the body, where they are digested.

The tentacles of this sea anemone show radial symmetry.

Flatworms

As their name suggests, flatworms are flat and thin. Their bodies have a left half and a right half that are the same. This type of body plan is known as **bilateral symmetry**. There are more than 20,000 species of flatworms. Most are parasites that live on or inside other animals. An example of a flatworm that is a parasite is the tapeworm. Tapeworms live in the intestines of vertebrates, including humans. In the intestine, tapeworms absorb nutrients through their skin. People can get tapeworms when they eat infected meat that has not been cooked completely.

Roundworms

Roundworms have long, round bodies that come to a point at the ends. Like flatworms, roundworms have bilateral symmetry. Most of the 80,000 species of roundworms are not parasitic. They may live in the soil or in water. Some soil-dwelling roundworms help plants by eating insect pests. About 150 species of roundworms are parasites, and many of them live in humans. For example, hookworms settle in the intestine and feed on blood. Hookworms enter the body by boring through the skin. That usually happens when people walk barefoot in places that are not clean.

Segmented Worms

Segmented worms have a body that is divided into many sections, or segments. These worms may live in the soil, in freshwater, or in the ocean. The earthworm is the most familiar of the 15,000 species of segmented worms. Earthworms tunnel through the soil, eating small food particles. Their tunnels loosen the soil and allow air to enter it, which helps plants grow. Leeches are another kind of segmented worm. Many leeches eat small invertebrates, but some leeches are parasites. Leeches that are parasites attach to the skin of a vertebrate and feed on its blood. While feeding, leeches release a chemical that keeps the blood flowing.

Mollusks

There are more than 112,000 species of mollusks. These are invertebrates that are divided into three parts: head, body, and foot. Some live on land, while others live in freshwater

A squid uses its tentacles to capture prey.

or in the ocean. Snails and slugs make up the largest group of mollusks. Snails have a coiled shell, but slugs have no shell at all. Another group of mollusks includes clams, scallops, and oysters. Their shell is made of two hinged pieces that can open and close. Squids and octopuses have no outer shells. These mollusks can swim quickly as they hunt for fish and other animals.

Arthropods

Arthropods are the largest group of invertebrates. They make up more than three-fourths of all animal species. The major groups of arthropods are crustaceans, arachnids, centipedes, millipedes, and insects. Arthropods are segmented animals with jointed legs. Most arthropods also have antennae, which they use to feel, taste, or smell.

Arthropods shed their external skeleton as they grow.

All arthropods have an external skeleton that supports the body and protects the tissues inside. If you ever cracked open the claw of a crab, you know how hard this skeleton can be. Arthropods can bend their bodies because they have joints in their legs and between their body segments. However, an external skeleton is not able to grow as an internal skeleton does. For that reason, an arthropod must shed its skeleton to grow in size. The shedding process shown in the photo is called **molting.** An arthropod begins to produce a new skeleton before it molts. After the animal molts, the skeleton takes a few days to harden completely. The soft-shelled crabs served in restaurants are crabs that have just molted.

Crabs, lobsters, and crayfish are crustaceans. Most of the 40,000 species of crustaceans live in rivers, lakes, and oceans. Crustaceans have five pairs of legs. Some of the legs have small claws that help the animal handle food. The two legs closest to the head usually have powerful claws used for protection. Sow bugs and pill bugs are crustaceans that live on land. You can often find them under rocks and in other moist places.

Spiders, scorpions, mites, and ticks are arachnids. There are about 70,000 species of arachnids. Almost all arachnids live on land. They have four pairs of legs. Spiders produce threads of silk to spin webs and build nests. Most spiders eat insects, but some also catch small fish or frogs. Spiders capture their prey by injecting it with a poison. Scorpions also use poison to capture prey. They use a stinger to inject the poison. Mites and ticks include species that live on the human body. Mites feed on hair and dead skin. Ticks pierce the skin and feed on blood.

All of the 2,500 species of centipedes and the 10,000 species of millipedes live on land. Their bodies have up to 175 segments. Notice in the photo below that centipedes have one pair of legs on each body segment. They can run quickly because their legs are long. Centipedes use their poison claws to kill insects and other prey. Millipedes have two pairs of legs on each body segment. Their legs are short, so millipedes move slowly. Most millipedes eat dead plant matter in the soil.

Centipedes have a pair of legs on each body segment.

Tube foot

A small structure used by echinoderms for movement

Insects are also arthropods. The nearly one million species of insects live almost everywhere except in the deep ocean. Insects include mosquitoes, flies, ants, and beetles. Insects have three pairs of legs. Most have one or two pairs of wings. Insects are the only invertebrates that can fly. Like frogs, most insects go through metamorphosis. Study the metamorphosis of a butterfly in the diagram. Metamorphosis is a change in form during development.

Metamorphosis

Stage 1:
A butterfly egg hatches into a caterpillar.

Stage 4:
After a few weeks, the pupa molts into an adult butterfly.

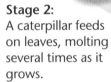

Stage 2:
A caterpillar feeds on leaves, molting several times as it grows.

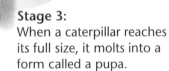

Stage 3:
When a caterpillar reaches its full size, it molts into a form called a pupa.

Echinoderms

Echinoderms, such as this sea star, are invertebrates with tube feet and radial symmetry.

Echinoderms include sea stars, sea urchins, sand dollars, and sea cucumbers. All 7,000 species of echinoderms live in the ocean. Like cnidarians, echinoderms have radial symmetry. Find the echinoderm's **tube feet** in this photo. The tube feet attach firmly to surfaces. Echinoderms use their tube feet to move.

Lesson 3   R E V I E W

Write your answers to these questions on a separate sheet of paper. Write complete sentences.

1. How do sponges feed?

2. Contrast radial symmetry and bilateral symmetry.

3. Give an example of a flatworm, roundworm, and segmented worm.

4. Explain why arthropods molt.

5. How do echinoderms move?

Achievements in Science

Study of Invertebrates Begins

In the late 1700s, few scientists thought that insects and worms were important enough to study. The word *invertebrate* did not even exist. The classification of this group of organisms was not made until a French professor began to study insects and worms.

In 1793 Jean Lamarck became a professor of insects and worms at France's National Museum of Natural History. He was not familiar with these organisms, and the collection at the museum was poorly organized. Lamarck studied, researched, and classified these organisms. He was the first person to use the word *invertebrate*. His work resulted in the study of invertebrates becoming a new field of biology.

By studying invertebrates, we know how important they are to our ecosystems. Invertebrates help build a healthy environment, and they serve as food for countless other animals. Today scientists continue to study and identify all the different invertebrates.

How Animals Get and Digest Food

Objectives

After reading this lesson, you should be able to

◆ describe three main ways animals get food.

◆ explain the importance of digestion.

◆ tell the difference between a gastrovascular cavity and a digestive tract.

Filter feeding

A way of getting food by straining it out of the water

Unlike plants, algae, and some bacteria, animals cannot make their own food. Animals must get food from other organisms. Different animals have different ways of getting food.

Filter Feeding

Many animals that live in water get food by filtering, or straining, it. This way of getting food is called **filter feeding**. Sponges strain bacteria and protists from the water that passes through their body. Sponges cannot move around as adults, and filter feeding allows them to gather food without chasing it. Barnacles also remain in place. They collect food particles with their legs. The legs act as screens. Mollusks, such as clams and oysters, tend to remain in one spot. They use their gills to strain food out of the water. Some filter-feeding animals do move. Many whales harvest millions of tiny animals by swimming with their mouths open.

Feeding on Fluids

Some animals get food from the fluids of plants or other animals. The fluids are rich in nutrients. Aphids and cicadas are insects that have piercing mouthparts. They draw sap from roots, leaves, and stems. Bees, butterflies, and hummingbirds draw nectar from flowers. Spiders and assassin bugs capture insects and suck the fluid from their bodies. Leeches, mosquitoes, and horseflies feed on the blood of vertebrates, including humans.

Consuming Large Pieces of Food

Most animals consume, or eat, large pieces of solid food. Sometimes they eat entire organisms. Such animals use different kinds of body structures to capture and consume their food. For example, hydras, jellyfish, and other cnidarians have tentacles armed with stinging cells. The tentacles catch small animals in the water and bring them to the mouth. Cnidarians consume their food whole.

Many insects have mouthparts that are suited for cutting and chewing. The mouthparts turn the food into pieces that are small enough to swallow. Grasshoppers, termites, and beetles use their chewing mouthparts to feed on plants. Animals that eat plants are known as herbivores. Dragonflies and praying mantises also have chewing mouthparts but eat other insects. Animals that eat other animals are called carnivores.

Vertebrates are the only animals that have teeth. Mammals have teeth of different shapes and sizes. Each kind of tooth does a certain job. Chisel-like teeth at the front of the mouth cut food into pieces. Long, pointed teeth grip and pierce food. Teeth that have a flat surface grind and crush food. A mammal's teeth indicate what kind of food it eats. Carnivores have sharp, pointed teeth that tear flesh. Herbivores have large teeth that have a flat surface. These teeth are suited for grinding plants. Look at the teeth of these skulls. Which is the skull of a carnivore? of a herbivore?

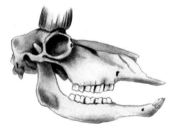

Digesting Food

Foods usually contain fats, proteins, and carbohydrates. These chemicals provide the energy an animal needs. However, they are too large for most animal cells to absorb. These large chemicals must be broken down into smaller chemicals before cells can absorb them. The process of breaking down food into small chemicals is digestion. Animals digest food by **secreting** digestive **enzymes**. An enzyme is a substance that speeds up chemical changes. *Secrete* means to "form and release."

In sponges, the digestive enzymes work inside cells. These cells line the inside of the sponge. The cells trap food that enters the sponge. They package the food in food vacuoles. Digestive enzymes break down the food into small chemicals. The cells then absorb the chemicals.

Digesting food inside cells has one drawback. The food must be small enough to fit inside food vacuoles. This means that sponges can eat only tiny food particles. Most other animals digest their food outside of cells. They have a space where digestion begins. These animals can eat much larger foods.

Secrete

Form and release, or give off

Enzyme

A substance that speeds up chemical changes

Gastrovascular cavity

A digestive space with a single opening

Gastrovascular Cavities

Cnidarians, such as the hydra in the diagram, and flatworms digest food in a hollow space called a **gastrovascular cavity**. This space has only one opening, the mouth. Food enters through the mouth. Special cells line the gastrovascular cavity. These cells secrete digestive enzymes. The enzymes break down the food into small particles. The cells can then absorb the particles. Material that is not digested leaves through the mouth.

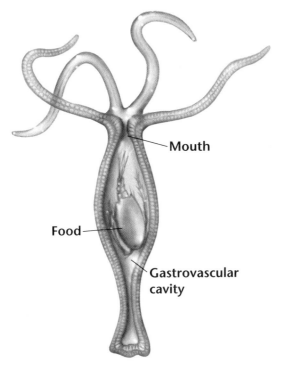

Mouth

Food

Gastrovascular cavity

Digestive tract

A tubelike digestive
space with an opening
at each end

Digestive Tracts

Animals that are more developed have a **digestive tract**. This is a tubelike digestive space with an opening at each end. Food moves through a digestive tract in one direction. Different parts of the tract carry out different functions. The main functions of digestive tracts are storing food, digesting food, and absorbing nutrients.

Most digestive tracts are organized the same way. The digestive tract of a bird provides a good example. Food enters the digestive tract through the mouth. It passes down the esophagus to the crop, where it is stored. In the stomach, the food mixes with acid and digestive enzymes. The mixture moves to the gizzard. The gizzard grinds it into a watery paste. More digestive enzymes are added in the intestine. This is where digestion is completed. The walls of the intestine absorb the small chemicals. Material that is not digested leaves the digestive tract through an opening called the anus.

The digestive tracts of animals have some differences. For example, humans do not have a crop or a gizzard. The human stomach carries out the functions of those organs.

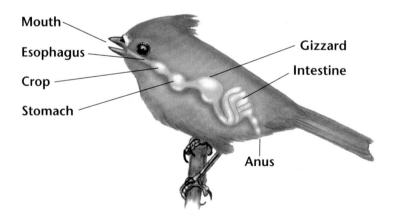

Mouth

Esophagus

Crop

Stomach

Gizzard

Intestine

Anus

Lesson 4 REVIEW

Write your answers to these questions on a separate sheet of paper. Write complete sentences.

1. Name three kinds of animals that use filter feeding to get food.

2. How are cicadas different from dragonflies in the way they feed?

3. Why must animals digest their food?

4. Name and describe the type of digestive space found in a cnidarian.

5. What functions does the digestive tract perform?

Achievements in Science

Aquariums Invented

Before the 1800s, scientists could study animals such as fish only in their natural habitat. Studying animals underwater was difficult. The scientists could not always gather complete information over a long period of time. The animals could not survive outside their environments, so it didn't help to take them out of the water. To study underwater animals well, the scientists needed to confine them in some way.

Jeanne Villepreux-Power was a self-taught naturalist and marine biologist. She became interested in the living organisms and the environment around her when she lived on an island in the Mediterranean Sea. In 1832, she invented aquariums. She was the first scientist to use aquariums to do experiments in an aquatic environment. Aquariums allowed scientists to confine aquatic organisms while they studied them.

Diffusion

The movement of materials from an area of high concentration to an area of low concentration

To obtain the energy in food, all animals must carry out chemical reactions. In these reactions, food molecules join with oxygen. Energy is released. Carbon dioxide forms as a waste product. Thus, animals must bring oxygen into their body. They must eliminate carbon dioxide. This process of gas exchange is called respiration. Animals respire in different ways.

Gas Exchange in Simple Animals

The body wall of sponges and cnidarians is made of just two cell layers. Water outside the animal touches the cells in one layer. Water inside the animal touches cells in the other layer. Both layers of cells get oxygen and get rid of carbon dioxide by **diffusion**. Diffusion is movement from an area of high concentration to an area of low concentration. The concentration of oxygen is higher in the water than in the cells. Therefore, oxygen diffuses from the water into the cells. The concentration of carbon dioxide is higher in the cells than in the water. Therefore, carbon dioxide diffuses from the cells into the water.

Flatworms have very thin body walls too. Most cells touch water, either outside or in the gastrovascular cavity. Gas exchange in flatworms also happens by diffusion. All cells in a hydra can exchange oxygen and carbon dioxide with the surrounding water.

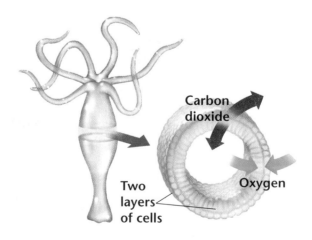

Carbon dioxide

Oxygen

Two layers of cells

Gas Exchange in Other Animals

Most animals are not just two cell layers thick. They contain many cells deep inside the body. These cells cannot exchange gases directly with the outside environment. Animals like these must have a special organ for gas exchange. Such organs come in many different forms.

Animals that live in water usually have gills. Fish have one type of gills. Tadpoles, lobsters, and clams also have gills. Gills often have a feathery structure. This structure provides a large surface area. This allows diffusion to happen quickly. Oxygen diffuses from the water into the gills. Carbon dioxide diffuses in the opposite direction.

The gills on this brown trout provide a large surface area for exchanging gases quickly.

Land animals exchange oxygen and carbon dioxide with the air. Insects use a system of tubes to carry air into the body. The tubes have very fine branches that reach almost all of the animal's cells. The entrances to the tubes are scattered over the insect's body. Watch a bee that has landed on a flower. You will see its abdomen move in and out. It is pumping air into and out of the tubes.

Most other land animals use lungs for gas exchange. Lungs are like balloons inside the body. When you inhale, or breathe in, you draw air into your lungs. Exhaling, or breathing out, forces the air back out. Like gills, lungs provide a large surface area for gas exchange.

Circulatory Systems

Animals must transport oxygen from their gills or lungs to the rest of their body. They must transport carbon dioxide from the rest of their body to their gills or lungs. A **circulatory** system performs these jobs. *Circulatory* means "flowing in a circle." This system moves blood through the body. In the gills or lungs, oxygen enters the blood. Carbon dioxide leaves. As the blood circulates, it delivers oxygen and picks up carbon dioxide. Blood also carries nutrients from the digestive tract to cells.

All circulatory systems have a set of tubes and one or more pumps. The tubes are called blood vessels. The pumps are called hearts. When a heart contracts, or pulls together, it squeezes blood through the blood vessels.

Arthropods and most mollusks have an **open circulatory system**. The grasshopper in the diagram below has an open circulatory system. In this system, blood leaves the vessels and enters spaces around the organs. The blood flows slowly through the spaces and makes direct contact with cells.

Earthworms, vertebrates, and some mollusks have a **closed circulatory system**. The blood stays inside vessels at all times. The smallest vessels have very thin walls. Oxygen and carbon dioxide diffuse into or out of the blood across these walls.

Circulatory

Flowing in a circle

Open circulatory system

A system in which blood makes direct contact with cells

Closed circulatory system

A system in which blood stays inside vessels at all times

Did You Know?

A shrew's heart can beat as fast as 1,300 times per minute. An elephant's heart beats only about 25 times per minute.

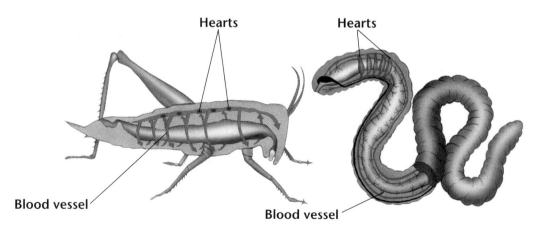

Open Circulatory System	Closed Circulatory System

Vertebrate Circulatory Systems

The circulatory system of a vertebrate includes a single heart. The heart is divided into enclosed spaces called chambers. The **atria** are chambers that receive blood that returns to the heart. The **ventricles** are chambers that pump blood out of the heart. Fish have one atrium and one ventricle. Amphibians and most reptiles have two atria and one ventricle. Birds, mammals, and some reptiles have two atria and two ventricles.

The diagram below shows how blood circulates through the body of a mammal or bird. The left atrium receives blood from the lungs. This blood has a lot of oxygen that was picked up in the lungs. The blood has little carbon dioxide. The left atrium sends the blood to the left ventricle. The left ventricle pumps it to the rest of the body. The blood delivers oxygen to body tissues. It picks up carbon dioxide that has formed as waste. The blood returns to the right atrium. The blood has little oxygen and a lot of carbon dioxide. The blood moves from the right atrium to the right ventricle. The right ventricle pumps the blood to the lungs. In the lungs, oxygen enters the blood. Carbon dioxide leaves the blood. The carbon dioxide is exhaled as waste. The blood returns to the left atrium, completing the cycle.

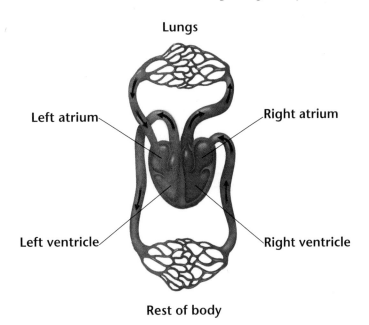

Lungs

Left atrium

Right atrium

Left ventricle

Right ventricle

Rest of body

Lesson 5   R E V I E W

Write your answers to these questions on a separate sheet of paper. Write complete sentences.

1. How are gases exchanged in a sponge?

2. Describe the system that insects use to respire.

3. What is the difference between an open and a closed circulatory system?

4. What is the function of the atria in a vertebrate heart?

5. In a bird's heart, where does blood go from the right ventricle?

Technology Note

Studying animals that live in water became easier after the invention of the Aqua-Lung. This equipment allows people to breathe underwater. Jacques Cousteau and Emile Gagnan invented the Aqua-Lung in 1943. Today, it is more commonly known as scuba (**s**elf-**c**ontained **u**nderwater **b**reathing **a**pparatus). The equipment consists of a tank of compressed air, regulators, hoses, pressure chambers, valves, and a mouthpiece. All these things make exploring animals underwater possible and safer.

After reading this lesson, you should be able to

◆ compare asexual reproduction and sexual reproduction.

◆ recognize the advantages and disadvantages of each type of reproduction.

◆ compare the gestation times of different mammals.

Asexual reproduction

Reproduction that involves one parent and no egg or sperm

Sexual reproduction

Reproduction that involves both a female and a male parent

Egg cell

A female sex cell

Sperm cell

A male sex cell

Some animals need only one parent to reproduce. Other animals reproduce with two parents. In this lesson, you will learn about these two types of reproduction.

Asexual Reproduction

Some simple animals reproduce by **asexual reproduction.** This form of reproduction involves only one parent. The new organisms are identical to the parent organism. For example, a piece of a parent sponge can fall off and grow into a new sponge. If a sea star is broken into pieces, new sea stars can grow from the larger pieces. A sea anemone can split apart to form two or more sea anemones.

One advantage of asexual reproduction is that an organism can reproduce alone. It does not have to find a mate. A disadvantage of asexual reproduction is that the offspring are exact copies of the parent. They are likely to respond to changes in the environment in the same way. If a change kills one of the offspring, it will probably kill them all. Thus, asexual reproduction is favorable in environments that do not change much.

Sexual Reproduction

Most animals reproduce by **sexual reproduction.** During sexual reproduction, a cell from one parent joins with a cell from the other parent.

Sexual reproduction involves both a female parent and a male parent. The female produces **egg cells.** The male produces **sperm cells.** Sperm cells and egg cells are called sex cells.

In many animals, **testes** are the male sex organs that produce sperm cells. **Ovaries** are the female sex organs that produce egg cells. An egg cell contains food for the early stage of the developing offspring.

A sperm cell usually has a tail that allows it to move toward an egg. When a sperm reaches an egg, the nucleus of the sperm cell and the nucleus of the egg cell join. **Fertilization** is the process by which a sperm cell and an egg cell join to form one cell. The cell, called a **zygote,** begins to develop into a new organism.

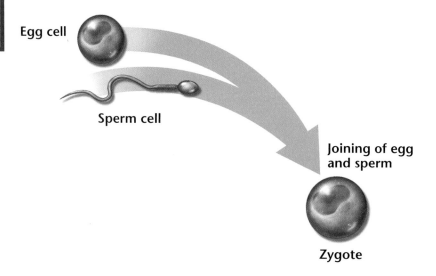

Egg cell

Sperm cell

Joining of egg and sperm

Zygote

A disadvantage of sexual reproduction is that an organism must find a mate to reproduce. However, a big advantage of sexual reproduction is that each offspring is unique. Its combination of traits is different from the combination of traits in either parent.

Animal Gestation Times

Different mammals have different **gestation times,** depending on the size of the animal. Gestation time is the period of time from the fertilization of an egg until birth occurs. Gestation times for a variety of mammals are shown in the chart. As you can see, an elephant develops inside its mother for almost two years. But the gestation time of a mouse is only 20 days. In general, the larger the mammal, the longer is its gestation time.

Mammal	Approximate Number of Days
Mouse	20
Rabbit	31
Cat, dog	63
Pig	115
Monkey	210
Human	275
Cattle	281
Horse	336
Whale	360
Elephant	624

The gestation time of a pig is about 115 days.

Lesson 6   R E V I E W

Write your answers to these questions on a separate sheet of paper. Write complete sentences.

1. What is an advantage and a disadvantage of asexual reproduction?

2. Name some animals that reproduce by asexual reproduction.

3. What is the main advantage of sexual reproduction?

4. What method of reproduction is used by most animals?

5. Describe the process of fertilization.

▼◄▲▼◄▲▼◄▲▼◄▲▼◄▲▼◄▲▼◄▲▼◄▲▼◄▲▼◄▲▼◄▲▼◄▲▼◄▲▼◄▲▼◄▲▼◄▲▼

Science at Work

Veterinary Assistant

A veterinary assistant must be able to communicate effectively and use correct medical terms. Being able to observe, measure, and record is important. Working as part of a team and following procedures are part of this job. A veterinary assistant may receive on-the-job training or take classes at a trade school or community college.

Veterinary assistants help a veterinarian examine and care for animals. They also help keep the office running smoothly. They should like working with animals and be interested in medical science. Duties might include holding the animal while a veterinarian examines and treats it. A veterinary assistant may also prepare an animal for surgery and help during surgery. This person may also perform laboratory tests and provide for the needs of animals that stay during the day or overnight. Veterinary assistants may answer phones and make appointments. They work not only with the veterinarian but also with the pet owners.

- Biologists classify animals based on the animals' similar features.

- The classification system used by biologists has seven levels.

- Every species has a two-word scientific name consisting of its genus and its species label.

- Vertebrates are animals that have a backbone.

- Invertebrates are animals that do not have a backbone.

- Animals feed by filtering food, sucking fluids, or consuming large pieces of food.

- Animals digest food in their cells, in a gastrovascular cavity, or in a digestive tract.

- Most animals that live in water use gills to exchange oxygen and carbon dioxide. Land animals use lungs or tubes.

- In an open circulatory system, blood leaves the vessels and makes direct contact with cells. In a closed circulatory system, blood stays inside vessels.

- Asexual reproduction involves one parent and no egg or sperm. It produces offspring that are identical to the parent.

- Sexual reproduction involves an egg from a female parent and a sperm from a male parent. It produces offspring that are unique.

- In fertilization, a sperm cell and an egg cell unite to form a zygote. The zygote develops into a new organism.

Science Words

amphibian, 441	egg cell, 461	metamorphosis, 441	species, 433
asexual reproduction, 461	enzyme, 453	molting, 447	sperm cell, 461
atrium, 459	fertilization, 462	open circulatory system, 458	swim bladder, 441
bilateral symmetry, 446	filter feeding, 451	ovary, 462	tentacle, 445
cartilage, 440	gastrovascular cavity, 453	phylum, 433	testes, 461
circulatory, 458	genus, 433	radial symmetry, 445	tube foot, 449
closed circulatory system, 458	gestation time, 463	reptile, 442	ventricle, 459
cold-blooded, 442	gill, 441	scientific name, 436	vertebra, 440
diffusion, 456	invertebrate, 445	secrete, 453	vertebrate, 440
digestive tract, 454	mammary gland, 443	sexual reproduction, 461	warm-blooded, 443
			zygote, 462

Chapter 19 REVIEW

Word Bank

bilateral symmetry

closed circulatory system

filter feeding

invertebrates

mammary glands

radial symmetry

scientific name

swim bladder

ventricle

vertebrates

Vocabulary Review

Choose the word or words from the Word Bank that best complete each sentence. Write the answer on a sheet of paper.

1. Animals that have a backbone are called _____.

2. A fish uses its _____ to move up or down in water.

3. Animals with _____ have bodies with a left half and right half that are the same.

4. An animal's _____ consists of its genus and its species label.

5. Animals with _____ have body parts arranged like spokes on a wheel.

6. Female bears produce milk from their _____.

7. Sponges, cnidarians, and mollusks are all _____.

8. A chamber that pumps blood out of a vertebrate heart is called a _____.

9. Blood stays inside vessels at all times in a _____.

10. A sponge gets food by _____.

Concept Review

Choose the answer that best completes each sentence. Write the answer on your paper.

11. The genus of the western rattlesnake, *Crotalus viridis*, is _____.
    A rattlesnake   **C** *Crotalus*
    B *viridis*   **D** western

12. Animals break down food by secreting _____.
    A digestive enzymes   **C** neurotransmitters
    B hormones   **D** impulses

13. _____ allows crustaceans to grow larger in size.
    A Bilateral symmetry   **C** Metamorphosis
    B Molting   **D** Bone growth

14. The bodies of _____ are made of segments.
    A insects   **C** cnidarians
    B flatworms **D** sponges

15. All vertebrates have a(n) _____ skeleton.
    A internal **B** external **C** bony **D** soft

16. _____ allow animals to live on land.
    A Gills   **C** Scales
    B Swim bladders **D** Lungs

17. Reproduction that involves one parent is _____.
    A sexual reproduction   **C** fertilization
    B asexual reproduction **D** diffusion

18. An advantage of sexual reproduction is that _____.
    A offspring all have the same traits
    B each offspring is unique
    C an organism must find a mate to reproduce
    D a zygote is formed

Critical Thinking

Write the answer to each of the following questions.

19. Suppose you found a small arthropod under a rock. Using only a hand lens, how could you tell whether the animal is an arachnid or an insect?

20. Some animals live in water that has a low oxygen concentration. They often have large gills. Why would large gills be helpful to these animals?

Test-Taking Tip When answering multiple-choice questions, first identify the choices you know are untrue.

20 Classifying Plants

S ome plants have flowers. Some have needles. Some have green leaves. Plants come in different shapes and sizes— from tiny mosses to giant redwood trees. However, all plants are alike in some ways. In this chapter, you will learn how plants are classified into different groups. You will also find out how plants make food, carry water, produce oxygen, and reproduce.

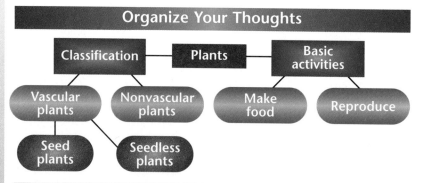

Organize Your Thoughts

Classification — Plants — Basic activities

Vascular plants — Nonvascular plants — Make food — Reproduce

Seed plants — Seedless plants

Goals for Learning

◆ To explain the differences between vascular and nonvascular plants

◆ To explain the differences between plants with seeds and seedless plants

◆ To describe angiosperms, gymnosperms, ferns, and mosses

◆ To identify the main parts of a plant

◆ To explain how plants make food, transport food and water, and produce oxygen

◆ To describe how plants reproduce

After reading this lesson, you should be able to

◆ explain how plants are classified and the history of the classification.

◆ tell the difference between vascular and nonvascular plants.

◆ explain how seed plants are different from the other plant groups.

◆ explain the differences between angiosperms and gymnosperms.

◆ list vascular and nonvascular plants that are seedless.

◆ describe ferns and mosses.

Seed

A plant part that contains a beginning plant and stored food

Fern

A seedless plant with tubelike cells that transport water

Moss

A plant with no tubelike cells to transport water

Scientists have identified more than 260,000 kinds of plants. That sounds like a lot. However, scientists think even more kinds have yet to be discovered. About 1,000,000 kinds of plants may exist that have not been found and named. Most of these plants live in the tropical rain forests.

Scientists divide this huge number of plants into groups to make them easier to study. They classify plants according to whether they have body parts such as **seeds**, tubes, roots, stems, and leaves. The three main groups of plants are seed plants, **ferns**, and **mosses**. The groups that contain ferns and mosses also contain related plants. However, ferns and mosses form the greatest number in each of these groups.

History of Classification

The classification of plants started more than 2,000 years ago. The Greek philosopher Aristotle first classified plants and animals. His student Theophrastus listed the names of over 500 plants. In 1753, Carolus Linnaeus, a Swede, developed a new method to classify plants and animals. Today, organisms are classified based on his system.

Under this system, organisms have a two-word name. The first word is the genus. For example, maple trees belong to the genus *Acer*. The scientific name of all maple trees begins with the word *Acer*. The second word is the species. Each kind of maple tree has its own species name. The scientific name of the sugar maple tree is *Acer saccharum*. The scientific name of the red maple is *Acer rubrum*.

Vascular and Nonvascular Plants

Vascular plant

A plant that has tubelike cells

Vascular tissue

A group of plant cells that form tubes through which food and water move

Nonvascular plant

A plant that does not have tubelike cells

Did You Know?

The tallest living thing in the world is a redwood tree in California. It is 112 meters tall. The oldest living thing in the world is a bristlecone pine tree in California, which is over 4,700 years old.

Seed plants and ferns are **vascular plants**. Vascular plants have tubelike cells. *Vascular* means "vessel" or "tube." These cells form tissue called **vascular tissue**. The tissue forms tubes that transport food and water through the plant. Vascular plants have well-developed leaves, stems, and roots.

Vascular tissue is important in two ways. First, it allows food and water to be transported through the plant. The plant can grow larger because its leaves and stems do not need to be near water. Second, vascular

The veins of a leaf are vascular tissue.

tissue is thick and provides support for a plant. This also allows plants to grow tall.

Mosses are **nonvascular plants**. Nonvascular plants do not have tubelike cells. These plants are short and must have constant contact with moisture. They do not have tubes to transport water or to support them. These small plants usually grow in damp, shady places on the ground and on the sides of trees and rocks. Unlike vascular plants, nonvascular plants do not have true leaves, stems, or roots.

Technology Note

To study some plant tissues, scientists use equipment to make very thin slices of a plant's stem. These thin slices are used to prepare microscope slides. When scientists first used microscopes, they had to draw what they saw. Today, they can use special cameras to take pictures of what they see. They can also store the pictures on a computer. This allows scientists to share their work with others.

Seed Plants

Embryo
A beginning plant

Angiosperm
A flowering plant

Recall that scientists classify plants into three main groups. Seed plants are different from the other plant groups because they use seeds to reproduce. A seed is a plant part that contains a beginning plant and stored food. The beginning plant is called an **embryo.** A seed has a seed coat that holds in moisture. When conditions are right, the embryo grows into a full-sized plant.

Seed plants have the most advanced vascular tissue of all plants. They have well-developed leaves, stems, and roots.

Seed plants come in many sizes and shapes. The duckweed plant that floats on water may be just one millimeter long. Giant redwood trees are the largest plants in the world. A pine tree has long, thin needles. A rose has soft petals. The different sizes and shapes of seed plants help them to live in many different places. Grass, trees, garden flowers, bushes, vines, and cacti are all seed plants.

Seed plants are the largest group of plants. They are divided into two subgroups. One group is flowering plants and the other group is nonflowering plants.

Most species of plants are **angiosperms,** or flowering plants. The word *angiosperm* is made from the Greek words *angeion,* "capsule," and *sperma,* "seed." A capsule, or fruit, protects the seeds of angiosperms. The fruit forms from part of the flower. Flowers come in many shapes and colors.

The flowers of some plants are colorful and showy.

Nonflowering seed plants are called **gymnosperms**. They do not produce flowers. The word *gymnosperm* means "naked seed." The seeds of gymnosperms are not surrounded by a fruit. The seeds are produced inside cones. For example, the seeds of pine trees form on the scales of cones.

There are over 700 species of gymnosperms. The major group of gymnosperms is conifers. Conifers are cone-bearing gymnosperms. There are about 600 species of conifers. All conifers are woody shrubs or trees. They make up 30 percent of the forests around the world. Pines, spruces, and firs are conifers. Plants such as junipers, yews, and spruces decorate the landscape of many homes.

Most conifers have green leaves all year. Therefore, they are called evergreens. They lose only some of their leaves at any time. The leaves of conifers are shaped like needles. They do not lose water as easily as the broad leaves on other trees do. This makes it easier for conifers to live in dry places where trees must store water for a long time.

Besides conifers, there are other gymnosperms. The ginkgo tree is one of the most familiar. Ginkgo trees have peculiar fan-shaped leaves. These trees are planted along many city streets because they are able to survive pollution better than other trees.

Conifers have cones and needle-shaped leaves.

The leaves of the ginkgo tree are shaped like fans.

Seedless Plants

There are two main groups of seedless plants. The largest group includes ferns and related plants. Like seed plants, ferns are vascular plants. Unlike seed plants, they do not have seeds. The second group of seedless plants includes mosses and related plants. They are different from ferns because they are nonvascular plants.

The largest group of seedless vascular plants is ferns. There are over 10,000 species of ferns in the world. Many of them are tropical plants. They range in size from tiny plants to large treelike plants. Like other vascular plants, ferns have well-developed leaves, stems, and roots.

The leaves, or **fronds**, usually are large and flat. They are divided into small sections, or leaflets, that spread out from a center rib. If you look closely, you can see new fronds that are curled up. They uncurl as they grow.

On the underside of fronds, you can see small dots called **sori**. Sori are clusters that contain the reproductive cells of ferns. These cells are called **spores**. When the spores are ripe, the sori burst open and release the spores into the air.

The **rhizome** is a plant part that has shoots aboveground and roots belowground.

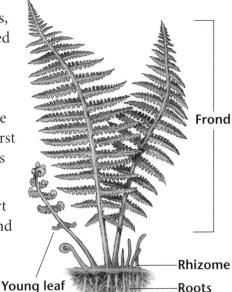

Frond

Young leaf

Rhizome

Roots

Fern

Water in a nonvascular plant moves from one cell to another. Since water can't travel far this way, each cell must be near water. This limits the number of cells a nonvascular plant can have.

After they are released, spores must land in a moist place. Spores that drop in a moist place produce a tiny plant. The plant must have constant moisture to grow. Seeds, on the other hand, have food stored inside and seed coats. The seed coat protects a seed until it has the right conditions to grow. Seeds usually survive longer than spores when conditions are dry. This explains why there are more seed plants than seedless plants.

A moss is a nonvascular plant that has simple leaflike and stemlike parts. Scientists have found more than 9,000 species of mosses. It does not have well-developed leaves, stems, and roots. Mosses do not have vascular tissue to transport water. They must live in moist, shady places.

Mosses grow best where the air is full of moisture and the soil is wet. They get water through rootlike threads called **rhizoids**. Woodlands and the edges of streams are common homes for mosses. Mosses look like little trees and often form carpetlike mats on the forest floor.

Like ferns, mosses reproduce by means of spores. You can see spores in the photo on page 485. Millions of tiny spores form inside spore cases on special stalks. The spore case breaks open when it is ripe. It shoots the spores into the air. The spores make new plants when they fall on moist soil. One reason for moss survival is that mosses produce great numbers of spores.

Mosses cover the roots of this tree.

Write your answers to these questions on a separate sheet of paper. Write complete sentences.

1. What are the three main groups of plants?

2. Who developed the classification system of organisms that is used today?

3. What are two ways that vascular tissue is important?

4. What are other names for flowering plants and nonflowering seed plants?

5. What's the largest group of seedless vascular plants?

6. Why are the seeds of gymnosperms called "naked seeds"?

7. Why are conifers able to live where other plants cannot?

8. What groups of plants do not have seeds?

9. Why are there more seed plants than seedless plants?

10. Where do mosses need to live and why?

Science in Your Life

How do ferns and mosses provide energy?

Ferns that lived millions of years ago are important to your life today. About 300 million years ago, forests and swamps contained many ferns, some the size of trees. Over time, these ferns died, and layers of dead ferns and other plants built up. Pressure and heat on the deep layers of plant material caused coal to form. Coal is burned to produce steam in power plants, which produce electricity.

Peat is formed in much the same way. It is also used as a source of energy, especially in parts of Europe. In Ireland, for example, peat is cut into loaf-sized chunks and burned in stoves and fireplaces. The peat burns slowly, like charcoal.

A vascular system of tiny tubes runs through the roots, leaves, and stems of most plants. It connects all parts of the plant. To make food and to survive, plant roots take water and minerals from the soil. Plant leaves collect light from the sun and carbon dioxide from the air. Without this system, the parts of the plant could not do their jobs.

What Roots Do

Have you ever tried to pull a weed out of the ground? You were probably surprised by how hard you had to pull. You discovered an important function of roots. They hold plants firmly in the ground. Roots also have three other functions. First, they absorb water and minerals from the soil. Roots push their way through the soil to reach the water and minerals they need. Second, roots store water and minerals. They can also store food that is made in leaves. Third, the root vascular system brings water and minerals to other parts of the plant.

Roots hold a plant in the ground, absorb water and minerals, and store food.

The Parts of a Root

The tip of a root is always growing. Millions of tiny root hairs cover the tip of each root. As it grows, it pushes its way through the soil. It is the root hairs that absorb water and minerals from the soil. Roots can store the water and minerals until needed. Water and minerals can also move to the stems and leaves through the root's vascular tissue. **Xylem** vascular tissue forms tubes that carry water and minerals from roots to stems and leaves. The leaves use the water and minerals to make food. **Phloem** vascular tissue forms tubes that carry food from leaves to stems and roots. The roots can also store food.

What Stems Do

Stems are the parts of plants that connect the leaves with the roots. Most stems are above the ground. Stems have three functions. First, stems support the leaves. They hold the leaves up so that they can receive sunlight. Second, stems transport food, water, and minerals through the plant. Third, stems can store food.

The Parts of a Stem

Xylem and phloem form the annual growth rings of trees.

Like roots, stems contain xylem and phloem. They also contain a special layer of growth tissue. It produces new layers of xylem and phloem cells. These layers build up in some plants, so stems become thicker as they get taller. In trees, these layers become wood. In a tree trunk, one layer forms a new ring each year. You can count these rings, called annual growth rings, to tell the tree's age.

What Leaves Do

Leaves are the parts of the plant that trap sunlight. Leaves have four functions. First, they make food. Second, they store food. Third, they transport food to stems. Fourth, they allow gases to enter and leave the plant.

The Parts of a Leaf

Leaves have three main parts: the **petiole**, the blade, and the veins. The petiole, or stalk, attaches the leaf to a stem or a branch. The blade is the main part of the leaf. It collects light from the sun to make food. Many leaves are thin and have flat surfaces. A tree full of leaves can gather large amounts of energy from the sun.

The veins are part of the plant's vascular system. They are thin tubes that are arranged in a pattern. Veins run throughout the blade. They also run through the petiole to the stem. The veins of leaves transport food and water between the stem and the leaf.

The underside of each leaf has many small openings called **stomata**. Each opening is called a stoma. Stomata allow gases, such as carbon dioxide and oxygen, to enter and leave the leaf. Water vapor also leaves through stomata.

The parts of a leaf are the petiole, the blade, and the veins.

Lesson 2 REVIEW

Write your answers to these questions on a separate sheet of paper. Write complete sentences.

1. What are the functions of roots?

2. What is the difference between xylem and phloem tissue?

3. How are annual growth rings made?

4. What are the main parts of a leaf?

5. What do stomata do?

Science at Work

Tree Technician

Tree technicians need strength and balance. They need the ability to climb and to use equipment such as chain saws and wood chippers. Tree technicians need knowledge of trees and their growth. Tree technicians need a high school diploma. A two-year degree is encouraged but not required.

Tree technicians trim trees, get rid of dead limbs, and remove trees. To do this, they often climb up into a tree and use ropes and pulleys to keep from falling. Other times they use trucks with buckets that lift them into the air. The work of tree technicians helps trees grow correctly and helps prevent problems.

Tree technicians might be hired by homeowners to trim trees on their property. They also might be hired by companies to trim trees that could damage electrical wires or phone lines. After natural disasters, such as tornadoes and hurricanes, tree technicians help clean up damaged trees.

Objectives

After reading this lesson, you should be able to

◆ describe where plants make food.

◆ explain how plants make food.

◆ discuss the meaning of the chemical equation for photosynthesis.

◆ identify the importance of oxygen for living things.

Pigment

A chemical that absorbs certain types of light

Chlorophyll

The green pigment in plants that absorbs light energy for photosynthesis

All plants make food in a process called photosynthesis. Why is this important to you? To live, people need the food that plants make. Much of the food you eat comes directly from plants. The rest may come from animals that eat plants or that feed on plant-eating animals.

The Process of Photosynthesis

The process of photosynthesis is the connection between the energy of the Sun and the energy needs of living things. During photosynthesis, plants use the energy of sunlight to turn carbon dioxide and water into simple sugars (food) and oxygen. How do plants get the energy, carbon dioxide, and water they need for photosynthesis? Carbon dioxide comes from the air. It enters the leaves through the stomata. Water comes up from the roots through the xylem. The minerals that the roots absorb also help the plant make food.

Chloroplasts are organelles in plant cells where photosynthesis takes place. Chloroplasts contain a green **pigment** called **chlorophyll**. A pigment is a chemical that absorbs certain types of light. The cells of the green parts of plants, such as leaves, contain many chloroplasts. When sunlight hits the chloroplasts in the leaves, the chlorophyll absorbs light. The sunlight then supplies the energy for photosynthesis.

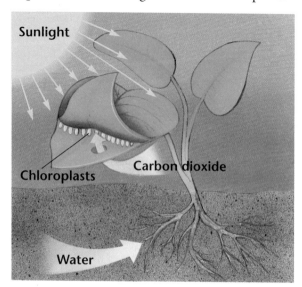

Sunlight

Chloroplasts

Carbon dioxide

Water

Plants use the energy to split water into hydrogen and oxygen. The oxygen leaves the plant through the stomata and goes into the air. The hydrogen combines with the carbon dioxide to make simple sugar. Plants store the energy of sunlight in the sugar as chemical energy.

Chemical Energy

Chemical energy is energy stored in the bonds that hold a chemical's molecules together. When the chemical breaks apart, the energy is released. Glucose is the simple sugar that plants make during photosynthesis. Glucose contains stored chemical energy. Plants and animals that eat plants use that stored energy.

The Chemical Equation for Photosynthesis

You can write a chemical equation that shows how photosynthesis works. In an equation, the left side and the right side are equal. Each side of this equation has the same number of oxygen, hydrogen, and carbon atoms. The chemical equation for photosynthesis looks like this:

$$6CO_2 + 6H_2O + \text{light energy} \longrightarrow C_6H_{12}O_6 + 6O_2$$

$$\text{carbon dioxide} + \text{water} + \text{light energy} \longrightarrow \text{makes sugar} + \text{oxygen}$$

The substances to the left of the arrow are those needed for photosynthesis: carbon dioxide (CO_2), water (H_2O), and light from the sun. The substances to the right of the arrow are the products of photosynthesis: sugar ($C_6H_{12}O_6$) and oxygen (O_2). In photosynthesis, six molecules of carbon dioxide ($6CO_2$) join with six molecules of water ($6H_2O$). They form one molecule of sugar ($C_6H_{12}O_6$) and six molecules of oxygen ($6O_2$).

The Importance of Oxygen

Two of the most important gases in the air that you breathe are carbon dioxide and oxygen. Oxygen is important to most living things. They use oxygen to break down food to release the chemical energy stored in it. This process is called cellular respiration.

Photosynthesis happens only in plants. Respiration happens in both plants and animals. Cellular respiration is a special low-temperature kind of burning that breaks down glucose. Glucose is the simple sugar that plants make during photosynthesis. Glucose is also your body's main source of energy. You get that energy when your cells burn sugars and starches that come from the plants you eat. Your body cells use oxygen to break apart the sugar molecules. During cellular respiration, oxygen combines with hydrogen to make water. Carbon dioxide is released as a waste product. Does this sound familiar? It is the opposite of photosynthesis.

Photosynthesis and respiration are part of the carbon dioxide-oxygen cycle. Plants take in carbon dioxide and water and give off oxygen during photosynthesis. Plants and animals take in oxygen and give off carbon dioxide and water during respiration. This cycle is necessary for life on Earth.

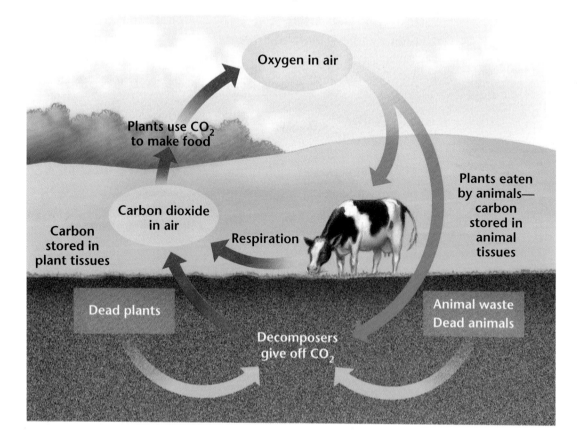

Did You Know?

Most of the oxygen that we breathe comes from plants.

Producing Oxygen

The oxygen that plants produce comes from water. During photosynthesis, plants use water and carbon dioxide to make sugars. Photosynthesis splits water into hydrogen and oxygen. The hydrogen combines with the carbon dioxide to make sugar and more water. The oxygen forms into oxygen gas. The plant uses some of the oxygen for cellular respiration. A plant, however, makes more oxygen than it needs. The rest of the oxygen leaves the plant and goes into the air.

Releasing Oxygen

The oxygen that goes out of the plant into the air leaves through the stomata. Remember that stomata are small openings on a leaf. Each stoma has two special cells called **guard cells**. The size and shape of the guard cells change as they take up and release water. When the guard cells take up water and swell, the stomata open. Oxygen, carbon dioxide, and water vapor can move in and out of the leaf through the openings. When the guard cells lose water, the stomata close.

The amount of light affects the opening and closing of stomata. The stomata of most plants close at night. They open during the day when photosynthesis takes place. The amount of water also affects the opening and closing of stomata. When the soil and air are dry, stomata close, even during the day. This prevents the plant from losing water during short dry periods.

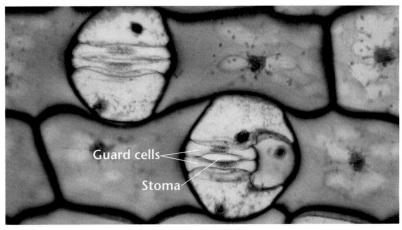

Guard cells open and close a stoma.

Write your answers to these questions on a separate sheet of paper. Write complete sentences.

1. What is photosynthesis and where does it occur?

2. What is the source of the chemical energy stored in plants?

3. Why do living things need oxygen?

4. How is respiration the opposite of photosynthesis?

5. What do guard cells do?

Achievements in Science

The Discovery of Photosynthesis

Today you can study about photosynthesis because of many scientific experiments performed over the years. You know that in photosynthesis, plants use carbon dioxide, water, and light to make sugars (food). Plants give off oxygen during photosynthesis. The discovery of the way photosynthesis works was a process. It did not happen all at once.

The process started in the 1770s, when a scientist discovered that plants give off oxygen. His experiments involved burning a candle in a closed container with a plant. When the burning used all the oxygen in the container, the flame went out. After a few days, the plant replaced the oxygen, and the candle could be burned again.

Several years later, another scientist heard about this discovery and decided to experiment further. His experiments showed that plants need light to produce oxygen. Other scientists went on to discover that plants need carbon dioxide and water for photosynthesis. They also discovered that plants change solar energy to chemical energy. When scientists share information, other scientists can build on it to plan their own experiments. Even today, research on plants and photosynthesis continues.

Objectives

After reading this lesson, you should be able to

◆ identify the difference between sexual and asexual reproduction.

◆ describe how mosses and ferns reproduce.

◆ discuss sexual reproduction in angiosperms and gymnosperms.

Plants can reproduce by sexual reproduction or by asexual reproduction. Sexual reproduction involves two parents. The female parent provides the egg. The male parent provides the sperm. The sperm and egg cells join to form a new plant. Asexual reproduction involves only one parent and no egg or sperm. Many plants can reproduce both sexually and asexually.

Reproduction in Seedless Plants

Mosses and ferns are seedless plants. They reproduce asexually and sexually. Asexual reproduction happens in mosses when a small piece of the parent plant breaks off. That piece forms a new plant. Asexual reproduction happens in ferns when a new plant grows from an underground stem.

Seedless plants reproduce sexually from spores. A spore is a reproductive cell with a thick protective coating. Spores develop into tiny plants that are male, female, or both male and female. The plants produce sperm and eggs. A sperm cell swims to an egg cell through the moisture around the plants. The egg and sperm come together during fertilization. The fertilized cell is called a zygote. The zygote is the beginning of a new plant. When the plant matures, it produces spores that create a new generation of plants.

Seedless plants such as ferns reproduce from spores.

Reproduction in Seed Plants

There are two types of seed plants: flowering plants and nonflowering plants. Seed plants can reproduce asexually. New plants can grow from a piece of a plant called a cutting. A single leaf or stem can grow roots and become a new plant. However, seed plants usually reproduce sexually.

Sexual Reproduction in Angiosperms

Flowering plants are angiosperms. The flower is the part of an angiosperm that contains eggs and sperm. In a flower, the **stamens** are the male organs of reproduction. The stamen includes the anther and filament. They produce **pollen**, which are tiny grains containing sperm. The **pistil** is the female organ of reproduction. The upper part of the pistil is the **stigma**, on the tip of the style. The lower part of the pistil is the **ovary**, which contains eggs.

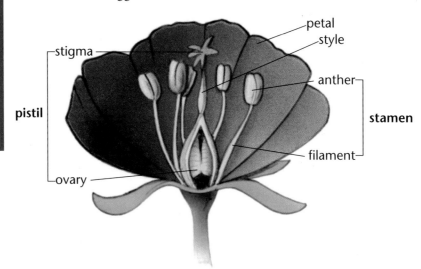

For reproduction to take place, the sperm in pollen must fertilize the egg. Flowers have many colors and shapes to attract insects and birds. They land on flowers to drink nectar, which is a sweet liquid that many kinds of flowers produce. While insects and birds drink, pollen sticks to their bodies. They carry the pollen to the pistil of other flowers or to the same flower. Wind also spreads pollen. The process by which pollen is transferred from the stamen to the pistil is called **pollination.**

Stamen

The male organ of reproduction in a flower, which includes the anther and filament

Pollen

Tiny grains containing sperm

Pistil

The female organ of reproduction in a flower

Stigma

The upper part of the pistil, on the tip of the style

Ovary

The lower part of the pistil that contains eggs

Pollination

The process by which pollen is transferred from the stamen to the pistil

Fertilization

After pollination, the pollen grain grows a tube. The tube reaches down through the pistil to the eggs in the ovary. When the pollen inside the tube meets an egg, fertilization takes place. The ovary grows and becomes a fruit with seeds inside. The fruit protects the seeds.

Seeds

Seeds contain the embryo, or beginning stages of a new plant. If the temperature and amount of water are just right, the seed **germinates**. That means it starts to grow into a new plant. Seeds also contain stored food. The young plant uses this food until it can make its own. If the new plant is fertilized, a new set of seeds develops in the ovary.

Sexual Reproduction in Gymnosperms

Gymnosperms are nonflowering plants. The largest group of gymnosperms are conifers, or cone-bearing plants. Most evergreen trees are gymnosperms. The reproductive organs of gymnosperms are in cones, not flowers. Some cones are male. Some are female. Male cones are usually smaller than female cones.

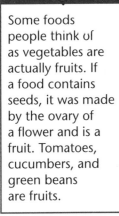

Germinate

Start to grow into a new plant

Some foods people think of as vegetables are actually fruits. If a food contains seeds, it was made by the ovary of a flower and is a fruit. Tomatoes, cucumbers, and green beans are fruits.

During reproduction, male cones release millions of pollen grains into the air. Some of the pollen reaches female cones. As in flowering plants, the pollen grain grows a tube that reaches eggs in the ovary. When the pollen and egg meet, fertilization takes place. But unlike angiosperms, a fruit does not cover gymnosperm seeds. The uncovered seeds are under the scales of the cones.

How do male and female cones differ from each other?

Lesson 4   REVIEW

Write your answers to these questions on a separate sheet of paper. Write complete sentences.

1. What is the difference between sexual reproduction and asexual reproduction?

2. Which type of plants uses spores to reproduce?

3. Describe the process of fertilization in angiosperms.

4. What happens when a seed germinates?

5. Describe the process of reproduction in a conifer.

Achievements in Science

World's Oldest Flowering Plant Discovered

A fossil of the oldest flowering plant ever found was discovered recently in China. It was in rock that used to be at the bottom of a lake. The plant did not have a flower with petals, but it did have characteristics of a flowering plant. It had seeds in an undeveloped fruit. Only flowering plants have seeds in fruits. This discovery has challenged existing ideas about the ancestors of flowering plants. Their ancestors were thought to be shrubs similar to small trees. This fossil plant is at least 125 million years old and was only about 20 inches high. Scientists believe it lived underwater with its thin stems extending upward above the water. Now scientists wonder if the ancestors of today's flowering plants were aquatic plants.

Materials

- ◆ African violet plant
- ◆ water
- ◆ 2 paper cups
- ◆ aluminum foil
- ◆ potting soil

Growing an African Violet from a Leaf

Purpose

Can one leaf grow into a whole new plant? In this investigation, you will grow a plant, using asexual reproduction.

Procedure

1. Have your teacher cut a leaf with a long stem from the African violet plant.

2. Fill a cup with water. Then cover it with aluminum foil. With a pencil, poke a hole in the center of the foil.

3. Insert the leaf into the hole. The end of the stem should be in the water.

4. Place the leaf and cup in a window where the leaf will get sunlight.

5. Change the water in the cup every few days. As you do, observe the end of the stem. Observe and record any changes.

6. When roots appear and begin to grow, plant your leaf in a cup of potting soil. Bury the roots and part of the stem in the soil. Water the soil.

7. Place the potted leaf on a windowsill. Keep the soil moist. What eventually happens?

Questions and Conclusions

1. What was the first change that you observed in the leaf? Describe your observation.

2. Why do you think the plant produced this type of new growth?

3. How does the plant change after the leaf is planted in soil?

4. What type of reproduction occurred in this investigation? Explain your answer.

Explore Further

Many plants will grow from leaf or stem cuttings. Try to grow some other plants this way. You may want to use a book on houseplants as a reference.

- Plants are classified according to whether they have body parts such as seeds, tubes, roots, stems, and leaves.

- The three main groups of plants are seed plants, ferns and related plants, and mosses and related plants.

- Vascular plants have vascular tissue that forms tubes for transporting food and water.

- Flowering plants are called angiosperms. The seeds of angiosperms are surrounded by a fruit.

- Gymnosperms are nonflowering plants that have seeds. Their seeds are not surrounded by a fruit.

- Ferns and mosses have no seeds. Ferns are vascular plants. Mosses are nonvascular plants.

- Roots hold plants in the ground and absorb water and minerals.

- Stems support the leaves, store food, and transport food, water, and minerals through the plant.

- Plants make food in the green parts of the plant. The cells in these parts contain chloroplasts, where photosynthesis takes place.

- Plants need carbon dioxide and water to make food. Food stores chemical energy. The process of releasing energy from food is cellular respiration.

- Plants give off oxygen gas. Most living things need oxygen for cellular respiration.

- Plants can reproduce by sexual reproduction, which involves two parents, or by asexual reproduction, which involves only one parent.

Science Words

angiosperm, 471	guard cell, 483	pistil, 486	spore, 473
chlorophyll, 480	moss, 469	pollen, 486	stamen, 486
embryo, 471	nonvascular	pollination, 486	stigma, 486
fern, 469	plant, 470	rhizoid, 474	stoma, 478
frond, 473	ovary, 486	rhizome, 473	vascular plant, 470
germinate, 487	petiole, 478	seed, 469	vascular tissue, 470
gymnosperm, 472	phloem, 477	sori, 473	xylem, 477
	pigment, 480		

Chapter 20 REVIEW

Word Bank

chlorophyll
embryo
fern
frond
guard cell
nonvascular plants
photosynthesis
pistil
pollination
seed
spores
stamen
stomata
vascular plant

Vocabulary Review

Choose the word or words from the Word Bank that best complete each sentence. Write the answer on a sheet of paper.

1. The large feathery leaf of a fern is called a(n) _____.

2. A(n) _____ has a protective coat around a plant embryo.

3. Mosses are examples of _____.

4. A(n) _____ is a seedless, vascular plant.

5. _____ are reproductive cells of ferns and mosses.

6. A plant that has tissue that forms tubes is called a(n) _____.

7. A seed contains stored food and a(n) _____.

8. Gases move in and out of a leaf through _____.

9. The type of cell that opens and closes a stoma is a(n) _____.

10. Plants make simple sugars during _____.

11. Pollen is transferred from the stamen to the top of the pistil in the process of _____.

12. The male part of a flower is the _____.

13. The green pigment, _____, absorbs light energy for photosynthesis.

14. The female part of a flower is the _____.

Concept Review

Choose the answer that best completes each sentence. Write the letter of the answer on your paper.

15. Vascular tissue forms _____ that transport food and water.
  A tubes   **C** leaves
  B hollows   **D** embryos

16. Plants that must live in moist, shady places are

_____.
  A angiosperms   **C** conifers
  B mosses   **D** gymnosperms

17. The main parts of a plant are roots, stems, and _____.
  A leaves   **C** pollen
  B stomata   **D** chlorophyll

18. The food that is made during photosynthesis contains
_____ energy.
  A little   **C** cellular
  B light   **D** chemical

Critical Thinking

Write the answer to each of the following questions.

19. The chemical formula for glucose is $C_6H_{12}O_6$. How many carbon, hydrogen, and oxygen atoms does one molecule of glucose have?

20. Explain how energy for animals comes originally from the sun.

Test-Taking Tip Prepare for a test by making a set of flash cards. Write a word or phrase on the front of each card. Write the definition on the back. Use the flash cards in a game to test your knowledge.

21 Ecology

Living things depend on one another and on the nonliving things in the world around them. Animals depend on plants for food. They also use air, water, soil, and energy from the sun to help them meet their needs. In this chapter, you will learn about the levels of organization of living and nonliving things. You will learn how food and energy flow through the environment. You also will learn about the cycle of different materials through the environment.

Organize Your Thoughts

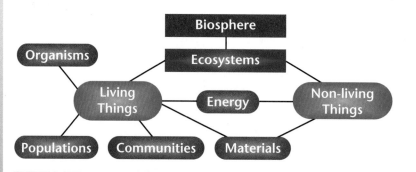

Goals for Learning

◆ To identify ways in which living things interact with one another and with nonliving things

◆ To understand that human activities have an impact on ecosystems

◆ To describe feeding relationships among the organisms in a community

◆ To explain how energy flows through ecosystems

◆ To identify materials that cycle through ecosystems

Objectives

After reading this lesson, you should be able to

◆ explain the relationships among organisms, populations, communities, and ecosystems.

◆ describe the process of succession.

◆ describe how pollution affects ecosystems.

◆ understand how human activities affect the environment.

◆ list examples of biomes.

◆ describe two types of natural resources.

Interact

To act upon or with something

Ecology

The study of the interactions among living things and the nonliving things in their environment

Habitat

The place where an organism lives

Organisms act upon, or **interact** with, one another and with nonliving things in their environment. For example, you interact with the air when you inhale oxygen and exhale carbon dioxide. You interact with plants when you eat fruits and vegetables. **Ecology** is the study of the interactions among living things and the nonliving things in their environment.

Levels of Organization

Organisms interact at different levels. For example, organisms of the same species interact with one another. Organisms of different species also interact. The diagram below shows the organization of living things into different levels. The higher the level, the more interactions there are.

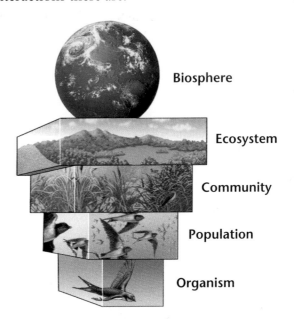

Biosphere

Ecosystem

Community

Population

Organism

Notice that the lowest level of organization is the individual organism. The place where an organism lives is its **habitat**. Each organism is adapted to live in its habitat. For example, tuna use their fins to swim through the ocean. A spider monkey uses its long tail to hang from trees.

Populations

The next level of organization is a **population**. A group of organisms of the same species that lives in the same area form a population. The grizzly bears in Yellowstone National Park make up a population. All the people in the United States make up the country's human population.

Carrying capacity is the number of individuals of a species that can live in an environment without harming it. There are limits to the population an environment can support. The resources and space available to the population determine the carrying capacity.

The individual members of a population interact with one another. For example, the males and females in a population interact when they mate. The individuals also interact when they compete for food, water, and space.

Communities

A **community** is the third level of organization of living things. Populations of different species that live in the same area make up a community. Bears, rabbits, pine trees, and grass are different populations of organisms, but they all may live together in the same forest community.

The populations in a community interact with one another in many ways. In a forest, large trees determine how much light gets through to the shrubs and grass on the forest floor. The trees also provide shelter and food for animals, such as squirrels. Some of the nuts that squirrels bury grow to become new trees.

Ecosystems

Living things are the **biotic** factors in the environment. Nonliving things, such as light, temperature, water, and air are **abiotic** factors. All the interactions among the populations of a community and the nonliving things in their environment make up an **ecosystem**. Organisms interact with nonliving things when they breathe air, drink water, or grow from the soil. Ecosystems occur on land, in water, and in air.

Population

A group of organisms of the same species that lives in the same area

Carrying capacity

The number of individuals that an environment can support

Community

A group of different populations that live in the same area

Biotic

Living

Abiotic

Nonliving

Ecosystem

The interactions among the populations of a community and the nonliving things in their environment

---

Changes in Ecosystems

Succession

The process by which a community changes over time.

As the community of organisms and the nonliving things of an ecosystem interact, they may cause changes. These changes may result in the community changing into a different type of community. For example, a pond community may change into a forest community. The changes that occur over time in a community are called **succession**.

The diagrams below show the succession of a pond community into a forest community. Notice that small organisms and few plants live in a young pond. The bottom of the pond has little soil. When these organisms die, their bodies sink to the bottom and decay. The dead matter helps to form a layer of soil on the bottom of the pond. Soil is also washed into the pond from the surrounding land. Soon, larger plants are able to grow from the soil in the pond. Larger animals that feed on those plants move into the pond. Over the years, the pond fills up with even more soil. Grasses and other small land plants begin to grow on the dry edges of the pond. Small land animals, such as mice and rabbits, move into the area. Changes continue. The pond completely fills in. Bushes shade out the grass. Then trees overgrow the bushes. Squirrels and deer move into the area. The area that was once a pond becomes a forest.

Succession of Pond to Forest

Climax community

A community that changes little over time

Pollution

Anything added to the environment that is harmful to living things

Acid rain

Rain that is caused by pollution and is harmful to organisms because it is acidic

It is estimated that the population of people on Earth will grow from just over 6 billion in 2003 to over 7 billion in 2013 and to over 9 billion by 2050.

Eventually, a community reaches a point at which it changes little over time. A community that is stable is called a **climax community**. A climax community, such as an oak-hickory forest, may stay nearly the same for hundreds of years. A climax community usually has a great diversity of organisms. However, a volcano, a forest fire, or an earthquake can destroy large parts of a climax community within a short time. When that happens, the community goes through succession once again.

Human Impact on Ecosystems

People produce a variety of wastes and waste products that affect ecosystems. **Pollution** is anything added to the environment that is harmful to living things. Pollution is most often caused by human activities. For example, the burning of coal, oil, or gasoline releases a colorless, poisonous gas called sulfur dioxide. This gas poisons organisms that breathe it. Sulfur dioxide in the air also makes rainwater more acidic. This **acid rain** decreases the growth of plants and harms their leaves. Acid rain that falls into lakes and streams can harm or kill organisms living in the water.

Succession of Pond to Forest Continues

Other types of pollution affect lakes and other bodies of water as well. Topsoil is washed off the land because of construction and bad farming practices. It fills up streams and lakes. Fertilizer washes off the land into bodies of water. This pollutes the water with chemicals. Factories dump chemicals into lakes and streams. The chemicals kill plants and animals in the water.

Another way that human activities affect wildlife is by causing the loss of habitat. In order to build roads and shopping centers, animal habitats are sometimes destroyed. Birds and other animals that live nearby can no longer build nests or eat the plants in the developed area. It becomes harder for those animals to survive. If habitat destruction becomes widespread, there are fewer animals to reproduce.

Over time, this can result in a species being classified as **threatened**. This means that there are fewer of these animals than there used to be. If there are almost no animals left of a certain species, that species is **endangered**. When all the members of a species are dead, that species has become **extinct**. In Chapter 22, you will learn about dinosaurs, which became extinct millions of years ago. But there are many other animals that have become extinct more recently. They will never return. Pollution and habitat destruction are two reasons animals become extinct.

Tundra

Tropical rain forest

Biomes

Some ecosystems are found over large geographic areas. These ecosystems are called **biomes**. Some biomes, such as deserts, pine forests, and grasslands, are on land. Water biomes include the oceans, lakes, and rivers.

Temperature, sunlight, and rainfall are all part of a biome's climate. For example, tropical rain forests get plenty of rainfall and are hot. Tundras are found in areas that are dry and cold. A desert is the driest of all biomes. Some deserts get only two centimeters of rain in a year.

Science Myth

Acid rain falls only in cities, which are sources of air pollution.

Fact: Winds carry air pollution from cities to ecosystems away from cities. Acid rain falls on forests, in ponds, or wherever the winds carry it.

The types of organisms found in a particular biome depend on the available **resources.** Resources are things that organisms use to live. Resources include water, air, sunlight, and soil. Fish are not found in a desert biome because a desert has little water. Most cactuses do not grow in a tropical rain forest because the soil in the forest is too wet.

In order to be good citizens of Earth, we should use our natural resources wisely. Some resources, such as water, air, and sunlight, are **renewable resources.** This means that they are resources that are replaced constantly by nature. Other resources, such as coal, minerals, and natural gas, are **nonrenewable resources.** These materials cannot be replaced once they are used up.

Both kinds of resources are important. One thing you can do to reduce the use of nonrenewable resources is to recycle, or reuse, some materials. Another way to save resources is to use alternative energy resources. This kind of energy does not use **fossil fuels**, or fuels formed millions of years ago from the remains of plants and animals. You can learn more about different kinds of energy in Appendix A at the end of this book.

The Biosphere

Look back at the diagram on page 495. Notice that the highest level of organization of life is the **biosphere**. All the biomes on Earth together form the biosphere. The biosphere is the part of Earth where living things can exist.

Think of Earth as an orange or an onion. The biosphere is like the peel of the orange or the skin of the onion. It is the thin layer on a large sphere. The biosphere includes the organisms living on Earth's surface, in water, underground, and in the air. The biosphere also includes nonliving things, such as water, minerals, and air.

The biosphere is a tiny part of Earth. This thin surface layer can easily be damaged. Thus, humans need to be aware of how they can protect the biosphere. One way is to avoid polluting it. The survival of living things depends on the conditions of the nonliving parts of the biosphere.

Lesson 1 REVIEW

Write your answers to these questions on a separate sheet of paper. Write complete sentences.

1. What is the difference between a population and a community?

2. What kinds of interactions make up an ecosystem?

3. Describe the difference between renewable and nonrenewable resources.

4. How does acid rain affect plants and animals?

5. Define *biome* and list three or more examples of biomes.

▼◄▲▼◄▲▼◄▲▼◄▲▼◄▲▼◄▲▼◄▲▼◄▲▼◄▲▼◄▲▼◄▲▼◄▲▼◄▲▼

Science at Work

Ecologist

An ecologist needs to be able to identify and solve problems and must communicate well. Ecologists usually need a master's degree in science or a Ph.D. in ecology or environmental science. Jobs are also available for ecologists with a bachelor's degree in biology, ecology, or a related field. There are some jobs in ecology that require a two-year associate of science degree.

Ecologists are scientists who study the relationships between organisms and their environments. Ecologists study organisms in ecosystems as different as a city, a desert, a tropical rain forest, or the ocean. Some ecologists work for universities, parks, museums, and government agencies. As a part of their jobs, ecologists do research, help identify and solve environmental problems, and manage resources. Ecologists also provide advice to different agencies and communicate what they have learned to others.

INVESTIGATION

Testing the pH of Rain

Materials

◆ 3 small
  trash cans
◆ 3 new plastic
  trash bags
◆ pH paper
◆ pH scale
◆ distilled
  water

Purpose

How can you tell if rain is acid rain? In this investigation, you will find out if the rain in your area is acid rain.

Procedure

1. Copy the data table below on a sheet of paper.

Date	pH of Sample 1	pH of Sample 2	pH of Sample 3	Average pH of Samples
pH of distilled water:				

2. On a rainy day, place open plastic bags inside the trash cans.

3. If there is no thunder and lightning, place the containers outside in the rain. Make sure that the containers collect rainwater that has not touched anything on the way down, such as a roof or the leaves of a tree.

4. When a small amount of rainwater has been collected, touch the edge of the pH paper to the rainwater in one of the containers.

5. Notice the change in color of the pH paper. Compare the color of the pH paper to the colors on the pH scale. The matching color on the scale indicates the pH of the sample of rainwater. In your data table under sample 1, record the pH value of the rainwater.

6. Repeat steps 4 and 5 for the other two samples of rainwater. Record the pH of the samples in the correct columns.

7. If the pH values that you recorded for the three samples are not the same, compute the average pH of the samples. To do this, add all of the pH values and divide by 3. Record this number in the last column in your data table.

8. Use the pH paper to determine the pH of distilled water. Record the pH in your data table.

9. Repeat this investigation on one or two more rainy days. Record in your data table the dates on which you collected the rainwater.

Questions and Conclusions

1. How does the pH of distilled water compare with the pH of the rainwater you tested?

2. When water has a pH lower than 7, it is acidic. Normal rain is always slightly acidic and has a pH between 4.9 and 6.5. When rain has a pH of less than 4.9, it is called acid rain. Were any of the samples of rainwater you tested acid rain?

3. Was the pH of the rainwater the same every day you collected samples? What are some reasons the pH of rainwater could vary from day to day?

Explore Further

Test the pH of the water in a local pond, lake, or stream. **Safety Alert: Wear protective gloves when you collect the water samples.** Is the pH of the body of water the same as that of rainwater? Why might the values be different?

A water plant captures the energy from sunlight. It uses the energy to make sugars and other molecules. A small fish eats the plant. A bigger fish eats the small fish. A bird eats the big fish. This feeding order is called a **food chain**. Almost all food chains begin with plants or other organisms that capture the energy of the sun.

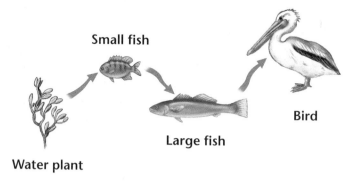

Small fish

Bird

Large fish

Water plant

A Food Chain

Producers

Plants, some protists, and some bacteria make their own food. Organisms that make, or produce, their own food are called **producers**. Every food chain begins with a producer. Most producers use the energy of sunlight to make food by the process of photosynthesis.

Consumers

Organisms that cannot make their own food must get food from outside their bodies. These organisms get their food from other organisms. **Consumers** are organisms that feed on, or consume, other organisms. All animals and fungi and some protists and bacteria are consumers.

Consumers may eat plants or other consumers. Consumers, such as rabbits, that eat only plants are called herbivores. Consumers, such as lions, that eat only animals are carnivores. Some consumers, such as bears, are **omnivores**. They eat both plants and animals.

The consumers in a food chain are classified into different feeding levels, called orders, depending on what they consume. First-order consumers eat plants. Rabbits are first-order consumers. Second-order consumers eat animals that eat plants. A snake eats rabbits. Thus, a snake is a second-order consumer. A hawk that eats the snake is a third-order consumer.

Numbers of Producers and Consumers

You might think of a food chain as a pyramid with the highest-level consumers at the top. Notice in the **pyramid of numbers** that a food chain begins with a large number of producers. There are more producers in a community than there are first-order consumers feeding on the producers. The sizes of the populations decrease at each higher level of a food chain.

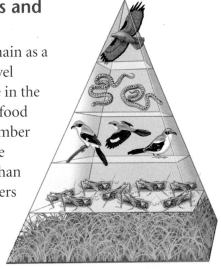

A Pyramid of Numbers

Food Webs

The frogs in a pond eat a variety of foods, including insects and worms. The frogs in turn may be eaten by snakes or birds. Thus, frogs are part of more than one food chain. The diagram shows some food chains in a community. Trace the different food chains. Notice that the food chains are linked to one another at certain points. Together, the food chains form a **food web.**

Hawks

Birds

Snakes

Frogs

Mice

Worms

Insects

Decaying material

Plants with seeds

A Food Web

Decomposers

Suppose that a high-level consumer, such as a lion, dies but is not eaten by another animal. Does the food chain stop there? No, because decomposers continue the food chain by feeding on the dead animal. Recall that decomposers are certain bacteria, fungi, and protists that feed on dead organisms. Decomposers feed on dead organisms at each level of a food chain. They feed on producers and consumers.

Decomposers get food by breaking down complex chemicals in dead organisms into simple chemicals. The simple chemicals become part of the soil. Plants take in these chemicals through their roots and use them to grow. Over time, the chemicals are used again and again. They are taken up by plants, transferred to herbivores and carnivores, and returned to the soil by decomposers. The total amount of the chemicals stays the same even though their form and location change.

Achievements in Science

Crop Rotation Recommended

By the late 1800s, the soil in the southern states of the United States could not produce as much cotton as it once did. Decades of growing crops such as cotton had taken nitrogen out of the soil without replacing it. Farmers did not know that plants need nitrogen. Even if the farmers did know this, fertilizers were not available to add nitrogen to the soil.

George Washington Carver was one of the United States' greatest plant researchers. He found that crops such as cotton take nitrates, a form of nitrogen needed for plant growth, out of the soil. Rotating these crops with other crops such as peanuts put nitrates back into the soil. The soil was improved, and crops grew better.

Carver shared his research and helped improve the productivity of farmers. Even today, crop rotation is used. It is better for the soil and the environment than using fertilizers.

Lesson 2   REVIEW

Write your answers to these questions on a separate sheet of paper. Write complete sentences.

1. What is the difference between a producer and a consumer?

2. Define the terms *herbivore*, *carnivore*, and *omnivore*.

3. Diagram a food chain that includes three levels of consumers. Which level of consumers has the smallest population size?

4. What is the relationship between food chains and food webs?

5. What is the role of decomposers in a community?

Science in Your Life

What kind of consumer are you?

Like all consumers, you cannot make your own food. You must eat, or consume, food. Are you a first-order, second-order, or third-order consumer? When you eat plants or parts of plants, you are a first-order consumer. For example, if you eat an apple or a peanut, you are a first-order consumer.

When you eat the meat or products of animals that feed on plants, you are a second-order consumer. For example, if you eat a hamburger or drink a glass of milk, you are a second-order consumer. Milk and hamburger come from cows, which feed on plants. When you eat the meat or products of animals that feed on other animals, you are a third-order consumer. If you eat swordfish or lobster for dinner, you are a third-order consumer.

You probably eat many different kinds of food. Depending on what you eat, you are part of different food chains. The diagram shows the food chains that you are a part of when you eat a chicken sandwich. Trace the different food chains. What kind of consumer are you when you eat a chicken sandwich?

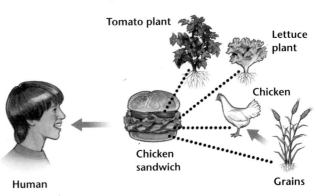

Objectives

After reading this lesson, you should be able to

◆ explain why organisms need energy.

◆ describe how energy flows through a food chain.

◆ compare the amount of energy available at different levels of a food chain.

◆ explain how the amount of available energy affects the sizes of populations.

Plants use energy from the sun to make food. You get energy from the food you eat. What is energy? Energy is the ability to do work, to move things, or to change things. Energy comes in many forms. For example, light from the sun is energy. Heat from the sun also is energy. Batteries store chemical energy. A moving bicycle has mechanical energy.

You and all organisms need energy to live. Your muscles use energy to contract. Your heart uses energy to pump blood. Your brain uses energy when you think. Your cells use energy when they make new molecules.

You probably get tired when you work hard. You might even say that you have "run out of energy" to describe how you feel. You might take a break and eat some lunch to "get your energy back." Food contains chemical energy.

Energy in Food

Recall from Chapter 20 that plants absorb energy from sunlight. A plant's chlorophyll and other pigments absorb some of the light energy. By the process of photosynthesis, the plant uses the absorbed energy to make sugar molecules. Photosynthesis is a series of chemical reactions. During these reactions, light energy is changed into chemical energy. The chemical energy is stored in the sugar molecules.

Plants use the sugar to make other food molecules, such as starches, fats, and proteins. All these nutrients store chemical energy. When plants need energy, they release the energy stored in the nutrients. Plants need energy to grow, reproduce, make new molecules, and perform other life processes. To use the energy stored in nutrients, plant cells break down the molecules into simpler molecules. As the molecules are broken down, they release the stored energy.

Energy pyramid

A diagram that compares the amounts of energy available to the populations at different levels of a food chain

Did You Know?

Only about one-tenth of the available energy at each level of a food chain is passed on to the next level.

Plants also use the nutrients they make to produce tissues in their leaves, roots, and stems. The nutrients' chemical energy is stored in the tissues. When you eat potatoes, asparagus, or other plant parts, you are taking in the plants' stored chemical energy.

Flow of Energy Through Food Chains

The flow of energy in a food chain begins with the producers, such as plants. As you know, plants absorb the sun's energy to make food. They use some of the energy in the food for life processes. As plants use this energy, some is changed to heat. The heat becomes part of the environment. The rest of the energy is stored as chemical energy in the plants' tissues.

The energy stored in plants is passed on to the organisms that eat the plants. These first-order consumers use some of the food energy and lose some energy as heat. The rest of the energy is stored as chemical energy in the nutrients in their body.

The energy stored in the first-order consumers is passed on to the second-order consumers. Then, energy stored in the second-order consumers is passed on to the third-order consumers. At each level of the food chain, some energy is used for life processes, some is lost as heat, and the rest is stored in the organisms.

Energy Pyramid

The **energy pyramid** on the next page compares the amounts of energy available to the populations at different levels of a food chain. The most energy is available to the producers. They get energy directly from the sun. Less energy is available to the insects, the first-order consumers that feed on the producers. That is because the producers have used some of the sun's energy for their own needs. Also, some of the energy was lost as heat. Only the energy that is stored in the producers is passed on to the insects.

The insects use some of the energy they take in for their own needs. Again, some energy is lost as heat. Thus, the amount of energy available to the birds, the second-order consumers, is less than the amount of energy available to the insects. The amount of available energy decreases at each higher level of a food chain. The foxes have the least amount of energy available. They are at the highest level of the food chain.

The amounts of energy available to the different populations of a food chain affect the sizes of the populations. Look back to the pyramid of numbers shown on page 505. Recall that the size of the population decreases at each higher level of a food chain. That is because less energy is available to the population at each higher level.

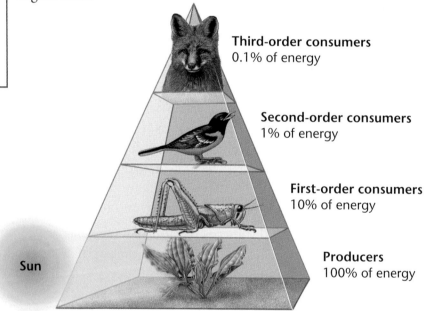

Third-order consumers
0.1% of energy

Second-order consumers
1% of energy

First-order consumers
10% of energy

Sun

Producers
100% of energy

An Energy Pyramid

Importance of the Sun

Without the sun, there would be no life on Earth. Plants, the animals that eat plants, and most other organisms depend on energy from the sun. Energy flows in one direction from sunlight to producers, and then to consumers. Communities lose energy as it flows through food chains. The sun continuously replaces the lost energy.

Lesson 3 REVIEW

Write your answers to these questions on a separate sheet of paper. Write complete sentences.

1. Why do organisms need energy?

2. Which organisms in a community get energy directly from the sun?

3. How does energy flow through a food chain?

4. Explain why less energy is available at each higher level of a food chain.

5. How does the amount of energy available to a population affect the size of the population?

Groundwater

Water that sinks into the ground

The planet Earth is sometimes compared to a spaceship. Like a spaceship, Earth is isolated in space. All the materials we use to build homes, to make tools, and to eat come from the biosphere. If a material is in short supply, there is no way to get more of it. Materials in the biosphere must be used over and over again. For example, chemicals continuously cycle between organisms and the nonliving parts of Earth. Some chemicals important for life are water, carbon, oxygen, and nitrogen.

The Water Cycle

The diagram shows the water cycle between the living and nonliving parts of an ecosystem. The most noticeable water in ecosystems is the liquid water in lakes, rivers, and the ocean. In addition, **groundwater** exists beneath the surface of the land.

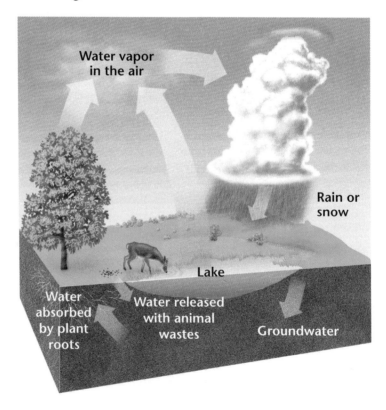

What happens when a puddle of water dries up? As the puddle dries, the liquid water changes into a gas, or evaporates. This gaseous water is called water vapor. Water from the ocean, lakes, and rivers evaporates and becomes part of the air. Water vapor comes from other places, too. Organisms produce water when they get energy from food during the process of cellular respiration. Plants release water vapor through their leaves. Animals release water vapor with their breath. They also release liquid water with their wastes.

Water vapor is always in the air, but you cannot see it. Have you ever noticed that the outside of a glass of ice water becomes wet? Water vapor from the air condenses, or changes into a liquid, on the outside of the glass. The ice water cools the air next to the glass, causing the water vapor to condense.

Water vapor in the air may cool and condense into water droplets in a cloud. When enough water gathers in the cloud, rain or snow may fall. That water may be used by organisms. Organisms need water for various life processes. For example, plants need water to make food during photosynthesis. Plants take in water from the soil through their roots. Animals may drink water from ponds or streams. Animals also get water from the food they eat.

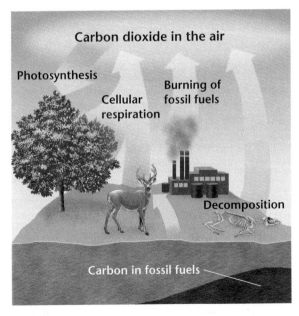

Carbon dioxide in the air

Photosynthesis

Cellular respiration

Burning of fossil fuels

Decomposition

Carbon in fossil fuels

The Carbon Cycle

All living things are made up of chemicals that include carbon. Carbohydrates, fats, and proteins contain carbon. Carbon also is found in the nonliving parts of the environment. For example, carbon dioxide gas is in the air and in bodies of water. Carbon is found in fossil fuels, such as coal and oil. Plants and other organisms that undergo photosynthesis take in carbon dioxide and use it to make food. Animals take in carbon-containing chemicals when they eat plants or other animals.

During cellular respiration, plants, animals, and other organisms produce carbon dioxide. Plants release carbon dioxide through their leaves and other plant parts. Animals release carbon dioxide when they exhale. Decomposers release carbon dioxide as they break down dead organisms. The carbon dioxide that is released by organisms may become part of the air or a body of water. People also produce carbon dioxide when they burn fossil fuels. In these ways, carbon continues to cycle through ecosystems.

The Oxygen Cycle

Oxygen is a gas that is essential to almost every form of life. Oxygen is found in air and in bodies of water. Organisms use oxygen for cellular respiration. The oxygen is used to release energy that is stored in food.

Most of the oxygen that organisms use comes from producers, such as plants. Producers release oxygen as a waste product during photosynthesis. Producers use some of the oxygen for cellular respiration. Consumers take in some of the oxygen and use it themselves. Thus, oxygen continuously cycles between producers and consumers in an ecosystem.

The Nitrogen Cycle

Nitrogen is a gas that makes up about 78 percent of the air. Many chemicals important to living things, such as proteins and DNA, contain nitrogen. However, the nitrogen in the air is not in a form that organisms can use. Certain bacteria are able to change nitrogen gas into a chemical, called ammonia, that plants can use. These bacteria live in the soil and in the roots of some plants. The process by which the bacteria change nitrogen gas into ammonia is called **nitrogen fixation**.

The diagram on the next page shows that plants take in the ammonia through their roots. Some of the ammonia, however, is changed by certain bacteria into chemicals called nitrates. Plants use both ammonia and nitrates to make proteins and other chemicals they need.

Nitrogen fixation

The process by which certain bacteria change nitrogen gas from the air into ammonia

Not all of the nitrates are used by plants. Notice in the diagram below that bacteria change some of the nitrates back into nitrogen gas. The return of nitrogen gas to the air allows the nitrogen cycle to continue.

Animals get the nitrogen they need by feeding on plants or on animals that eat plants. When organisms die, decomposers change the nitrogen-containing chemicals in the organisms into ammonia. The ammonia may then be used by plants or may be changed into nitrates by bacteria.

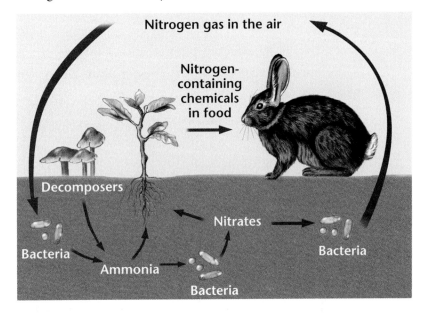

System of Cycles

The different cycles in an ecosystem interact with one another. For example, the carbon cycle, oxygen cycle, and water cycle are linked by photosynthesis and cellular respiration. Plants take in carbon dioxide and water for photosynthesis, and release oxygen. Animals, plants, and other organisms use the oxygen for cellular respiration and release carbon dioxide and water.

When plants make nitrogen-containing chemicals from ammonia and nitrates, they use carbon and oxygen. Many other materials cycle through ecosystems. Iron, calcium, phosphorus, and other chemicals used by living organisms are cycled.

Lesson 4   R E V I E W

Write your answers to these questions on a separate sheet of paper. Write complete sentences.

1. Describe how water may move from a plant to a cloud and back to a plant.

2. Why is carbon important to living things?

3. How are photosynthesis and cellular respiration part of the carbon cycle?

4. How are photosynthesis and cellular respiration part of the oxygen cycle?

5. How is nitrogen gas from the air changed into a form that plants can use?

Technology Note

Farmers need to add nitrogen to soil to help plants grow. Adding too much nitrogen, though, causes pollution of groundwater, lakes, and streams. Different kinds of technology can help farmers apply just the amount the crop needs. As farmers drive tractors across fields, sensors can collect information about the soil and the plants. Computers on the tractors use this information. They calculate how much nitrogen is needed. The right amount of nitrogen is then applied to different parts of the field.

- A population is a group of organisms of the same species that lives in the same area.

- A community is a group of different populations that live in the same area.

- Communities may change over time by a process called succession.

- All the interactions among populations and the nonliving things in their environment make up an ecosystem.

- Human activities can cause pollution and loss of habitat.

- Natural resources can be renewable or nonrenewable.

- The feeding order of organisms is called a food chain. Every food chain begins with producers, which can make their own food. Consumers must take in food.

- Energy flows through food chains. All the food chains in a community that are linked make up a food web.

- Water, carbon, oxygen, and nitrogen cycle through ecosystems.

- Water evaporates and condenses as it cycles between organisms and the environment.

- Oxygen and carbon dioxide are cycled through the environment by the processes of respiration and photosynthesis.

- In the nitrogen cycle, bacteria change nitrogen gas from the air into ammonia. Other bacteria change nitrates back to nitrogen gas.

Science Words

abiotic, 495	consumer, 504	groundwater, 512	producer, 504
acid rain, 498	ecology, 495	habitat, 495	pyramid of
biome, 499	ecosystem, 496	interact, 495	numbers, 505
biosphere, 500	endangered, 499	nitrogen	renewable
biotic, 495	energy	fixation, 514	resources, 500
carrying	pyramid, 509	nonrenewable	resource, 500
capacity, 496	extinct, 499	resources, 500	succession, 497
climax	food chain, 504	omnivore, 504	threatened, 499
community, 498	food web, 505	pollution, 498	
community, 496	fossil fuels, 500	population, 496	

Chapter 21 R E V I E W

Word Bank

biomes

biosphere

climax community

consumers

ecology

ecosystems

food chains

habitat

nitrogen fixation

omnivores

pollution

population

producers

succession

Vocabulary Review

Choose the word or words from the Word Bank that best complete each sentence. Write your answer on your paper.

1. _____ absorb the energy of the sun.

2. The study of how living things interact with one another and with nonliving things in their environment is _____.

3. Consumers that eat both plants and animals are _____.

4. Deserts, grasslands, and the ocean are all examples of _____.

5. Anything added to the environment that is harmful to living things is _____.

6. The place where an organism lives is its _____.

7. All the biomes on Earth together form the _____.

8. _____ feed on other organisms.

9. All the _____ in a community that are linked to one another make up a food web.

10. _____ are made up of several populations and the nonliving things in their environment.

11. The process by which a community changes over time is called _____.

12. A community that changes very little over time is called a(n) _____.

13. All the deer of the same species living in a forest make up a(n) _____.

14. Certain bacteria change nitrogen gas from the air into ammonia by the process of _____.

Concept Review

Choose the answer that best completes each sentence. Write the letter of the answer on your paper.

15. Water, air, and sunlight are examples of _____.
   A organisms   **C** nonrenewable resources
   B renewable resources   **D** pollution

16. Photosynthesis and cellular respiration help to cycle _____ through ecosystems.
   A carbon, oxygen,   **C** only carbon
      and water
   B nitrogen   **D** only oxygen

17. When water in a pond _____, it changes into water vapor.
   A condenses   **C** evaporates
   B falls as rain   **D** becomes groundwater

18. Plants store _____ energy in their tissues.
   A mechanical   **C** light
   B heat   **D** chemical

Critical Thinking

Write the answer to each of the following questions.

19. What would Earth be like if there were no decomposers?

20. Identify the producers and the first-order, second-order, and third-order consumers in the food web shown here. Remember that organisms may be part of more than one food chain.

Test-Taking Tip When choosing answers from a word bank, answer all of the questions you know first. Then, study the remaining words to choose the answers for the questions you are not sure about.

22 Heredity and Evolution

Are birds and dinosaurs related? How does evolution happen? Why do new kinds of organisms develop over time? How are characteristics passed from one generation to the next? In this chapter, you will learn how genes and chromosomes are passed on to offspring and how they affect an organism's appearance. You also will find out what scientists have learned from fossils about how living things change.

Organize Your Thoughts

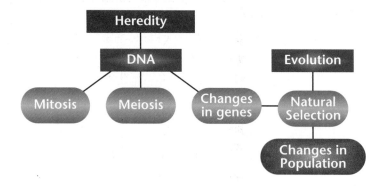

Goals for Learning

◆ To describe the role of DNA in heredity

◆ To compare mitosis and meiosis

◆ To recognize how populations change over time

◆ To explain the theory of natural selection

◆ To give examples of evidence that supports evolution

After reading this lesson, you should be able to

◆ describe how traits are passed from parent to offspring.

◆ compare mitosis and meiosis.

Heredity

The passing of traits from parents to offspring

Gene

A section of DNA that carries a trait

Chromosome

A rod-shaped structure that contains DNA and is found in the nucleus of a cell

Genetics

The study of heredity

Environment

An organism's surroundings

Mutation

A change in a gene

Family members have many of the same characteristics, or traits. The passing of traits from parents to their children is called **heredity**. All organisms pass information about traits to their children, or offspring. That is why bluebirds produce bluebird chicks, and lions produce lion cubs.

Some traits are controlled by a single **gene.** Other traits are the result of several genes. In some cases a gene can have an effect on more than one trait. A **chromosome** may contain hundreds of genes. Chromosomes are rod-shaped bodies located in the nucleus of a cell. Chromosomes are made of proteins and a chemical called DNA. Sections of DNA make up an organism's genes, which determine all the traits of an organism.

Heredity and Environment

Genetics is the study of heredity. You are born with certain genes. That is your heredity. Your genes determine your skin color, eye color, body shape, and other characteristics. But your **environment** also may affect your characteristics. Your family, the air you breathe, and everything else in your surroundings make up your environment. To find out how environment affects a person's characteristics, scientists study identical twins who have been separated since birth. Both twins have the same genes, but they grew up in different environments. Food, sunlight, air, and other parts of the environment can affect a person's characteristics. Scientists look for differences in the characteristics of the twins. If they find any different characteristics, they know the environment caused those differences.

The environment can directly affect a person's genes. For example, X rays and some types of chemicals cause changes in genes. These changes are called **mutations**. Mutations can cause problems in humans and other organisms. How do mutations occur? Before you can understand mutations better, you need to know more about DNA.

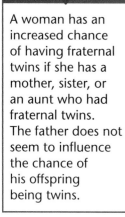

A woman has an increased chance of having fraternal twins if she has a mother, sister, or an aunt who had fraternal twins. The father does not seem to influence the chance of his offspring being twins.

DNA

DNA in chromosomes is the material that contains an organism's genes. Each DNA molecule in a cell makes one chromosome. During cell division, genes on DNA are passed from parent cell to offspring. All the information needed to carry out life activities is in DNA. All the information that makes a duck a duck is in the duck's DNA. All the information that makes you a human is in your DNA.

You can see below that DNA is a large molecule shaped like a twisted ladder. The rungs of the ladder are made of four different kinds of molecules called **bases**. The letters *T*, *A*, *C*, and *G* are used as abbreviations for the names of the four bases. The order of the bases in the DNA molecules of a cell provides a code for all the information that the cell needs to live.

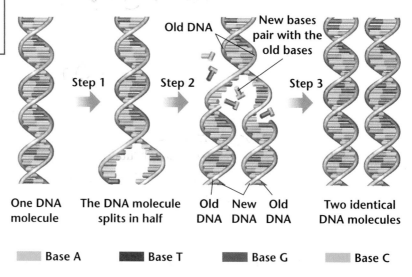

Old DNA

New bases pair with the old bases

Step 1 Step 2 Step 3

One DNA molecule | The DNA molecule splits in half | Old DNA New DNA Old DNA | Two identical DNA molecules

Base A   Base T   Base G   Base C

The DNA molecules of different organisms have different orders of bases. The greater the differences between the organisms, the greater the differences in the order of their bases. Thus, the order of bases in a frog's DNA is very different from the order of bases in your DNA. The difference in the order of bases between your DNA and your friend's DNA is not as great.

Recall that a gene is a section of a DNA molecule. Each DNA molecule has thousands of genes. A gene is made up of bases arranged in a certain order. Different genes have a different order of bases. This difference allows genes to provide different kinds of information. For example, the order of bases in a gene for hair color determines whether the hair will be black, brown, red, or blonde.

An important feature of DNA is that it can **replicate**, or copy, itself. A DNA molecule is held together at its rungs. Notice in the diagram on page 522 that each rung is made of a pair of bases. The bases pair in certain ways. Base A pairs with base T. Base C pairs with base G. When DNA replicates, it first splits down the middle of its rungs. The paired bases separate. Then, new bases pair with the separated bases on each half of the DNA molecule. The result is two identical copies of the original DNA molecule.

DNA replication occurs every time a cell divides normally. The new cells receive copies of the DNA molecules. In this way, genetic information is passed on from cell to cell.

Since genes determine traits, mutations may affect the traits of an organism. For example, white eye color in fruit flies is the result of a mutation. Mutations may be harmful or helpful to organisms or may have no effect at all. Only gene mutations in sex cells can be passed on to offspring.

Achievements in Science

The Human Genome Project

The Human Genome Project (HGP) was a joint international research program to map the different genes in the human body. A genome is all the DNA in an organism.

The project began in 1990 and was completed in April of 2003. Scientists have put in order the 3.1 billion units of DNA that make up the human genome.

Genes carry various hereditary conditions, ranging from cystic fibrosis to Alzheimer's. Now it's possible to test whether people might have certain genetic disorders. Rapid technological advances in genetics testing has greatly improved our ability to make the detection of genetic conditions earlier, simpler, and more precise.

Mitosis and Cell Division

One-celled organisms, such as amoebas, reproduce by splitting in half. Before doing so, the amoeba's chromosomes make a copy of themselves. Then, the amoeba's nuclear membrane dissolves. The two sets of chromosomes separate, and a nucleus forms around each set. The division of the nucleus into two new nuclei is called **mitosis.**

Following mitosis, the entire cell divides. When the amoeba becomes two amoebas, each new amoeba gets one nucleus with a complete set of chromosomes. Each set of chromosomes is identical to the parent amoeba's chromosomes. Thus, each new amoeba is identical to the parent amoeba.

Just as amoebas go through mitosis and cell division, so do the cells that make up the human body. The photo below shows a human cell dividing. Body cells divide by mitosis and cell division as the body grows and repairs itself. However, to reproduce itself, the body uses a different kind of process.

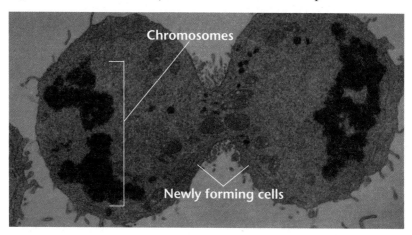

Sexual Reproduction

Humans and most other many-celled organisms reproduce sexually. In sexual reproduction, two cells called gametes join to form one complete cell. Males produce gametes called sperm cells. Females produce gametes called egg cells. Each gamete has only one-half of the chromosomes found in the organism's body cells. When gametes join, they form a cell that has a complete set of chromosomes.

Diversity

The range of differences found among the members of a population

Adaptation

A change or adjustment that makes an organism better able to survive in its environment

Humans have 46 chromosomes in their body cells. These include two copies of each of 22 different chromosomes, plus a pair of sex chromosomes. Male sex chromosomes are identified as Y, and female chromosomes as X. There are only 23 chromosomes in human sperm cells. Human egg cells also have only 23 chromosomes. When humans reproduce, a sperm and an egg join to form a cell called a zygote. If a zygote contains two female chromosomes, XX, it will become a female. If it contains a male chromosome and a female chromosome, XY, it will be a male. A zygote with its complete set of 46 chromosomes and eventually develops into an adult.

Together, the 46 human chromosomes contain two copies of each gene. The mix of chromosomes from both parents during sexual reproduction produces an offspring that is different from either parent. It also explains the variations in traits of offspring.

Humans and other species that produce unique offspring are said to have **diversity.** Diversity is the range of differences found among the members of a population. If a population's environment changes suddenly, the population's diversity can help it continue to survive. For example, suppose a disease sweeps through a population of deer, killing many of them. If none of the deer are able to fight the disease, then the population will die off. However, in a diverse population, a few deer may be able to resist the disease. As a result of this difference, or **adaptation,** in some deer, the population will survive. Adaptations result from the information in an organism's DNA.

Meiosis

As you know, mitosis results in two new cells. Each cell has a complete set of chromosomes. Gametes form by a different kind of process. They form by a division of the nucleus called **meiosis.**

The diagram below compares the process of meiosis with that of mitosis. As in mitosis, meiosis begins with the copying of the chromosomes in a parent cell. Then, the cell divides into two new cells. However, in meiosis, each new cell divides again. Thus, one parent cell results in four new sex cells. Each sex cell contains one-half the number of chromosomes of the parent cell.

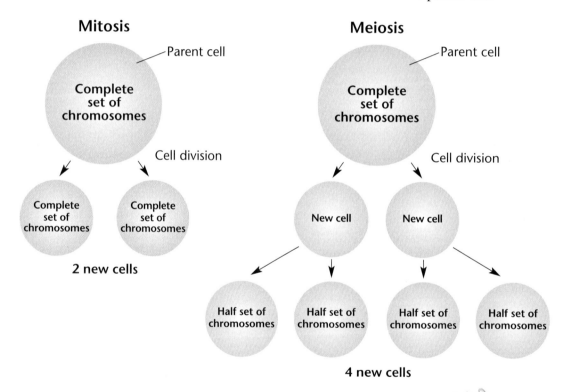

Science Myth

Eye color is determined by one pair of genes with one gene from the father and one gene from the mother.

Fact: Your eye color is an example of a trait that is determined by many different pairs of genes. Each pair is inherited independently from the other pairs. That explains why blue eyes are not all the same blue.

Write your answers to these questions on a separate sheet of paper. Write complete sentences.

1. What is heredity?

2. What are chromosomes?

3. What is a gene?

4. Describe mitosis.

5. Describe meiosis.

▼◄▲▼◄▲▼◄▲▼◄▲▼◄▲▼◄▲▼◄▲▼◄▲▼◄▲▼◄▲▼◄▲▼◄▲▼◄▲▼◄▲▼◄▲▼◄▲▼◄▲▼◄▲▼

Science at Work

Genetic Counselor

A genetic counselor must be good at solving problems, interpreting medical information, and studying patterns and risks. A college degree in a field such as biology, genetics, nursing, or psychology is needed. A graduate degree in genetic counseling is also needed. Certification as a genetic counselor requires clinical experience and passing the examination of the American Board of Genetic Counseling (ABGC).

Genetic counselors counsel families who might have offspring with genetic diseases or birth defects. Genetic counselors identify possible risks, investigate the problem in the family's history, and explain information to the family. Most genetic counselors work in medical centers or hospitals. Some work in research laboratories that diagnose genetic problems, at drug companies, in private practice, or in public-health agencies.

Evolution

The changes in a population over time

You have probably noticed that there are many different kinds of organisms alive today. Many of these organisms are quite different in their structure and behavior from organisms that lived in the past. For example, modern reptiles are smaller than dinosaurs and other ancient reptiles. Modern reptiles also eat different foods. The diversity of organisms today and in the past is the result of a process called **evolution**, or change over time.

Organisms, Populations, and Change

An organism changes as it grows and develops. However, these changes are not evolution. Individual organisms do not evolve. Evolution is the changes that occur in a population of organisms over time. As you learned in Chapter 21, a population is made up of individuals of the same species that live in the same place. A species is made up of individuals of the same kind that are able to interbreed and reproduce. What species makes up the population shown in the picture?

Evolution occurs within populations.

Most populations of organisms exist over long periods of time. A population exists much longer than any individual in the population. For example, as individual penguins die and leave the population, other penguins are born into it. The population of penguins continues even though individuals die.

Lethal mutation

A mutation that results in the death of an organism

The process of evolution takes place over many generations. For example, it may take millions of years for a population of short-necked animals to change, or evolve, into a population of long-necked animals. Evolution involves changes in populations over extremely long periods of time. Evolution has occurred on Earth over many millions of years.

Changes in Genes

As you know, genes determine the traits of all living things. Thus, genes determine the characteristics of a population. Evolution involves changes in a population's gene pool. As you learned in Lesson 1, radiation and chemicals in the environment can cause genes to change. Genes also change if they are copied incorrectly during DNA replication.

Mutations may occur in two different kinds of cells. Some mutations occur in an organism's body cells. These mutations can cause cancers and other changes in the organism. In organisms that reproduce sexually, body-cell mutations are not passed on to the offspring. For this reason, body-cell mutations are not involved in the evolution of most plants and animals.

Mutations can also occur in an organism's gametes. If the genes in an organism's gametes change, these mutations usually do not affect the organism itself. However, the mutations are passed on to the organism's offspring. The mutations can affect the traits of the offspring and of future generations.

Effects of Mutations over Time

Often, mutations cause harmful changes in traits. A **lethal mutation** is one that results in an organism's death. Organisms that inherit a lethal mutation usually do not live long enough to reproduce. As a result, the mutation is not passed on to offspring.

Sometimes a mutation results in a trait that improves an organism's chances for survival. An organism that survives is more likely to reproduce. The favorable mutation is then passed on to the offspring. As the mutation is passed on to future generations, it becomes more and more common within the population. Over time, all of the members of the population may have the mutation.

Mutations usually occur at a slow rate in populations. For example, the mutation rate in one generation of a population of fruit flies is about 0.93. This means that less than one fly per generation is likely to have a mutation. Because mutations are rare, populations usually evolve slowly.

If a population's environment changes, members of the population that have certain traits may be more likely to survive. For example, if the environment turns cold and snowy, an animal with white fur may be more likely to survive. The white fur helps to hide the animal against the white background of snow.

Organisms that survive and reproduce pass their genes on to following generations of the population. In this way, traits that help animals survive in the environment become more common within the population. Over time, the population evolves.

Scientific Theory

In science, the term *theory* is used in a way that is different from its use in common language. In everyday language, you might say that you have a theory about why a friend did not go to a party. That is, you might have a hunch. But in science, *theory* indicates more than a hunch. A **scientific theory** is an explanation that has undergone many tests. Many different kinds of evidence support a scientific theory and no evidence can contradict, or disagree with, the explanation. As scientists find new evidence, they compare the evidence to the theory. If the evidence contradicts the theory, the theory is changed.

The Theory of Evolution

Hypothesis

A testable explanation of a question or problem (plural is hypotheses)

Descent with modification

The theory that more recent species of organisms are changed descendants of earlier species

Natural selection

The process by which organisms best suited to the environment survive, reproduce, and pass their genes to the next generation

Adaptive advantage

The greater likelihood that an organism will survive, due to characteristics that allow it to be more successful than other organisms

Charles Darwin spent five years traveling around the world, from 1831 to 1836. During his travels, Darwin studied fossils from rock formations that were known to be very old. He compared those fossils with fossils from younger rock formations. Darwin found similar organisms in the different rock formations. He noted that the similar organisms had undergone change. The fossil evidence showed Darwin that species change over time.

Based on his observations and collections, Darwin came up with ideas of how evolution occurs. When Darwin first proposed his ideas about evolution, the ideas were **hypotheses**. A hypothesis is a testable explanation of a question or problem. Today, Darwin's ideas about evolution are stated as two theories.

The first theory is called **descent with modification**. It states that more recent species found in the fossil record are changed descendants of earlier species. In other words, all organisms have descended from one or a few original life-forms. Descent with modification basically says that evolution occurs in nature.

The second theory is called **natural selection**. It explains how evolution occurs. Natural selection occurs in all populations of organisms. An example is the natural selection of snakes that have a specialized upper tooth. Young snakes use the tooth to cut their way out of their shell. Snakes that are able to leave their shell with ease are more likely to survive and reproduce. The presence and use of the specialized tooth give the young snakes an **adaptive advantage**. They have a greater likelihood of surviving because of their characteristics. The environment selects individuals in a population that have an adaptive advantage. Young snakes that do not have the specialized tooth do not live to reproduce. Their genes are lost from the population. This process results in the evolution of a new species over a long period of time.

The fossils of dinosaur skeletons can deteriorate in museums. Using computer technology and scanners, digital copies of the dinosaur skeleton are stored in electronic files. Some fossil bones are used to make molds and casts. Then, the fossils are preserved and stored. The electronic files can be used to make molds of bones that are missing. A computer-guided laser can form the missing bones from a vat of liquid plastic.

The following four points summarize Darwin's theory of natural selection to explain how evolution occurs.

1. Organisms tend to produce more offspring than can survive. For example, fish lay thousands of eggs, but only a few live to be adult fish.

2. Individuals in a population have slight variations. For example, fish in a population may differ slightly in color, length, fin size, or speed.

3. Individuals struggle to survive. Individuals that have variations best suited to the environment are more likely to survive.

4. Survivors pass on their genes to their offspring. Gradually, the population changes.

Behaviors also evolve through natural selection. Behavior is an interaction of heredity and experience. It is the way an organism acts. There are two main types of behavior: innate and learned.

A behavior that is present at birth is called an innate behavior. The behavior is inherited. It does not have to be learned. An animal usually performs the behavior correctly on the first try.

Unlike innate behaviors, learned behaviors are not present at birth. They are behaviors that are the result of experience. Learned behaviors can change over the lifetime of an organism.

Birdsongs are both innate and learned. The behavior is innate because birds are born knowing how to sing. A bird that is raised alone will sing. However, the song is different from songs by other birds of the same species. Birds must learn their songs by hearing other adult birds sing. Songs are behaviors that help males and females of the same species identify each other so they can mate.

Evidence of Evolution

Vestigial structure

A body part that appears to be useless to an organism but was probably useful to the organism's ancestors

Homologous structure

A body part that is similar in related organisms

If populations really do change slowly over time, then there should be evidence of the change. As you know, the fossil record shows recent species that are slightly different from earlier species. This is one type of evidence that supports the theory of evolution.

Other evidence is that the embryos of some kinds of organisms go through similar stages of development. For example, an early human embryo has a tail and gill pouches, just as an early fish embryo has. Similarities in the development of vertebrate embryos are an indication that all vertebrates descended from a common ancestor.

Another indication that certain organisms are related to one another is the presence of **vestigial structures**. A vestigial structure is a body part that appears to be useless to an organism. For example, snakes and whales have the remnants of leg bones and pelvic bones. These vestigial structures are not used to help snakes and whales move. They are probably "leftover" structures from ancestors of snakes and whales that had legs for walking on land.

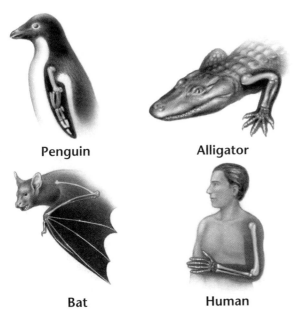

Penguin   Alligator

Bat   Human

Homologous Structures in Vertebrates

Still more support comes from the way living things are connected. Look at the front limbs of the vertebrates in the diagram on the left. Notice how similar they are. The limbs are **homologous structures**. Homologous structures are body parts that are similar in related organisms. Homologous structures are thought to have first appeared in an ancestor that is common to all the organisms that have the homologous structures. Thus, vertebrates probably share a common ancestor that had front limbs like those you see in the diagram.

Write your answers to these questions on a separate sheet of paper. Write complete sentences.

1. What is evolution?

2. Do individual organisms evolve? Explain your answer.

3. In organisms that reproduce sexually, through what type of cells are mutations passed to offspring?

4. Explain the process of natural selection.

5. Give two types of evidence other than fossils that support the theory of evolution.

Science in Your Life

How long is 4.6 billion years?

Many scientists think that Earth is about 4.6 billion years old. That is a long time compared to the time spans we deal with every day. One way to understand how long 4.6 billion years is would be to make a model of the geologic time scale.

You will need to gather colored pencils, a meterstick, tape, scissors, and sheets of unlined paper. Then, follow the steps below.

1. Using the meterstick and scissors, tape the sheets of paper together end-to-end until you reach 4.6 meters. On the paper, 1 meter will represent 1 billion years.
2. Find an area of the floor where you can spread out the sheets of paper. Then, tape the paper to the floor. This will be your model.
3. Mark one end of your model "Origin of Earth." Mark the opposite end of your model "Today."
4. Refer to the geologic time scale on page 306. Using the chart to the right, map each event in the geologic time scale on your model.
5. Where is the year of your birth on the time scale? Is it possible to find it?

Geological Time Scale	
Length	**Number of Years**
1 meter =	1 billion years
10 centimeters =	100 million years
1 centimeter =	10 million years
1 millimeter =	1 million years

INVESTIGATION

22

Materials

♦ clear jar with lid
♦ paper towels
♦ water
♦ 3 bean seeds

Observing a Plant Adaptation

Purpose

Have you ever wondered what effect gravity has on plants? In this investigation, you will observe how plants adapt to gravity.

Procedure

1. Moisten paper towels so they are damp but not wet.

2. Fill the jar with the damp paper towels.

3. Insert bean seeds between the towels and the side of the jar, as shown in the illustration. Screw the lid on the jar.

4. Put the jar in a warm place out of sunlight. Check the jar every day to see if the seeds have germinated. When they do, draw what you see.

5. Let the plants' stems and roots grow until they are at least 2 cm long. Then turn the jar upside down.

6. Examine the seeds each day for three days. Draw what you see.

7. Turn the jar rightside up again. Repeat step 6.

Questions and Conclusions

1. When the seeds germinated in step 4, how did their stems and roots grow?

2. What did the stems and roots do when you turned the jar upside down?

3. What did the stems and roots do when you turned the jar rightside up again?

4. How does this adaptation help plants survive?

Explore Further

Compare a cactus and a leafy plant like a philodendron. A cactus is adapted for life in a hot, dry environment. Make a list of cactus features that are different from the features of the philodendron. Next to each, explain how you think that feature helps a cactus survive in the desert.

■ Heredity is the passing of traits from parents to their offspring.

■ Genes are located on chromosomes, which are found in the nucleus of a cell.

■ Chromosomes are able to make copies of themselves. During mitosis and cell division, each new cell gets an exact copy of the parent cell's chromosomes.

■ Meiosis is the process by which sex cells form. Each sex cell contains one-half the number of chromosomes in the parent cell.

■ Mutations are changes in DNA. Harmful mutations cause genetic diseases, such as diabetes and hemophilia.

■ Evolution is the result of changes in the gene pools of populations over long periods of time. Populations are the smallest units in which evolution occurs. Mutations and changes in a population's environment may cause the population's gene pool to change.

■ Darwin's ideas about evolution are stated as two theories. The first theory is called descent with modification. Darwin's second theory is called natural selection.

Science Words

adaptation, 525	diversity, 525	homologous structure, 533	natural selection, 531
adaptive advantage, 531	environment, 521	hypothesis, 531	replicate, 523
base, 522	evolution, 528	lethal mutation, 529	scientific theory, 530
chromosome, 521	gene, 521	mitosis, 524	vestigial structure, 533
descent with modification, 531	genetics, 521	meiosis, 526	
	heredity, 521	mutation, 522	

Chapter 22 REVIEW

Word Bank

environment

evolution

genes

heredity

homologous structures

lethal mutations

mitosis

meiosis

mutations

natural selection

replicate

vestigial structures

Vocabulary Review

Choose the word or words from the Word Bank that best complete each sentence. Write the answer on a sheet of paper.

1. The passing of traits from parents to offspring is _____.

2. Everything in your surroundings make up your _____.

3. Changes in an organism's DNA are _____.

4. Parents pass traits to their offspring through their _____.

5. Before a cell can divide normally, its DNA molecules have to _____.

6. The process called _____ is the changes in a population over time.

7. _____ result in the death of organisms.

8. The theory of _____ states that organisms that are best suited to live in a certain environment are more likely to reproduce.

9. The process of _____ produces four sex cells.

10. The process of _____ produces two new cells exactly like the parent cell.

11. Body parts that are similar in related organisms are called _____ .

12. _____ are body parts that appear to be useless to organisms but were probably useful to their ancestors.

Concept Review

Choose the answer that best completes each sentence. Write the letter of the answer on your paper.

13. After _____ and cell division, each new cell has the same number of chromosomes as the parent cell.

    A meiosis   C reproduction

    B mitosis   D genetics

14. After _____, each new cell has half the number of chromosomes as the parent cell.
- **A** meiosis
- **B** mutation
- **C** reproduction
- **D** mitosis

15. Offspring resemble their parents because they have copies of their parents' _____.
- **A** DNA
- **B** sex cells
- **C** body cells
- **D** variations

16. _____ can cause either harmful or helpful changes in traits.
- **A** Genetics
- **B** Adaptations
- **C** Mutations
- **D** Gametes

17. Evolution occurs in the gene pool of a(n) _____.
- **A** individual
- **B** organism
- **C** cell
- **D** population

18. The rod-shaped structures in a cell's nucleus that contain DNA are called _____.
- **A** genes
- **B** chromosomes
- **C** mutations
- **D** vestigial structures

19. Evolution involves changes in the gene pool of a(n) _____.
- **A** individual
- **B** population
- **C** body cell
- **D** gamete

Critical Thinking

Write the answer to each of the following questions.

20. Suppose a mouse loses its tail in a mousetrap. Will the mouse's offspring be born without tails? Explain your answer.

Test-Taking Tip Read the directions carefully. Don't assume that you know what you're supposed to do.

UNIT 3   S U M M A R Y

- All living things are made of cells. Cells are organized into tissues and tissues are organized into organs.

- Plant cells and animal cells have many of the same parts. Plant cells have cell walls and chloroplasts. Animal cells do not.

- Living things are divided into five kingdoms based on how they are related. The kingdoms are plant, animal, protist, fungi, and monera.

- Animals eat other organisms for food. They move around to get their food. They have many cells that are organized into tissues and organs.

- Plants make their own food and do not move around from place to place. They have many cells that are organized into tissues and sometimes organs.

- Most protists are one-celled. They have properties of both animals and plants. Some make their own food. Others absorb their food. Some do both.

- Fungi absorb their food from other organisms or the remains of other organisms. Some are parasites.

- Monerans are bacteria. They are usually one-celled organisms that do not have organelles. Some make their own food and others absorb their food.

- Plants make food in their chloroplasts during photosynthesis. Plants need carbon dioxide and water to make food. As a result of photosynthesis, plants give off oxygen gas.

- Food stores chemical energy. The process of releasing energy from food is called cellular respiration. Most living things need oxygen for cellular respiration.

- Vertebrates are animals that have a backbone.

- Invertebrates are animals that do not have a backbone.

■ Every species has a two-word scientific name consisting of its genus and its species level.

■ Asexual reproduction involves one parent and no egg or sperm. The offspring are exactly like the parent.

■ Sexual reproduction involves an egg from a female parent and a sperm from a male parent. The offspring are different from either parent.

■ The three main groups of plants are: seed plants, ferns and related plants, and mosses and related plants.

■ Plants can reproduce by sexual reproduction or by asexual reproduction.

■ The feeding order of organisms is called a food chain. Every food chain begins with producers, which can make their own food. Consumers must take in food. Energy flows through food chains from producers to consumers.

■ Water, carbon, oxygen, and nitrogen cycle through ecosystems.

■ Heredity is the passing of traits from parents to their offspring.

■ Traits are carried on genes. The genes are located on the chromosomes within the nuclei of cells. Chromosomes are able to make copies of themselves. During mitosis and cell division, each new cell gets an exact copy of the parent cell's chromosomes.

■ Meiosis is the process by which sex cells form. Each sex cell contains one-half the number of chromosomes in the parent cell.

■ Evolution is the result of changes in populations over long periods of time. Mutations and changes in a population's environment may cause the population's gene pool to change.

Word Bank

cell

cellular respiration

consumer

genes

heredity

kingdoms

mutation

photosynthesis

producer

tissues

Vocabulary Review

Choose the word or words from the Word Bank that best complete each sentence. Write the answer on a sheet of paper.

1. Living things are divided into five major groups or _____.

2. The process by which plants make their own food is _____.

3. _____ are made of a group of similar cells that work together.

4. A(n) _____ is an organism that feeds on other organisms.

5. A(n) _____ is a change in an organism's DNA.

6. The basic unit of all living things is the _____.

7. A _____ is an organism that uses the sun's energy to make its own food.

8. During the process of _____, living things break down the molecules of food to release energy.

9. The passing of traits from parent to offspring is _____.

10. Traits that can be passed along to offspring are carried on _____ of chromosomes.

Concept Review

Choose the answer that best completes each sentence. Write the letter of the answer on your paper.

11. After _____, each new cell has half the number of chromosomes as the parent cell.
    A meiosis   **C** metamorphosis
    B mitosis   **D** mutation

12. Reproduction that involves only one parent is _____.
    A asexual reproduction   **C** fertilization
    B sexual reproduction   **D** metamorphosis

13. Organisms that absorb their food from other organisms or from dead matter are classified as _____.
  A plants   **C** fungi
  B animals   **D** protists

14. _____ are consumers that move around to get their food.
  A plants   **C** fungi
  B producers   **D** animals

15. One-celled organisms that do not contain organelles are classified as _____.
  A fungi   **C** protists
  B monerans   **D** consumers

16. _____ is a change in a population over time.
  A heredity   **C** evolution
  B reproduction   **D** mitosis

17. In a food chain, energy travels from _____.
  A producers to consumers   **C** decomposers to producers
  B consumers to producers   **D** producers to producers

18. During photosynthesis, plants use _____ and water to make food.
  A oxygen   **C** chemical energy
  B carbohydrates   **D** carbon dioxide

Critical Thinking

Write the answer to each of the following questions

19. Suppose a biologist discovers a new living thing. It is a one-celled organism that can move around. Within its cell are organelles that contain chloroplasts. In what kingdom does this organism belong? Why?

20. What type of molecule is shown in the diagram to the left? Explain how this molecule passes traits from parents to offspring.

Unit 4

The Human Body

Thereare millions of human beings on Earth. No two humans are exactly alike. Yet all have a lot in common. Every human body is built by the same basic plan.

The human body could be called a machine. But compared to other machines, it is remarkable. The body machine is light weight, but very durable. It can take in raw materials and use them to build new structures, make repairs, and power all of its work.

The control systems for the human body are more complex than any machine or computer on Earth. In less than a second, the body can take in information, process it, and respond. At the same time, the body carries on hundreds of different jobs, such as breathing and growing. In this unit, you will find out how the body works. You will also learn more about the systems that control the body.

Chapters in Unit 4

545

Meeting the Body's Basic Needs

Imagine that you're running in a race. The muscles in your legs spring into action when you hear the starting pistol. You feel your feet hit the ground as you move ahead of the other runners. You breathe deeply as air moves into and out of your lungs. You feel your heart pounding. Before long, you begin to sweat. Different systems in your body work together to make all this possible. In this chapter, you will learn about the body systems and what they do.

Organize Your Thoughts

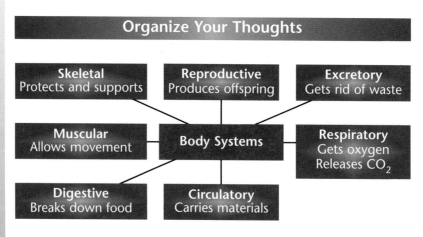

Skeletal
Protects and supports

Reproductive
Produces offspring

Excretory
Gets rid of waste

Muscular
Allows movement

Body Systems

Respiratory
Gets oxygen
Releases CO_2

Digestive
Breaks down food

Circulatory
Carries materials

Goals for Learning

◆ To identify seven systems of the human body

◆ To describe the structure and function of each body system

◆ To recognize that body systems work together to carry out basic life activities

The Skeletal System

The 206 bones of the human body make up the **skeletal system**. Bones have several functions. First, bones support the body. They give the body a shape. Bones form a framework that supports the softer tissues of the body. Second, bones protect organs. For example, a rib cage protects the heart and lungs. Vertebrae protect the spinal cord. Vertebrae are the 33 bones that make up the backbone. The pelvis protects reproductive organs. The skull protects the brain. Find these bones in the diagram below.

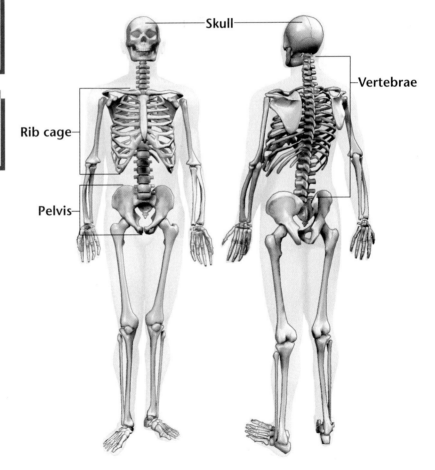

Skull — Vertebrae — Rib cage — Pelvis

The Skeletal System

A third function of bones is to allow movement. Muscles attach to bones and move them. The body has big bones, small bones, flat bones, wide bones, and bones that have unusual shapes. The variety of bones helps a person to move in different ways. Fourth, bones are the place where blood cells are formed. Bones contain spongy material called red marrow. Red marrow has special cells that make blood cells. Finally, bones store minerals, such as calcium, phosphorus, and magnesium.

Cartilage to Bone

Most bones start out as cartilage. Cartilage is a thick, smooth tissue. It is not as hard as bone. Before birth, the entire skeleton is cartilage. It is gradually replaced by bone. A baby is born with more than 300 bones. Over time, some of the bones join so that a person ends up with 206 bones. However, some parts of the body continue to have cartilage. Feel the end of your nose. It is cartilage and will never become bone. Your outer ear contains cartilage. Inside your body, cartilage surrounds your **trachea.**

How Bones Change

Bones are organs that are made of tissue. They are always changing. Bones are built up and broken down throughout life. This is a normal process. For example, enzymes break down bone tissue when the body needs calcium. Calcium is released into the bloodstream. However, if calcium is not replaced properly, a person can develop osteoporosis. The bones of people with this disease become less solid and break more easily than before. Osteoporosis most often affects older people. Regular exercise and a diet higher in calcium can help prevent osteoporosis.

Joints

Bones come together at joints. Cartilage covers bones at the joints. This cartilage acts like a cushion. It protects bones from rubbing against one another. At the movable joints, strips of strong tissue called **ligaments** connect bones to each other. Ligaments stretch to allow the bones to move.

There are several kinds of joints. The ball-and-socket joint allows the greatest range of motion. This type of joint is located at the hips and shoulders. It allows you to move your arms and legs forward, backward, side to side, and in a circular motion. The knee joint is the largest and most complex joint. The knee joint is a hinge joint. Some joints, such as your rib and spine joints, can move only a little. A few joints, such as those in your skull, do not move at all.

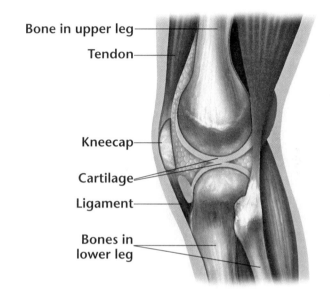

Bone in upper leg
Tendon
Kneecap
Cartilage
Ligament
Bones in lower leg

The Knee Joint

The Muscular System

The muscular system consists of the more than 600 muscles in your body. The skeletal and muscular systems work together to produce movement. Tough strips of tissue called tendons attach muscles to bones.

Most muscles work in pairs. When a muscle contracts, or shortens, it pulls on the tendon. The tendon pulls on the attached bone, and the bone moves. A muscle cannot push. Therefore, a different muscle on the opposite side of the bone contracts to return the bone to its starting position.

The diagram below shows an example of muscles working in pairs. When you bend your arm, the biceps muscle contracts. You can feel how the muscle shortens and hardens as it contracts. The biceps pulls on the tendon, which pulls your lower arm toward you. The triceps muscle on the underside of your arm is relaxed. It is long and thin. When you straighten your arm, the triceps contracts. It pulls the lower arm back to its starting position. Now the biceps muscle is relaxed.

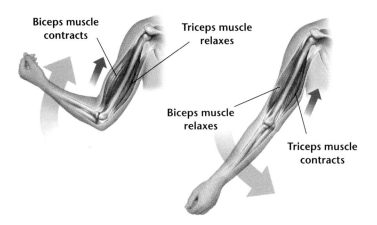

Biceps muscle contracts

Triceps muscle relaxes

Biceps muscle relaxes

Triceps muscle contracts

Kinds of Muscle Tissue

The body has three kinds of muscle tissue—skeletal, smooth, and cardiac. Most muscle tissue is skeletal muscle. Skeletal muscles are attached to bones. Skeletal muscles are voluntary muscles. That is, you can choose when to use them. The muscles in your arms, legs, and face are voluntary.

The second kind of muscle tissue is smooth muscle. These muscles form layers lining the walls of organs. Smooth muscles are found in the esophagus, stomach, and intestines. These muscles move in wavelike actions to move food through the digestive system. The walls of the blood vessels also are lined with smooth muscles. These muscles contract and relax to maintain blood pressure. Smooth muscles are involuntary muscles. You cannot choose when to use them. They react to changes in the body.

The third kind of muscle tissue is cardiac muscle. These muscles make up the heart. They contract regularly to pump blood throughout your body. Cardiac muscles are involuntary.

Lesson 1 REVIEW

Write your answers to these questions on a separate sheet of paper. Write complete sentences.

1. What are the five functions of bone?

2. How does bone change during a person's lifetime?

3. What is the difference between ligaments and tendons?

4. How do muscles make bones move?

5. What are the three kinds of muscle tissue?

Achievements in Science

Artificial Joints

In a condition called osteoarthritis, bone and cartilage are damaged. Osteoarthritis can be both crippling and painful. The disease can strike any joint of the body, but the hip joints are often affected. These large joints get a lot of wear and tear because they support the weight of the upper body. Each hip joint is made of a socket and a head. The socket is an indention in the bone of the pelvis. The head is a round part of the top of the leg bone. Until the early 1900s, people suffering from severe osteoarthritis in a hip joint endured years of pain and limited movement.

The skill of two doctors changed all that. In 1923, Dr. Marius Smith-Peters tried something never done before. He surgically covered the damaged head of a leg bone with a glass cup. Smith-Peters' patient was able to enjoy many pain-free years because the glass cup improved motion in the joint. However, the glass eventually wore out. In 1961 Sir John Charnley took Smith-Peters' idea and improved it. With the better materials available to him, Charnley used plastic to reinforce a patient's hip socket and steel to rebuild the head on his leg bone. Charnley's version of the artificial hip lasted a long time. The work of both doctors laid the groundwork for modern day hip-replacement surgery.

Digestion

Your body is made up of systems that work together to maintain your good health. One of these systems is your digestive system, which breaks down food for your body to use. Food contains energy for your body's cells. However, this food is too large to enter cells. The food must be broken down into smaller pieces. This process is called digestion. Food contains carbohydrates, proteins, and fats. In digestion, these nutrients are broken down into a form that your cells can use for energy. As you read about digestion, refer to the diagram of the digestive system shown below.

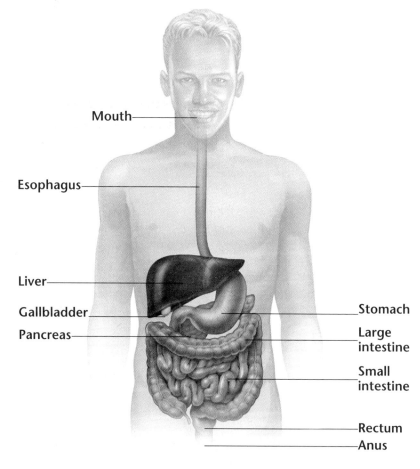

Mouth

Esophagus

Liver

Gallbladder

Pancreas

Stomach

Large intestine

Small intestine

Rectum

Anus

The Digestive System

Digestion Begins Inside Your Mouth

Your teeth and jaws chew and crush food while your tongue turns it over. This mechanical action makes pieces of food smaller. As you chew, salivary glands secrete saliva, a fluid that has a digestive enzyme. An enzyme is a protein that causes chemical changes. The enzyme in saliva changes carbohydrates into sugars as you chew. Digestive enzymes help to break down food. Different parts of the digestive system have their own special digestive enzymes.

The Esophagus

As you chew, food moves around in your mouth. When you swallow, the food moves into your **pharynx,** or throat. From there, it moves into the esophagus. This long tube connects the mouth to the stomach. Smooth muscles in the esophagus contract, or squeeze together, to push food toward the stomach. This movement is called **peristalsis.**

The Stomach

Digestion continues in the stomach. Strong muscles of the stomach walls contract. This action churns and mixes the food. The stomach walls secrete digestive juices. These juices are hydrochloric acid and digestive enzymes. A special moist lining protects the stomach from being eaten away by the acids. The acid and enzymes break down large molecules of food. Solid food becomes liquid. This liquid food is called **chyme.**

Pharynx

The passageway between the mouth and the esophagus for air and food

Peristalsis

The movement of digestive organs that pushes food through the digestive tract

Chyme

Partly digested liquid food in the digestive tract

Technology Note

Medical technology is often used to study the digestive system. One test involves taking an X ray of the esophagus, stomach, and small intestine. The person being tested swallows a liquid that coats the lining of these organs. The barium in the liquid makes these organs show up on the X ray. This test, along with others, can help doctors determine the health of the digestive system.

The Small Intestine

Peristalsis squirts chyme from the stomach into the small intestine. The small intestine is a coiled tube that is about 4 to 7 meters long. This is where most digestion takes place.

Two organs and a gland close to the small intestine aid digestion. These are the liver, the **gallbladder**, and the pancreas. The liver makes a fluid called **bile**. Bile breaks apart fat molecules. The gallbladder stores the bile. The bile enters the small intestine through a tube called a bile duct. **Glands** are organs that produce chemicals for the body to use. The pancreas is a gland that secretes enzymes that complete the digestion of carbohydrates, proteins, and fats.

By this time, the food molecules are ready to be absorbed, or taken in, by body cells. They are absorbed through tiny, fingerlike structures called **villi**. Thousands of villi line the small intestine. Villi make the surface area of the intestine larger. Many food molecules can be absorbed through the blood vessels of the villi. Blood carries the food molecules to cells all through the body.

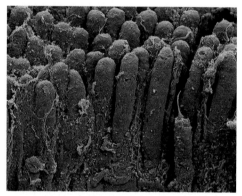

Villi provide a large surface area through which food molecules can pass into the blood.

The Large Intestine

Peristalsis moves material that cannot be digested to the large intestine. The main function of the large intestine is to remove water from undigested material. The water is returned to the body. The undigested material forms a solid mass called **feces**. Feces are stored in the **rectum** for a short time. The rectum is the last part of the large intestine. Smooth muscles line the large intestine. They contract and push the feces out of the body through an opening called the anus. The journey of food through your digestive system takes about 24 to 33 hours.

Gallbladder
The digestive organ that stores bile

Bile
A substance made in the liver that breaks down fats

Gland
An organ that produces chemicals for the body to use

Villi
Tiny fingerlike structures in the small intestine through which food molecules enter the blood

Feces
Solid waste material remaining in the large intestine after digestion

Rectum
Lower part of the large intestine where feces are stored

Did You Know?

If the villi in the small intestine could be laid out flat, the area would be as big as a baseball diamond.

Lesson 2   R E V I E W

Write your answers to these questions on a separate sheet of paper. Write complete sentences.

1. What does the digestive system do?

2. Where and how does digestion begin?

3. Describe the path that food takes through the digestive system.

4. Why are villi shaped the way they are?

5. How do feces leave the body?

Achievements in Science

Human Digestion Observed

Today, doctors can view the human stomach with a tiny camera. They understand the digestive process and the way the stomach works. But many years ago, doctors didn't know what the stomach did. Some thought it cooked the food and others thought it ground up the food. The first opportunity for a doctor to actually observe digestion taking place in the stomach occurred by accident.

In 1822, Alexis St. Martin was badly injured by a shotgun. Dr. William Beaumont, an Army doctor assigned to Fort Mackinac, Michigan, took care of him. Even after St. Martin was treated, he had a permanent hole in his stomach. With St. Martin's permission, Dr. Beaumont began experiments.

Beaumont was the first person to observe human digestion as it was occurring. His experiments showed that digestion is a chemical process and that digestive juices need heat to work. Beaumont carefully recorded his observations. He published a book containing the results of his work.

23

Materials

◆ watch or clock with a second hand

◆ graph paper

How Does Exercise Change Heart Rate?

Purpose

Does your heart beat faster when you're very active? In this investigation, you will observe the changes in heart rate during different amounts of activity.

Procedure

1. Copy the table below on a sheet of paper.

2. Sit quietly for three minutes. Then find your pulse. Hold two or three fingers of one hand on the thumb side of the other wrist.

3. Take your pulse. To do this, count the number of times you feel your pulse for 15 seconds. Multiply this number by 4. Your answer is your pulse for one minute. Record this number as your resting heart rate.

Activity	Heart Rate
Sitting (resting heart rate)	
Standing up	
After running in place	
Resting 30 seconds	
Resting 1 minute	
Resting $1\frac{1}{2}$ minutes	
Resting 2 minutes	
Resting $2\frac{1}{2}$ minutes	
Resting 3 minutes	

4. Stand up and immediately take your pulse again. Record this number.

5. Run in place for 200 steps. Then immediately take your pulse and record it.

6. Sit quietly for 30 seconds and take your pulse again. Record this number.

7. Repeat step 6 until you have taken your pulse every 30 seconds for three minutes. Remember to record your data.

8. Graph all of your data. Set up the graph so that time is on the *x*-axis (the line that runs the same direction as the bottom of the page). Put your heart rate on the *y*-axis (which runs the same direction as the side of the page).

Questions and Conclusions

1. How does the amount of activity affect heart rate?

2. Describe the demands on your heart when the heart rate was lowest and when it was highest.

3. Why does the heart rate change as the amount of activity changes?

Explore Further

Design an investigation about heart rate. You could investigate one of the following questions or one of your own: What activities increase heart rate the most? How much do people's resting heart rates differ? Once you choose a purpose for your investigation, write a procedure and do the investigation.

Objectives

After reading this lesson, you should be able to

◆ identify the major parts of the circulatory system and their functions.

◆ tell how arteries and veins are alike and different.

◆ trace the flow of blood through the heart.

◆ describe the parts of the blood and explain their functions.

Cardiac

Relating to the heart

Body cells must have a way to get oxygen and nutrients. They must get rid of wastes. The circulatory system performs these functions. The circulatory system consists of the heart and blood vessels. The heart pumps blood throughout the body through blood vessels. Blood carries food and oxygen to all the body cells. Blood also carries away wastes from the body cells.

The Heart

The main organ of the circulatory system is the heart. The heart is about the size of a human fist. It is located between the lungs in the chest cavity. The heart is the most powerful organ in the body. It is made mostly of muscle tissue called **cardiac** muscle. *Cardiac* means "of the heart" or "relating to the heart." The heart contracts and relaxes in a regular rhythm known as the heartbeat. The heartbeat is automatic. A person does not have to think about it to make it happen.

The heart beats about 70 times a minute in adults who are sitting or standing quietly. That is over 100,000 beats per day pumping more than 7,000 liters of blood per day. Each time the heart contracts, it squeezes blood out of itself and into blood vessels. Pressure increases inside the walls of certain blood vessels, and they bulge. This bulge can be felt at the wrist and on the side of the neck as the pulse.

How Blood Circulates

Look at the diagram of the heart on the next page. Notice that it has two sides, left and right. Each side has an upper chamber called the atrium and a lower chamber called the ventricle. Use your finger to trace over the diagram as you read how blood moves through the heart.

The right atrium receives blood from the rest of the body. The blood is low in oxygen and high in carbon dioxide. The blood moves into the right ventricle. The right ventricle pumps the blood to the lungs. In the lungs, the blood is filled with oxygen. Carbon dioxide leaves the blood and is exhaled, or breathed out. From the lungs, blood that is high in oxygen goes back to the heart. It goes first to the left atrium and then to the left ventricle. The left ventricle is a thick, powerful muscle. It sends the blood surging out through a large vessel called the aorta. The blood then moves to the rest of the body.

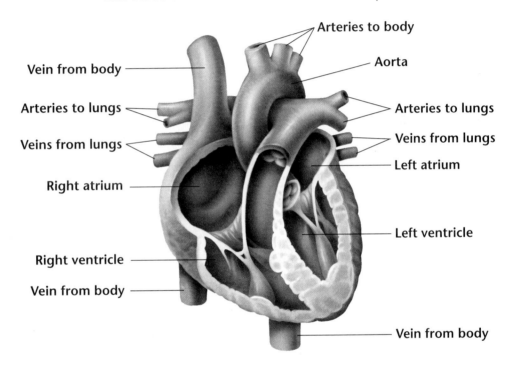

The Human Heart

Blood Vessels

Blood travels in only one direction, forming a circle pattern. Blood vessels that carry blood away from the heart are called **arteries**. Arteries carry blood full of oxygen. The aorta is the largest artery. The aorta leads to the rest of the body. The arteries become smaller as they move away from the heart. Only one artery carries blood high in carbon dioxide. This artery carries blood from the right ventricle to the lungs.

Capillary

A blood vessel with a wall one cell thick through which oxygen and food molecules pass to body cells

Vein

A blood vessel that carries blood to the heart

Tiny arteries branch into blood vessels called **capillaries**. The walls of the capillaries are only one cell thick. Oxygen and food molecules pass easily through the capillary walls to cells. Wastes, such as carbon dioxide, move into the capillaries from cells. The body has so many capillaries that each of its millions of cells is next to a capillary wall.

Capillaries that branched out from arteries join up again to form **veins**. Veins are blood vessels that carry blood to the heart. They carry carbon dioxide from the cells. Veins become larger as they move toward the heart. Pressure from the heart is not as great in veins as in arteries. Veins have one-way valves that keep the blood from flowing backward. Some veins are squeezed by muscles. This helps blood flow back to the heart.

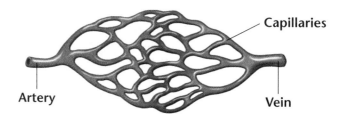

Blood Vessels

Blood Pressure

Blood pressure is the force of blood against the walls of blood vessels, usually arteries. When your heart beats, blood is pushed into the arteries. This forces the artery walls to bulge for a moment. The heart works hard to pump blood so that it reaches every part of the body. If blood vessels lose their ability to stretch, blood pressure rises. If blood pressure goes up too high, the heart can be damaged.

Blood and Its Parts

Blood does more than deliver oxygen and carry wastes to the lungs. It also delivers nutrients from the digestive system to cells. Food molecules pass through blood vessels in the villi. Blood carries waste products to the kidneys. You will learn more about that in Lesson 5. Blood also contains materials that fight infections and heal wounds.

Plasma

The liquid part of blood

Hemoglobin

A substance in red blood cells that carries oxygen

Platelet

A tiny piece of cell that helps form clots

Plasma, the liquid part of blood, is mostly water. It makes up half of your blood. Plasma contains dissolved oxygen, food molecules, minerals, and vitamins. Some proteins in plasma, called antibodies, fight disease. They help a person resist disease and harmful organisms. Your body makes antibodies against these foreign substances.

Red blood cells make up almost half of the blood. These cells are filled with hemoglobin, a protein that carries oxygen in the blood. Oxygen plus **hemoglobin** gives blood its bright red color. Hemoglobin carries oxygen from the lungs to the cells. There it picks up carbon dioxide and carries it back to the lungs.

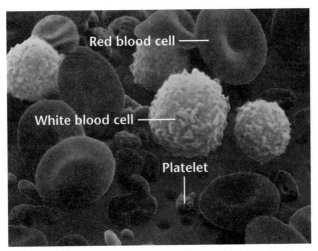

Find the red blood cells, white blood cells, and platelets.

As you can see in the photo at the left, white blood cells are larger than red blood cells. There is only about one white blood cell for every 700 red blood cells. Like antibodies, white blood cells protect the body against foreign substances. They move through the walls of capillaries to wrap themselves around invaders.

Platelets are tiny cell pieces that help blood to clot. A clot is a thick mass of blood. Platelets do not have a regular shape like red and white blood cells. Platelets collect at the place where a vessel is cut. They stick to each other and to the broken blood vessel. Red blood cells stick to the platelets, and together they form a clot.

Blood Types

People have one of four blood types. These are type A, type B, type AB, and type O. These different types are caused by different proteins in the red blood cells. Sometimes people may need a blood transfusion to replace lost blood. Blood banks can provide all types of blood. First health care workers must identify the patient's blood type. If they give the wrong blood type, the person's blood clumps. This blocks the tiny capillaries. Oxygen does not get to cells, and the cells die.

Lesson 3   R E V I E W

Write your answers to these questions on a separate sheet of paper. Write complete sentences.

1. What are the two main parts of the circulatory system?

2. What is the difference between arteries and veins?

3. What does blood do?

4. What are the functions of red blood cells, white blood cells, and platelets?

5. Why is it important to know your blood type?

Achievements in Science

Human Blood Groups Discovered

When people were given blood transfusions before the early 1900s, they often died because they were not given the correct blood. Doctors didn't know about blood groups. In 1901, an important discovery was made that has helped to save lives.

Austrian doctor Karl Landsteiner discovered that people have different blood groups. He identified these groups as A, B, and O. Later the blood group AB was discovered. With this information, doctors could make sure that blood types matched during blood transfusions. In 1930, Landsteiner received a Nobel Prize for his discovery of blood groups.

Identifying the different blood groups has increased the safety of transfusions and has saved many lives. Today, there are more than four million people in the United States who get blood transfusions each year.

Objectives

After reading this lesson, you should be able to

◆ identify the function and parts of the respiratory system.

◆ describe the process of gas exchange in the lungs.

◆ explain how the diaphragm moves when a person breathes.

Larynx

The voice box

Bronchus

A tube that connects the trachea to a lung (plural is bronchi)

Bronchiole

A tube that branches off the bronchus

Alveolus

A tiny sac at the end of each bronchiole that holds air (plural is alveoli)

The Respiratory System

The function of the respiratory system is to get oxygen into the body and to get rid of carbon dioxide. Lungs are the most important organs in the respiratory system. They connect your body to the outside air. The circulatory system then carries the oxygen from your lungs to the rest of your body. You have two lungs. One is in the right side of your chest, and one is in the left side. Your heart lies between them.

How Air Moves to the Lungs

Look at the diagram on page 564. Air comes into your body through your nose and mouth. It travels through the pharynx. Air and food share this passageway. From the pharynx, the air moves through the **larynx**, or voice box. A flap of tissue covers the larynx when you swallow. This tissue prevents food from going into your airways. From the larynx, air moves into a large tube called the trachea, or windpipe. The trachea branches into two smaller tubes called **bronchi**. One bronchus goes into each lung. In the lungs, each bronchus branches into smaller tubes called bronchial tubes. The bronchial tubes continue to branch and become **bronchioles**.

Respiration

At the end of each bronchiole are tiny sacs that hold air. They are so small that you need a microscope to see them. These microscopic air sacs are called **alveoli.** The walls of alveoli are only one cell thick. They are always moist. Many tiny capillaries act like nets and wrap around the alveoli.

Blood returning to the heart from the rest of the body is full of carbon dioxide. The right ventricle pumps blood through an artery to the lungs. Recall that this is the only artery in the body that is high in carbon dioxide instead of oxygen. It is called the pulmonary artery. *Pulmonary* means "lung." The carbon dioxide passes out of the capillaries around the alveoli. Carbon dioxide leaves the body when you exhale, or breathe out.

When you inhale, or breathe in, oxygen comes into the lungs. The oxygen moves through the walls of the alveoli. Oxygen then moves through the walls of the tiny capillaries and into the blood. The exchange of carbon dioxide and oxygen is called respiration.

A vein carries the blood that is high in oxygen to the left atrium. This vein is called the pulmonary vein. Recall that it is the only vein that carries blood high in oxygen.

Breathing

At rest, you usually breathe about 12 times a minute. With each breath, the lungs stretch and you take in about half a liter of air. A strong muscle below your lungs helps you breathe. This muscle is called the diaphragm. It separates the lung cavity from the abdominal cavity.

Breathing happens partly because the pressure inside the chest cavity changes. When the diaphragm contracts, or tightens, it moves down. The ribs move upward. This movement increases the volume of the chest cavity. Air is inhaled, or pulled in, to fill this larger volume. When the diaphragm relaxes, it moves up. The ribs move downward. This movement reduces the volume of the chest cavity. Air is exhaled, or forced out of the lungs. Just like the heartbeat, breathing is automatic.

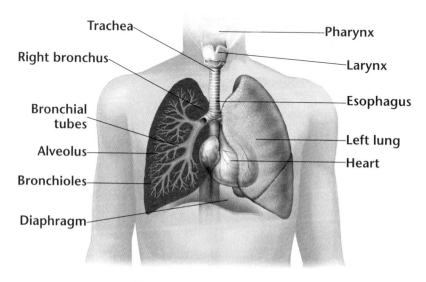

The Respiratory System

Write your answers to these questions on a separate sheet of paper. Write complete sentences.

1. What is the function of the respiratory system?

2. Describe the path of air from the nose to the alveoli.

3. What is respiration?

4. Where and how does respiration take place?

5. How does the diaphragm move when you inhale and exhale?

Science Myth

Air exhaled from the lungs contains carbon dioxide but no oxygen.

Fact: The air a person breathes in usually contains about 20 percent oxygen. Only about 5 percent of the oxygen in the air moves through the walls of alveoli in the lungs. The air that is exhaled is about 15 percent oxygen.

Epidermis

The thin outer layer of skin

Dermis

The thick layer of cells below the epidermis

Perspiration

Liquid waste made of heat, water, and salt released through the skin

You know that when you exhale, you get rid of carbon dioxide. Carbon dioxide is one of the wastes that cells make when they use oxygen and food to release energy. Other wastes that your cells make include water, heat, salt, and nitrogen. Exhaling releases some of the extra water and heat.

Perspiration

Many wastes leave your body through its largest organ, the skin. There are three layers of skin. The outer layer, the **epidermis**, is the thinnest. It protects the deeper layers of the skin. The **dermis** is a thicker layer under the epidermis. It contains blood vessels, nerves, and glands. The fatty layer protects the body's organs and keeps in heat. Your blood carries heat, water, and salt to sweat glands in your skin. These wastes form a salty liquid called **perspiration**. Thousands of sweat glands in the skin release perspiration through pores onto the skin's surface. Perspiration cools your body as the water evaporates from the skin.

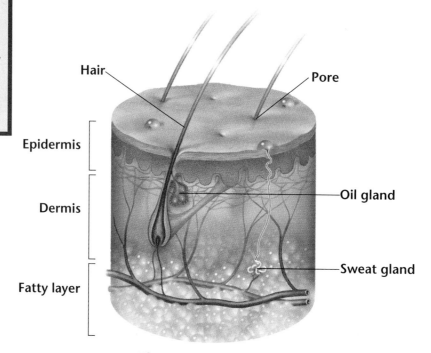

Three Layers of Skin

The Excretory System

Excretory system

A series of organs that get rid of cell wastes in the form of urine

Urine

Liquid waste formed in the kidneys

Ureter

A tube that carries urine from the kidney to the urinary bladder

Urethra

The tube that carries urine out of the body

Your cells make nitrogen wastes, which are poisonous. The **excretory system** gets rid of these wastes. The kidneys are the main organs of the excretory system. The body has two kidneys, located in the lower back. Kidneys filter nitrogen wastes out of the blood. The kidneys also remove some extra water and salt from the blood.

The filtered wastes form a liquid called **urine**. Tubes called **ureters** carry urine from each kidney. The urine collects in the urinary bladder. This muscular bag stretches as it fills. When the urinary bladder is almost full, you feel the need to urinate. When you do, the urinary bladder squeezes urine out of your body through a tube called the **urethra**. Follow the path of urine through the excretory system in the diagram.

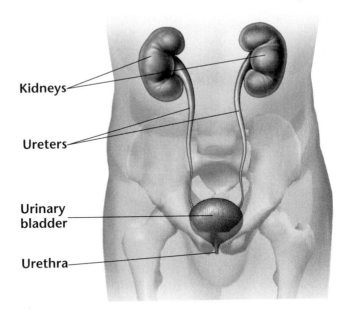

Kidneys

Ureters

Urinary bladder

Urethra

The Excretory System

Lesson 5   R E V I E W

Write your answers to these questions on a separate sheet of paper. Write complete sentences.

1. List four wastes that your cells produce.

2. What is perspiration?

3. What is the function of kidneys?

4. What is urine made of?

5. Describe how urine travels through the excretory system.

Technology Note

If the kidneys do not work properly, the body cannot get rid of wastes in the blood. These wastes can build up to dangerous levels. The patient could die. A patient with damaged kidneys can have those wastes removed by an artificial kidney called a kidney dialysis machine.

During dialysis, the patient relaxes in a chair or bed. The patient's blood is routed out of the body into a tube made of thin membrane. The tube runs through a tank of fluid. As the patient's blood travels through the tube, wastes in the blood pass through the membrane and into the surrounding fluid. The clean blood stays inside the membrane and is returned to the body. Depending on the patient, the treatment lasts about four hours, and it needs to be repeated every three or four days. Some patients with kidney failure have depended on dialysis for many years.

Objectives

After reading this lesson, you should be able to

◆ identify the parts of the male and female reproductive systems in humans.

◆ describe the main events of pregnancy.

Like other mammals, humans reproduce sexually. A male parent and a female parent together produce a fertilized egg that develops inside the female's body.

The Male Reproductive System

The diagram shows the main reproductive organs of a human male. The testes produce sperm cells. The testes lie outside the body in a sac called a **scrotum**. Because the scrotum is outside the body, it is about 2°C cooler than the rest of the body. Sperm cells are sensitive to heat. The lower temperature of the scrotum helps the sperm to live.

Scrotum

The sac that holds the testes

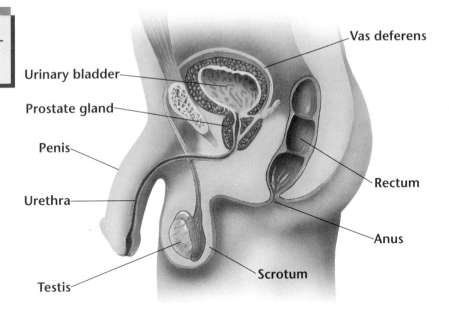

Urinary bladder

Prostate gland

Penis

Urethra

Testis

Vas deferens

Rectum

Anus

Scrotum

The Organs of the Male Reproductive System

Testosterone

Male sex hormone

Hormone

A chemical signal that glands produce

Penis

The male organ that delivers sperm to the female body

Vagina

The tubelike canal in the female body through which sperm enter the body

Prostate gland

The gland that produces the fluid found in semen

Semen

A mixture of fluid and sperm cells

The testes produce **testosterone**. This male sex **hormone** is important in the development of male sexual traits and in production of sperm. Beginning at puberty, the testes make more that 200 million sperm cells every day. Males are usually able to produce sperm from puberty through the rest of their life.

The external male organ, called the **penis**, delivers sperm to the female body. Before this happens, blood flows into the tissues of the penis. The blood causes the penis to lengthen and become rigid, or erect. The erect penis is inserted into a tubelike canal, called a **vagina**, in the female's body.

Sperm cells leave the male body through a tube in the penis called the urethra. The **prostate gland** connects to the urethra. The prostate gland produces fluid that mixes with the sperm cells and carries them through the urethra. The mixture of sperm and fluid is called **semen**. The semen flows through the urethra to the outside of the body. Urine also leaves the body through the urethra. However, urine and semen do not flow through the urethra at the same time.

All egg cells have an X chromosome. Half the sperm cells have an X and half have a Y chromosome. If a sperm with an X chromosome unites with an egg, the zygote (with two X chromosomes) becomes a girl. If a sperm with a Y chromosome unites with an egg, the zygote (with an X and a Y chromosome) will become a boy.

The Female Reproductive System

You can see the main female reproductive organs in the diagram below. Females are born with about 400,000 egg cells that are produced and stored in the ovaries. The ovaries also produce **estrogen** and **progesterone**. These female sex hormones regulate the reproductive development in females. One egg is usually released from one of the ovaries about every 28 days. The release of an egg is called **ovulation**.

After its release, an egg travels through one of the **fallopian tubes**. If sperm are present, a sperm cell may fertilize the egg cell in the fallopian tube. There, the fertilized egg will develop into an embryo, which travels to the **uterus.** If the egg is not fertilized, it eventually passes out of the female's body.

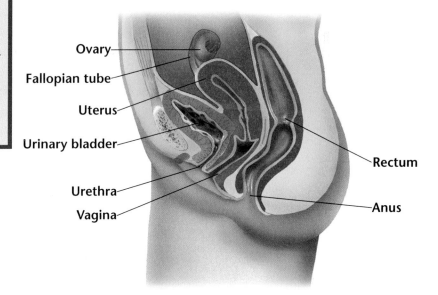

Ovary

Fallopian tube

Uterus

Urinary bladder

Urethra

Vagina

Rectum

Anus

The Organs of the Female Reproductive System

Menstruation

Each month, the lining of the uterus thickens to form a blood-rich cushion. The lining can hold and nourish a developing embryo. If the egg is not fertilized and no embryo forms, the lining of the uterus breaks down. The unfertilized egg, blood, and pieces of the lining pass out of the female's body through the vagina. This process is called **menstruation**.

Estrogen

Female sex hormone

Progesterone

Female sex hormone

Ovulation

The process of releasing an egg from an ovary

Fallopian tube

A tube through which eggs pass from an ovary to the uterus

Uterus

An organ in most female mammals that holds and protects an embryo

Menstruation

The process during which an unfertilized egg, blood, and pieces of the lining of the uterus exit the female body

Pregnancy

When the male's penis releases semen into the female's vagina,
the sperm cells swim to the uterus and fallopian tubes. If a
sperm cell fertilizes an egg cell in a fallopian tube, the female
begins a period of **pregnancy**. During pregnancy, the fertilized
egg develops into a baby.

The diagram below shows the fertilized egg, or zygote, dividing
in the fallopian tube. The zygote becomes an embryo. When the
embryo reaches the uterus, it soon attaches to the blood-rich
lining of the uterus.

The embryo forms a placenta. The **umbilical cord**, which
contains blood vessels, connects the placenta to the embryo.
The embryo's blood flows through blood vessels in the placenta.
The mother's blood flows through blood vessels in the lining of
the uterus. The two blood supplies usually do not mix.
However, they come so close together that food and oxygen
pass from the mother's blood to the embryo's blood. The
embryo's waste products pass from the embryo's blood to the
mother's blood. The embryo's wastes pass out of the mother's
body along with her own wastes.

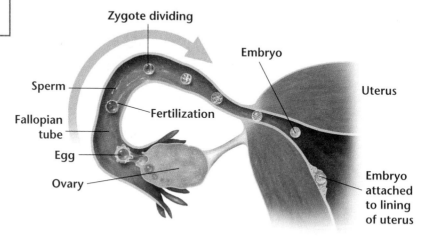

The embryo is made of cells formed by the kind of cell division
called mitosis. As they divide, cells specialize or differentiate.
Later, these cells form tissues, organs, and organ systems. After
eight weeks, the embryo has grown to be a **fetus.** The embryo
takes about nine months to become a fully developed baby.

Birth of a Baby

Usually, when the fetus reaches full size, the uterus begins to squeeze together, or contract. At first, the uterus contracts about every half hour. Then gradually, it contracts more often. As the uterus contracts, it pushes the baby out of the uterus and through the vagina.

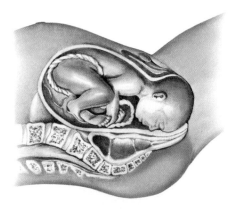

Birth

After much work, the mother gives birth to the baby. The mother's body pushes out the placenta soon after the baby is born. The doctor clamps and cuts the umbilical cord. Now the baby can survive outside of the mother's body. The part of the umbilical cord that remains attached to the baby eventually falls off. A person's "belly button," or navel, is where the umbilical cord was once attached.

▼◀▲▼◀▲▼◀▲▼◀▲▼◀▲▼◀▲▼◀▲▼◀▲▼◀▲▼◀▲▼◀▲▼◀▲▼◀▲▼◀▲▼◀▲▼

Science at Work

Obstetrician/gynecologist

An obstetrician/gynecologist (ob/gyn) needs to have good observation, communication, problem-solving, and decision-making skills. An ob/gyn needs to be able to deal with emergencies and work with other medical professionals. A college degree followed by four years of medical school is required for ob/gyns. They are also required to do up to seven years of residency (caring for patients in a hospital under supervision). They must be licensed and pass an oral and written exam for certification.

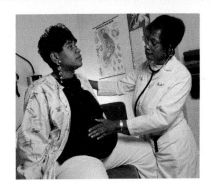

An ob/gyn is a doctor who specializes in the health of women. The doctor focuses on the reproductive system, pregnancy, and birth. These doctors may see healthy patients for a checkup or women experiencing health problems. Listening to the patients, answering questions, and providing health information are important parts of every exam. Women who are pregnant visit an ob/gyn regularly to check on their health. The ob/gyn also checks the growth and development of the fetus. Ob/gyns help women deliver their babies. These doctors never stop learning because they need to keep up with new discoveries and new technology.

Lesson 6 REVIEW

Write your answers to these questions on a separate sheet of paper. Write complete sentences.

1. Describe the path followed by sperm from the testes to the site of fertilization.

2. What happens during ovulation?

3. What is menstruation?

4. How does an embryo get nutrients during pregnancy?

5. What happens during the birth of a baby?

Science in Your Life

What substances are harmful during pregnancies?

An embryo and a fetus undergo many changes during development. During this time, the unborn baby is sensitive to substances in its environment. The baby's environment is its mother's body.

Any substance that a pregnant woman takes into her body can reach her unborn baby. A woman may take substances into her body by eating, drinking, breathing, and absorbing them through her skin. Just as food and oxygen can cross the placenta to the baby, so can drugs and other harmful substances.

What is wrong with drinking alcohol or smoking during pregnancy?

Alcohol has a more serious effect on a developing baby than it has on an adult. Even small amounts of alcohol drunk during pregnancy can cause fetal alcohol syndrome (FAS). Babies with FAS have various birth defects, including mental retardation. There is no safe amount of alcohol that a woman can drink during pregnancy.

The chemicals in tobacco also may harm an unborn baby. Pregnant women who smoke or are exposed to secondhand smoke are more likely to have babies with asthma, allergies, and other breathing problems.

How do other drugs affect unborn babies?

Pregnant women who take illegal drugs, such as cocaine, are likely to have babies who are addicted to the drugs. The babies also may have birth defects caused by the drugs. Even medicines such as aspirin and cold medications can harm a developing baby. It is important to read the information on the package of a medicine before taking it. Also, a woman should always tell her doctor if she is pregnant before taking a prescription drug.

Chapter 23 SUMMARY

- Bones support and protect the body's soft tissues. Blood cells are made inside some bones. Bones also store minerals.

- Skeletal muscles work in pairs to pull on bones.

- During digestion, food changes into a form that can enter cells. The large intestine eliminates undigested food.

- The circulatory system moves materials to and from cells.

- Red blood cells carry oxygen in hemoglobin. White blood cells protect the body from disease. Platelets help blood to clot.

- The respiratory system brings oxygen into your lungs and releases carbon dioxide from your lungs.

- The kidneys filter the blood to get rid of toxic wastes. The filtered wastes form urine.

- A male produces sperm cells. A female produces egg cells. When a sperm cell and an egg cell unite in fertilization, pregnancy occurs.

Science Words

alveolus, 563	excretory	ovulation, 571	skeletal system, 547
artery, 559	system, 567	penis, 570	testosterone, 570
bile, 554	fallopian tube, 571	perspiration, 566	trachea, 548
bronchiole, 563	feces, 554	pharynx, 553	umbilical cord, 572
bronchus, 563	fetus, 573	plasma, 561	ureter, 567
capillary, 560	gallbladder, 554	platelet, 561	urethra, 567
cardiac, 558	gland, 554	pregnancy, 572	urine, 567
chyme, 553	hemoglobin, 561	progesterone, 571	uterus, 571
dermis, 566	hormone, 570	prostate gland, 570	vagina, 570
epidermis, 566	larynx, 563	rectum, 554	vein, 560
estrogen, 571	ligament, 548	scrotum, 569	villi, 554
	menstruation, 571	semen, 570	

Vocabulary Review

Word Bank

alveoli

bile

chyme

fetus

hemoglobin

ligament

ovulation

plasma

platelets

umbilical cord

uterus

villi

Choose the word or words from the Word Bank that best complete each sentence. Write the answer on a sheet of paper.

1. The liver produces _____, which breaks down fats.

2. _____ carries oxygen in the blood.

3. Oxygen from outside the body enters tiny air sacs in the lungs called _____.

4. Food molecules enter the blood through _____ that line the small intestine.

5. Partly digested liquid food called _____ passes from the stomach to the small intestine.

6. Tiny pieces of cells called _____ help blood clot.

7. A(n) _____ connects a bone to another bone.

8. The liquid part of blood is called _____.

9. The _____ holds and protects a developing embryo.

10. The _____ connects the developing baby to the placenta.

11. The release of an egg cell by the ovary is called _____.

12. After eight weeks of development, a human embryo is called a(n) _____.

Concept Review

Choose the answer that best completes each sentence. Write the letter of the answer on your paper.

13. The heart is made of _____ muscle.
    - **A** smooth
    - **B** cardiac
    - **C** skeletal
    - **D** voluntary

14. The process of _____ occurs when a released egg cell has not been fertilized.
   A menstruation   **C** pregnancy
   B ovulation   **D** mitosis

15. Perspiration leaves the body through the _____.
   A kidneys   **C** skin
   B lungs   **D** feces

16. You get oxygen into your lungs when you _____.
   A swallow   **C** exhale
   B relax   **D** inhale

17. Most digestion takes place in the _____.
   A esophagus   **C** small intestine
   B stomach   **D** large intestine

18. The _____ of the heart forces blood to the rest of the body.
   A right ventricle   **C** right atrium
   B left ventricle   **D** left atrium

Critical Thinking

Write the answer to each of the following questions.

19. The statement "All arteries carry blood that is high in oxygen" is incorrect. Why? Write a statement that describes all arteries.

20. What are four waste products made by the body?

Test-Taking Tip   Make sure you have the same number of answers on your paper as the number of items on the test.

24 The Body's Control Systems

Your body systems work 24 hours a day, seven days a week to take care of the business of living. Together, the body systems handle a lot of jobs. They break down food to supply energy for every cell. They also bring in oxygen and get rid of wastes. At the same time, the body systems make it possible for you to jog around the track, talk on the phone, or watch a movie. To carry out all of these functions, plus many more, the body systems must stay in touch with each other. In this chapter, you will learn how all of life's activities are coordinated.

Organize Your Thoughts

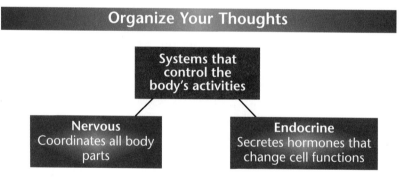

Systems that control the body's activities

Nervous
Coordinates all body parts

Endocrine
Secretes hormones that change cell functions

Goals for Learning

◆ To identify the structures and functions of the nervous system

◆ To explain how the sense organs function

◆ To identify the structures and functions of the endocrine system

◆ To explain what hormones are and what they do

◆ To explain changes that occur in puberty

Objectives

After reading this lesson, you should be able to

◆ identify the structures and functions of the nervous system.

◆ describe how impulses travel.

◆ explain how the eyes "see" objects.

◆ trace a sound wave as it travels through the ear.

◆ describe how the senses of taste and smell work together.

Your body systems constantly work together to keep you healthy and functioning. For your systems to work, however, they have to be coordinated. All the different parts have to know what to do and when to do it. Your body has to respond to changes in the environment. For example, if you run, the heart has to know to pump faster. Your nervous system coordinates all of your body parts. It is your body's communication network.

The Nervous System

The nervous system is divided into two main parts. The central nervous system is made of the brain and the spinal cord. This system controls the activities of the body. The peripheral nervous system is made of nerves outside the central nervous system. This system carries messages between the central nervous system and other parts of the body.

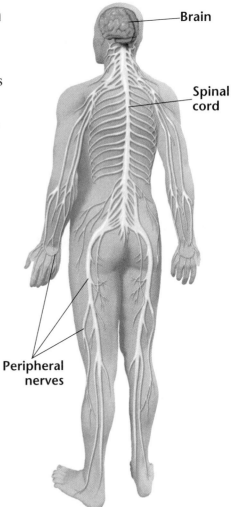

Brain

Spinal cord

Peripheral nerves

The Central and Peripheral Nervous Systems

The Brain

Cerebrum

The largest part of the brain that controls thought, memory, learning, feeling, and body movement

Cerebellum

The part of the brain that controls balance

Brain stem

The part of the brain that controls automatic activities and connects the brain and the spinal cord

The three parts of the brain are the **cerebrum,** the **cerebellum,** and the **brain stem**. The largest part is the cerebrum, as the diagram below shows. The cerebrum controls the way you think, learn, remember, and feel. It controls muscles that let you move body parts, such as your arms and legs. It interprets messages from the sense organs, such as the eyes and ears. The cerebrum is divided into two halves. The left half controls activities on the right side of the body. The right half controls activities on the left side of the body.

The cerebellum lies beneath the cerebrum. The cerebellum controls balance. It helps muscles work together so that you walk and write smoothly.

Under the cerebellum is the brain stem. It connects the brain and the spinal cord. The brain stem controls the automatic activities of your body. These include heart rate, gland secretions, digestion, respiration, and circulation. The brain stem coordinates movements of muscles that work without your thinking about them, such as your stomach muscles.

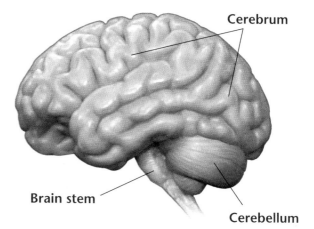

Cerebrum

Brain stem

Cerebellum

The Brain

The Spinal Cord

The spinal cord is a thick bunch of nerves that starts at the brain stem and goes down the back. The spinal cord is protected inside a backbone. The brain sends and receives information through the spinal cord. Thirty-one pairs of spinal nerves branch off from this cord. The spinal nerves send nerve messages all over the body. The spinal cord and brain are the central controls of the sense organs and body systems.

Neurons

Nerve cells are called **neurons**. They send messages in the form of electrical signals all through the body. These messages are called **impulses.** An impulse rapidly carries information from one nerve cell to the next. Neurons do not touch each other. Impulses must cross a small gap, or **synapse**, between neurons. This happens when an impulse travels from one end of a neuron to the other. When the impulse reaches the end of the cell, a chemical is released. The chemical moves out into the synapse and touches the next neuron. This starts another impulse. Information moves through your body by traveling along many neurons.

There are three kinds of neurons in your nervous system. Sensory neurons carry impulses from sense organs to the spinal cord or the brain. Motor neurons carry impulses from the brain and spinal cord to muscles and glands. Association neurons carry impulses from sensory neurons to motor neurons. Dendrites carry messages to the cell body. The axon carries messages away from the cell body.

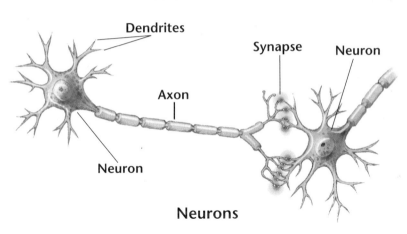

Neurons

Reflex Actions

Sneezing, coughing, and blinking are reflex actions. They happen automatically. What happens if you touch a hot frying pan? Sensory neurons send the "It is hot!" message to the spinal cord. Inside the spinal cord, association neurons receive the impulses and send them to the motor neurons. All of this happens in an instant, as you feel the heat. You pull your hand away quickly. You have been saved from a serious burn. Many other reflex actions protect the body from injury. For example, if an object comes flying toward your eyes, you blink without thinking.

The Sense Organs

The body connects with the outside world through sense organs. The five main sense organs are the eyes, ears, skin, nose, and tongue. Your skin is the largest organ in your body. **Receptor cells** in these organs receive information about the outside world. Receptor cells send impulses to your brain through sensory neurons. Your brain makes sense of the impulses. Then you see, hear, feel, smell, and taste.

The Sense of Sight

Your eyes are your organs of sight. When you look at one of your eyes in a mirror, you see the white outer layer that protects your eye. The part of the outer layer of your eye that isn't white is a clear layer. Light enters the eye through this clear layer called the **cornea**. The colored part of your eye is the **iris**. It is made of tiny muscles arranged in a ring. The black circle in the center of the iris is an opening called the **pupil**. Light passes from the cornea through the pupil. The iris controls the amount of light that enters by making the pupil larger or smaller. The pupil opens wide in a dark room. The larger opening lets in more light, and you can see more clearly. Likewise, the pupil becomes smaller in bright sunlight.

Find the cornea, iris, and pupil in the diagram of the eye. Then find the other parts of the eye as you read more about how the eye works.

Receptor cell

A cell that receives information about the environment and starts nerve impulses to send that information to the brain

Cornea

A clear layer of the eye that light passes through

Iris

The part of the eye that controls the amount of light that enters

Pupil

The black circle in the center of the iris

Retina

The back part of the eye where light rays are focused

Optic nerve

A bundle of nerves that carry impulses from the eye to the brain

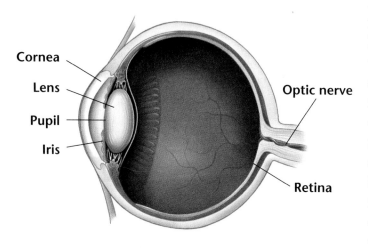

Cornea
Lens
Pupil
Iris
Optic nerve
Retina

Behind the pupil is a lens that focuses light. The lens focuses light rays onto the **retina** at the back of the eye. Receptor cells on the retina send impulses to a nerve bundle called the **optic nerve**. Nerve impulses travel along the optic nerve to the brain. The brain translates the impulses into images you can see. All of this happens faster than you can blink.

The Sense of Hearing

Just as your eyes collect light, your ears collect sound. Review the diagram below as you read about how the ears work. The outer ear acts like a funnel to collect sound waves. The waves travel through the ear canal to the middle ear. The middle ear, just behind the **eardrum,** contains three small bones. The eardrum is a thin tissue that vibrates, or shakes, when sound waves strike it. The sound waves then travel through each of the three bones. The sound waves enter the inner ear. They cause fluid in the **cochlea** to vibrate. The cochlea is a hollow coiled tube that contains fluid and thousands of receptor cells. These cells vibrate when sound waves strike them. The cells send impulses to the **auditory nerve**, which goes to the brain. The brain translates the impulses into sounds you can hear.

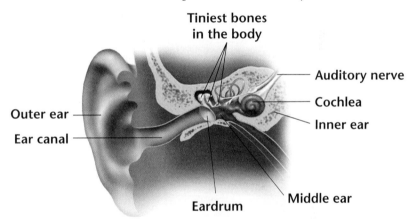

Tiniest bones in the body — Auditory nerve — Cochlea — Inner ear — Outer ear — Ear canal — Eardrum — Middle ear

Achievements in Science

Hearing Aids

People who lose all or part of their hearing may choose to wear a hearing aid. A hearing aid is an object that makes sound louder. The earliest hearing aids were large, horn-shaped appliances that users held to ears. They simply funneled sound waves into the ear canal.

Today's hearing aids are smaller and more efficient. Most of them are made of the same basic parts. A microphone picks up sound and changes it into electrical signals. The signals are amplified, or made louder. A receiver changes these signals back into sound. Sound from the receiver is directed into the ear canal by an ear mold. A battery provides the power to operate the microphone, processor, and receiver. Some hearing aids are also made with volume control and other adjustments that help the wearer fine-tune it for their particular needs.

The Sense of Touch

The skin receives messages about heat, cold, pressure, and pain. Receptor cells in the skin send nerve impulses to the brain. Then you can tell if something is cold, hot, smooth, or rough. Your fingertips and lips are most sensitive to touch because they have the most receptor cells.

The Senses of Taste and Smell

Taste buds are tiny receptor cells on the tongue that distinguish four basic kinds of tastes. The four tastes are sweet, sour, bitter, and salty. Notice in the diagram that certain parts of the tongue are sensitive to each taste. The taste buds send impulses to the brain. The brain uses these impulses along with impulses from the nose and interprets them as tastes.

Much of the sense of taste depends on the sense of smell. Receptor cells in the nose sense smells. If you hold your nose while you chew, much of your sense of taste goes away. Why does this happen? As you chew and swallow, air carrying the smell of the food reaches the nose. When you hold your nose, the air cannot flow freely. The smells never reach the receptor cells in your nose. The brain doesn't have impulses from the nose to use with impulses from the tongue to interpret taste.

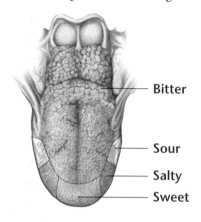

Bitter

Sour

Salty

Sweet

The Tongue

Technology Note

Biometrics is a new type of technology that provides unique ways to identify human characteristics. There are a number of biometric technologies, including fingerprint identification, voice identification, and even body odor identification. One company is working on a product that can record your body odor. A sensor is used to "capture" your body odor from your hand.

Lesson 1 **REVIEW**

Write your answers to these questions on a separate sheet of paper. Write complete sentences.

1. How is the central nervous system different from the peripheral nervous system?

2. Name the activities that each part of the brain controls.

3. How do impulses travel between neurons?

4. Name the three parts of the eye that light passes through in the order it travels from outside the eye to the retina.

5. Explain how holding your nose would affect how you taste food.

Science in Your Life

What can smart drugs do?

You may have seen advertisements for "smart drugs" in stores, in magazines, or on the Internet. The drugs may be in the form of pills, drinks, or powders. They may be advertised as herbs, natural ingredients, nutritional supplements, or food additives. The ads might promise improved memory, more alertness, and better performance in school or on the job. But do smart drugs work?

Smart drugs are supposed to work by increasing the amount of blood that flows to the brain. They may also increase the level of neurotransmitters involved in learning and memory. These ideas originated with research on people who had strokes and people who have Alzheimer's disease. People who had a stroke often suffer from memory loss. This is because the blood supply to some parts of the brain is reduced. In Alzheimer's disease, memory loss is due to destruction of neurons in the brain. Research on Alzheimer's continues. So far, a few drugs have been developed that may slow symptoms but can't cure the disease.

Some drugs may help people with diseases affecting the brain. There are few scientific studies that have been done on healthy people. The studies that have been done provide conflicting information. Most scientists agree that, in healthy people, the brain receives enough blood.

Many smart drugs have not been part of reliable scientific experiments. There is no evidence that these drugs will improve memory. Claims are usually false and do not mention possible side effects of using the drugs. Sorry, but taking a smart drug will not improve your memory or help you pass your next test.

Materials

- large index card
- pencil
- scissors
- round, clear glass bowl
- white tissue paper
- tape
- large, round magnifying glass
- clay
- flashlight

Modeling the Human Eye

Purpose

How do your eyes work? In this investigation, you will learn how parts of the eye work to focus an image.

Procedure

1. Do this investigation with a partner.

2. Fold the index card in half lengthwise. On the fold, draw half of a shape that has a definite top and bottom—for example, a valentine heart or a triangular pine tree. Cut out the shape and unfold the card.

3. Tape a sheet of white tissue paper to one side of the bowl.

4. Set up the magnifying glass near the other side of the bowl. Use clay to hold the magnifying glass up straight on the table.

5. Set up the opened card on the same side of the bowl as the magnifying glass but farther away from the bowl. Use clay to stand the card up straight. Your finished setup should look like the picture on the next page.

6. Darken the room as much as possible. Then shine the flashlight at the card so the light passes through the shape you cut out, the magnifying glass, and the bowl.

7. Look closely at the white paper. Move the bowl back and forth until the image is clear. What do you see?

Questions and Conclusions

1. What do you see on the white paper? How is the image different from the shape on the card?

2. In your model, what does the bowl represent?

3. What does the white paper represent?

4. What does the magnifying glass represent?

Explore Further

Move the bowl closer and farther from the lens. What happens to the image?

Did You Know?

Scientists have changed some bacteria so that they produce growth hormone. This hormone is used to treat children who do not produce enough of it themselves.

The Endocrine Glands

The endocrine system works closely with the nervous system to control certain body activities. Together the two systems respond to changes inside and outside the body. They adjust the body's activities to meet its needs. By doing so, they keep the body conditions within the range required for survival.

The endocrine system is made of glands. Some of them are circled in the illustration on the next page. These glands secrete substances called hormones. Hormones are chemical messengers. Glands release hormones into the bloodstream. The hormones then travel all through the body.

What Hormones Do

There are more than 30 different hormones. They affect everything from kidney function to growth and development. Hormones work by attaching to certain cells. They change the function of the cells. Some examples of hormones are aldosterone, insulin, and growth hormone. The adrenal glands secrete aldosterone. This hormone helps direct the kidneys to put more sodium and water back into the bloodstream. This may happen when a person has lost fluids. The pancreas secretes insulin, which changes cells so that glucose can enter them. The pituitary gland secretes growth hormone, which causes bones and muscles to grow.

The Feedback Loop

Glands must secrete the correct amounts of hormones for the body. The body has built-in systems that control the amount of hormone a gland releases. In one system, the feedback loop, a gland produces a hormone until levels of that hormone are high. Then production slows or stops. In another system, a change in the body triggers the release of a hormone. Eating a meal can alter hormone levels. These two mechanisms, plus the genes that direct the activities of cells, keep the human body operating correctly.

The pancreas is a part of both the endocrine system and the digestive system. As an endocrine gland, it releases the hormone insulin into the blood. As a gland of the digestive system, it secretes digestive enzymes into the small intestine.

Science Myth

Hormones in the body are responsible only for regulating reproductive activity.

Fact: There are more than 30 different hormones. Some hormones do regulate reproductive activity. But many other hormones control other activities in the body.

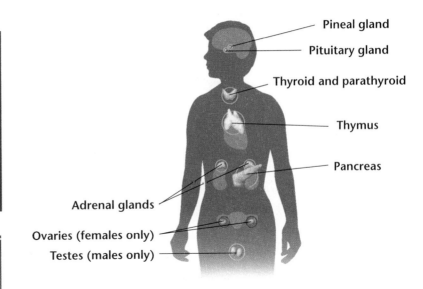

- Pineal gland
- Pituitary gland
- Thyroid and parathyroid
- Thymus
- Pancreas
- Adrenal glands
- Ovaries (females only)
- Testes (males only)

Endocrine Glands

Hormones and Stress

When you feel scared or excited, your adrenal glands secrete a hormone called adrenaline. Adrenaline can trigger a stress response. It may cause your palms to sweat and your heart to speed up. If the stress response continues for a long time, it could have a negative effect on your body.

At times, the stress response can be positive. Suppose you are running a race. The increase in your heart rate causes more oxygen to be delivered to your muscles. Adrenaline also increases the amount of glucose to your muscles. After the race, your body returns to normal.

Hormones and Puberty

The teenage years are called **adolescence.** At the beginning of adolescence, hormones cause rapid growth and physical changes. This period of growth and change is called **puberty.**

During puberty in males, a boy's voice changes to a low pitch. Hair begins to grow on the face, under the arms, and in the area around the sex organs. The sex organs become more fully developed. During puberty in females, hair also begins to grow under the arms and around the sex organs. The breasts enlarge and menstruation begins.

Lesson 2   R E V I E W

Write your answers to these questions on a separate sheet of paper. Write complete sentences.

1. What is the function of the endocrine system?

2. What are hormones? How do they affect the body?

3. How does the feedback loop work?

4. Give examples that show how the stress response can be positive and how it can be negative.

5. What are some changes that occur in males and females during puberty?

▼◄▲▼◄▲▼◄▲▼◄▲▼◄▲▼◄▲▼◄▲▼◄▲▼◄▲▼◄▲▼◄▲▼◄▲▼

Science at Work

Nurse

A nurse needs good observation, decision-making, and communication skills. Nurses also need to keep accurate records, pay attention to detail, and perform medical tests and procedures carefully. The training for a nurse varies from about one year at a vocational school or a community college to four to five years at a university. All nurses must take and pass a state licensing exam.

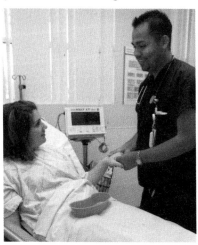

Nurses understand how all the human body systems work. They help people prevent disease and take care of people when they are sick, injured, or disabled. Nurses work in hospitals, doctors' offices, clinics, nursing homes, or other offices. The duties of a nurse include taking measurements such as blood pressure, giving injections, and monitoring.

- The nervous system controls and coordinates all body activities.

- The nervous system has two main parts. They are the central nervous system and the peripheral nervous system.

- The brain and the spinal cord make up the central nervous system.

- The brain has three major parts—the cerebrum, the cerebellum, and the brain stem. The three parts control different body activities.

- Impulses carry information from one nerve cell to the next.

- The five main sense organs are the eyes, ears, skin, nose, and tongue.

- Special cells in each of the sense organs receive information from the environment and send impulses to the brain.

- The glands of the endocrine system release hormones into the bloodstream.

- Hormones help control certain body activities. Hormones also cause the rapid growth and physical changes that occur during puberty.

Science Words

adolescence, 589	cochlea, 583	neuron, 581	receptor cell, 582
auditory nerve, 583	cornea, 582	optic nerve, 582	retina, 583
brain stem, 580	eardrum, 583	peristalsis, 553	synapse, 581
cerebellum, 580	impulse, 581	puberty, 589	
cerebrum, 580	iris, 582	pupil, 582	

Chapter 24 REVIEW

Word Bank

adolescence

cerebellum

cornea

impulse

iris

neuron

puberty

pupil

synapse

Vocabulary Review

Choose a word from the Word Bank that best completes each sentence. Write the answer on a sheet of paper.

1. A nerve cell is called a(n) _____.

2. _____ is the period of rapid growth and physical changes during the early teen years.

3. The _____ is the part of the brain that controls balance.

4. A _____ is a tiny gap between neurons.

5. The teen years are known as _____.

6. The _____ controls the amount of light that can enter the eye.

7. A message that travels from one neuron to another is a(n) _____.

8. The black hole in the center of the iris is called the _____.

9. A clear layer of tissue covering the front of the eye is the _____.

Concept Review

Choose the answer that best completes each sentence. Write the letter of the answer on your paper.

10. The _____ controls automatic activities such as digestion and circulation.

    A cerebrum   **C** brain stem

    B cerebellum   **D** spinal cord

11. Neurons send messages in the form of _____ signals.

    A visual   **C** chemical

    B electrical   **D** sound

12. _____ protect the body from injury.

    A synapses   **C** hormones

    B reflex actions   **D** neurons

13. Increased heart rate and breathing rate are signs of _____.

    A reflex actions   **C** associative neurons

    B the stress response   **D** growth

14. The retina sends impulses to the _____ nerve.

    A outer   **C** motor

    B auditory   **D** optic

15. The lens in the human eye focuses images on the _____.

    A pupil   **C** cornea

    B retina   **D** iris

16. The _____ vibrates when sound waves strike it.

    A auditory nerve   **C** ear canal

    B outer ear   **D** eardrum

17. The organ in the ear that sends impulses to the auditory nerve is the _____.

    A eardrum   **C** inner ear

    B cornea   **D** cochlea

18. Insulin and adrenaline are examples of _____.

    A reflexes   **C** receptor cells

    B glands   **D** hormones

Critical Thinking

Write the answer to each of the following questions.

19. How are the "messengers" of the endocrine system different from those of the nervous system?

20. Why is it important for your brain to control many functions automatically?

Test-Taking Tip Make a labeled drawing to help you remember the names of the parts in a figure.

UNIT 4   S U M M A R Y

- Bones support and protect the soft tissues and organs of the body.

- Skeletal muscles work in pairs to pull on bones.

- During digestion, food changes into a form that can enter cells. The large intestine eliminates undigested food.

- The circulatory system moves materials to and from cells.

- Red blood cells carry oxygen in hemoglobin. White blood cells protect the body from disease. Platelets help blood to clot.

- The respiratory system brings oxygen into your lungs and releases carbon dioxide from your lungs.

- The kidneys filter the blood to get rid of toxic wastes. The filtered wastes form urine.

- A male produces sperm cells. A female produces egg cells. When a sperm cell and an egg cell unite in fertilization, pregnancy occurs.

■ All body activities are controlled by the nervous system.

■ The nervous system has two main parts: the central nervous system and the peripheral nervous system. The brain and spinal cord make up the central nervous system.

■ The brain has three major parts—the cerebrum, the cerebellum, and the brain stem. The three parts control different body activities.

■ The five main sense organs are the eyes, ears, skin, nose, and tongue. Special cells in each of the sense organs gather information for the brain.

■ The glands of the endocrine system release hormones into the blood. Hormones help control body activities.

UNIT 4   R E V I E W

Word Bank

alveolus
auditory nerve
cardiac
cerebellum
eardrum
epidermis
glands
hormones
optic nerve
perspiration
pregnancy
prostate gland

Vocabulary Review

Choose the word or words from the Word Bank that best complete each sentence. Write the answer on a sheet of paper.

1. _____ is a liquid waste product released through the skin.

2. The term _____ means "of the heart."

3. _____ are chemicals that carry messages through the body.

4. A tiny sac-like structure in the lung is a(n) _____.

5. A thin tissue that vibrates when struck by sound is the _____.

6. _____ is a period of time during which a fertilized egg develops into a baby.

7. The outermost layer of skin is called the _____.

8. _____ are structures in the body that release hormones.

9. The _____ is the part of the brain that controls balance.

10. The _____ is a bundle of nerves that carries impulses from the eye to the brain.

11. In the ear, nerves that carry impulses to the brain make up the _____.

12. Fluid from the _____ mixes with sperm to form semen.

Concept Review

Choose the answer that best completes each sentence. Write the letter of the answer on your paper.

13. The _____ supports the body and protects the internal organs.
    A excretory system   **C** skeletal system
    B nervous system   **D** digestive system

14. The _____ breaks down food for the body to use as fuel.
   A excretory system   **C** skeletal system
   B respiratory system   **D** digestive system

15. The _____ is made up of the brain, spinal cord, and nerves.
   A excretory system   **C** skeletal system
   B nervous system   **D** digestive system

16. In males, the _____ produce sex hormones that cause the growth of facial hair.
   A scrotum   **C** cochlea
   B liver   **D** testes

17. Most digestion takes place in the _____.
   A stomach   **C** large intestine
   B small intestine   **D** gallbladder

18. A bone is held to another bone by _____.
   A ligaments   **C** muscles
   B villi   **D** neurons

Critical Thinking

Write the answer to each of the following questions

19. How do the respiratory system, the digestive system, and the circulatory system work together?

20. Why is it important for your brain to control many functions automatically?

Appendix A: Alternative Energy Sources

Fossil Fuels

We fly through the air in planes. We roll down highways in cars. On the coldest days, our homes are warm. Our stores are full of products to satisfy our needs and wants.

The power that runs our lives comes from fossil fuels. A fossil is the remains of ancient life. Fossil fuels formed from the remains of dead matter—animals and plants. Over millions of years, forests of plants died, fell, and became buried in the earth. Over time, the layers of ancient, dead matter changed. The carbon in the animals and plants turned into a material we now use as fuel. Fossil fuels include coal, oil, natural gas, and gasoline.

Fossil fuels power our lives and our society. In the United States, electricity comes mainly from power plants that burn coal. Industries use electricity to run machines. In our homes, we use electricity to power lightbulbs, TVs, and everything else electric. Heat and hot water for many homes come from natural gas or oil, or from fuels that come from oil.

Of course, cars and trucks run on gasoline, which is also made from oil. Powering our

society with fossil fuels has made our lives more comfortable. Yet our need for fossil fuels has caused problems. Fossil fuels are a nonrenewable source of energy. That means that there is a limited supply of these fuels. At some point, fossil fuels will become scarce. Their cost will increase. And one day the supply of fossil fuels will run out. We need to find ways now to depend less and less on fossil fuels.

Fossil fuels cause pollution. The pollution comes from burning them. It is like the exhaust from a car. The pollution enters the air and causes disease. It harms the environment. One serious effect of burning fossil fuels is global warming. Carbon dioxide comes from the burning of fossil fuels. When a large amount of this gas enters the air, it warms the earth's climate. Scientists believe that warming of the climate will cause serious problems.

Renewable Energy

Many people believe that we should use renewable fuels as sources of energy. Renewable fuels never run out. They last forever.

What kinds of fuels last forever? The energy from the sun. The energy in the wind. The energy in oceans and rivers. We can use these forms of energy to power our lives. Then we will never run out of fuel. We will cut down on pollution and climate warming. Using renewable energy is not a dream for the future. It is happening right now—right here—today.

Energy from the Sun

As long as the sun keeps shining, the earth will get energy from sunlight. Energy from the sun is called solar energy. It is the energy in light. When you lie in the sun, your skin becomes hot. The heat comes from the energy in sunlight. Sunlight is a form of renewable energy we can use forever.

We use solar energy to make electricity. The electricity can power homes and businesses. Turning solar energy into electricity is called photovoltaics, or PV for short. Here's how PV works.

Flat solar panels are put near a building or on its roof. The panels face the direction that gets the most sunlight. The panels contain many PV cells. The cells are made from silicon—a material that absorbs light. When sunlight strikes the cells, some of the light energy is absorbed. The energy knocks some electrons loose in the silicon. The electrons begin to flow. The electron flow is controlled. An electric current is produced. Pieces of metal at the top and bottom of each cell make a path for electrons. The path leads the electric current away from the solar panel. The electric current flows through wires to a battery. The battery stores the electrical energy. The electrical wiring in a building is connected to the battery. All the electricity used in the building comes from the battery.

Today, PV use is 500 times greater than it was 20 years ago. And PV use is growing about 20 percent per year. Yet solar energy systems are still not perfect. PV cells do not absorb all the sunlight that strikes them, so some energy is lost. Solar energy systems also are not cheap. Still, every year, PV systems are improved. The cost of PV electricity has decreased. The amount of sunlight PV cells absorb has increased.

On a sunny day, every square meter of the earth receives 1,000 watts of energy from sunlight. Someday, when PV systems are able to use all this energy, our energy problems may be solved.

Energy from the Wind

Sunlight warms different parts of the earth differently. The North Pole gets little sunlight, so it is cold. Areas near the equator get lots of sunlight, so they are warm. The uneven warming of the earth by the sun creates the wind. As the earth turns, the wind moves, or blows. The blowing wind can be used to make electricity. This is wind energy. Because the earth's winds will blow forever, the wind is a renewable source of energy.

Wind energy is not new. Hundreds of years ago, windmills created energy. The wind turned the large fins on a windmill. As the fins spun around, they turned huge stones inside the mill. The stones ground grain into flour.

Modern windmills are tall, metal towers with spinning blades, called wind turbines. Each wind turbine has three main parts. It has blades that are turned by blowing wind. The turning blades are attached to a shaft that runs the length of the tower. The turning blades spin the shaft. The spinning shaft is connected to a generator.

A generator changes the energy from movement into electrical energy. It feeds the electricity into wires, which carry it to homes and factories.

Wind turbines are placed in areas where strong winds blow. A single house may have one small wind turbine near it to produce its electricity. The electricity produced by the wind turbine is stored in batteries. Many wind turbines may be linked together to produce electricity for an entire town. In these systems, the electricity moves from the generator to the electric company's wires. The wires carry the electricity to homes and businesses.

Studies show that 34 of the 50 United States have good wind conditions. These states could use wind to meet up to 20 percent of their electric power needs. Canada's wind conditions could produce up to 20 percent of its energy from wind, too. Alberta already produces a lot of energy from wind, and the amount is expected to increase.

Energy from Inside the Earth

Deep inside the earth, the rocks are burning hot. Beneath them it is even hotter. There, rocks melt into liquid. The earth's inner heat rises to the surface in some places. Today,

people have developed ways to use this heat to create energy. Because the inside of the earth will always be very hot, this energy is renewable. It is called geothermal energy (*geo* means earth; *thermal* means heat).

Geothermal energy is used where hot water or steam from deep inside the earth moves near the surface. These areas are called "hot spots." At hot spots, we can use geothermal energy directly. Pumps raise the hot water, and pipes carry it to buildings. The water is used to heat the space in the buildings or to heat water.

Geothermal energy may also be used indirectly to make electricity. A power plant is built near a hot spot. Wells are drilled deep into the hot spot. The wells carry hot water or steam into the power plant. There, it is used to boil more water. The boiling water makes steam. The steam turns the blades of a turbine. This energy is carried to a generator, which turns it into electricity. The electricity moves through the electric company's wires to homes and factories.

Everywhere on the earth, several miles beneath the surface, there is hot material. Scientists are improving ways of tapping the earth's inner heat. Some day, this renewable, pollution-free source of energy may be available everywhere.

Energy from Trash

We can use the leftover products that come from plants to make electricity. For example, we can use the stalks from corn or wheat to make fuel. Many leftover products from crops and lumber can fuel power plants. Because this fuel comes from living plants, it is called bioenergy (*bio* means life or living). The plant waste itself is called biomass.

People have used bioenergy for thousands of years. Burning wood in a fireplace is a form of bioenergy. That's because wood comes from trees. Bioenergy is renewable, because people will always grow crops. There will always be crop waste we can burn as fuel.

Some power plants burn biomass to heat water. The steam from the boiling water turns turbines. The turbines create electricity. In other power plants, biomass is changed into a gas. The gas is used as fuel to boil water, which turns the turbine.

Biomass can also be made into a fuel for cars and trucks. Scientists use a special process to turn biomass into fuels, such as ethanol. Car makers are designing cars that can run on these fuels. Cars that use these fuels produce far less pollution than cars that run on gas.

Bioenergy can help solve our garbage problem. Many cities are having trouble finding places to dump all their trash. There would be fewer garbage dumps if we burned some trash to make electricity.

Bioenergy is a renewable energy. But it is not a perfect solution to our energy problems. Burning biomass creates air pollution.

Energy from the Ocean

Have you ever been knocked over by a small wave while wading in the ocean? If so, you know how much power ocean water has. The motion of ocean waves can be a source of energy. So can the rise and fall of ocean tides. There are several systems that use the energy in ocean waves and tides. All of them are very new and still being developed.

In one system, ocean waves enter a funnel. The water flows into a reservoir, an area behind a dam where water is stored. When the dam opens, water flows out of the reservoir. This powers a turbine, which creates electricity. Another system uses the waves' motion to operate water pumps, which run an electric generator. There is also a system that uses the rise and fall of ocean waves. The waves compress air in a container. During high tide, large amounts of ocean water enter the container. The air in the container is under great pressure. When the high-pressure air in the container is released, it drives a turbine. This creates electricity.

Energy can also come from the rise and fall of ocean tides. A dam is built across a tidal basin. This is an area where land surrounds the sea on three sides. At high tide, ocean water is allowed to flow through the dam. The water flow turns turbines, which generate electricity. There is one serious problem with tidal energy. It damages

the environment of the tidal basin and can harm animals that live there.

The oceans also contain a great deal of thermal (heat) energy. The sun heats the surface of the oceans more than it heats deep ocean water. In one day, ocean surfaces absorb solar energy equal to 250 billion barrels of oil! Deep ocean water, which gets no sunlight, is much colder than the surface.

Scientists are developing ways to use this temperature difference to create energy. The systems they are currently designing are complicated and expensive.

Energy from Rivers and Dams

Dams built across rivers also produce electricity. When the dam is open, the flowing water turns turbines, which make electricity. This is called hydroelectric power (*hydro* means water). The United States gets 7 percent of its electricity from hydroelectric power. Canada gets up to 60 percent of its electricity from hydroelectric plants built across its many rivers.

Hydroelectric power is a nonpolluting and renewable form of energy—in a way. There will always be fresh water. However, more and more people are taking water from rivers for different uses. These uses include

drinking, watering crops, and supplying industry. Some rivers are becoming smaller and weaker because of the water taken from them. Also, in many places dams built across rivers hurt the environment. The land behind the dam is "drowned." Once the dam is built, fish may not be able swim up or down the river. In northwestern states, salmon have completely disappeared from many rivers that have dams.

Energy from Hydrogen Fuel

Hydrogen is a gas that is abundant everywhere on the earth. It's in the air. It is a part of water. Because there is so much hydrogen, it is a renewable energy source. And hydrogen can produce energy without any pollution.

The most likely source of hydrogen fuel is water. Water is made up of hydrogen and oxygen. A special process separates these elements in water. The process produces oxygen gas and hydrogen gas. The hydrogen gas is changed into a liquid or solid. This hydrogen fuel is used to produce energy in a fuel cell.

Look at the diagram on page 603. Hydrogen fuel (H_2) is fed into one part of the fuel cell. It is then stripped of its electrons. The free electrons create an electric current (e). The electric current powers a lightbulb or whatever is connected to the fuel cell.

Meanwhile, oxygen (O_2) from the air enters another part of the fuel cell. The stripped hydrogen (H+) bonds with the oxygen, forming water (H_2O). So a car powered by a fuel cell has pure water leaving its tailpipe. There is no exhaust to pollute the air.

When a regular battery's power is used up,

the battery dies. A fuel cell never runs down as long as it gets hydrogen fuel.

A single fuel cell produces little electricity. To make more electricity, fuel cells come in "stacks" of many fuel cells packaged together. Stacked fuel cells are used to power cars and buses. Soon, they may provide electric power to homes and factories.

Hydrogen Fuel Cell

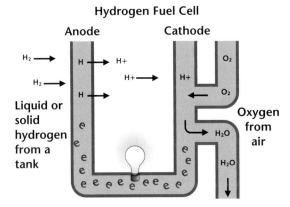

Hydrogen fuel shows great promise, but it still has problems. First, hydrogen fuel is difficult to store and distribute. Today's gas stations would have to be changed into hydrogen-fuel stations. Homes and factories would need safe ways to store solid hydrogen.

Second, producing hydrogen fuel by separating water is expensive. It is cheaper to make hydrogen fuel from oil. But that would create pollution and use nonrenewable resources. Scientists continue to look for solutions to these problems.

Energy from Atoms

Our sun gets its energy—its heat and light—from fusion. Fusion is the joining together of parts of atoms. Fusion produces enormous amounts of energy. But conditions like those on the sun are needed for fusion to occur. Fusion requires incredibly high temperatures.

In the next few decades, scientists may find ways to fuse atoms at lower temperatures. When this happens, we may be able to use fusion for energy. Fusion is a renewable form of energy because it uses hydrogen atoms. It also produces no pollution. And it produces no dangerous radiation. Using fusion to produce power is a long way off. But if the technology can be developed, fusion could provide us with renewable, clean energy.

Today's nuclear power plants produce energy by splitting atoms. This creates no air pollution. But nuclear energy has other problems. Nuclear energy is fueled by a substance we get from mines called uranium. There is only a limited amount of uranium in the earth. So it is not renewable. And uranium produces dangerous radiation, which can harm or kill living things if it escapes the power plant. Used uranium must be thrown out, even though it is radioactive and dangerous. In 1999, the United States produced nearly 41 tons of radioactive waste from nuclear power plants. However, less uranium is being mined. No new nuclear power plants have been built. The amount of energy produced from nuclear power is expected to fall. People are turning toward less harmful, renewable energy sources: the sun, wind, underground heat, biomass, water, and hydrogen fuel.

Fuel That U.S. Electric Utilities Used to Generate Electricity in 2000

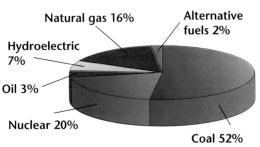

Source: U.S. Dept. of Energy Hydropower Program

Appendix B: Measurement Conversion Factors

Metric Measures

Length
1,000 meters (m) = 1 kilometer (km)
100 centimeters (cm) = 1 m
10 decimeters (dm) = 1 m
1,000 millimeters (mm) = 1 m
10 cm = 1 decimeter (dm)
10 mm = 1 cm

Area
100 square millimeters (mm^2) = 1 square centimeter (cm^2)
10,000 cm^2 = 1 square meter (m^2)
10,000 m^2 = 1 hectare (ha)

Volume
1,000 cubic meters (m^3) = 1 cubic centimeter (cm^3)
1,000 cubic centimeters (cm^3) = 1 liter (L)
1 cubic centimeter (cm^3) = 1 milliliter (mL)
100 cm^3 = 1 cubic decimeter (dm^3)
1,000,000 cm^3 = 1 cubic meter (m^3)

Capacity
1,000 milliliters (mL) = 1 liter (L)
1,000 L = 1 kiloliter (kL)

Mass
100 grams (g) = 1 centigram (cg)
1,000 kilograms (kg) = 1 metric ton (t)
1,000 grams (g) = 1 kg
1,000 milligrams (mg) = 1 g

Temperature Degrees Celsius (°C)
0°C = freezing point of water
37°C = normal body temperature
100°C = boiling point of water

Time
60 seconds (sec) = 1 minute (min)
60 min = 1 hour (hr)
24 hr = 1 day

Customary Measures

Length
12 inches (in.) = 1 foot (ft)
3 ft = 1 yard (yd)
36 in. = 1 yd
5,280 ft = 1 mile (mi)
1,760 yd = 1 mi
6,076 feet = 1 nautical mile

Area
144 square inches (sq in.) = 1 square foot (sq ft)
9 sq ft = 1 square yard (sq yd)
43,560 sq ft = 1 acre (A)

Volume
1,728 cubic inches (cu in.) = 1 cubic foot (cu ft)
27 cu ft = 1 cubic yard (cu yard)

Capacity
8 fluid ounces (fl oz) = 1 cup (c)
2 c = 1 pint (pt)
2 pt = 1 quart (qt)
4 qt = 1 gallon (gal)

Weight
16 ounces (oz) = 1 pound (lb)
2,000 lb = 1 ton (T)

Temperature Degrees Fahrenheit (°F)
32°F = freezing point of water
98.6°F = normal body temperature
212°F = boiling point of water

To change	To	Multiply by		To change	To	Multiply by
centimeters	inches	0.3937		meters	feet	3.2808
centimeters	feet	0.03281		meters	miles	0.0006214
cubic feet	cubic meters	0.0283		meters	yards	1.0936
cubic meters	cubic feet	35.3145		metric tons	tons (long)	0.9842
cubic meters	cubic yards	1.3079		metric tons	tons (short)	1.1023
cubic yards	cubic meters	0.7646		miles	kilometers	1.6093
feet	meters	0.3048		miles	feet	5,280
feet	miles (nautical)	0.0001645		miles (statute)	miles (nautical)	0.8684
feet	miles (statute)	0.0001894		miles/hour	feet/minute	88
feet/second	miles/hour	0.6818		millimeters	inches	0.0394
gallons (U.S.)	liters	3.7853		ounces avdp	grams	28.3495
grams	ounces avdp	0.0353		ounces	pounds	0.0625
grams	pounds	0.002205		pecks	liters	8.8096
hours	days	0.04167		pints (dry)	liters	0.5506
inches	millimeters	25.4000		pints (liquid)	liters	0.4732
inches	centimeters	2.5400		pounds advp	kilograms	0.4536
kilograms	pounds avdp	2.2046		pounds	ounces	16
kilometers	miles	0.6214		quarts (dry)	liters	1.1012
liters	gallons (U.S.)	0.2642		quarts (liquid)	liters	0.9463
liters	pecks	0.1135		square feet	square meters	0.0929
liters	pints (dry)	1.8162		square meters	square feet	10.7639
liters	pints (liquid)	2.1134		square meters	square yards	1.1960
liters	quarts (dry)	0.9081		square yards	square meters	0.8361
liters	quarts (liquid)	1.0567		yards	meters	0.9144

Appendix C: The Periodic Table of Elements

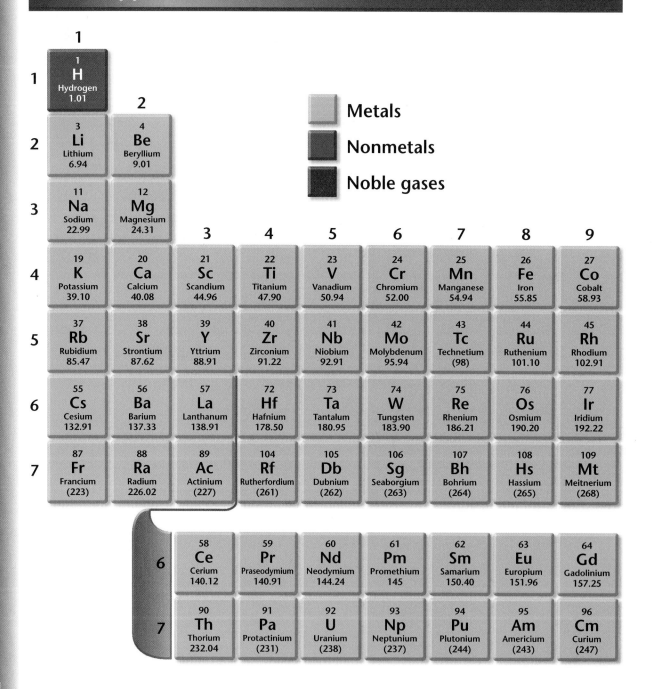

Metals

Nonmetals

Noble gases

			13	**14**	**15**	**16**	**17**	**18**
								2 **He** Helium 4.00
			5 **B** Boron 10.81	6 **C** Carbon 12.01	7 **N** Nitrogen 14.01	8 **O** Oxygen 16.00	9 **F** Fluorine 19.00	10 **Ne** Neon 20.18
10	**11**	**12**	13 **Al** Aluminum 26.98	14 **Si** Silicon 28.09	15 **P** Phosphorus 30.97	16 **S** Sulfur 32.07	17 **Cl** Chlorine 35.45	18 **Ar** Argon 39.95
28 **Ni** Nickel 58.70	29 **Cu** Copper 63.55	30 **Zn** Zinc 65.39	31 **Ga** Gallium 69.72	32 **Ge** Germanium 72.59	33 **As** Arsenic 74.92	34 **Se** Selenium 78.96	35 **Br** Bromine 79.90	36 **Kr** Krypton 83.80
46 **Pd** Palladium 106.42	47 **Ag** Silver 107.90	48 **Cd** Cadmium 112.41	49 **In** Indium 114.82	50 **Sn** Tin 118.69	51 **Sb** Antimony 121.75	52 **Te** Tellurium 127.60	53 **I** Iodine 126.90	54 **Xe** Xenon 131.30
78 **Pt** Platinum 195.09	79 **Au** Gold 196.97	80 **Hg** Mercury 200.59	81 **Tl** Thallium 204.40	82 **Pb** Lead 207.20	83 **Bi** Bismuth 208.98	84 **Po** Polonium 209	85 **At** Astatine (210)	86 **Rn** Radon (222)
110 **Uun** Ununnilium (269)	111 **Uuu** Unununium (272)	112 **Uub** Ununbium (277)		114 **Uuq** Ununquadium (289)		116 **Uuh** Ununhexium (289)		

65 **Tb** Terbium 158.93	66 **Dy** Dysprosium 162.50	67 **Ho** Holmium 164.93	68 **Er** Erbium 167.26	69 **Tm** Thulium 168.93	70 **Yb** Ytterbium 173.04	71 **Lu** Lutetium 174.97
97 **Bk** Berkelium (247)	98 **Cf** Californium (249)	99 **Es** Einsteinium (254)	100 **Fm** Fermium (257)	101 **Md** Mendelevium (258)	102 **No** Nobelium (259)	103 **Lr** Lawrencium (260)

Note: *The atomic masses listed in the table reflect current measurements.*
The atomic masses listed in parentheses are those of the element's most stable or most common isotope.

Appendix D: The Solar System

The planets in our solar system are very different from each other. Some are huge balls of gas, and others are small, rocky worlds. Some are frozen, and others are burning hot. Some have violent storms raging in their atmosphere, and others have almost no atmosphere. The table below lists many facts about each planet. As you study these facts, look for similarities, differences, and patterns.

Features	Mercury	Venus	Earth	Mars	Jupiter	Saturn	Uranus	Neptune	Pluto
Unique Characteristics	fastest moving planet; closest planet to sun	hottest planet; brightest planet in Earth's night sky	only planet that has liquid water and supports life	reddish color; only planet explored by exploration robots	fastest rotation; largest planet; Great Red Spot	biggest ring system; great storms	rotates on its side; blue-green color	storms; blue-green color; Great Dark Spot	coldest and smallest planet; longest revolution time
Diameter (kilometers)	4,879	12,014	12,756	6,794	142,984	120,536	51,118	49,528	2,390
Relative Mass (Earth = 1)	0.055	0.82	1	0.11	318	95	15	17	0.002
Average Distance from Sun (millions of kilometers)	58	108	150	228	779	1,434	2,873	4,496	5,870
Rotation (Earth time)	59 days	243 days*	1 day	24 hours and 38 minutes	10 hours	11 hours	17 hours*	16 hours	6 days*
Revolution (Earth time)	88 days	224 days	365 days	687 days	12 years	29 years	84 years	164 years	248 years
Surface Temperature (°C)	−183 to 427	460	−89 to 58	−82 to 0	−150	−170	−200	−210	−220
Atmospheric Composition	very thin: sodium and helium gas	thick: carbon dioxide gas	thick: nitrogen and oxygen gas	thin: carbon dioxide gas	thick: hydrogen and helium gas	thick: hydrogen and helium gas	thick: hydrogen, helium, and methane gas	thick: hydrogen, helium, and methane gas	thin: methane gas
Surface Composition	rocky	rocky	rocky	rocky	gaseous	gaseous	gaseous	gaseous	rocky
Number of Moons	0	0	1	2	60	31	22	11	1
Ring System	no	no	no	no	yes	yes	yes	yes	no

*planet rotates from east to west, the opposite direction of Earth's rotation

Source: NASA

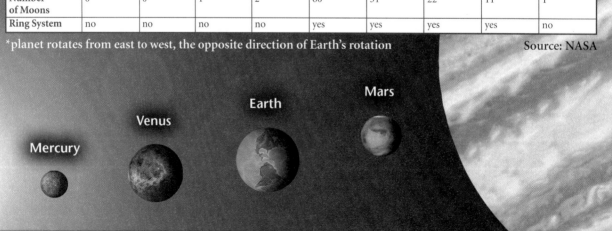

Mercury Venus Earth Mars

Pluto

Neptune

Uranus

Saturn

Jupiter

Appendix E: Space Exploration

Our knowledge of outer space has grown tremendously since the space age began in the 1950s. Orbiters, landers, probes, satellites, and space stations—as well as crews and scientists—continue to uncover new information about the solar system and beyond. The following timeline displays some of the important missions of space exploration. Each entry lists the name of the spacecraft, the country sponsoring it, and the mission's significance.

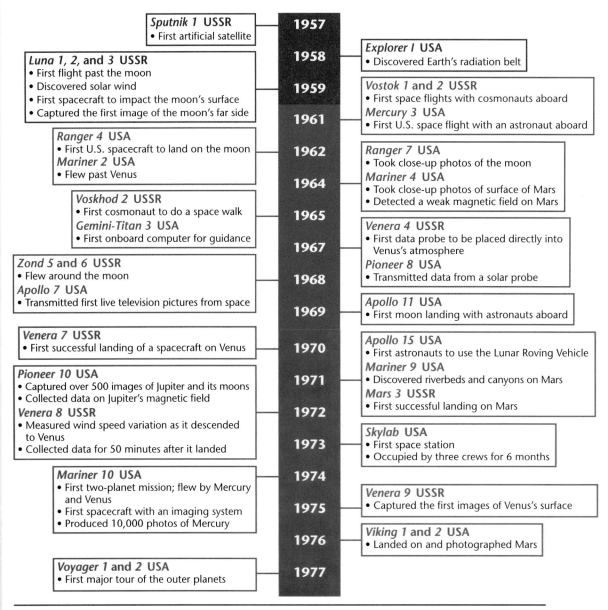

Sputnik 1 USSR
- First artificial satellite

1957

Explorer I USA
- Discovered Earth's radiation belt

1958

Luna 1, 2, and 3 USSR
- First flight past the moon
- Discovered solar wind
- First spacecraft to impact the moon's surface
- Captured the first image of the moon's far side

1959

Vostok 1 and 2 USSR
- First space flights with cosmonauts aboard

Mercury 3 USA
- First U.S. space flight with an astronaut aboard

1961

Ranger 4 USA
- First U.S. spacecraft to land on the moon

Mariner 2 USA
- Flew past Venus

1962

Ranger 7 USA
- Took close-up photos of the moon

Mariner 4 USA
- Took close-up photos of surface of Mars
- Detected a weak magnetic field on Mars

1964

Voskhod 2 USSR
- First cosmonaut to do a space walk

Gemini-Titan 3 USA
- First onboard computer for guidance

1965

Venera 4 USSR
- First data probe to be placed directly into Venus's atmosphere

Pioneer 8 USA
- Transmitted data from a solar probe

1967

Zond 5 and 6 USSR
- Flew around the moon

Apollo 7 USA
- Transmitted first live television pictures from space

1968

Apollo 11 USA
- First moon landing with astronauts aboard

1969

Venera 7 USSR
- First successful landing of a spacecraft on Venus

1970

Apollo 15 USA
- First astronauts to use the Lunar Roving Vehicle

Mariner 9 USA
- Discovered riverbeds and canyons on Mars

Mars 3 USSR
- First successful landing on Mars

1971

Pioneer 10 USA
- Captured over 500 images of Jupiter and its moons
- Collected data on Jupiter's magnetic field

Venera 8 USSR
- Measured wind speed variation as it descended to Venus
- Collected data for 50 minutes after it landed

1972

Skylab USA
- First space station
- Occupied by three crews for 6 months

1973

Mariner 10 USA
- First two-planet mission; flew by Mercury and Venus
- First spacecraft with an imaging system
- Produced 10,000 photos of Mercury

1974

Venera 9 USSR
- Captured the first images of Venus's surface

1975

Viking 1 and 2 USA
- Landed on and photographed Mars

1976

Voyager 1 and 2 USA
- First major tour of the outer planets

1977

1980

Voyager 1 USA
- Flew past Titan, one of Saturn's moons

Solar Maximum Mission USA
- Monitored the sun, especially solar flares

1981

STS-1 Columbia USA
- First winged, reusable space shuttle to be launched

Venera 13 USSR
- First color views of Venus's surface

1982

1983

Venera 15 and *16* USSR
- Produced maps of Venus

1984

Suisei Japan
- Flew past and studied comet Halley

1985

Soyuz T-14 USSR
- First relief mission to replace cosmonauts on *Soyuz-T13*

1986

Mir USSR
- First space station to conduct research and deploy other spacecraft

Voyager 2 USA
- Flew past Uranus

1987

Ginga Japan
- Studied sources of gamma rays and X-rays in the Milky Way galaxy

1988

1989

Voyager 2 USA
- Flew past Neptune

Magellan USA
- Began mapping the surface of Venus

1990

***STS-31 Discovery* USA, Europe**
- Deployed the Hubble Space Telescope

***Soyuz TM-1* USSR**
- First commercial passenger to make a space shuttle flight

***Galileo* USA**
- Flew past Venus

1991

1992

***Ulysses* Europe and USA**
- Orbited Jupiter on its way to the sun

1993

***STS-61 Endeavor* USA**
- Repaired the Hubble Space Telescope

1994

***Clementine* USA**
- Generated the first lunar topographic map

1995

***Galileo* USA**
- Began orbiting Jupiter

1996

***NEAR* USA**
- Orbited and studied asteroids near Earth

1997

***Mars Pathfinder* USA**
- Returned data about Mars, including thousands of images
- Landed on Mars and released an exploration robot to explore its surface

***Cassini* Europe**
- Began a 7-year flight to Saturn

1998

International Space Station
- First orbiting research facility

1999

***Stardust* USA**
- Collected sample from a comet

2000

***IMAGE* USA**
- First weather satellite to monitor space storms

2001

***Mars 2001 Odyssey* USA**
- Mapping surface minerals, looking for water, and studying potential radiation hazards to future missions

2002

***Muses-C* Japan**
- Collected sample from an asteroid

2003

***Mars Express* Europe**
- Will attempt to study Mars's surface and atmosphere in great detail

2004

***Deep Impact* USA**
- Will attempt to excavate the interior of a comet

2005

***Venus Express* Europe**
- Will attempt to study Venus's atmosphere in great detail

2006 and beyond

***Europa* USA**
- Will attempt to orbit Jupiter's moon Europa

***BepiColumbo* Europe**
- Will attempt to orbit Mercury

Appendix F: Body Systems

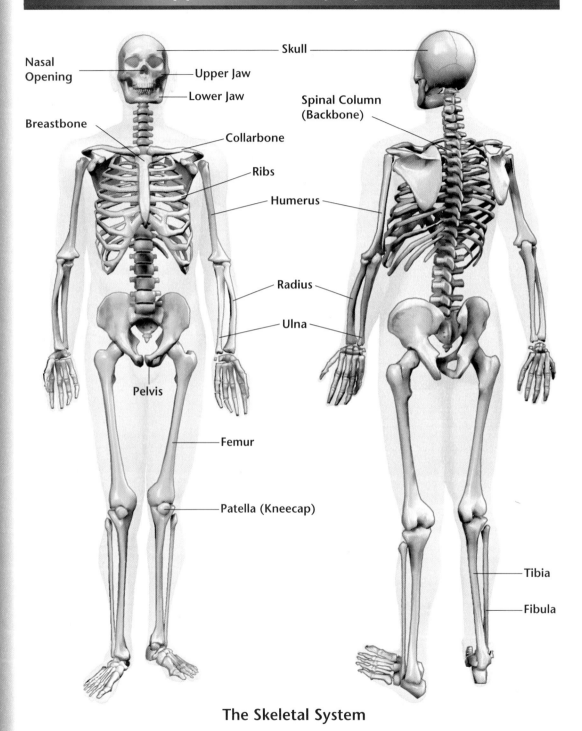

Nasal Opening

Skull

Upper Jaw

Lower Jaw

Breastbone

Collarbone

Ribs

Spinal Column (Backbone)

Humerus

Radius

Ulna

Pelvis

Femur

Patella (Kneecap)

Tibia

Fibula

The Skeletal System

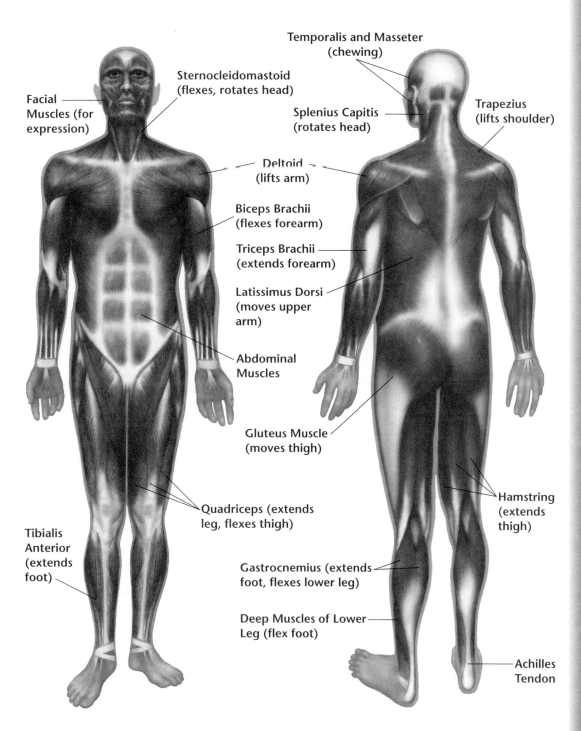

Temporalis and Masseter
(chewing)

Sternocleidomastoid
(flexes, rotates head)

Facial
Muscles (for
expression)

Splenius Capitis
(rotates head)

Trapezius
(lifts shoulder)

Deltoid
(lifts arm)

Biceps Brachii
(flexes forearm)

Triceps Brachii
(extends forearm)

Latissimus Dorsi
(moves upper
arm)

Abdominal
Muscles

Gluteus Muscle
(moves thigh)

Quadriceps (extends
leg, flexes thigh)

Hamstring
(extends
thigh)

Tibialis
Anterior
(extends
foot)

Gastrocnemius (extends
foot, flexes lower leg)

Deep Muscles of Lower
Leg (flex foot)

Achilles
Tendon

The Muscular System

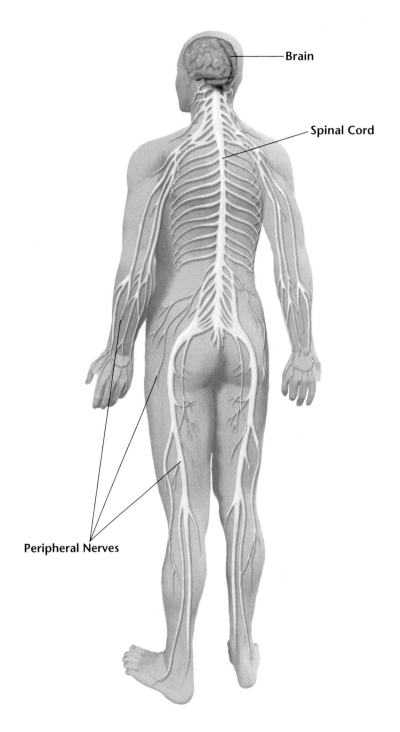

Brain

Spinal Cord

Peripheral Nerves

The Nervous System

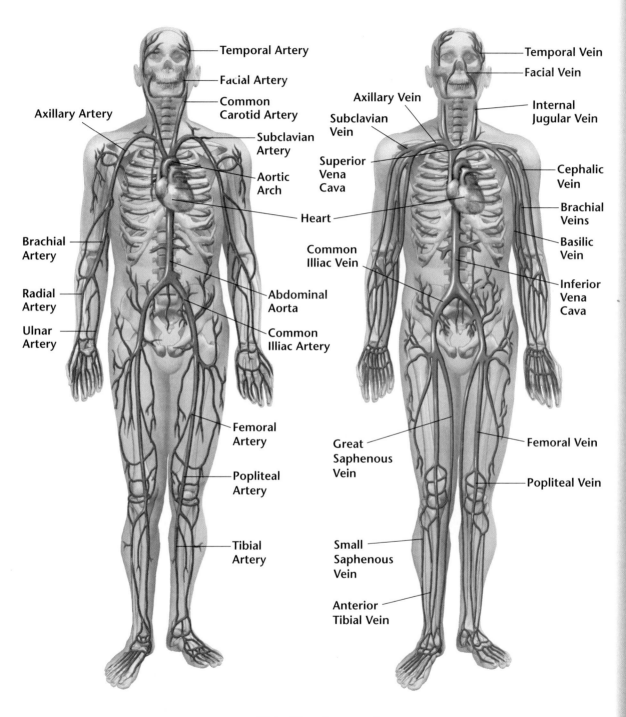

Temporal Artery

Facial Artery

Common
Carotid Artery

Axillary Artery

Subclavian
Artery

Aortic
Arch

Brachial
Artery

Heart

Radial
Artery

Abdominal
Aorta

Ulnar
Artery

Common
Illiac Artery

Femoral
Artery

Popliteal
Artery

Tibial
Artery

Temporal Vein

Facial Vein

Axillary Vein

Internal
Jugular Vein

Subclavian
Vein

Superior
Vena
Cava

Cephalic
Vein

Brachial
Veins

Common
Illiac Vein

Basilic
Vein

Inferior
Vena
Cava

Great
Saphenous
Vein

Femoral
Vein

Popliteal
Vein

Small
Saphenous
Vein

Anterior
Tibial Vein

The Circulatory System

Glossary

A

Abiotic (ā bī ot´ik) nonliving (p. 496)

Absolute dating (ab´sə lüt dā´ting) a method that estimates the actual age of a rock or fossil (p. 300)

Acceleration (ak sel ə rā´shən) the rate of change in velocity (p. 102)

Acid rain (as´id rān) rain that is caused by pollution and is harmful to organisms because it is acidic (p. 498)

Adaptation (ad ap tā´shən) a change or adjustment that makes an organism better able to survive in its environment (p. 525)

Adaptive advantage (ə dap´tiv ad van´tij) the greater likelihood that an organism will survive, due to characteristics that allow it to be more successful than other organisms (p. 531)

Adolescence (ad l es´ns) the teenage years of a human (p. 589)

Air mass (âr mas) a large section of the atmosphere with the same temperature and humidity throughout (p. 357)

Air pressure (âr presh´ər) the force of air against a unit of area (p. 352)

Algae (al´jē) protists that have plantlike qualities and usually live in water (p. 424)

Alluvial fan (ə lü´vē əl fan) a fan-shaped area of land deposited where a mountain stream moves onto flat land (p. 260)

Altitude (al´tə tüd) the height above the earth's surface (p. 339)

Alveolus (al vē´ə ləs) a tiny sac at the end of each bronchiole that holds air (plural is *alveoli*) (p. 563)

Amoeba (ə mē´bə) a protozoan that moves by pushing out parts of its cell (p. 425)

Ampere (am´pir) the unit used to describe how much electric current flows through a wire (p. 178)

Amphibian (am fib´ē ən) a vertebrate that lives at first in water and then on land (p. 441)

Anemometer (an ə mom´ə tər) an instrument used to measure wind speed (p. 354)

Angiosperm (an´jē ə spėrm) a flowering plant (p. 471)

Area (âr´ē ə) the amount of space the surface of an object takes up (p. 12)

Artery (är´tər ē) a blood vessel that carries blood away from the heart (p. 559)

Asexual reproduction (ā sek´shü əl rē prə duk´shən) reproduction that involves one parent and no egg or sperm (p. 461)

Asteroid (as´tə roid) a rocky object, smaller than a planet, that orbits a star (p. 390)

Asteroid belt (as´tə roid belt) the region between Mars and Jupiter where most asteroids orbit the sun (p. 390)

Astronomy (ə stron´ə mē) the study of outer space and objects in it (p. 213)

Atmosphere (at´mə sfir) the layer of gases that surrounds the earth (p. 333); the envelope of gas surrounding an object in space (p. 375)

Atom (at´əm) the building block of matter (p. 37)

Atomic mass (ə tom´ik mas) the average mass of all the isotopes of a particular element (p. 60)

Atomic number (ə tom´ik num´bər) a number equal to the number of protons in the nucleus of an atom (p. 48)

ATP high energy molecules that store energy in a form the cells can easily use (p. 410)

Atrium (ā´trē əm) a heart chamber that receives blood returning to the heart (plural is *atria*) (p. 459)

Attract (ə trakt´) to pull together (p. 189)

Auditory nerve (ȯ´də tôr ē nėrv) a bundle of nerves that carry impulses from the ear to the brain (p. 583)

Axis (ak´sis) an imaginary line through the earth that connects the North and South Poles (p. 219)

B

Bacteria (bak tir´ē ə) the simplest organisms that carry out all basic life activities (p. 405)

Balance (bal´əns) an instrument used to measure mass (p. 26); to keep the number of atoms the same on both sides of the equation (p. 86)

Barometer (bə rom′ə tər) an instrument used to measure air pressure (p. 352)

Base (bās) a molecule found in DNA that is used to code information (p. 522)

Battery (bat′erē) a source of voltage (energy) that changes chemical energy into electrical energy (p. 182)

Benthos (ben′thos) organisms that live on the ocean floor (p. 327)

Bilateral symmetry (bī lat′ər əl sim′ə trē) a body plan that consists of left and right halves that are the same (p. 446)

Bile (bīl) a substance made in the liver that breaks down fats (p. 554)

Biome (bī′ōm) an ecosystem found over a large geographic area (p. 499)

Biosphere (bī′ə sfir) the part of Earth where living things can exist (p. 500)

Biotic (bī ot′ik) living (p. 496)

Boiling point (boi′ling point) the temperature at which a substance changes from a liquid to a gas under normal atmospheric pressure (p. 147)

Brain stem (brān stem) the part of the brain that controls automatic activities and connects the brain and the spinal cord (p. 580)

Bronchiole (brong′kē ōl) a tube that branches off the bronchus (p. 563)

Bronchus (brong′kəs) a tube that connects the trachea to a lung (plural is *bronchi*) (p. 563)

C

Capillary (kap′ə ler ē) a blood vessel with a wall one cell thick through which oxygen and food molecules pass to body cells (p. 560)

Carbohydrate (kär bō hī′drāt) a sugar or starch, which living things use for energy (p. 414)

Cardiac (kär′dē ak) relating to the heart (p. 558)

Carrying capacity (kar′e ing kə pas′ə tē) the number of individuals that an environment can support (p. 496)

Cartilage (kär′tl ij) a soft material found in vertebrate skeletons (p. 440)

Cast (kast) a type of fossil that forms when minerals fill a mold; a model of an organism (p. 297)

Cell (sel) the basic unit of life (p. 405)

Cell membrane (sel mem′brān) a thin layer that surrounds and holds a cell together (p. 408)

Cell wall (sel wôl) the outer part of a plant cell that provides shape to the cell (p. 409)

Celsius scale (sel′sē əs skāl) the temperature scale used by scientists and by people in many countries, in which water freezes at 0° and boils at 100° (p. 144)

Cenozoic Era (sen ə zō′ik ir′ə) the era described as the Age of Mammals; began about 65 million years ago and continues today (p. 309)

Centigram (cg) (sen′tə gram) a unit of mass in the metric system that is $\frac{1}{100}$ of a gram (p. 25)

Centimeter (cm) (sen′tə mē tər) a metric unit of measure that is $\frac{1}{100}$ of a meter (p. 9)

Cerebellum (ser ə bel′əm) the part of the brain that controls balance (p. 580)

Cerebrum (sə rē′brəm) the largest part of the brain that controls thought, memory, learning, feeling, and body movement (p. 580)

Chemical bond (kem′ə kəl bond) the attractive force that holds atoms together (p. 76)

Chemical change (kem′ə kəl chānj) a change that produces one or more new substances with new chemical properties (p. 69)

Chemical equation (kem′ə kəl i kwā′zhən) a statement that uses symbols, formulas, and numbers to stand for a chemical reaction (p. 85)

Chemical formula (kem′ə kəl fôr′myə lə) tells the kinds of atoms and how many of each kind are in a compound (p. 78)

Chemical reaction (kem′ə kəl rē ak′shən) a chemical change in which elements are combined or rearranged (p. 82)

Chemical weathering (kem′ə kəl weᴛʜ′ər ing) the breaking apart of rocks caused by a change in their chemical makeup (p. 254)

Chemistry (kem′ə strē) the study of matter and how it changes (p. 3)

a	hat	e	let	ī	ice	ô	order	ù	put	sh	she	ə {	a in about
ā	age	ē	equal	o	hot	oi	oil	ü	rule	th	thin		e in taken
ä	far	ėr	term	ō	open	ou	out	ch	child	ᴛʜ	then		i in pencil
â	care	i	it	ȯ	saw	u	cup	ng	long	zh	measure		o in lemon
													u in circus

Chlorophyll (klôr´ə fil) the green pigment in plants that absorbs light energy for photosynthesis (p. 480)

Chloroplast (klôr´ə plast) captures the light energy from the sun to make food (p. 409)

Chromosome (krō´mə sōm) a rod-shaped structure that contains DNA and is found in the nucleus of a cell (p. 521)

Chyme (kīm) partly digested liquid food in the digestive tract (p. 553)

Cilia (sil´ē ə) hairlike structures that help some one-celled organisms move (p. 425)

Cinder cone (sin´dər kōn) a small volcano with steep sides and explosive eruptions; made of ash and rock (p. 279)

Circuit (ser´kit) a path for electric current (p. 178)

Circulatory (ser´kyə lə tôr ē) flowing in a circle (p. 458)

Cirrus cloud (sir´əs kloud) a high, wispy cloud made of ice crystals (p. 340)

Climate (klī´mit) the average weather of a region over a long period of time (p. 363)

Climax community (klī´maks kə myü´nə tē) a community that changes little over time (p. 498)

Closed circuit (klōzd ser´kit) a complete, unbroken path for electric current (p. 178)

Closed circulatory system (klōzd´ ser´kyə lə tôr ē sis´təm) a system in which blood stays inside vessels at all times (p. 458)

Cochlea (kok´lē ə) the organ in the ear that sends impulses to the auditory nerve (p. 583)

Coefficient (kō ə fish´ənt) a number placed before a formula in a chemical equation (p. 87)

Cold-blooded (kōld´ blud´id) having a body temperature that changes with temperature of surroundings (p. 442)

Cold front (kōld frunt) the boundary ahead of a cold air mass that is pushing out and wedging under a warm air mass (p. 357)

Comet (kom´it) a ball of ice, rock, frozen gases, and dust that orbits the sun (p. 391)

Community (kə myü´nə tē) a group of different populations that live in the same area (p. 496)

Composite volcano (kəm poz´it vol kā´nō) a tall volcano; formed from quiet lava flows that alternate with eruptions of ash and rock (p. 279)

Compound (kom´pound) a substance that is formed when atoms of two or more elements join together (p. 62)

Concave lens (kon kav´ lenz) a lens that is thin in the middle and thick at the edges (p. 171)

Concave mirror (kon kav´ mir´ər) a mirror that curves in at the middle (p. 170)

Condensation (kon den sā´shən) a change from a gas to a liquid (p. 137)

Condense (kən dens´) to change from a gas to a liquid (p. 338)

Conduction (kan duk´shən) the movement of heat energy from one molecule to the next (p. 151)

Conductor (kan duk´tər) a material through which heat travels easily (p. 151)

Consumer (kən sü´mər) an organism that feeds on other organisms (p. 504)

Continent (kon´tə nənt) one of the seven major land areas of the earth (p. 216)

Continental drift (kon tə nən´təl drift) the theory that the major landmasses of the earth move (p. 274)

Continental shelf (kon tə nən´təl shelf) a part of a continent that extends from a shoreline out into an ocean (p. 326)

Continental slope (kon tə nən´təl slōp) a steep slope between the continental shelf and the deep ocean floor (p. 326)

Contract (kən trakt´) to become smaller in size (p. 138)

Convection (kən vek´shən) the flow of energy that occurs when a warm liquid or gas rises (p. 152)

Convection current (kən vek´shən kėr´ənt) the circular motion of a gas or liquid as it heats (p. 276)

Convex lens (kon veks´ lenz) a lens that is thick in the middle and thin at the edges (p. 171)

Convex mirror (kon veks´ mir´ər) a mirror that curves outward at the middle (p. 170)

Core (kôr) the dense center of the earth made of solid and melted metals (p. 273)

Cornea (kôr´nē ə) a clear layer of the eye that light passes through (p. 582)

Crust (krust) the outer layer of the earth (p. 273)

Cubic centimeter (cm³) (kyü´bik sen´tə mē tər) a metric unit of measure that means centimeter × centimeter × centimeter (p. 16)

Cumulus cloud (kyü´myə ləs kloud) a puffy, white cloud occurring at medium altitudes (p. 340)

Current (kėr´ənt) a large stream of water flowing in oceans, in rivers, and in some large lakes (p. 325)

Customary (kus´tə mer ē) ordinary (p. 6)

Cytoplasm (sī´tə plaz əm) a gel-like substance containing chemicals needed by the cell (p. 408)

D

Decompose (dē kəm pōz´) to break down or decay matter into simpler substances (p. 426)

Degree (di grē´) a unit of measurement on a temperature scale (p. 144); unit for measuring angles in a circle or sphere (p. 228)

Delta (del´tə) a fan-shaped area of land formed when sediment is deposited where a river empties into a lake or an ocean (p. 260)

Density (den´sə tē) a measure of how tightly the matter of a substance is packed into a given volume (p. 38)

Deposition (dep ə zish´ən) the dropping of eroded sediment (p. 260)

Dermis (dėr´mis) the thick layer of cells below the epidermis (p. 566)

Descent with modification (di sent´ wiŦH mod ə fə kā´shən) the theory that more recent species of organisms are changed descendants of earlier species (p. 531)

Deuterium (dü tir´ē əm) an isotope of hydrogen that has one proton and one neutron (p. 57)

Development (di vel´əp mənt) the changes that occur as a living thing grows (p. 421)

Diffusion (di fyü´zhən) the movement of materials from an area of high concentration to an area of low concentration (p. 456)

Digestion (də jes´chən) the process by which living things break down food (p. 419)

Digestive tract (də jes´tiv trakt) a tubelike digestive space with an opening at each end (p. 454).

Displacement of water method (dis plās´mənt ov wo´tər) a method of measuring volume of irregularly shaped objects (p. 21)

Dissolve (di zolv´) to break apart (p. 83)

Distance (dis´təns) the length of the path between two points (p. 98)

Diversity (də vėr´sə tē) the range of differences found among the members of a population (p. 525)

Divide (də vīd´) a ridge that separates drainage basins (p. 318)

DNA the chemical inside cells that stores information about an organism (p. 408)

Drainage basin (drā´nij bā´sn) a land area that is drained by a river and its tributaries (p. 318)

E

Eardrum (ir´drum) a thin tissue in the middle ear that vibrates when sound waves strike it (p. 583)

Earthquake (ėrth´kwāk) a shaking of the earth's crust (p. 286)

Earth science (ėrth sī´əns) the study of the earth's land, water, air and outer space (p. 213)

Ecology (ē kol´ə jē) the study of the interactions among living things and the nonliving things in their environment (p. 495)

Ecosystem (ē´kō sis təm) the interactions among the populations of a community and the nonliving things in their environment (p. 496)

Effort force, F_e (ef´ərt fôrs) the force applied to a machine by the user (p. 116)

Egg cell (eg sel) a female sex cell (p. 461)

Elapsed time (i lapsd´ tim) the length of time that passes from one event to another (p. 97)

Electric current (i lek´trik kėr´ənt) the movement of electrons from one place to another (p. 178)

Electricity (i lek tris´ə tē) a flow of electrons (p. 177)

Electromagnet (i lek trō mag´nit) a temporary magnet made by passing a current through a wire wrapped around an iron core (p. 197)

a	hat	e	let	ī	ice	ô	order	u̇	put	sh	she	ə	a in about
ā	age	ē	equal	o	hot	oi	oil	ü	rule	th	thin		e in taken
ä	far	ėr	term	ō	open	ou	out	ch	child	ŦH	then		i in pencil
â	care	i	it	ȯ	saw	u	cup	ng	long	zh	measure		o in lemon
													u in circus

Electromagnetism (i lek trō mag′ni tism) the relationship between magnetism and electricity (p. 197)

Electron (i lek′tron) a tiny particle of an atom that moves around the nucleus (p. 42)

Element (el′ə mənt) matter that has only one kind of atom (p. 46)

Embryo (em′brē ō) a beginning plant or other organism(p. 471)

Endangered (en dān′jərd) there are almost no animals left of a certain species (p. 499)

Endoplasmic reticulum (en də plaz′mik ri ti′kyə ləm) a system of tubes that process and transport proteins within the cell (p. 408)

Energy (en′ər jē) the ability to do work (p. 93)

Energy level (en′ər jē lev′əl) one of the spaces around the nucleus of an atom in which an electron moves (p. 74)

Energy pyramid (en′ər jē pir′ə mid) a diagram that compare the amounts of energy available to the populations at different levels of a food chain (p. 509)

Environment (en vī′rən mənt) an organism's surroundings (p. 521)

Enzyme (en′zīm) a substance that speeds up chemical changes (p. 453)

Epicenter (ep′ə sen′tər) a point on the earth's surface directly over the focus of an earthquake (p. 288)

Epidermis (ep ə dėr′mis) the thin outer layer of skin (p. 566)

Equator (i kwā′tər) the line of 0° latitude halfway between the poles (p. 228)

Erosion (i rō′zhən) a wearing away and moving of weathered rock and soil (p. 259)

Estrogen (es′trə jən) female sex hormone (p. 571)

Euglena (yü glē′nə) a protozoan that behaves like both plants and animals (p. 425)

Evaporate (i vap′ə rāt) to change from a liquid to a gas (p. 137; p. 338)

Evolution (ev ə lü′shən) the changes in a population over time (p. 528)

Excretion (ek skrē′shən) the process by which living things get rid of wastes (p. 419)

Excretory system (ek′skrə tôr ē sis′təm) a series of organs that get rid of cell wastes in the form of urine (p. 567)

Expand (ek spand′) to become larger in size (p. 138)

Exponent (ek spō′nənt) a number that tells how many times another number is a factor (p. 12)

Extinct (ek stingkt′) all the members of a species are dead (p. 499)

Extrusive rock (ek strü′siv rok) igneous rock that forms from cooled lava on the earth's surface (p. 246)

F

Fahrenheit scale (far′ən hīt skāl) the temperature scale commonly used in the United States, in which water freezes at 32° and boils at 212° (p. 144)

Fallopian tube (fə lō′pē ən tüb) a tube through which eggs pass from an ovary to the uterus (p. 571)

Fat (fat) a chemical that stores large amounts of energy (p. 414)

Fault (fȯlt) a break in the earth's crust along which movement occurs (p. 282)

Feces (fē′sēz) solid waste material remaining in the large intestine after digestion (p. 554)

Fern (fėrn) a seedless plant with tubelike cells that transport water (p. 469)

Fertilization (fėr tl ə zā′shən) the joining of an egg cell and a sperm cell (p. 462)

Fetus (fē′təs) an embryo after eight weeks of development in the uterus (p. 572)

Filter feeding (fil′tər fēd′ing) a way of getting food by straining it out of the water (p. 451)

Flagellum (flə jel′əm) a whiplike tail that helps some one-celled organisms move (plural is *flagella*) (p. 425)

Focus (fō′kəs) a point inside the earth where rock first moves, starting an earthquake (p. 288)

Fog (fog) a stratus cloud that forms near the ground (p. 339)

Folding (fōld′ing) the bending of rock layers that are squeezed together (p. 281)

Food chain (füd′ chān) the feeding order of organisms in a community (p. 504)

Food web (füd′ web) all the food chains in a community that are linked to one another (p. 505)

Force (fôrs) a push or a pull (p. 102)

Fossil (fos′əl) the traces or remains of an organism preserved in the earth's crust (p. 296)

Fossil fuels (fos′əl fyü′əls) the fuels formed millions of years ago from the remains of plants and animals (p. 500)

Freezing point (frēz′ing point) the temperature at which a liquid changes to a solid (p. 146)

Friction (frik′shən) a force that opposes motion and that occurs when things slide or roll over each other (p. 102)

Frond (frond) a large feathery leaf of a fern (p. 473)

Front (frunt) a moving boundary line between two air masses (p. 357)

Fulcrum (ful′krəm) a fixed point around which a lever rotates (p. 116)

Fungus (fung′gəs) an organism that usually has many cells and decomposes material for its food (plural is *fungi*) (p. 425)

Fusion (fyü′zhən) the process by which particles combine to form a new particle (p. 372)

G

Galaxy (gal′ək sē) a group of billions of stars (p. 374)

Gallbladder (gȯl′blad ər) the digestive organ that stores bile (p. 554)

Gas (gas) a form of matter that has no definite shape or volume (p. 39)

Gastrovascular cavity (gas trō vas′kyə lər kav′ə tē) a digestive space with a single opening (p. 453)

Gene (jēn) a section of DNA that carries a trait (p. 521)

Generator (jen′ə rā tər) a device used to convert mechanical energy to electrical energy (p. 95)

Genetics (jə net′iks) the study of heredity (p. 521)

Genus (jē′nəs) a group of living things that includes separate species (p. 433)

Geologic time (jē ə loj′ik tīm) all the time that has passed since the earth formed (p. 295)

Geologic time scale (jē ə loj′ik tīm skāl) an outline of the events of the earth's history (p. 305)

Geology (jē ol′ə jē) the study of the solid parts of the earth (p. 213)

Germinate (jėr′mə nāt) to start to grow into a new plant (p. 487)

Gestation time (je stā′shən tīm) the period of time from fertilization of an egg until birth occurs (p. 463)

Geyser (gī′zər) a place where hot groundwater and steam blast into the air (p. 317)

Gill (gil) a body part used by some animals to breathe in water (p. 441)

Glacier (glā′shər) a thick mass of ice that covers a large area (p. 263)

Gland (gland) an organ that produces chemicals for the body to use (p. 554)

Golgi body (gȯl′jē bod′ē) packages and distributes proteins outside the cell (p. 408)

Graduated cylinder (graj′ü ā tid sil′ən dər) a glass or plastic cylinder used to measure the volume of liquids (p. 19)

Gram (g) (gram) the basic unit of mass in the metric system (p. 24)

Gravity (grav′ə tē) the force of attraction between any two objects that have mass (p. 106)

Greenhouse effect (grēn′hous ə fekt′) the warming of the atmosphere because of trapped heat energy from the sun (p. 379)

Groundwater (ground′wȯ tər) water that sinks into the ground (p. 315, 512)

Guard cell (gärd sel) a cell that opens and closes stomata (p. 483)

Gymnosperm (jim′nə spėrm) a nonflowering seed plant (p. 472)

H

Habitat (hab′ə tat) the place where an organism lives (p. 495)

Half-life (haf′ līf) the length of time it takes for half of the atoms of a radioactive element to decay (p. 300)

Hardness (härd′nəs) the ability of a mineral to resist being scratched (p. 239)

Heat (hēt) a form of energy resulting from the motion of particles in matter (p. 133)

a	hat	e	let	ī	ice	ȯ	order	u̇	put	sh	she	ə	a in about
ā	age	ē	equal	o	hot	oi	oil	ü	rule	th	thin		e in taken
ä	far	ėr	term	ō	open	ou	out	ch	child	ŦH	then		i in pencil
â	care	i	it	ȯ	saw	u	cup	ng	long	zh	measure		o in lemon
													u in circus

Heat source (hēt sôrs) a place from which heat energy comes (p. 134)

Hemisphere (hem´ə sfir) half of the earth (p. 231)

Hemoglobin (hē´mə glō bən) a substance in red blood cells that carries oxygen (p. 561)

Heredity (hə red´ə tē) the passing of traits from parents to offspring (p. 521)

High (hī) cold area of high air pressure (p. 358)

Homeostatsis (hō mē ō stā´səs) the ability of organisms to maintain their internal conditions (p. 420)

Homologous structure (hō mo´lə gəs struk´chər) a body part that is similar in related organisms (p. 533)

Hormone (hôr´mōn) a chemical signal that glands produce (p. 570)

Humidity (hyü mid´ə tē) the amount of water vapor in the air (p. 353)

Hurricane (hėr´ə kān) a severe tropical storm with high winds that revolve around an eye (p. 359)

Hypothesis (hī poth´ə sis) a testable explanation of a question or problem (plural is *hypotheses*) (p. 531)

I

Igneous rock (ig´nē əs rok) rock formed from melted minerals that have cooled and hardened (p. 244)

Image (im´ij) a copy or likeness (p. 170)

Impulse (im´puls) a message that travels along nerve cells (p. 581)

Inclined plane (in klīnd´ plān) a simple machine made up of a ramp, used to lift an object (p. 125)

Index fossil (in´deks fos´əl) a fossil that can be used to establish the relative age of the rock in which the fossil occurs (p. 300)

Inertia (in ėr´shə) the tendency of an object to resist changes in its motion (p. 103)

Insulator (in´sə lā tər) material that does not conduct heat well (p. 151)

Interact (in tər akt´) to act upon or with something (p. 495)

International date line (in tər nash´ə nəl dāt līn) an imaginary line that defines the start of a day (p. 221)

Intrusive rock (in trü´siv rok) igneous rock that forms underground from cooled magma (p. 246)

Invertebrate (in vėr´tə brit) an animal that does not have a backbone (p. 445)

Ion (ī´ən) an atom that has either a positive or a negative charge (p. 76)

Ionosphere (ī on´ə sfir) the layer of the atmosphere containing ions, or electrically charged particles (p. 336)

Iris (ī´ris) the part of the eye that controls the amount of light that enters (p. 582)

Isobar (ī´sə bär) a line on a weather map connecting areas of equal air pressure (p. 358)

Isotope (ī´sə tōp) one of a group of atoms of an element with the same number of protons and electrons but different numbers of neutrons (p. 57)

J

Joule (jül) the metric unit of work (p. 114)

K

Kilogram (**kg**) (kil´ə gram) a unit of mass in the metric system that equals 1,000 grams (p. 25)

Kilometer (**km**) (kə lom´ə tər) a metric unit of measure that is equal to 1,000 meters (p. 10)

Kinetic energy (ki net´ik en´ər jē) the energy of motion (p. 93)

Kingdom (king´dəm) one of the five groups into which living things are classified (p. 423)

L

Larynx (lar´ingks) the voice box (p. 563)

Latitude (lat´ə tüd) an angle that describes the distance north or south of the equator (p. 228)

Law of conservation of energy (lȯ ov kon´sər vā shən ov en´ar jē) energy cannot be created or destroyed (p. 95)

Law of conservation of matter (lȯ ov kon´sər vā shən ov mat´ər) matter cannot be created or destroyed in chemical and common physical changes (p. 86)

Law of universal gravitation (lȯ ov yü nə vėr´səl grav ə tā´shən) gravitational force depends on the mass of the two objects involved and on the distance between them (p. 107)

Lens (lenz) a curved piece of clear material that refracts light waves (p. 171)

Lethal mutation (lē´thəl myü tā´shən) a mutation that results in the death of an organism (p. 529)

Lever (lev´ər) a simple machine containing a bar that can turn around a fixed point (p. 116)

Life science (līf sī´əns) the study of living things (p. 403)

Ligament (lig´ə mənt) a tissue that connects bone to bone (p. 548)

Light (līt) a form of energy that can be seen (p. 164)

Lines of force (līnz ov fôrs) lines that show a magnetic field (p. 192)

Liquid (lik´wid) a form of matter that has a definite volume but no definite shape (p. 38)

Liter (L) (lē´tər) the basic unit of volume in the metric system (p. 17)

Longitude (lon´jə tüd) an angle that describes the distance east or west of the prime meridian (p. 230)

Low (lō) a warm area of low air pressure (p. 358)

Luster (lus´tər) how a mineral reflects light (p. 238)

Lysosome (lī´sə sōm) contains chemicals that break down materials (p. 409)

M

Magma (mag´mə) hot, liquid rock inside the earth (p. 246)

Magnet (mag´nit) an object that attracts certain kinds of metals, such as iron (p. 189)

Magnetic field (mag net´ik fēld) the area around a magnet in which magnetic forces can act (p. 192)

Magnetic pole (mag net´ik pōl) the end of a magnet, where magnetic forces are greatest (p. 190)

Mammary gland (mam´ər ē gland) a milk-producing structure on the chest or abdomen of a mammal (p. 443)

Mantle (man´tl) the layer of the earth that surrounds the core (p. 273)

Mass (mas) the amount of material an object has (p. 3)

Mass number (mas num´bər) a number equal to the sum of the numbers of protons and neutrons in an atom of an element (p. 60)

Matter (mat´ər) anything that has mass and takes up space (p. 3)

Mechanical advantage (MA) (mə kan´ə kəl ad van´tij) the factor by which a machine multiplies the effort force (p. 119)

Mechanical weathering (mə kan´ə kəl weŦH´ər ing) the breaking apart of rocks without changing their mineral composition (p. 253)

Meiosis (mī ō´sis) the process that results in sex cells (p. 526)

Melting point (melt´ing póint) the temperature at which a solid changes to a liquid (p. 146)

Meniscus (mə nis´kəs) the curved surface of a liquid (p. 19)

Menstruation (men strü ā´shən) the process during which an unfertilized egg, blood, and pieces of the lining of the uterus exit the female body (p. 571)

Meridian (mə rid´ē ən) a line of longitude (p. 230)

Mesosphere (mes´ə sfir) the third layer of the atmosphere; the coldest layer (p. 336)

Mesozoic Era (mes ə zō´ik ir´ə) an era characterized by dinosaurs; began about 245 million years ago and ended about 65 million years ago (p. 308)

Metamorphic rock (met ə môr´fik rok) rock that has been changed by intense heat, pressure, and chemical reactions (p. 245)

Metamorphosis (met ə môr´fə sis) a major change in form that occurs as some animals develop into adults (p. 441)

Meter (m) (mē´tər) the basic unit of length in the metric system; it is about 39 inches long (p. 8)

Meteor (mē´tē ər) a brief streak of light seen when an asteroid enters the earth's atmosphere and burns up (p. 390)

Meteorite (mē´tē ə rīt) an asteroid that hits the surface of a planet or moon after traveling through space (p. 391)

a	hat	e	let	ī	ice	ó	order	ů	put	sh	she	ə	a in about
ā	age	ē	equal	o	hot	oi	oil	ü	rule	th	thin		e in taken
ä	far	ėr	term	ō	open	ou	out	ch	child	ŦH	then		i in pencil
â	care	i	it	ȯ	saw	u	cup	ng	long	zh	measure		o in lemon
													u in circus

Meteorology (mē tē ə rol´ə jē) the study of the earth's air and weather (p. 213)

Meterstick (mē´tər stik) a common tool for measuring length in the metric system (p. 9)

Metric system (met´rik sis´təm) the system of measurement used by scientists (p. 6)

Microorganism (mī krō ôr´gə niz əm) an organism that is too small to be seen without a microscope (p. 424)

Microscope (mī´krə skōp) an instrument used to magnify things (p. 405)

Mid-ocean ridge (mid´ ō´shən rij) a mountain chain on the ocean floor (p. 326)

Milligram (mg) (mil´ə gram) a unit of mass in the metric system that is $\frac{1}{1,000}$ of a gram (p. 25)

Milliliter (mL) (mil´ə lē tər) a metric unit of measure that is $\frac{1}{1,000}$ of a liter; it equals one cubic centimeter (p. 18)

Millimeter (mm) (mil´ə mē tər) a metric unit of measure that is $\frac{1}{1,000}$ of a meter (p. 9)

Mineral (min´ər əl) an element or compound found in the earth (p. 237); a natural substance needed for fluid balance, digestion, and other bodily functions (p. 417)

Mitochondrion (mī tə kon´drē ən) an organelle that uses oxygen to break down food and release the energy in food's chemical bonds (plural is *mitochondria*) (p. 408)

Mitosis (mī tō´sis) the process that results in two cells identical to the parent cells (p. 524)

Mixture (miks´chər) a combination of substances in which no reaction takes place (p. 82)

Model (mod´l) a picture, an idea, or an object that is built to explain how something else looks or works (p. 41)

Mold (mōld) the type of fossil that forms when the shape of a plant or an animal is left in rock (p. 297)

Molecule (mol´ə kyül) the smallest particle of a substance that has the same properties as the substance (p. 36)

Molting (mōlt´ing) the process by which an arthropod sheds its external skeleton (p. 447)

Moneran (mə nir´ən) an organism, usually one-celled, that does not have organelles (p. 426)

Moon (mün) a natural satellite that orbits a planet (p. 371)

Moraine (mə rān´) a ridge of sediment deposited by a glacier (p. 264)

Moss (mȯs) a plant with no tubelike cells to transport water (p. 469)

Motion (mō´shən) a change in position (p. 93)

Motor (mō´tər) a device that converts electrical energy to mechanical energy (p. 200)

Mouth (mouth) the place where a river flows into a larger body of water (p. 260)

Mutation (myü tā´shən) a change in a gene (p. 521)

N

Natural element (nach´ər əl el´ə mənt) an element found in nature (p. 47)

Natural selection (nach´ər əl si lek´shən) the process by which organisms best suited to the environment survive, reproduce, and pass their genes to the next generation (p. 531)

Nekton (nek´ton) free-swimming ocean animals (p. 327)

Neuron (nùr´on) a nerve cell (p. 581)

Neutron (nü´tron) a tiny particle in the nucleus of an atom that is similar to a proton in size (p. 43)

Newton (nüt´n) the metric unit of weight (p. 23)

Nitrogen fixation (nī´trə jən fik sā´shən) the process by which certain bacteria change nitrogen gas from the air into ammonia (p. 514)

Nonrenewable resources (non ri nü´ə bel ri sôrs´əz) resources that cannot be replaced (p. 500)

Nonvascular plant (non vas´kyə lər plant) a plant that does not have tubelike cells (p. 470)

Normal fault (nôr´məl fȯlt) a break in the crust in which the overhanging block of rock has slid down (p. 282)

North Pole (nôrth pōl) the point farthest north on the earth (p. 219)

Nuclear fission (nü´klē ar fish´ən) the reaction that occurs when the nucleus of an atom splits and energy is released as heat and light (p. 135)

Nuclear fusion (nü´klē ar fyü´zhan) the reaction that occurs when atoms are joined together and energy is released (p. 135)

Nucleus (nü′klē əs) the central part of an atom (p. 42); the information and control center of the cell (p. 408)

Nutrient (nü′trē ənt) any chemical found in foods that is needed by living things (p. 417)

O

Oceanography (o shə nog′rə fē) the study of the earth's oceans (p. 213)

Omnivore (om′nə vôr) a consumer that eats both plants and animals (p. 504)

Open circuit (ō′pən sėr′kit) an incomplete or broken path for electric current (p. 179)

Open circulatory system (ō′pən sėr′kyə lə tôr ē sis′təm) a system in which blood makes direct contact with cells (p. 458)

Optic nerve (op′tik nėrv) a bundle of nerves that carry impulses from the eye to the brain (p. 582)

Organ (ôr′gən) a group of different tissues that work together (p. 407)

Organelle (ôr gə nel′) a tiny part inside a cell (p. 406)

Organism (ôr′gə niz əm) a living thing that can carry out all the basic life activities (p. 405)

Ovary (ō′vər ē) the female sex organ that produces egg cells (p. 462); the lower part of the pistil that contains eggs (p. 486)

Ovulation (ō vyə lā′shən) the process of releasing an egg from an ovary (p. 571)

Oxidation (oks sə dā′shən) the process in which minerals combine with oxygen to form new substances (p. 254)

P

Paleozoic Era (pā lē ə zō′ik ir′ə) an era marked by great development in sea life; began about 540 million years ago and ended about 245 million years ago (p. 307)

Pangaea (pan jē′ə) a single landmass from which Alfred Wegener thought the continents separated millions of years ago (p. 274)

Parallel (par′ə lel) a line of latitude (p. 228)

Parallel circuit (par′ə lel sėr′kit) a circuit in which there is more than one path for current (p. 186)

Paramecium (par ə mē′sē əm) A protozoan that moves by using hairlike cilia (plural is *paramecia*) (p. 425)

Parasite (par′ə sīt) an organism that absorbs food from a living organism and harms it (p. 426)

Penis (pē′nis) the male organ that delivers sperm to the female body (p. 570)

Periodic table (pir ē od′ik tā′bəl) an arrangement of elements by increasing atomic number (p. 56)

Peristalsis (per ə stòl′sis) the movement of digestive organs that pushes food through the digestive tract (p. 553)

Perspiration (pėr spə rā′shən) liquid waste made of heat, water, and salt released through the skin (p. 566)

Petiole (pet′ē ōl) the stalk that attaches a leaf to a stem (p. 478)

Petrification (pet rə fə kā′shən) the replacement of the original parts of a buried organism with minerals (p. 296)

Pharynx (far′ingks) the passageway between the mouth and the esophagus for air and food (p. 553)

Phloem (flō′em) the vascular tissue in plants that carries food from leaves to other parts of the plant (p. 477)

Photons (fō′tonz) small bundles of energy that make up light (p. 164)

Photosynthesis (fō tō sin′thə sis) the process in which a plant makes food (p. 409)

Phylum (fī′ləm) a subdivision of a kingdom (plural is *phyla*) (p. 433)

Physical change (fiz′ə kəl chānj) a change in which the appearance (physical properties) of a substances changes but its chemical properties stay the same (p. 70)

Physics (fiz′iks) the study of how energy acts with matter (p. 3)

Pigment (pig′mənt) a chemical that absorbs certain types of light (p. 480)

a	hat	e	let	ī	ice	ȯ	order	u̇	put	sh	she	ə	a in about
ā	age	ē	equal	o	hot	oi	oil	ü	rule	th	thin		e in taken
ä	far	ėr	term	ō	open	ou	out	ch	child	ᴛʜ	then		i in pencil
â	care	i	it	ȯ	saw	u	cup	ng	long	zh	measure		o in lemon
													u in circus

Pistil (pis´tl) the female organ of reproduction in a flower (p. 486)

Plane mirror (plān mir´ər) a flat, smooth mirror (p. 170)

Planet (plan´it) a large object in space that orbits a star such as the sun (p. 371)

Plankton (plangk´tən) tiny organisms that live at or near the ocean surface (p. 327)

Plasma (plaz´mə) a very hot gas made of particles that have an electric charge (p. 39); the liquid part of blood (p. 561)

Plate (plāt) a large section of the earth's crust that moves (p. 275)

Platelet (plāt´lit) a tiny piece of cell that helps form clots (p. 561)

Plate tectonics (plāt tek ton´iks) the theory that the earth's surface is made of large sections of crust that move (p. 275)

Polar easterly (pō´lər ē´stər lē) the wind near a pole; blows from the east (p. 345)

Pollen (pol´ən) tiny grains containing sperm (p. 486)

Pollination (pol ə nā´shən) the process by which pollen is transferred from the stamen to the pistil (p. 486)

Pollution (pə lü´shən) anything added to the environment that is harmful to living things (p. 498)

Population (pop yə lā´shən) a group of organisms of the same species that lives in the same area (p. 496)

Porous (pôr´əs) containing many spaces through which air and water can move (p. 317)

Potential energy (pə ten´shəl en´ər jē) stored energy (p. 93)

Precambrian Era (prē kam´brē ən ir´ə) the oldest and longest era of the earth's history; began about 4.6 billion years ago and ended about 540 million years ago (p. 305)

Precipitation (pri sip ə tā´shən) moisture that falls to the earth from the atmosphere (p. 339)

Pregnancy (preg´nən sē) the development of a fertilized egg into a baby inside a female's body (p. 572)

Prevailing westerly (pri vā´ling wes´tər lē) a wind generally between 30°N and 60°N latitudes (or 30°S and 60°S); blows from the west (p. 345)

Prime meridian (prīm mə rid´ē ən) a line of 0° longitude (p. 230)

Prism (priz´əm) a clear piece of glass or plastic that can be used to separate white light (p. 166)

Producer (prə dü´sər) an organism that makes its own food (p. 504)

Product (prod´əkt) a substance that is formed in a chemical reaction (p. 85)

Progesterone (prō jes´tə rōn) female sex hormone (p. 571)

Property (prop´ər tē) a characteristic that helps identify an object (p. 33)

Prostate gland (pros´tāt gland) the gland that produces the fluid found in semen (p. 570)

Protein (prō´tēn) a chemical used by living things to build and repair body parts and control body activities (p. 414)

Protist (prō´tist) an organism that usually is one-celled and has plantlike or animal-like properties (p. 424)

Proton (prō´ton) a tiny particle in the nucleus of an atom (p. 42)

Protozoan (prō tə zō´ən) a protist that has animal-like qualities; some have properties of both plants and animals (p. 424)

Pseudopod (sü´də pod) a part of some one-celled organisms that sticks out like a foot to move the cell along (p. 425)

Psychrometer (sī krom´ə tər) an instrument used to measure relative humidity (p. 353)

Puberty (pyü´bər tē) the period of rapid growth and physical changes that occurs in males and females during early adolescence (p. 589)

Pulley (pul´ē) a simple machine made up of a rope, chain, or belt wrapped around a wheel (p. 123)

Pupil (pyü´pəl) the black circle in the center of the eye (p. 582)

Pyramid of numbers (pir´ə mid ov num´bərz) a diagram that compares the sizes of populations at different levels of a food chain (p. 505)

R

Radial symmetry (rā´dē əl sim´ə trē) an arrangement of body parts that resembles the arrangement of spokes on a wheel (p. 445)

Radiation (rā de ā´shən) the movement of energy through a vacuum (p. 150)

Radical (rad´ə kal) a group of two or more atoms that acts like one atom (p. 80)

Radioactive element (rā dē ō ak´tiv el´ə mənt) an element that breaks apart, or decays, to form another element (p. 300)

Rain gauge (rān gāj) an instrument used to measure the amount of rainfall (p. 355)

Reactant (rē ak´tənt) a substance that is altered in a chemical reaction (p. 85)

Receptor cell (ri sep´tər sel) a cell that receives information about the environment and starts nerve impulses to send that information to the brain (p. 582)

Rectum (rek´təm) the lower part of the large intestine where feces are stored (p. 554)

Reflect (ri flekt´) to bounce back (p. 164)

Refraction (ri frak´shən) the bending of a light wave as it moves from one material to another (p. 170)

Relative dating (rel´ə tiv dāt´ing) a method that compares two rock layers to find out which is older (p. 299)

Relative humidity (rel´ə tiv hyü mid´ə tē) the amount of water vapor in the air compared to the maximum amount of water vapor the air can hold (p. 353)

Renewable resources (ri nü´ə bəl ri sôrs´əz) a resource that is replaced by nature (p. 500)

Repel (ri pel´) to push apart (p. 190)

Replicate (rep´lə kāt) to make a copy of (p. 523)

Reproduction (rē prə duk´shən) the process by which living things produce offspring (p. 420)

Reptile (rep´tīl) an egg-laying vertebrate that breathes with lungs (p. 442)

Reservoir (rez´ər vwär) an artificial lake created by placing a dam across a river (p. 319)

Resistance force (F_r) (ri zis´təns fôrs) the force applied to a machine by the object to be moved (p. 116)

Resource (ri sôrs´) a thing that an organism uses to live (p. 500)

Respiration (res pə rā´shən) the process by which living things release energy from food (p. 419)

Retina (ret´n ə) the back part of the eye where light rays are focused (p. 582)

Reverse fault (ri vėrs´ fôlt´) a break in the crust in which the overhanging block of rock has been raised (p. 282)

Revolution (rev ə lü´shən) the movement of one object in its orbit around another object in space (p. 225)

Rhizoid (rī´zoid) a tiny rootlike thread of a moss plant (p. 474)

Rhizome (rī´zōm) a plant part that has shoots aboveground and roots belowground (p. 473)

Ribosome (rī´bə sōm) a protein builder of the cell (p. 408)

Richter scale (rik´tər skāl) a scale used to measure the strength of an earthquake (p. 288)

RNA a molecule that works together with DNA to make proteins (p. 410)

Rock (rok) a natural, solid material made of one or more minerals (p. 244)

Rock cycle (rok sī´kəl) a series of natural changes that cause one type of rock to become another type of rock (p. 246)

Rotation (rō tā´shən) the spinning of the earth (p. 219)

Runoff (run´ôf) water that runs over the earth's surface and flows into streams (p. 315)

S

Salinity (sə lin´ə tē) the saltiness of water (p. 323)

Schematic diagram (ski mat´ik dī´ə gram) a diagram that uses symbols to show the parts of a circuit (p. 180)

Scientific name (sī ən tif´ik nām) the name given to each species, consisting of its genus and its species label (p. 436)

Scientific theory (sī ən tif´ik thē´ər ē) a generally accepted and well-tested scientific explanation (p. 530)

Screw (skrü) a simple machine made up of an inclined plane wrapped around a straight piece of metal (p. 126)

Scrotum (skrō´təm) the sac that holds the testes (p. 569)

a	hat	e	let	ī	ice	ȯ	order	ù	put	sh	she	ə	a in about
ā	age	ē	equal	o	hot	oi	oil	ü	rule	th	thin		e in taken
ä	far	ėr	term	ō	open	ou	out	ch	child	ŦH	then		i in pencil
â	care	i	it	ȯ	saw	u	cup	ng	long	zh	measure		o in lemon
													u in circus

Sea-floor spreading (sē´flôr spred´ing) the theory that the ocean floor spreads apart as new crust is formed at mid-ocean ridges (p. 275)

Seamount (sē´mount) an underwater mountain that is usually a volcano (p. 326)

Secrete (si krēt´) to form and release, or give off (p. 453)

Sedimentary rock (sed ə mən´tər ē rok) rock formed from pieces of other rock and remains of living things that have been pressed and cemented together (p. 245)

Seed (sēd) a plant part that contains a beginning plant and stored food (p. 469)

Seismograph (sīz´mə graf) an instrument that detects and records earthquake waves (p. 287)

Semen (sē´mən) a mixture of fluid and sperm cells (p. 570)

Series circuit (sir´ēz sėr´kit) a circuit in which all current (electrons) flows through a single path (p. 182)

Sexual reproduction (sek´shü əl rē prə duk´shən) reproduction that involves both a female and a male parent (p. 461)

Shield volcano (shēld vol kā´nō) a low, broad volcano with a wide crater; formed from thin layers of lava (p. 279)

Simple machine (sim´pəl mə shēn´) a tool with few parts that makes it easier or possible to do work (p. 116)

Sinkhole (singk´hōl) a funnel-shaped depression that results when the roof of a cave collapses (p. 317)

Skeletal system (skel´ə təl sis´təm) the network of bones in the body (p. 547)

Soil (soil) a mixture of tiny pieces of weathered rock and the remains of plants and animals (p. 255)

Solar system (sō´lər sis´təm) a star, such as the sun, and all the objects that revolve around it in space (p. 372)

Solid (sol´id) a form of matter that has a definite shape and volume (p. 38)

Solute (sol´yüt) the substance that is dissolved in a solution (p. 83)

Solution (sə lü´shən) a mixture in which one substance is dissolved in another (p. 83)

Solvent (sol´vənt) a substance capable of dissolving one or more other substances (p. 83)

Sori (sôr´ī) clusters of reproductive cells on the underside of a frond (p. 473)

Sound wave (sound wāv) a wave produced by vibrations (p. 160)

South Pole (south pōl) the point farthest south on the earth (p. 219)

Species (spē´shēz) a group of organisms that can breed with each other to produce offspring like themselves (p. 433)

Speed (spēd) the rate at which the position of an object changes (p. 97)

Sperm cell (spėrm sel) a male sex cell (p. 461)

Spore (spôr) the reproductive cells of some organisms (p. 473)

Spring (spring) a place where groundwater flows naturally out of the ground (p. 317)

Stamen (stā´mən) the male organ of reproduction in a flower; includes the anther and filament (p. 486)

Standard mass (stan´dard mas) a small object that is used with a balance to determine mass (p. 26)

Standard time zone (stan´dərd tīm zōn) an area that has the same clock time (p. 221)

Star (stär) a glowing ball of hot gas that makes its own energy and light (p. 371)

State of matter (stāt ov mat´ər) the form that matter has—solid, liquid, or gas (p. 39)

Static electricity (stat´ik i lek tris´ə tē) the buildup of electrical charges (p. 177)

Stigma (stig´mə) the upper part of the pistil, on the tip of the style (p. 486)

Stoma (stō´mə) a small opening in a leaf that allows gases to enter and leave (plural is *stomata*) (p. 478)

Stratosphere (strat´ə sfir) the second layer of the atmosphere; includes the ozone layer (p. 336)

Stratus cloud (strā´təs kloud) a low, flat cloud that forms in layers (p. 339)

Streak (strēk) the color of the mark a mineral makes on a white tile (p. 239)

Strike-slip fault (strīk´slip fôlt) a break in the crust in which the blocks of rock move horizontally past each other (p. 282)

Subscript (sub´skript) a number in a formula that tells the number of atoms of an element in a compound (p. 79)

Subsoil (sub´soil) the layer of soil directly below the topsoil (p. 255)

Succession (sək sesh´ən) the process by which a community changes over time (p. 497)

Sunspot (sun´spot) a dark area on the sun's surface that gives off less energy than the rest of the sun (p. 375)

Swim bladder (swim blad´ər) a gas-filled organ that allows a bony fish to move up and down in water (p. 441)

Symbol (sim´bəl) one or two letters that represent the name of an element (p. 51)

Synapse (sin´aps) a tiny gap between neurons (p. 581)

T

Temperature (tem´pər ə char) a measure of how fast an object's particles are moving (p. 142)

Tentacle (ten´tə kəl) an armlike body part in invertebrates that is used for capturing prey (p 445)

Testes (tes´tēz) the male sex organ that produces sperm cells (p. 462)

Testosterone (te stos´tə rōn) male sex hormone (p. 570)

Thermocline (thėr´mō klīn) the ocean layer between about 300 and 1,000 meters below the surface, where the temperature drops sharply (p. 324)

Thermometer (thər mom´ə tər) a device that measures temperature (p. 143)

Thermosphere (thėr´mə sfir) the outermost layer of the atmosphere; includes most of the ionosphere (p. 336)

Threatened (thret´nd) there are fewer of a species of animal than there used to be (p. 499)

Tissue (tish´ü) groups of cells that are alike and work together (p. 406)

Topsoil (top´soil) the top layer of soil, rich with oxygen and decayed organic matter (p. 255)

Tornado (tôr nā´dō) a powerful wind storm with a whirling, funnel-shaped cloud and extremely low pressure (p. 359)

Trachea (trā´kē ə) the tube that carries air to the bronchi (p. 548)

Trade wind (trād wind) strong, reliable wind just north or south of the equator; blows from the east (p. 345)

Trench (trench) a deep valley on the ocean floor (p. 326)

Tributary (trib´yə ter ē)a river that joins another river of equal or greater size (p. 318)

Tritium (trit´ē əm) an isotope of hydrogen that has one proton and two neutrons (p. 57)

Troposphere (trop´ə sfir) the bottom layer of the atmosphere, extending from ground level up to about 16 kilometers above the earth (p. 335)

Tsunami (sü nä´mē) a large sea wave caused by vibrations of the earth (p. 289)

Tube foot (tüb fůt) a small structure used by echinoderms for movement (p. 449)

U

Umbilical cord (um bil´ə kəl kôrd) the cord that connects an embryo to the placenta (p. 572)

Unit (yü´nit) a known amount used for measuring (p. 5)

Ureter (yů rē´tər) a tube that carries urine from the kidney to the urinary bladder (p. 567)

Urethra (yů rē´thrə) the tube that carries urine out of the body (p. 567)

Urine (yůr´ən) liquid waste formed in the kidneys (p. 567)

Uterus (yü´tər əs) an organ in most female mammals that holds and protects an embryo (p. 571)

V

Vacuole (vak´yü ōl) stores substances such as food, water, and waste products (p. 408)

Vacuum (vak´yü əm) space that contains no matter (p. 150)

a	hat	e	let	ī	ice	ò	order	ů	put	sh	she	ə	a	in about
ā	age	ē	equal	o	hot	oi	oil	ü	rule	th	thin		e	in taken
ä	far	ėr	term	ō	open	ou	out	ch	child	ᴛн	then		i	in pencil
â	care	i	it	ȯ	saw	u	cup	ng	long	zh	measure		o	in lemon
													u	in circus

Vagina (və jī´nə) the tubelike canal in the female body through which sperm enter the body (p. 570)

Vascular plant (vas´kyə lər plant) a plant that has tubelike cells (p. 470)

Vascular tissue (vas´kyə lər tish´ü) a group of plant cells that form tubes through which food and water move (p. 470)

Vein (vān) a blood vessel that carries blood to the heart (p. 560)

Velocity (və los´ə tē) the speed and direction in which an object is moving (p. 102)

Vent (vent) a round opening through which magma reaches the surface of the earth (p. 278)

Ventricle (ven´trə kəl) a heart chamber that pumps blood out of the heart (p. 459)

Vertebra (vėr´tə brə) one of the bones or blocks of cartilage that make up a backbone (p. 440)

Vertebrate (vėr´tə brit) an animal with a backbone (p. 440)

Vestigial structure (ve stij´ē əl struk´chər) a body part that appears to be useless to an organism but was probably useful to the organism's ancestors (p. 533)

Vibrate (vī´brāt) to move rapidly back and forth (p. 159)

Villi (vil´ī) tiny fingerlike structures in the small intestine through which food molecules enter the blood (p. 554)

Visible spectrum (viz´ə bəl spek´trəm) the band of colors that make up white light; the colors in a rainbow (p. 166)

Vitamin (vī´tə mən) a substance your body needs for growth and activity (p. 417)

Volcano (vol kā´nō) a mountain that develops where magma pushes up through the earth's surface (p. 278)

Volume (vol´yəm) the amount of space an object takes up (p. 16)

W

Warm-blooded (wôrm´ blud´id) having a body temperature that stays the same (p. 443)

Warm front (wôrm frunt) the boundary ahead of a warm air mass that is pushing out and riding over a cold air mass (p. 357)

Water cycle (wȯ´tər sī´kəl) the movement of water between the atmosphere and the earth's surface (p. 315)

Water table (wȯ´tər tā´bəl) the top of the groundwater layer (p. 317)

Water vapor (wȯ´tər vā´pər) water in the form of a gas (p. 338)

Wave (wāv) the up-and-down motion of water caused by wind energy moving through the water (p. 324)

Weather (weŦH´ər) a state of the atmosphere at a given time and place (p. 351)

Weathering (weŦH´ər ing) the breaking down of rocks on the earth's surface (p. 253)

Wedge (wej) a simple machine made up of an inclined plane or pair of inclined planes that are moved (p. 126)

Weight (wāt) the measure of how hard gravity pulls on an object (p. 23)

Wheel and axle (wēl and ak´səl) a simple machine made up of a wheel attached to a shaft (p. 127)

Wind belt (wind belt) the pattern of wind movement around the earth (p. 345)

Wind cell (wind sel) a continuous cycle of rising warm air and falling cold air (p. 344)

Wind vane (wind vān) an instrument used to find wind direction (p. 354)

Work (wėrk) what happens when an object changes its position by moving in the direction of the force that is being applied (p. 113)

X

Xylem (zī´lem) the vascular tissue in plants that carries water and minerals from roots to stems and leaves (p. 477)

Z

Zygote (zī´gōt) a fertilized cell (p. 462)

Index

Atoms. *See also individual
element by name*
  atomic charge, 44
  atomic mass defined, 60
  atomic number defined, 48
  compounds, formation of,
    75–76
  dcfined, 37
  electrons, arrangement of, 74
  energy levels in, 74, 75
  models of, 42–45
  Science Myths, 43, 48
ATP defined, 410
Atrium (heart) defined, 459
Attract defined, 189
Auditory nerve defined, 583
Australia, 216
Axis defined, 219

B

Babies, birth of, 572–574
Bacteria, 405, 428, 588
Baking soda described, 63
Balances, 26–27, 86
Barium, 51
Barometer defined, 352
Base (genetic) defined, 522
Batteries, 182, 183–184, 187
Beaumont, William and
  digestion, 555
Bees, 451
Beetles, 452
Behaviors, innate vs. learned, 532
Benthos defined, 327
Beryllium, 44, 48
Bilateral symmetry defined, 446
Bile defined, 554
Biology defined, 402
Biome defined, 499–500
Biometrics, 584
Biosphere defined, 500
Biotic defined, 496
Birds, 443, 454, 459
Blood, 446, 558–561
Blood pressure, 560
Blood types, 561, 562
Blood vessels, 458, 559–560
Bohr, Niels and atoms, 45

Boiling point defined, 147
Bones, 548
Bopp, Thomas, 391
Boron, 44, 48, 51
Botany defined, 402.
    See also Plants
Boyle, Robert and elements, 63
Brain, human, 580
Brain stem defined, 580
Bromine, 51
Bronchiole defined, 563
Bronchus defined, 563
Brown, Robert, 42
Brownian motion, 42
Bureau of Weights and
  Measures, France, 11
Butterflies, 451

C

Cady, Hamilton P., 61
Calcite, 237, 239, 240
Calcium, 49, 51
Capillary defined, 560
Carbohydrate defined, 414, 415
Carbon
  atomic number of, 48
  –14, half-life of, 301
  properties of, 44
  sources of, 47, 48
  symbol for, 51
Carbonate radical, formula for, 80
Carbon cycle, 513–514
Carbon dioxide-oxygen cycle, 482
Cardiac defined, 558
Careers
  See Science at Work
Carnivore defined, 452
Carob beans and measurement, 5
Carrying capacity defined, 496
Carson, Rachel, 328
Cartilage, 440, 548
Carver, George Washington, 506
Cassini spacecraft and space
  exploration, 384
Cast (fossil) defined, 297
Catalyst defined, 83
Cats, 463
Cattle, 463

Cells
  brain cells, 179
  cell membrane defined, 408
  cell wall defined, 409
  comparing cells,
    Investigation, 412–413
  defined, 405
  egg defined, 461
  and energy, 410
  guard cell defined, 483
  information and, 410
  load cells, electronic scales, 24
  observing, 405–406
  plant vs. animal, 408–409
  receptor cell defined, 582
  solar, 392
  sperm cell defined, 461
  wind cell defined, 344
Cellular phones, 3
Cellular respiration and
  oxygen, 481, 482
Celsius scale defined, 144, 148
Cenozoic Era defined, 306, 309
Centigram defined, 25
Centimeter defined, 9
Centipedes, 448
Cerebellum defined, 580
Cerebrum defined, 580
Charnley, Sir John, 551
Chemical bond defined, 76
Chemical change defined, 69
Chemical energy, 94, 135, 481
Chemical equations, 85–87
Chemical formula defined, 78
Chemical reactions, 68, 82
Chemical weathering defined, 254
Chemistry defined, 3
Chlorate radical, formula for, 80
Chlorine, 52
Chlorine, source of, 47
Chlorophyll defined, 480
Chloroplast defined, 409
Chromium, 52
Chromosome defined, 521
Chromosphere defined, 375
Chyme defined, 553
Cicadas, 451
Cilia defined, 425

Evolution
    Darwin, Charles and, 531–532
    defined, 528
    descent with modification
        theory, 531
    evidence of, 533
    natural selection theory,
        531–532
Excretion defined, 419
Excretory system, 566–568
Expand defined, 138
Exponent defined, 12
Extinct defined, 499
Extrusive rock defined, 246

Moon defined, 371
Moraine defined, 264
Mosquitoes, 451
Moss, 469, 470, 475, 485.
    See also Plants
Motion
    Brownian, 42
    defined, 93, 97
    laws of, 102–104, 108
    solar system, 372
Motor defined, 200
Mountains, 281–282
Mouse, 463
Mouth (river) defined, 260
Mouveine, history of, 71
Movement and living, 419
Muscular system, human,
    549–551
Mushrooms, 426
Mutations, 521, 529–530

N

National Institute of Standards
    and Technology,
    United States, 11
Natural element defined, 47
Natural resources, 95, 237, 241,
    244, 316, 317–319, 328, 346,
    380, 500, 598–603
Natural selection theory of
    evolution defined, 531–532
Nekton defined, 327
Neon, 44, 47, 48, 51
Neptune, 385–386
Nervous system, 579–585
Neuron defined, 581
Neutron defined, 43
Newcomen, Thomas, 136
Newton, Isaac, 381
Newton defined, 23
Night and day, 220
Nitrate radical, formula for, 80
Nitrates and plants, 514–515
Nitrogen
    atomic number of, 48
    cycle, 334, 514–515

fixation defined, 514
    properties of, 44
    source of, 47, 48
    symbol for, 51
Nonrenewable resources
    defined, 500
Nonvascular tissue defined, 470
Normal faults defined, 282
Norphel, Chewang and artificial
    glaciers, 265
Northern lights, 193
North Pole defined, 219
Notes
    atomic charge, 44
    atoms and energy levels, 75
    batteries, 183
    boys or girls, 570
    Brownian motion, 42
    carbohydrates, 415
    chemical change, 69
    chemical equations, 85
    chemical equations,
        balanced, 86
    climates, 364
    color, determining, 166
    decibels and sound
        intensity, 160
    dissolved gases, 316
    Earth's origins, 305
    Earth's surface
        temperature, 379
    elements, 47
    elements and compounds, 63
    fossils, 296
    fruits and vegetables, 487
    fusion, 135
    glaciers, forming, 264
    gulfs, bays, and seas, 324
    Hale-Bopp Comet, 391
    human population, 498
    inclined planes, 125
    ionic compounds, 76
    iron, 273
    Kilauea Volcano, 279
    kinetic energy, 93

landslides, 267
mad cow disease
    and proteins, 416
magnets, 201
measurements,
    requirements of, 10
Metric Conversion Act, 16
miners and precious
    metals, 239
molecules and chemical
    bonds, 410
motion, changes in, 104
motion of objects, 97
oceans, 217
pancreas, 589
penguins, ostriches,
    and emus, 443
photosynthesis, 150
properties of matter, 33, 34
proteins and Alzheimer's
    disease, 416
radioactivity and
    radioisotopes, 60
reference points, 98
science and technology, 3
solar system, motion of, 372
solenoids, 199
speedboats, 126
systems, 213
theories, 274
twins and heredity, 522
viruses, 423
water and nonvascular
    plants, 474
waves, 165
Nuclear energy defined, 94, 135
Nuclear fission defined, 135
Nuclear fusion defined, 135
Nucleus defined, 42, 408
Nurse, 590
Nutrients, 417
Nutrition, 49, 240, 414–417
Nylon, 88

Pregnancy, 572–573, 574
Prevailing westerly defined, 345
Prime meridian defined, 230
Prism defined, 166
Producer defined, 504, 505
Product defined, 85
Progesterone defined, 571
Property defined, 33
Prostate gland defined, 570
Protein defined, 414, 416
Protist defined, 424
Protist Kingdom, 424–425
Proton defined, 42
Protozoan defined, 424
Pseudopod defined, 425
Psychrometer defined, 353
Puberty defined, 589
Pulley defined, 123–124
Pupil defined, 582
Pyramid of numbers defined, 505
Pyrite, 239

Q
Quarks, 50
Quartz, 237, 239, 240

R
Rabbits, 463
Radial symmetry defined, 445
Radiant energy defined, 94
Radiation defined, 150
Radicals defined, 80
Radioactive element defined, 300
Radioactivity and
   radioisotopes, 60
Radium, 51
Rain gauge defined, 355
Ramsay, Sir William
   and helium, 61
Reactant defined, 85
Receptor cell defined, 582
Rectangle area, computing, 12
Rectum defined, 554
Reference points, 98
Reflect defined, 164

Reflex actions, 581
Refraction defined, 170
Relative dating, principles of,
   299–300
Relative humidity defined, 353
Renewable resources defined, 500
Repel defined, 190
Replicate defined, 523
Reproduction
   animals, 461–464
   asexual defined, 461
   defined, 420
   human, 524–525, 569–574
   plants, 471, 485–487
   sexual defined, 461–462
Reproductive system, female, 571
Reproductive system, male,
   569–570
Reptile defined, 442
Reservoir defined, 319
Resistance force, defined, 116
Resource defined, 500
Respiration defined, 419,
   563–564
Respiratory system, 563–565
Retina defined, 582
Reverse faults defined, 282
Revolution defined, 225
Rhizoid defined, 474
Rhizome defined, 473
Ribosome defined, 408
Richter scale defined, 288
River deposits, 260
River erosion, 259
RNA defined, 410
Rock cycle defined, 246
Rock cycle theory, 247
Rocks, 236, 244–247, 295–297
Roller coasters, 96
Romans and measurement, 6
Roots (plant), 476–477
Rotation defined, 219
Roundworms, 446
Runoff defined, 315
Rutherford, Ernst and atoms, 45

S
Salinity defined, 323
Salt described, 63
Sand dunes, 266
Saturn, 384
Savery, Thomas, 136
Scanning electron microscope
   (SEM), 40
Schematic diagrams defined, 180
Science at Work
   accelerator technician, 64
   air traffic controller, 232
   appliance service
      technician, 185
   assayer, 53
   astronomer, 387
   atmospheric scientist, 356
   ecologist, 501
   environmental science
      technician, 346
   floodplain manager, 268
   genetic counselor, 527
   heating, ventilation, and air
      conditioning (HVAC)
      technician, 139
   hydroelectric power plant
      operator, 320
   instrument calibration
      technician, 22
   machine designer, 115
   microbiologist, 411
   nurse, 590
   obstetrician/gynecologist, 573
   optician, 172
   petroleum engineer, 302
   seismologist, 290
   space shuttle and International
      Space Station crews, 227
   stonemason, 248
   taxonomist, 427
   textile dye technologist, 77
   tree technician, 479
   veterinary assistant, 464
   wind tunnel technician, 105
   zookeeper, 444

Photo and Illustration Credits

p. xxiv (top left), Royalty-Free/Brand X Pictures; (top right) Royalty-Free/Photodisc Blue; (bottom left) Royalty-Free/Photodisc Green; (bottom right), Royalty-Free/Brand X Pictures; p. 2, © Jerome Wexler/Visuals Unlimited; p. 3, © Michael Newman/PhotoEdit; p. 5, © Mike Dobel/Masterfile; p. 22, © Jean Miele/Corbis; p. 24, © First Image West/Stock Montage; p. 33, 34 © Tom Neiman/First Image West/Stock Montage; p. 37, © Mark E. Gibson/Visuals Unlimited; p. 38, © Dean Conger/Corbis; p. 53, © Stephen Agricola/Stock Boston; p. 64, © Michael L. Abramson/Time Life Pictures/Getty Images; p. 69 (top), © Izzy Schwartz/ Getty Images; p. 69 (bottom), © E.R. Degginger/Color-Pic Inc.; p. 77, © Roger Tully/Getty Images; p. 82, © Stapleton Collection/Corbis; p. 84 (left), © Lawrence M. Sawyer/Getty Images; p. 84 (right), © Gibson Stock Photography; p. 94, © Stephen Wilkes/Getty Images; p. 96, © Jose Carillo/PhotoEdit; p. 105, © Ted Kawalerski Photography/Getty Images; p. 113, © Digital Vision; p. 115, © Casey McNamara/ Index Stock Imagery; p. 126, Royalty-Free/Corbis; p. 133, © David Young-Wolff/PhotoEdit; p. 134, © Barbara Stitzer/PhotoEdit; p. 139, © Jon Feingersh/Stock Boston, p. 142, © David Young-Wolff/PhotoEdit; p. 143, © J.K. West/Rainbow; p. 160, © John Foxx/Alamy; p. 165, © Don Bonsey/ Getty Images; p. 166 (top), © Craig Tuttle/Corbis; p. 166 (bottom), © Chris Ryan/Getty Images; p. 167, © Bob Daemmrich/Stock Boston; p. 171, © Bill Beatty/ Visuals Unlimited; p. 172, © Charles Gupton/ Stock Boston; p. 185, © Susan Van Etten/ PhotoEdit; p. 189, © Leslie Garland Picture Library/Alamy; p. 198, © Coco McCoy/Rainbow; p. 210, © Digital Vision;p. 213, © Brecelj Bojan/Corbis/Sygma; p. 227, Courtesy of NASA; p. 232, © David Lawrence/Corbis; p. 237, © Stan Osolinski/Dembinsky Photo Associates; p. 238 (top), © Alan Curtis/Leslie Garland Picture Library/Alamy; p. 238 (bottom), © Mark A. Schneider/Dembinsky Photo Associates; pp. 244, 246, © Hubert Stadler/Corbis; pp. 245 (top) and 246, © W. Cody/Corbis; pp. 245 (bottom) and 246, © David Muench/Corbis; p. 248,
© Annie Griffiths Belt/Corbis; p. 253, Royalty-Free/Corbis; p. 254 (left), © John Prior Images/Alamy; p. 254 (right), © John Lemker/Earth Scenes/Animals Animals; p. 255, © Adam Woolfitt/Corbis; p. 259, Royalty-Free/Corbis; p. 261, © Randy Wells/Getty Images; p. 262, © John Sohlden/Visuals Unlimited; p. 263 (top), © Gerald & Buff Corsi/Visuals Unlimited; p. 263 (bottom), © Visuals Unlimited; p. 267, Courtesy of Terry Taylor, Colorado State Patrol; p. 268, © Patti McConville/Getty Images; p. 279 (top), © Tom Bean/Corbis; p. 279 (middle), Courtesy of U.S. Geological Survey; p. 279 (bottom), © Getty Images; p. 280, © Dana White/PhotoEdit; p. 286, Courtesy of Robert E. Wallace, U.S. Geological Survey; p. 289, © Robert Yager/Getty Images; p. 290, © PhotoEdit; p. 295, © Danny Lehman/ Corbis; p. 296, © Phil Degginger/Getty Images; p. 297 (top), © Albert J. Copley/Getty Images; p. 297 (bottom), © Howard Grey/Getty Images; p. 302, © Keith Wood/Getty Images; p. 307, © A.J. Copley/Visuals Unlimited; p. 308, © Phil Martin/PhotoEdit; p. 310, © Michael Newman/PhotoEdit; p. 320, © Lester Lefkowitz/ Corbis; p. 337, Courtesy of NASA; p. 339, © Visuals Unlimited; p. 340 (top), © David Matherly/Visuals Unlimited; p. 340 (bottom), Royalty-Free/Corbis; p. 346, © Jerry Mason/Science Photo Library/Photo Researchers, Inc.; p. 352, © Leonard Lessin/Photo Researchers, Inc.; p. 354, © E.R. Degginger/Color-Pic Inc.; p. 355, © Runk/Schoenberger/Grant Heilman Photography; p. 356, © Shepard Sherbell/Corbis/SABA; p. 365 (top), © Kurt Scholz/ SuperStock; p. 365 (middle), © Dominique Braud/ Dembinsky Photo Associates; p. 365 (bottom), © Kjell B. Sandved/Visuals Unlimited; p. 376, © PhotoLink/Getty Images; p. 377, Courtesy of NASA, Mariner 10, U.S. Geological Survey Astrology Team; p. 378, Courtesy of Magellan Project, NASA Propulsion Laboratory; p. 380, Courtesy of NASA, James Bell (Cornell Univ.), Michael Wolff (Space Science Inst.), and the Hubble Heritage Team (STScI/AURA); p. 382, Courtesy of Hubble Heritage Team (STScI/AURA/NASA) and Amy Simon (Cornell U.);